Justice and Health Care: Comparative Perspectives

Justice and Health Care: Comparative Perspectives

Edited by

Andrew Grubb

Professor of Health Care Law, Director, Centre of Medical Law and Ethics, School of Law, King's College London, UK

and

Maxwell J. Mehlman

Professor of Law, The Law–Medicine Center, Case Western Reserve University, Cleveland, Ohio, USA

JOHN WILEY & SONS

Chichester · New York · Brisbane · Toronto · Singapore

Copyright © 1995 by John Wiley & Sons Ltd,
            Baffins Lane, Chichester,
            West Sussex PO19 1UD, England

            Telephone: National   01243 779777
                       International (+44) 1243 779777

All rights reserved.

No part of this book may be reproduced by any means,
or transmitted, or translated into a machine language
without the written permission of the publisher.

Other Wiley Editorial Offices

John Wiley & Sons, Inc., 605 Third Avenue,
New York, NY 10158–0012, USA

Jacaranda Wiley Ltd, 33 Park Road, Milton,
Queensland 4064, Australia

John Wiley & Sons (Canada) Ltd, 22 Worcester Road,
Rexdale, Ontario M9W 1L1, Canada

John Wiley & Sons (SEA) Pte Ltd, 37 Jalan Pemimpin #05-04,
Block B, Union Industrial Building, Singapore 2057

Library of Congress Cataloging-in-Publication Data

Justice and health care : comparative perspectives / edited by Andrew
   Grubb and   Maxwell J. Mehlman.
      p.   cm.
      Includes bibliographical references and index.
      ISBN 0 471 95526 4
      1. Medical care—Law and legislation—United States. 2. Medical
   care—Law and legislation—Great Britain. 3. Medical care—Law and
   legislation—Canada. I. Grubb, Andrew. II. Mehlman, Maxwell J.
   K3601.Z9J87   1995
   344′.0321—dc20
   [342.4321]
                                                                95-17812
                                                                    CIP

British Library Cataloguing in Publication Data

A catalogue record for this book is available from the British Library

ISBN 0 471 95526 4

Typeset in 10/12 pt Garamond by Pure Tech India Ltd, Pondicherry
Printed and bound in Great Britain by Biddles Ltd, Guildford

This book is printed on acid-free paper responsibly manufactured from sustainable
forestation, for which at least two trees are planted for each one used for paper production.

Contents

Contributors

James F. Blumstein is Professor of Law, Vanderbilt University School of Law, 21st Avenue South, Nashville, Tennessee 37240, USA.

Barry R. Furrow is Professor of Law, Widener University School of Law, PO Box 7474, 4601 Concord Pike, Wilmington, Delaware 19803, USA.

Dieter Giesen is Professor of Private and Comparative Law, Law Department, and Head, Working Center for Studies in German and International Medical Malpractice Law, Free University of Berlin, Van't-Hoff-Strasse 8, D 14195 Berlin (Dahlem) Germany.

Lawrence O. Gostin is Professor of Law, Georgetown University Law Center, 600 New Jersey Avenue, NW, Washington, DC, 20001, USA.

Andrew Grubb is Professor of Health Care Law and Director of the Centre of Medical Law and Ethics, King's College, London, UK.

Alan Maynard is Professor of Economics, Director of the Centre for Health Economics, University of York, York, Y01 5DD, UK.

Maxwell J. Mehlman is Professor of Law, Case Western Reserve University, The Law-Medicine Center, School of Law, 11075 East Boulevard, Cleveland, Ohio 44106, USA.

His Honour Judge David Pearl is Chief Adjudicator, Immigration Appeals; Visiting Professor, School of Law, King's College, London; and Honorary Professor, University of East Anglia, Norwich, UK.

Vernellia R. Randall is Assistant Professor of Law, University of Dayton, School of Law, Dayton, Ohio 45469, USA.

Robert L. Schwartz is Professor of Law, University of New Mexico School of Law, 1117 Stanford Drive, NE, Albuquerque, New Mexico 87106, USA.

Carolyn Hughes Tuohy is Professor of Political Science, Department of Political Science, University of Toronto, Toronto, Canada.

Preface

This is the ninth volume of essays on medical law and ethics published by the Centre of Medical Law and Ethics at King's College. It grew out of two conferences. The first, sponsored by the Law-Medicine Center at Case Western Reserve University School of Law, was held in Cleveland, Ohio in 1992. The second conference, which was co-sponsored by the Centre of Medical Law and Ethics, took place in London in 1993. The nine essays in this volume were presentations revised following the conferences. As with last year's volume, the papers in this volume adopt a thematic approach. It addresses a particular issue of importance in the provision of health care—"justice and health care". The papers consider first, the problems faced in the American health care system and subsequently, seek to broaden the debate by turning to consider approaches in other health care systems such as Britain and Canada. The papers display the essential need for interplay between law, economics, political science and moral philosophy when formulating health policy.

Finally, some acknowledgments must be made. The papers were published previously in volumes 3 and 4 of *Health Matrix: Journal of Law-Medicine*. The editors express their appreciation to the *Journal* for permission to publish the essays in book form. As ever, we are grateful to those at John Wiley who worked on this volume.

Andrew Grubb and Maxwell J. Mehlman

Introduction

Andrew Grubb and Maxwell J. Mehlman

The provision of health care is big business. In a number of countries it is, of course, literally a business. Sometimes, the ability to pay will define the individual's capacity to obtain health care but not always. Certainly, where state provision exists the limitation of available resources means that not everyone may be able to obtain everything they want (or need). Need (or want) will, history shows us, always exceed what can be reasonably afforded however much a particular society is prepared to spend on health care. Since state provision is usual to some extent, even in market based health systems such as the United States, access to health care and the need for a just allocation of limited resources are issues that ultimately must be confronted by every society. How, and on what basis, this should be done is, of course, a matter of social policy which will often be driven by the prevailing political will but it is not, nor could it ever properly be, a matter of naked political expression. The choices that have to be made must be informed by an understanding of a number of contributing disciplines such as law, moral philosophy, economics and political science. The nine essays which follow address the issues of access and allocation from this range of scholarly backgrounds.

The first set of five essays focuses on the health care system in the United States. However, these papers raise issues of universal application. Four of the five concern the relationship between economics and health care. James Blumstein proposes to use economic incentives to reduce the shortage of transplant organs. Vernellia Randall rejects an economic explanation for the lack of access of African-Americans to

Justice and Health Care: Comparative Perspectives. Edited by A. Grubb and M.J. Mehlman. © 1995 John Wiley & Sons Ltd.

health care services compared with European-Americans, and marshals the evidence pointing to discrimination on the basis of race. Barry Furrow explains how the law imposes treatment obligations on health care providers in an attempt to cope with gaps in access left by the patchwork system of US health care financing. Robert Schwartz argues that denying health care to persons with "unhealthy" life styles will do little to solve the problem of rising health care costs. The essay by Larry Gostin, although it deals with a different dimension of justice and health care, is no less far-ranging, since it explores the extent to which government can override individual rights in order to achieve public health objectives.

Several of the essays confront the failure of the US health care system to ensure that all people receive adequate health care. Each author concentrates on a different culprit. Furrow emphasizes how financial incentives discourage health care professionals and the organizations that they work within from providing uncompensated care. Randall blames institutionalized racism for the plight of African-American patients. Schwartz criticizes the tendency to make people's bad habits the scapegoat for rising health care costs instead of developing more meaningful solutions.

What is interesting is how unlikely it is that these particular problems will be solved by current US health reform efforts. The economic conflicts-of-interest between patients and care-givers that Furrow describes will be exacerbated, not relieved, by the reform-spurred growth of managed care organizations. Randall does not see national health reform as the solution to institutionalized racism; she believes that the problem must be combated by the aggressive use of anti-discrimination laws to punish wrongdoers. Schwartz's plea for a realistic appraisal of the relationship between life style and health status is being drowned out by the clamour for sin taxes and "personal responsibility." Nor will health reform alleviate the shortage of transplant organs that Blumstein's essay addresses.

Another theme shared by a number of the essays is the clash between individual freedom and the interests of the collective. Gostin approaches this topic from the standpoint of public health responses to communicable diseases. Historically, he points out, US courts have rarely invalidated public health laws. The US Constitution offers little protection for individuals with communicable diseases; the legislature must produce merely a plausible rationale to justify even the broadest assertion of public health powers. Gostin expects this to change with the emergence of a new body of US law prohibiting discrimination against persons with disabilities, which includes those with communicable diseases.

Blumstein takes a different tack: Why, he asks, should the law deny people the right to sell their organs? Reviewing the various opposing arguments, he finds none compelling enough to prevent experiments designed to see if commerce in transplantable organs is a feasible solution to the lack of organ donors.

Two other essays cover similar territory implicitly. Furrow's application of rescue doctrine to health care providers rejects the notion that their professional or commercial autonomy entitles them to ignore the health needs of those who are injured or ill. In the absence of a sufficient personal ethical imperative, he argues, the law simply should force providers to treat—or rescue—those in need. Schwartz challenges whether the government's interest in reducing health care spending justifies denying health services on the basis of personal life style choices Schwartz's argument centres largely on the practical flaws in such an approach, but one surmises that he would oppose singling out these individuals even if such a program were feasible and money would be saved.

The authors of these essays were selected on the basis of the breadth and depth of their previous scholarship, but it is striking how controversial the positions are that they espouse within these pages. All of their main theses conflict with conventional wisdom in the field of health policy. Blumstein's call for forward contracts of sale for the use of transplant organs runs head-on into federal laws prohibiting commerce in body parts, supported by vigorous opposition from medical ethicists. Randall eschews both the standard view that lack of access to health care is largely a function of socio-economic status, and the standard solution of guaranteeing access through national health financing reform. Gostin opposes public health advocates who argue that the law must give wholehearted support to efforts to eradicate disease. Furrow's challenge to the prerogatives of health care professionals conflicts with the common law's historic reluctance to compel professionals to render services involuntarily, and his willingness to force health care institutions to care for the indigent is at odds with the current fashion of relying on competition to solve the nation's health care woes. Meanwhile, except for industry lobbyists, hardly anyone besides Schwartz seems to disagree with the proposition that reducing smoking or drinking will reduce health care costs.

The controversial nature of the positions taken by these authors reflects the magnitude of the problems facing the US health care system, the degree to which the system is in flux, and the need to consider unconventional proposals in the absence of proven solutions. The essays have one final controversial viewpoint in common: They regard the law as a force for positive change, whether as a remedy for racism and hospital "dumping" of poor patients, or as a source of protection for the disabled and the unpopular, or as the framework for commercial transactions in human organs. Those who favour "getting the law off people's backs" will find little support in these pages.

The remaining four essays seek to bring a comparative perspective to the issues of access to health care and allocation of resources by looking to the health care delivery systems of Britain and Canada. The papers often reflect many of the issues raised by the American authors. Caroline Tuohy, a political scientist, both broadens the debate and puts it in context by exposing the range of models of 'welfare states' that may exist. She identifies four models. First, there is the *social democratic* model—where entitlement to benefits is based upon membership of the national community and is epitomized by the Swedish system. Secondly comes the *corporatist* model—where benefits are determined by membership of social insurance programmes and entitlement is based upon contribution. This model most closely corresponds to the German system. The third model she offers is the *residualist* model—where the market is the primary mechanism for distributing benefits although the state acts as a "long stop" for the most disadvantaged. This, of course, best describes the prevailing system in America where private insurance predominates with state provision for some through Medicare and Medicaid. Finally, Tuohy identifies the fourth option as the *Beveridge* model named after the architect of the British welfare state in the 1940s. This model combines social insurance (the "corporatist" model) but with two twists: the social democratic principle of universal access (a gain) and limited, albeit minimum, benefits (a loss).

Tuohy's main concern is to examine the Canadian health insurance system and its embodiment of the social democratic principle of universality. Her account of its structure and functioning illuminates the debate between those south of the 49th parallel who either proclaim the virtues of the Canadian system or condemn it through scepticism. Tuohy is undoubtedly a supporter. Its success, in terms of delivery and cost-effectiveness, she puts down to an accommodation between the medical profession and the state. In particular, the entrenchment of clinical autonomy was obtained in return for the doctors' abdication of any price-setting function to the state. In short, Tuohy states that Medicare "places physicians in a position of power/autonomy to determine the range of services provided while limiting their economic power and autonomy." Doctors retain a central role in determining access to health care even though the state pays the bills. The budgetary constraints on doctors (particularly fund-holding GPs) that are now a familiar feature of the British so-called "internal market" after the reforms of the National Health Service and Community Care Act 1990 are nowhere to be seen in Canada. In the words of Caroline Tuohy, "Medicare is Canada's social policy success story."

Dieter Giesen, in his paper, also follows the comparative path, this time of the comparative lawyer. While pointing out the absence of a *legal* right to health care, he argues the case for such a right as "an essential prerequisite to the exercise of personal autonomy and an irreducible condition of human flourishing." Giesen identifies two aspects to this right: first, one which would allow claims against *society*, i.e., would require diversion of resources to provide services; and secondly, one which would impose claims upon *individual doctors* to provide particular treatment or care to a patient. The English courts have been reluctant to impose *any* legally enforceable right to health care in either sense either because of their perception that this would involve them in resource allocation which is a political matter for Parliament (*R. v Secretary of State ex p Hincks* (1980) 1 B.M.L.R. 93 (C.A.)) or because it would be an unjustified interference with the doctor's clinical discretion (*Re J* [1993] Fam. 15 (C.A.)). Re-enforcing some of the points made earlier by Barry Furrow, he laments the common law's reluctance (by contrast to civil law systems) to recognize a doctor's duty to rescue a patient in emergency situations. Moving on to develop what he sees as the underlying right—that of autonomy—Giesen develops the argument that once treatment is given this moral right should be more vigorously reflected in English law. In particular, he criticizes the English courts' adherence to the "professional standard" of disclosure of information and its persistent refusal to accept that a patient should be given information which a "reasonable patient" or even "the particular patient" would want to know prior to deciding whether or not to undergo the treatment. England, as part of Europe, is no longer the island it once was. However, in this respect, as Giesen points out, English law is out of step with all major common law jurisdictions and the civil law world.

Alan Maynard, an economist, asks the central question addressed in a number of the other papers: "How do we allocate scarce resources?" As the gap between what can be done for patients and what can be afforded financially increases, there is no running away from this question. Maynard points out that in the UK, doctors have traditionally allocated resources on the basis of their clinical judgment of need and this remains largely the case today. General practitioners act as "gate-keepers" to hospital and other non-primary health care. Hospital consultants through their powers of admission and manipulation of waiting lists, further control the provision of non-emergency hospital care. Of course, this has been going on as long as the NHS has existed. Two factors, however, have brought the issue of allocation to the fore and, it could be said, given it a new impetus. First, there is a very real feeling that the system cannot bear the demands for care placed upon it. It seems a fact of life (and again this has been so since the inception of the NHS in 1948) that demand will always exceed supply when health care is the "commodity" in question. Today, however, the advent of "high-tech" medicine has quantitatively raised the costs of care that can be offered and further, there are unprecedented calls on the public purse from other sources, such as education and the welfare state. Secondly, the advent of the "internal market" since the National Health Service and Community Care Act 1990 has further squeezed resources and through the system of NHS contracts between purchasers (GP fund-holders and District Health Authorities) and providers (principally NHS Trusts) made these choices more explicit and transparent. Maynard acknowledges the realities of, and need for, allocation but warns of the dangers of erosion of patient trust and the inequalities that will inevitably occur when doctors are constrained by external funding decisions unconnected to their clinical judgment of the patient's need. After all, as Maynard states, inequality of access is "a sign of [the market's] success." Maynard calls for better data collecting systems so that decisions about what care is purchased with the available money can be better informed and the most cost-effective system created. But inequalities and patient dissatisfaction will remain. As Giesen points out in his paper, there has been a growth of legal actions in the last decade where, in essence, the claimant seeks to challenge the particular allocation of resources. What will the courts do if a doctor claims she could not give the care she wanted because the contract between the patient's purchaser of health care and the doctor's NHS Trust did not provide for it? The present singular failure of these actions does not mean that they will not succeed in the future.

In the final essay, David Pearl returns to the subject of Vernellia Randall's paper on health care and ethnic minorities. Like Randall, he reminds us that as a society we need to take account of ethnic diversity in the country lest the system fail the needs of ethnic groups. It is undoubtedly the case that ethnic groups have particular needs. Some groups have particular medical problems, for example, sickle cell disease, or particular needs, for example, special dietary requirements when in hospital. But, cultural differences should generally lead to the implementation of measures which are culturally sensitive. The government seems recently to have taken steps in the right direction. A special ethnic unit now exists in the Department of Health to monitor the NHS's care of ethnic groups. The Chief Medical Officer has, as Pearl points out, identified two general goals for the NHS: first, to ensure that black and ethnic groups understand the NHS and its services; and, secondly to ensure that such groups receive appropriate health care which is delivered in a culturally sensitive way. Pearl suggests that the courts may become more active in "policing" ethnic discrimination in the provision of health care through, for example, judicial review although, in a theme that runs throughout the papers in this volume, again this would often lead the courts headlong into questions of recourse allocation.

It is the issue of resource allocation which bedevils any judicial involvement and which, as the papers show, must be addressed if justice in health care is to be achieved through the courts.

The use of financial incentives in medical care: the case of commerce in transplantable organs*

James F. Blumstein

I. INTRODUCTION

As a relative newcomer to organ transplant issues, I liken my experience in the field to an anthropologist's exposure to a new culture, a new way of thinking. There are, I have learned, holy totems and sacred cows that permeate the thinking and have profoundly influenced the development of public policy in the organ transplant arena. Perhaps pushing the anthropological simile to the breaking point, I find my role to be that of the constructive archaeologist, investigating the existing landscape of values by uncovering layers of buried values that have been deemed fundamental but whose wisdom has been assumed and uncontested. These traditional values have achieved a sacrosanct status and have undergirded policy formulation in this field. It is important to subject these entrenched ways of thinking to careful scrutiny, to question whether some of these values are as self-evident as has been assumed, and to determine whether they are in need of reexamination

* An earlier version of this article appeared in 24 TRANSPLANTATION PROCEEDINGS 2190 (1992).

Justice and Health Care: Comparative Perspectives. Edited by A. Grubb and M.J. Mehlman © 1995 John Wiley & Sons Ltd.

and reevaluation given the evolution of organ transplantation into the status of mainstream, therapeutic medical care. This is particularly the case as society is forced to confront the specific set of problems associated with producing a better balance between the expanding demand for transplantable organs and the currently existing inadequate level of supply.

There is widespread agreement that a shortfall exists in the number of organs made available for purposes of organ transplantation and that the supply-side constraint is a major inhibition in the further utilization of therapeutically promising organ transplantation techniques. "For those with failing hearts or livers, transplantation . . . is the only therapy that can replace imminent certain death with the hope of new life. But as its benefits have become increasingly apparent and the medical barriers have fallen, the demand for transplantation has grown rapidly, far outstripping the supply of organs."[1] For example, the United Network for Organ Sharing reports that, as of May 31, 1992, 27,120 people were on waiting lists for organ transplants in the United States.[2] These waiting lists have gotten longer over time, with estimates suggesting that about 200 people are added to the lists each month for kidneys alone.[3] From 1986 to 1989, while kidney dialysis patients increased by 25,000,[4] kidney transplants did not increase in number and even declined slightly from 8976 to 8899.[5] Yet, evidence suggests that transplantation is a more successful and cost-effective procedure for many dialysis patients with end-stage renal disease.[6] It has been estimated that 30% of patients on dialysis are candidates for transplantation.[7]

---

1. Spital, *The Shortage of Organs for Transplantation: Where Do We Go From Here?*, 325 NEW ENG. J. MED. 1243 (1991).

2. United Network for Organ Sharing, *Patients Waiting for Transplants: Number of Patient Registrations on the National Waitlist*, 8(6) UNOS UPDATE 35 (1992) (containing the following breakdown, by organ, of the 27,120 people on the waiting list as of May 31, 1992: kidneys (20,741); hearts (2560); livers (2113); lungs (811); pancreases (726); and heart-lungs (169)).

3. Teri Randall, *Too Few Human Organs for Transplantation, Too Many in Need . . . and the Gap Widens*, 265 JAMA 1223 (1991).

4. HEALTH CARE FIN. ADMIN., DEP'T OF HEALTH AND HUMAN SERVS., END–STAGE RENAL DISEASE PROGRAM HIGHLIGHTS (1989).

5. *Id.*

6. *See* Paul W. Eggers, *Effect of Transplantation on the Medicare End-Stage Renal Disease Program*, 318 NEW ENG. J. MED. 223, 223–24 (1988).

7. F. T. Rapaport & D. Anaise, *Organ Donation—1990*, 23 TRANSPLANTA-TION PROC. 899 (1991).

Despite this fundamental supply-side problem, those in leadership roles in the organ transplant movement have been strikingly hostile to markets and to the use of financial incentives as a tool for increasing the availability of transplantable organs. There is a strong, visceral, adverse reaction to the introduction of commerce in the field of transplantable organs. This *weltanschauung* reflects a worldview more characteristic of an earlier era in medical care when the role of markets in health care was hotly contested. Shibboleth and shamanism have thrived at the expense of rigorous analysis. It is now time to frame the issues clearly and to distill and understand the nature of the deep-seated beliefs in the field.

II. ORGAN TRANSPLANTATION POLICY WITHIN THE BROADER HEALTH POLICY CONTEXT

The role of financial incentives in organ transplantation should be considered within the broader context of health policy. Ideology, as much as technology, has driven organ transplantation policy. An intellectual orthodoxy has permeated the field. The 1986 Report of the United States Department of Health and Human Services Task Force on Organ Transplantation (OTTF Report)[8] has set the tone. It has had remarkable influence on the development of thinking and the evolution of policy. Although many officials of the Department of Health and Human Services (DHHS) vigorously disagreed with the analysis and recommendations of the Task Force, and no evidence exists that the Department has ever adopted the recommendations of the Task Force as official departmental policy, it is clear that the OTTF Report has been extremely influential in the evolution of policy thinking of important constituencies within DHHS. The OTTF Report has clearly driven the policy of the United Network for Organ Sharing (UNOS), the organization that holds the federal contract to administer the Organ Procurement and Transplant Network (OPTN) mandated by federal law.[9] And the OTTF Report has been an extremely important

---

8. *See* U.S. DEP'T OF HEALTH AND HUMAN SERVS., REPORT OF THE TASK FORCE ON ORGAN TRANSPLANTATION, ORGAN TRANSPLANTATION: ISSUES AND RECOMMENDATIONS (1986) [hereinafter *OTTF Report*].

9. *See* James F. Blumstein, *Federal Organ Transplantation Policy: A Time for Reassessment?*, 22 U.C. DAVIS L. REV. 451, 476–78 (1989).

document in framing thinking about organ transplantation issues in the organ transplant community generally. From my initial exposure to organ transplantation issues, I concluded that another viewpoint and frame of reference needed expression.

A. Organ transplantation policy values

If ideology, as much as technology, has driven organ transplantation policy, it is appropriate to inquire what values have undergirded organ transplantation policy in the United States. I have identified at least five.

1. The ethical foundation of altruism

Even a superficial exposure to this field reveals an intense commitment to altruism. This is deemed a moral imperative. For example, the OTTF Report stated that a core value shaping organ transplantation policy was the goal of "promoting a sense of community through acts of generosity."[10] Despite the widespread recognition of the shortage of transplantable organs, there persists an insistence on the exclusion or elimination of commercial incentives from all facets of the organ transplant system of organ supply, acquisition or distribution. Yet, by reasonable hypothesis, one might expect a system of financial incentives to augment the supply of available organs for transplantation.[11]

2. The role of the potential donor's family

The focus of the organ transplant community is on the *family* of the dying patient, who is the potential donor. There is a great concern

---

10. OTTF Report, *supra* note 8, at 28.

11. There is clearly an empirical question whether commercial incentives will result in an increase in the supply of transplantable organs. Since such transactions have been illegal in the United States since 1984, there is no reliable data on the question from the United States. Some critics claim that the introduction of commercial incentives could result in reduced altruistic donating. Although experiences from abroad suggest that commercial incentives do work, the empirical issue is a serious and legitimate one. Where empirical, not ethical, disagreements split policy analysts, the appropriate resolution of the debate is to run an experiment to secure evidence on the matter. For a proposal to perform a pilot study of the effect on organ supply of a $1000 death benefit for organ donation, see Thomas G. Peters, *Life or Death: The Issue of Payment in Cadaveric Organ Donation*, 265 JAMA 1302 (1991).

expressed for the psychological well-being of family members of the potential organ donor as well as an emphasis on community-spirited commitment by the family through organ donation. There is a sense that families of a dying patient can be self-fulfilled by reaffirming their commitment to community solidarity through the donation of a loved one's organ for transplantation. This type of psychological fulfillment is "a demonstration of the principle that from a loved one's death may come some silver lining."[12]

A concomitant of this focus on the family is that there is an emphasis on the bedside of the dying patient (and potential organ donor) as the locus of decision making for organ donation. It is questionable whether the bedside is an optimal place for serious consideration of the complex set of issues that surround organ donation decisions. The family is facing the possible death of a loved one and is concentrating on efforts to save his or her life. It is quite natural for family members to feel ill at ease thinking about organ donation at a time when the grieving process has not yet commenced and the preferred focus of attention is on lifesaving not organ donation.

Further, it can be rather awkward for professional personnel to develop a sensitive conversation with the family of a potential donor because the family can perceive the very topic of organ donation as reflective of a certain prognostic pessimism. The so-called required request procedure, adopted in legislation at the federal level and imposed on all hospitals that participate in Medicare or Medicaid, mandates that hospitals institutionalize a policy of routinely asking families of potential donors whether or not they wish to donate the organs of their dying kin for purposes of transplantation.[13] Several assumptions underlie the policy of "required request" or "routine inquiry." Pragmatically, it was premised on the view that families would agree to donate organs of their next of kin if asked by trained organ procurement personnel. Public opinion surveys showed strong support for organ donation, so the objective was to make sure that the families of potential donors were actually asked about organ donation. At the same time, institutionalization was needed "because individual professionals typically feel squeamish about raising these sensitive issues with family members in such delicate circumstances. An institutional rule is needed to make the organ donation inquiry an

---

12. Blumstein, *supra* note 9, at 468.

13. *See* Maxwell J. Mehlman, *Presumed Consent to Organ Donation: A Reevaluation*, 1 HEALTH MATRIX 31, 37–39 (1991).

obligation."[14] Ideologically, "required request" of families of potential donors is a communitarian act that promotes altruism. It allows families of potential donors to "exercise . . . the virtue of generosity,"[15] performing an act that "strengthen[s] altruism and our sense of community."[16]

Disappointment with the pragmatic effects of routine inquiry policies has led some to seek out alternatives. Those alternatives, however, will be evaluated in terms of their ideological impact and propriety, with traditionalists likely to press for maintaining the role of the family at the potential donor's bedside as a means of promoting altruism and communitarianism.[17]

Focusing on the bedside seems at odds with the legal regime set up under the Uniform Anatomical Gift Act (UAGA), which emphasizes control of donation by the patient himself or herself and a determination regarding organ donation before that patient becomes ill. The revised (1987) UAGA explicitly states that a gift of an organ "does not require the consent or concurrence of any other person after the death of the donor. . . ."[18] This authority of the patient/donor to control the organ donation decision had been provided for in the original (1968) version, but subsequently was restated specifically for emphasis and for certainty.[19]

---

14. Blumstein, *supra* note 9, at 467.

15. PAUL RAMSEY, THE PATIENT AS PERSON 210 (1970).

16. OTTF Report, *supra* note 8, at 28 (quoting a report from the Hastings Center).

17. Disappointment with required request has led some to revisit the more drastic proposal of presumed consent—i.e., presuming that consent for organ donation exists in the absence of specific evidence on the question of intent. *See, e.g.,* Spital, *supra* note 1. The proposal for presumed consent was made as early as 1968 by Professors Dukeminier and Sanders. *See* Jesse Dukeminier, Jr. & David Sanders, *Organ Transplantation: A Proposal for Routine Salvaging of Cadaver Organs,* 279 NEW ENG. J. MED. 413 (1968). At least part of the rationale for presumed consent, even in its earliest iteration, was a sense of discomfort associated with asking for next-of-kin consent for organ donation. *See id.* at 416 (noting that "[t]o someone whose relative is about to die, asking for the kidneys may seem a ghoulish request").

18. UNIF. ANATOMICAL GIFT ACT (1987) § 2(h), 8A U.L.A. 13 (Supp. 1992) (superseding 1968 version).

19. The commentary to the 1987 UAGA makes it clear that the explicit language adopted in § 2(h) of the 1987 UAGA was designed to codify expressly the intention of § 2(f) (now § 2(h)) of the 1968 UAGA. What led to the explicit language in § 2(h) of the 1987 UAGA was evidence that family approval was routinely required by organ procurement agencies, despite the provisions of the UAGA. Section 2(f) was designed to "remove any uncertainty." UAGA (1987), *id.* at 14 (cmt.).

Despite this legal regime under the UAGA, apparently the fact is that family approval is always, or almost always, sought for organ donation.[20] This is the so-called family veto.[21] Opponents of shifting the locus away from the bedside worry that it de-emphasizes next-of-kin consent. That, in turn, deprives the family of an opportunity for "[p]romoting a sense of community through acts of generosity."[22] The DHHS Task Force Report clearly places in the value balance lifesaving that can come from transplantation, on the one hand, and "the value of social practices that enhance and strengthen altruism and our sense of community,"[23] on the other hand. Note that this value has nothing to do, strictly speaking, with transplants. Instead, it concerns itself with a vision of society, of community and solidarity, and deems it necessary and appropriate to balance lifesaving against this communal vision of the good society.

3. Elimination of donor/family control over organ distribution

Since the organ for transplant is deemed a "national resource" under the DHHS Task Force Report[24] and under controlling federal organ transplantation policies and principles, it is argued that the elimination of control by the patient/donor, or the family of the patient/donor, over the distribution of organs donated for transplant is an ethical imperative. Under this ideal, the donor and the family cannot assign an organ because it is simply not "theirs" to assign.[25] The UAGA, the

---

20. John A. Robertson, *Supply and Distribution of Hearts for Transplantation: Legal, Ethical, and Policy Issues*, 75 CIRCULATION 77, 78 (1987).

21. The authors of the original (1968) UAGA intended to eliminate this family veto. The Comments to the 1968 UAGA stated that the UAGA "recognizes and gives legal effect to the right of the individual to dispose of his own body without subsequent veto by others." Refusal by the transplant community to honor the decision of an individual to donate his or her own organs for transplantation without express family approval is, therefore, essentially lawless. UAGA, 8A U.L.A. 35, cmt. at 36 (1987).

22. OTTF Report, *supra* note 8, at 28.

23. *Id.* (quoting THE HASTINGS CENTER, ETHICAL, LEGAL AND POLICY ISSUES TRANSPLANTATION, 2 (Oct. 1985)).

24. *Id.* at 86.

25. Under the recommendations of the 1986 Department of Health and Human Services Task Force Report, OTTF Report, *id.*, donated organs are to be considered "a national resource to be used for the public good." In such a regime, "[o]rgans would become socialized, with individual donors stripped of power to control the destiny of their donated organs or to designate specific beneficiaries." *See* Blumstein, *supra* note 9, at 486.

state-adopted legal regime in this area, gives the donor and the family the right to assign the organ to a designated beneficiary. In fact, the UAGA creates a legally enforceable right in the beneficiary, if one is designated. So, the legal structure set up in the late 1960s and early 1970s created quite a different legal regime from the currently prevailing ethic in the field.[26]

4. Centralized criteria for organ distribution

The fourth organ transplantation policy value that I have identified—mandating that a centralized set of criteria govern the system of organ distribution—follows naturally from the notion that the organ, once donated, is a "national resource" that society is responsible for distributing. Once the family decides to donate the deceased's organ for the benefit of society, it is the duty of society to formulate criteria for the distribution of organs as a "national resource", thereby substituting collective decision making for patient or family determination. The approach of the DHHS Task Force and the prevailing view of the Organ Procurement and Transplantation Network are in direct tension with the patient/family control provisions of the UAGA.

5. An organized, unified, integrated system of organ procurement and distribution

As set forth in the DHHS Task Force Report, and as implemented by the Organ Procurement and Transplantation Network, the vision of appropriate public policy calls for centralized control and nationally uniform guidelines governing organ procurement and distribution, organ transplantation activities at the transplantation centers themselves, and histocompatibility laboratories. The notion is that a social services delivery network, organized and controlled by professionals, should dictate how organs are procured and transplanted.

B. Organ transplantation values within the broader health policy context

The values undergirding organ transplant policy are in distinct tension with the values that have emerged in the larger health policy context.

---

26. *See* Blumstein, *supra* note 9, at 486–90.

They also seem strangely at odds with a policy of encouraging an increased supply of transplantable organs.

A fundamental element of health policy over the last ten years has been competition and the role of markets. "Perhaps the most striking characteristic of the health care industry as it has developed in the last decade has been the recognition that competition and markets have an important role to play in the health policy arena."[27] What are the market-oriented values that so strikingly contrast with the values undergirding organ transplant policy?

1. The use of incentives

Not so long ago, the consideration of the use of incentives in the health policy arena was deemed inappropriate, a taboo, a subject not for polite company. The use of incentives in medical care was rejected on the related grounds of ethics and effectiveness. Ethically, the objection stemmed from the ideological commitment in some quarters that unrestricted access to medical care on the basis of medical need was the appropriate normative benchmark. This was a component of the rhetorical espousal of medical care as a right.[28] If one believes that access to medical care should be costless to users, the imposition of financial disincentives is directly in conflict with that principle. Obviously, if one starts from the premise that an individual's utilization of medical services should bear no economic consequences for the beneficiary of the treatment, the use of financial disincentives will have unacceptable distributive effects.[29]

In terms of effectiveness, financial incentives were questioned because of the prevailing medical view that money did not affect how

---

27. *See* James F. Blumstein, Reevaluating the Federal Role in Organ Transplantation Policy: The Relationship Between the Government and the Organ Procurement and Transplantation Network, 35 (June 1989) (unpublished paper, on file at Vanderbilt University School of Law). *See also* James F. Blumstein & Frank A. Sloan, *Redefining Government's Role in Health Care: Is a Dose of Competition What the Doctor Should Order?*, 34 VAND. L. REV. 849 (1981).

28. *See generally* James F. Blumstein, *Thinking About Government's Role in Medical Care*, 32 ST. LOUIS U.L.J. 853 (1988); Rand E. Rosenblatt, *Health Care, Markets, and Democratic Values*, 34 VAND. L. REV. 1067 (1981).

29. *See, e.g.*, T. R. Marmor et al., *Medical Care and Procompetitive Reform*, 34 VAND. L. REV. 1003, 1014 (1981) (stating that "[c]ost sharing amounts to a tax or user fee imposed on the sick and is a de facto transfer of wealth from the sick to the healthy").

patients were treated. It was assumed that there was a correct course of treatment, and that was a professionally determined decision. Science not economic incentives drove medical care diagnosis and treatment decisions. Therefore, financial incentives could not be effective because they did not influence medical care decision making. And, implicitly, to the extent that scientific and professional judgments might indeed be influenced by financial considerations, that was an inappropriate deviation from the clinically correct scientific pathway.

The ethical issue is now seen as more richly textured than it once was. The rhetoric of rights and equality has been deemphasized, replaced in responsible circles by concern about the role of government in providing for an adequate level of services to individuals unable to afford medical care.[30] Further, there is now a broader understanding that establishing a relationship between utilization of medical resources and expenditures by patients as consumers is not always inappropriate. Medical care is not monolithic; in some areas, it may be troublesome to use financial incentives, but with respect to other types of care, use of incentives to shape behavior might be acceptable.

With respect to effectiveness, it is now commonplace for analysts to examine the effects of incentives on conduct in the health arena. This is no longer an oddity. It is quite mainstream. And there is a recognition that economically unrestrained decision making in medical care, as in other areas, has consequences in terms of resource utilization. Thus, the ideological commitment to unrestricted access has run into a hitherto unrecognized economic reality. Not only are distributive values at issue when financial incentives are under consideration. Elimination of financial considerations from decisions about medical care resource allocation has the consequence of increasing the aggregate levels of resource utilization. This links the ethical and the effectiveness grounds for objecting to the use of financial disincentives. The cost of maintaining the ethical case against incentives is elevated once one accepts the position that overall patterns of utilization are affected (upwardly biased) by the absence of financial considerations in the medical care decisionmaking

---

30. *See* PRESIDENT'S COMMISSION FOR THE STUDY OF ETHICAL PROBLEMS IN MEDICINE AND BIOMEDICAL AND BEHAVIORAL RESEARCH, SECURING ACCESS TO HEALTH CARE, A REPORT ON THE ETHICAL IMPLICATIONS OF DIFFERENCES IN THE AVAILABILITY OF HEALTH SERVICES 18 (1983).

process.[31] Moreover, there is now greater recognition of the broad range of medical services; not all medical treatment fits the model of life-or-death treatment. Much care is palliative in character, and much expense in medical care involves careful consideration of the value of buying incremental levels of reduced uncertainty.[32] The existence of clinical uncertainty, reflected in the widely divergent and unexplained procedure rates across providers in seemingly similar circumstances,[33] further suggests an appropriate role for incentives. The evidence about divergent procedure rates undermines the assumption of a monolithically correct mode of treatment. In this world of uncertainty, it should no longer be inappropriate to allow financial considerations to enter into decisionmaking. The assumption can no longer be indulged that consideration of financial incentives undermines scientifically clear-cut clinical pathways. These factors—the many faces of medical care services and the existence of clinical uncertainty—lend further legitimacy to the use of incentives in many areas of medical care.

Now recognized to have an effect in influencing behavior, financial disincentives are widely in use, despite the earlier ideological objections. DRGs (diagnostic related groups), just to take one example, have shaped behavior. There has been an increasing emphasis on ambulatory care, and that is a direct result of the financial incentives created by DRGs. Hospitals downsized staffs, shortened lengths of stay, built outpatient clinics and outpatient surgery centers. At many medical centers, new construction emphasizes expansion of outpatient services. These are clearly supply-side responses to incentives.[34]

2. Enhanced respect for pluralism and decentralization

At one time in the broader health policy arena, commentators asked or inquired about the preferred way to organize the health care delivery system. In the early 1970s, Health Maintenance Organizations (HMOs)

---

31. For a general discussion of these trade-off issues, *see* Clark C. Havighurst & James F. Blumstein, *Coping with Quality/Cost Trade-offs in Medical Care: The Role of PSROs*, 70 Nw. U.L. Rev. 6 (1975).

32. *Id.* at 12–13.

33. *See* John Wennberg & Alan Gittelsohn, *Small Area Variations in Health Care Delivery*, 182 Science 1102 (1973).

34. Incentives have also played an augmented role on the demand side. For example, increased attention to competition and markets has resulted in a focus on individual consumer choice and patient involvement in decision making.

were promoted by some because they were seen as the good monolithic model by which to deliver health care. The mindset was that a consensus would form on the question of what is the single best way of organizing the system of health care delivery. The current trend, however, is toward pluralism and decentralization, that is toward diversity as in other segments of the economy. Much of this thinking has been influenced by the findings of Jack Wennberg[35] and others[36] concerning the existence of clinical uncertainty and the existence of striking, unexplained diversity in practice patterns. We now recognize that we do not have a monolithic system, and perhaps such a monolithic system is not a desirable objective.

In summary, then, the foregoing principles—competition and incentives, and pluralism and decentralization—have seemed to influence the rest of the health policy arena in the past decade. These principles appear to be strikingly at odds with the strongly held, fundamental principles that are so widespread in the organ transplanation arena. The logical next question is whether there might be some appropriate extrapolation from the broader health care context to the world of organ transplanation policy.

C. Mainstreaming organ transplanation policy

What would organ transplanation policy look like if it were more compatible with these other, mainstream trends in health policy? First, it would allow the introduction of incentives; that is, it would permit commerce in organ transplanation. Eliminating the exclusive reliance on altruism would recognize and acknowledge the priority of overcoming organ supply shortages and yet retain fidelity to principles of autonomy and individual choice of donors or their families.

Second, it would shift the exclusive focus from the family of the dying patient to the patient himself or herself. This, of course, is returning to the UAGA regime. It would shift decision making to a circumstance and time when the donor is capable of making competent choices regarding organ donation. It would restore patient and donor autonomy and basically restore the regime of the UAGA. Such a policy would undertake to make the organ donation vision of the UAGA work well rather than disregarding the philosophical underpinnings of the UAGA.

---

35. *See, e.g.*, Wennberg & Gittelsohn, *supra* note 33.
36. *See, e.g.*, Mark R. Chassin et al., *Variations in the Use of Medical and Surgical Services by the Medicare Population*, 314 NEW ENG. J. MED. 285 (1986).

Third, it would vest control over organ disposition with the donor or the donor's family. This would give the donor or the donor's family the psychological satisfaction of benefiting a human being. This has the ancillary benefit of allowing designated beneficiaries, persons or institutions, to have enforceable legal rights to the donated organs. This is an important potential counterforce to the present custom of requiring family consent, even though family consent is not now legally necessary.

Combining donor or family control over organ disposition with a forward contract of sale for the use of organs at death would alter the entire nature and perception of the transaction. Transplant procurement and surgical teams would have to defer to what is essentially a commercial judgment effectuated while the donor was alive and of sound mind. This would create a new calculus. At the present time the players are the procurement people, the physician of the potential donor, and the family. If the family objects, the prudent lawyer would advise the client, "look, the family members are the only ones around who can sue; they're the only ones who can cause trouble; they're the only ones who can go to the newspaper—so, defer to the family." With an enforceable contract, other players enter the game, and their interests must be taken into account. There is the patient/donor speaking not by means of an abstract donor card but specifically and compellingly through a commercial transaction. There is also the other party to the contract—the buyer/broker—who says "we did a deal and it's important to respect the contract." And third, and perhaps most importantly, there is an identified donee, a beneficiary who is lying in a hospital waiting to have his or her life saved. The beneficiary would say "the family may be finicky about this and I respect the family's judgment, but a deal was done, reliance on the transaction has been established, and the financial benefit has accrued or will accrue to the donor/seller or his or her beneficiary. My life and health are in the balance, and by enforcing the provisions of the contract I am respecting the autonomy of the donor, who made the choice to save lives by allowing use of his or her organs for transplantation."

Moreover, while one can understand the concerns of the family, those concerns must be put in context. The balance must appropriately not only consider the squeamishness of the family of the potential organ supplier but also examine the priority of saving an identified life and fulfilling a commitment made by the potential "donor" when he or she was competent to choose. The representative of the donee or of the contracting party would be facing a very different calculus on the evening news than currently exists. The public relations climate would inevitably concentrate on the primacy of lifesaving, especially when to save a life would be to fulfill the terms of a freely and fairly negotiated agreement and to honor the autonomy of the patient/donor/organ seller. So the introduction of commerce changes the legal advice, the public relations, the politics, and the whole nature of the transaction. The existence of a legally enforceable contract and the existence of enormous lifesaving stakes once there is an identified beneficiary create a tremendous counterforce to the current system.

Fourth, public policy would recognize a value to pluralism and diversity. It would allow for experimentation and innovation. There would be a substitution for the monolithic, national system of control that we currently have in the United Network for Organ Sharing (UNOS). The Organ Procurement and Transplantation Network (OPTN), administered by UNOS, still could be retained for education, for information, for the smooth transfer of organs, for matching of organs and so forth, but the OPTN would not have a regulatory, command-and-control function. It would recognize local and regional differences. It would respond to the need for clinical experimentation. In short, it would facilitate the smooth functioning of organ transplanation procedures and help to improve quality, but it would not seek to govern or control the process. Instead, the OPTN would respect pluralism and diversity.

Fifth, under a more mainstream policy orientation, there would be concern regarding the restrictive features of the current national system. There is considerable risk associated with the professional dominance that has characterized the medical care industry historically,[37] and that risk is particularly acute when the profession is in a position to exert control over potential competitors who seek to enter the market. The organ transplantation field has been characterized by professional control, and the OPTN provides a vehicle by which the professionals can impose their vision on potential competitors. The authority exercised by UNOS as administrator of the OPTN, if unconstrained, poses a considerable threat to the evolution of pluralism and competition in the organ transplantation marketplace.

At present, it is unclear who actually controls the OPTN policy-making process. Elsewhere, I have criticized the regulatory authority exercised by UNOS as administrator of the OPTN.[38] Partly in response to such

---

37. *See generally* PAUL STARR, THE SOCIAL TRANSFORMATION OF AMERICAN MEDICINE (1982).

38. *See* Blumstein, *supra* note 9, at 478.

criticism,[39] DHHS has asserted its power to review and approve of all OPTN regulatory policies.[40] Whether DHHS will rubber-stamp the regulatory vision of the OPTN embraced by UNOS, or whether it will strike out in a different direction is still unclear. It is within the power of DHHS, however, to alter the vision of the network so as to allow competition and encourage the promotion and preservation of different views on an array of organ transplantation issues. A particularly important objective, in this regard, would be to hold in check barriers to entry by new programs and to encourage young Turks to enter the field of organ transplantation.

III. DOES ORGAN TRANSPLANTATION WARRANT A DIFFERENT POLICY APPROACH FROM THAT OF MAINSTREAM MEDICAL CARE?

I have described mainstream public policy in the overall health care arena, explained how organ transplantation policy does not coincide with the mainstream, and analyzed how organ transplantation policy might look if it did coincide. Apart from different ideological perspectives, does the field of organ transplantation warrant such a different policy approach from that of mainstream medical care? I now want to present an approach toward consideration of that question.

A. The presumption for incentives in a market system

I would start with the assumption that organ transplantation policies should allow for financial incentives in the absence of convincing arguments to the contrary. Evidence from elsewhere in the health arena shows that incentives affect behavior. Evidence from abroad shows that financial incentives dramatically increase levels of transplantable organ supply.[41] The issue is increasingly being raised and discussed favorably in professional meetings and forums.[42] And a recent survey

---

39. *See id.* at 496 n: 245.

40. *See* Notice, Department of Health and Human Services, Health Care Financing Administration, 54 Fed. Reg. 51802 (1989).

41. *See* Raj Chengappa, *The Organs Bazaar*, INDIA TODAY, July 31, 1990, at 30.

42. *See, e.g.*, Thomas G. Peters, *Financial Incentives in Organ Donation: Current Issues*, 21 DIALYSIS & TRANSPLANTATION 270 (1992); Peters, *supra* note 11;

(*cont.*)

performed under the auspices of UNOS and published in *The Lancet* demonstrates that a majority of the respondents believed that some form of compensation should be offered in the United States to donors of transplantable organs; only 2% of those surveyed commented that use of financial incentives would be immoral or unethical.[43] I would require that those seeking to outlaw incentives in the area of organ transplantation persuasively make the case against commerce empirically or ethically. "In a nation whose institutions have relied on market mechanisms for making basic economic choices," governmental action that prohibits the use of incentives, which constitute a fundamental component of the market system, "bears a burden of persuasion."[44]

B. Organ procurement is a form of "commerce" and transplantable organs can be a form of "property" under the United States Constitution

In interesting ways, some courts have reinforced the case for allowing financial incentives to be introduced into the organ transplantation arena. A federal district court has found that organ procurement is "commerce" and is therefore protected by the commerce clause of the United States Constitution.[45] Also, a federal appeals court has held that a transplantable organ can be considered a form of "property" protected against deprivation under the due process clause of the Fourteenth Amendment.[46]

(42, *cont.*) TRANSPLANTATION AND COMMUNICATIONS IN THE '90S AND BEYOND 4 (unpublished consensus report of a forum presented by The Annenberg Washington Program of Northwestern University, The American Medical Association, and the Annenberg Center for Health Sciences at Eisenhower, April 22–25, 1990, (on file with the Annenberg Washington Program of Northwestern University)). *But see* Leon R. Kass, *Organs for Sale? Propriety, Property, and the Price of Progress*, 107 PUB. INTEREST 65 (1992).

43. *See* Dilip S. Kittur et al., *Incentives for Organ Donation?* 338 LANCET 1441 (1991).

44. James F. Blumstein & Frank A. Sloan, *Health Planning and Regulation Through Certificate of Need: An Overview*, 1978 UTAH L. REV. 3.

45. Delaware Valley Transplant Program v. Coye, 678 F. Supp. 479 (D.N.J. 1988) (granting injunction based upon the claim that state's designation of sole organ donor procurement agency for the State of New Jersey is violative of the commerce clause).

46. Brotherton v. Cleveland, 923 F.2d 477 (6th Cir. 1991) (holding that the wife of a deceased man had a property right in the decedent's corneas). The California Supreme Court, on the other hand, has held that cells from a removed spleen, used to form a commercially valuable cell line to produce

In *Delaware Valley Transplant Program v. Coye*,[47] the State of New Jersey forbade New Jersey hospitals from using an out-of-state organ procurement organization (OPO). A Philadelphia-based OPO that operated in sourthern New Jersey challenged the regulation as a violation of the commerce clause,[48] which prohibits state discrimination against interstate commerce.[49] The court found for the Philadelphia OPO and issued an injunction against New Jersey. Under commerce clause principles, New Jersey could not bar the interstate shipment of transplantable organs and could not ban the Philadelphia OPO from operating in New Jersey.[50]

In order to reach its decision, the court had to find that organ procurement and distribution constitute a form of commerce.[51] The court in *Delaware Valley Transplant Program* relied upon *Philadelphia v. New Jersey*,[52] a constitutional challenge under the commerce clause to New Jersey's banning of the dumping of garbage from Philadelphia in New Jersey landfills. The Supreme Court in *Philadelphia v. New Jersey* held that the traffic in garbage was a form of commerce and struck down New Jersey's ban on the importation of garbage as impermissible discrimination.[53] Just as the state in *Philadelphia v. New Jersey* could not ban the importation of an article of commerce (garbage), it could not ban the exportation of an article of commerce (transplantable organs) in *Delaware Valley Transplant Program*.[54]

In *Brotherton v. Cleveland*,[55] a "pulseless" person was found in an automobile, was taken to a hospital, and was pronounced dead on

---

lymphokines, are not a form of "property" protected under the state tort doctrine of conversion. Moore v. Regents of the University of Cal., 793 P.2d 479 (1990).

47. *Supra* note 45.

48. U.S. CONST. art. I, § 8, cl. 3.

49. Although the commerce clause is drafted as an authorization of power to the federal government, it has been interpreted for over a century to operate, in its dormant state, as an independent limitation on state police powers that unduly burden or discriminate against interstate commerce. *See* Hunt v. Washington State Apple Advertising Comm'n., 432 U.S. 333 (1977).

50. *Supra* note 45.

51. *Id.*

52. 437 U.S. 617 (1978).

53. *Id.*

54. The Supreme Court has held that bans on importation and on exportation of articles of commerce are presumptively unconstitutional. *See, e.g.,* Hughes v. Oklahoma, 441 U.S. 322 (1979).

55. Brotherton, *supra* note 46.

arrival. Because the death was considered a possible suicide, the body was taken to the county coroner's office for an autopsy. After the autopsy, the coroner permitted the decedent's corneas to be removed and used as "anatomical gifts." No approval for the anatomical gift was sought or received from the decedent's wife. The wife sued alleging that the county coroner had unconstitutionally deprived her of "property" (her husband's corneas) without due process of law.

The United States Court of Appeals for the Sixth Circuit noted that the wife's claim was "dependent upon her having a constitutionally protected property interest in her husband's corneas."[56] Upon an analysis of Ohio's laws, the Court of Appeals held that the wife had such a constitutionally protected property interest in her husband's corneas.[57]

The invocation of the commerce clause in *Delaware Valley Transplant Program* and the concept of property in *Brotherton* suggest that courts are not uncomfortable with the use of traditional commercial paradigms in considering organ transplantation issues. By analogy, these decisions lend support to the growing acceptance of adopting some form of a commercial paradigm in the organ transplantation context.

C. The advantages of a market approach

What are the advantages of the market approach, an approach that would allow individuals (or parents on behalf of their children) to enter into forward contracts while alive and in good health for the use of their organs for transplantation after their death?[58] I want to set forth two rationales simply and succinctly and then examine, at greater length, criticisms leveled at the use of markets.

---

56. *Id.* at 479.

57. For a discussion of the *Brotherton* case in the context of considering whether a presumed consent statute would constitute an unconstitutional taking of property, *see* Mehlman, *supra* note 13, at 53–9. On the general issue of body parts as property, *see* Guido Calabresi, *Do We Own Our Bodies?*, 1 HEALTH MATRIX 5 (1991).

58. In this article, I want to avoid specifying a specific market-based approach. My objective is to argue the general case. In practice, I would allow the market to function in developing effective strategies for inducing an increase in the supply of transplantable organs. The UNOS-sponsored article published in THE LANCET identified the following as "[s]ome of the more popular potential financial donor compensations" covered in the UNOS survey:

First, there is the libertarian argument in support of the use of incentives and markets. This position emphasizes respect for the autonomy of the donor (and the ability of the donor to choose), deemphasizes paternalism, and strengthens the hand of the individual rather than the family.[59] Payment to "donate"[60] allows a person to determine his or her own organs' fate, respects the right of the buyer to contract, and recognizes the ability of the medically needy donee beneficiary to benefit from the transaction.

In addition to the libertarian argument, there is also the utilitarian argument. That is, would or could incentives increase organ supply? Permitting contracts for the sale of organs and making provision for a

---

"(1) assistance in the payment of funeral expenses; (2) a cash award to the estate of the donor; (3) a cash award to a charity of the donor/donor family's choosing; (4) a limited low-cost life insurance policy redeemable upon the donation of organs by the deceased policy holder." *See* Kittur et al., *supra* note 43. Professor Henry Hansmann has proposed a reduction in medical insurance premiums for those who sign up to donate their organs at death. *See* Henry Hansmann, *The Economics and Ethics of Markets for Human Organs, in* ORGAN TRANSPLANTATION POLICY: ISSUES AND PROSPECTS 57 (James F. Blumstein & Frank A. Sloan eds., 1989). Dr. Thomas Peters has proposed a death benefit of $1000, analogous to a social insurance payment, for those whose organs are used in transplantation. *See* Peters, *supra* note 11. There have been numerous proposals for specific market-based systems designed to increase the supply of transplantable organs. I would like now to acknowledge those other proposals, although this is not designed to be a comprehensive listing. *See, e.g.*, Roger D. Blair & David L. Kaserman, *The Economics and Ethics of Alternative Cadaveric Organ Procurement Policies*, 8 YALE J. ON REG. 403 (1991); Lloyd R. Cohen, *Increasing the Supply of Transplant Organs: The Virtues of a Futures Market*, 58 GEO. WASH. L. REV. 1 (1989); Richard Schwindt & Aidan R. Vining, *Proposal for a Future Delivery Market for Transplant Organs*, 11 J. HEALTH POL., POL'Y & LAW 483 (1986); Aidan R. Vining & Richard Schwindt, *Have a Heart: Increasing the Supply of Transplant Organs for Infants and Children*, 7 J. POL'Y ANALYSIS & MGMT. 706 (1988). *See also* Erik S. Jaffe, Note, *"She's Got Bette Davis['s] Eyes": Assessing the Nonconsensual Removal of Cadaver Organs under the Takings and Due Process Clauses*, 90 COLUM. L. REV. 528 (1990). For critiques of these proposals, *see*, e.g., Kass, *supra* note 42; Richard D. Guttmann, *The Meaning of "The Economics and Ethics of Alternative Cadaveric Organ Procurement Policies,"* 8 YALE J. ON REG. 453 (1991).

59. *See, e.g.*, Lori B. Andrews, *My Body, My Property*, HASTINGS CTR. REP., Oct. 1986, at 28.

60. The term "donate" is a bit of an oxymoron in this context. It is noteworthy, however, that we are so imbued with the language of altruism that the term donor comes naturally, even when the proposal under consideration involves a mixture of altruism and the use of financial incentives rather than pure altruism through donation.

registry of potential donors would provide pressure to pursue transplants aggressively. A source of potential suppliers could be expected
to come forward,[61] and, once a contract had been entered into, the
purchaser and the ultimate beneficiary would be forceful advocates for
the effective use of transplantable organs to save lives.

D. Criticisms of markets

Criticisms leveled at the use of markets for increasing the supply of
transplantable organs can be either empirical or ethical in character. In
understanding and evaluating the criticisms of markets for transplantable organs, the analyst must bear in mind the framework within which
to consider objections to market-based proposals. In that context, it is
worth reiterating that the burden of persuasion should lie with those
advocating making market transactions illegal. Ultimately, the assign-
ment of the burden of persuasion may well be outcome determinative,
at least with regard to some portions of the argument.

1. Empirical criticisms

It is noteworthy that many critics of the use of markets and incentives
have focused on an empirical claim. Their argument is that the use of
financial incentives—allowing the market to function in this area—will
not result in an increase in the supply of transplantable organs. The
same claim was made ten to fifteen years ago regarding financial
incentives in medicine generally. But the empirical evidence from the
experience of the last ten years in the medical arena refutes this.
Incentives work. Objectors raise various concerns about the state of
mind of potential donors—fears, uncertainty and ignorance. These deal
not with the feasibility of a system of incentives but with the price that
would be needed to induce supply. Concerns concentrated on this type
of donor frame of mind do not address the question whether or not
incentives would work. If people are not inclined to donate, then that
means they will require more in the way of an inducement. Prospective
buyers would have to raise the price. This focuses, as an economist
would say, on the nature or characteristics of the supply curve, on its
price elasticity, not on whether inducements would ultimately work. It
is artificial to think in terms of absolutes—yes, people will contract for

---

61. See Chengappa, supra note 41 and accompanying text.

anatomical "gifts," or no, they will not enter into such contracts. It is better to think of what inducements are needed to encourage sufficient supply so as to satisfy the demand. That is, the issue is one of degree not one of absolutes.[62]

If the issue concerning commerce in transplantable organs is really an empirical argument—i.e., would it work to increase the supply of transplantable organs—then the scientist's view should come into operation: if in doubt, do a controlled experiment. Define a region, repeal the federal ban on the purchase and sale of organs for transplant in that area,[63] and, with proper controls and monitoring, let us see what happens.[64]

The problem is that this scientific approach of experimentalism is not satisfactory to many of the market critics. They worry that the altruistic system will be undermined and that the damage will be irreversible. The thought seems to be that the use of incentives is like an incurable infectious disease—once it is unleashed, it will deal a fateful and fatal blow to the altruistic underpinnings of the existing system of organ donation, a blow from which the existing system would not recover.

This is a hard position to counter because neither side has firm data. The evidence from India and Egypt indicates that inducements do work.[65] Evidence from other areas of health care suggest the same thing. It is not reasonable to maintain an empirically-based criticism of financial incentives and simultaneously deny society the opportunity at least to have an experiment, even if only in a region and not in the whole nation.[66]

---

62. Quality, which is a concern, arguably could be monitored where there is a contract and where patients have agreed to allow their organ to be used for transplant at their death. The purchaser would have an incentive to keep the seller's organ healthy, and in most scenarios the seller would have the same incentive. This makes the organ market distinguishable from the blood sale market, where quality is a serious concern.

63. Section 301(a) of the National Organ Transplant Act, enacted in 1984, bans the use of any "valuable consideration" for inducing potential donors to allow their organs to be used for transplantation. 42 U.S.C. § 274e(a) (1988).

64. The proposal for a controlled experiment accords, in broad brush, with the death-benefit idea recently advanced by Dr. Thomas Peters, although the contours of his proposal seem more narrowly drawn than the controlled experiment proposed in text. *See* Peters, *supra* note 11.

65. *See* Chengappa, *supra* note 41.

66. The empirical argument becomes linked to the ethical argument to some extent. Part of the concern about irreversibility is a fear that altruism will be

(*cont.*)

In appraising the empirical criticism, the analyst must return to first principles so as assess the argument within the appropriate analytical framework: the burden of persuasion is on those seeking to outlaw market-oriented behavior in our democratic society. In the absence of firm evidence, or an experiment, we should legalize commerce in organs for transplant, as other commerce in medical care is now permitted.

2. Ethical criticisms

I now consider the ethical criticisms of commerce in transplantable organs. I deal with these in specific contexts, taking on the harder claims first.

The effect of markets on the distribution of organs

Much of the ethical concern regarding commerce in transplantable organs focuses on the issue of distribution. That is, who gets the organ available for transplantation? What is the effect of a market in transplantable organs on the distribution of organs? This set of questions focuses on the demand side of the market.

The ethical thesis is that organs are different from other commodities or services that are distributed by the market system. Organs, argue critics of markets, should be allocated by medical criteria, not by financial considerations. This claim needs to be taken seriously. I would note, however, that some make the same claim for all medical care.[67] We know that financial considerations are taken into account in medical care generally, so the issue regarding transplantable organs

---

(66, cont.) eroded in practice. Critics of markets decry this, finding it lamentable as a policy development. Perhaps altruism has some immeasurable independent virtue worthy of some positive evaluation in the policy making process, but that virtue is hardly confined to the organ transplantation arena. When measured against the benefits of saving lives and improving health, the independent value of altruism surely must play second fiddle.

67. Ten years ago I was involved in a debate on rationing medical care in which the claim was made that medical care should be allocated purely on the basis of medical criteria. For opposing viewpoints on the debate, see James F. Blumstein, *Rationing Medical Resources: A Constitutional, Legal, and Policy Analysis*, 59 TEXAS L. REV. 1345 (1981); James F. Blumstein, *Distinguishing Government's Responsibility in Rationing Public and Private Medical Resources*, 60 TEXAS L. REV. 899 (1982); and Rand E. Rosenblatt, *Rationing "Normal" Health Care: The Hidden Legal Issues*, 59 TEXAS L. REV. 1401 (1981).

would have to be argued on the basis that organ transplantation is different from other forms of medical care—not only from medical care generally but also from comparable lifesaving therapies.[68]

In my view, the original banning of market transactions in transplantable organs stemmed from an understandable yet ultimately unsophisticated linkage of issues surrounding the demand and the supply sides of the market. A market in transplantable organs can function on the supply side and, if desired on ethical grounds. Society can leave the demand side to a non-market form of distribution.

The concern by ethical critics of commerce in transplantable organs is with the effect of wealth inequality on the distribution of available organs. There is a special claim that while wealth inequality is acceptable as a general matter, it is unacceptable as a basis for deciding which persons are to be recipients of organ transplants.[69] This is the notion that organ transplants constitute a "merit good."[70]

The problem, however, can be resolved by public subsidy for those whose inadequate level of wealth bars access. The kidney program is an example of a publicly financed program for a specific illness and a specific set of procedures. To establish a principled basis for this type of categorical public support for kidney transplantation, however, advocates must be prepared to justify a kidney transplant program in comparison to other transplant therapies, such as heart or liver transplants, which are more likely to deal with life-threatening situations and which are not funded as generously by the federal government.[71] Also, those who make claims of special consideration for transplant programs must be prepared to demonstrate that the justification for special status for organ transplantation does not apply as persuasively to non-transplant treatments of other life-threatening

---

68. On the question of government's role in paying for organ transplantation, see Blumstein, *supra* note 9, at 453–60.

69. Presumably, the life-or-death character of many transplants, coupled with the supply constraints on transplantable organs, distinguish organ transplantation from other areas of medical care. Of course, this is an incomplete basis for distinction since there are other lifesaving therapies and since not all transplants (*e.g.,* kidneys) are of a lifesaving character given the availability of alternative therapies (*e.g.,* dialysis).

70. *See* James F. Blumstein & Michael Zubkoff, *Perspectives on Government Policy in the Health Sector,* 51 MILBANK MEMORIAL FUND Q.: HEALTH & SOC'Y 395, 407–12 (1973).

71. *See generally* Peter H. Schuck, *Government Funding for Organ Transplants, in* ORGAN TRANSPLANTATION POLICY: ISSUES AND PROSPECTS 169 (James F. Blumstein & Frank A. Sloan eds., 1989).

illnesses (e.g., public financing of drugs such as AZT for AIDS patients). Does society have an obligation to provide a public subsidy to make available and distribute this type of life-enhancing or life-prolonging drug? And if so, must the drug be made available without a fee, so that commerce is completely eliminated in the allocation of the scarce resource? If wealth can make a difference with regard to AZT, for example, why is it unacceptable for financial considerations to enter into organ allocation decisions?

Special consideration for organ transplants must also distinguish not only other lifesaving but also other quality-of-life-enhancing procedures. Dialysis, after all, is an alternative to kidney transplantation, albeit less desirable therapeutically.[72] Thus, since an alternative treatment regimen exists, kidney transplantation is not necessarily a lifesaving procedure. Other parts of the kidney transplantation process require a fee. Whereas kidneys cannot be paid for by the patient, and kidney donors cannot receive compensation for their beneficence, organ procurement organizations can be paid for their organ procurement efforts by hospitals. Drugs are paid for, hospital stays are paid for, physicians are compensated. Money matters in every dimension of organ transplantation. It is not so clear why ethical critics become so fastidious, so squeamish, about paying for the lifegiving organ itself.

There is an irony at work here. Advocates for funding of organ transplants by third-party payers claim that organ transplantation is in fact ordinary and necessary medical care—mainstream, non-experimental medicine indistinguishable from other lifesaving and life-enhancing treatments for purposes of third-party reimbursement. The claim that organ transplantation be covered by insurance requires that organ transplantation be viewed as just another effective therapy, like many others covered and paid for under traditional medical insurance policies and programs. The claim for third-party coverage rests on the mainstream status, the lack of specialness of organ transplants. Yet that very specialness serves as the ethical foundation of the underlying hostility to commerce in transplantable organs. There is a clear tension between these two positions.

Further, for these ethical objections to commerce in organs to make sense, there must be a willingness on the part of the objectors to exalt these distributive values above overall lifesaving and quality-of-life-enhancing objectives. This is true because, for the ethical discussion, we

---

72. *See* Eggers, *supra* note 6.

must assume that, as an empirical matter, commerce in transplantable organs will result in an increased supply of such organs and, consequently, more saved and quality-of-life enhanced lives from transplantation procedures.

Some have made the forthright argument that it is better not to save lives in order to maintain distributional equity. I find that argument troubling. If one assumes that a price induces more supply, and that a wealthy person's life is thereby saved, how is the poor person harmed as compared with the status quo? One must take the position that it is better to deprive the wealthy person of a transplant, which by hypothesis would not otherwise be available, in order to preserve some sense of egalitarian justice. This is a difficult outcome to impose on a person in the name of fairness since the economically disadvantaged person is not benefited in any tangible way by prohibiting the wealthier person from using his or her resources to pay for a transplantable organ.

This is a genuinely troubling ethical dilemma that, as an intellectual matter, is worthy of further investigation, debate and discussion. As a pragmatic matter, however, the issue can be finessed in the name of incremental reform. For the time being, at least, market-oriented reformist efforts can be concentrated on the introduction of commercial incentives on the supply side of the marketplace, leaving intact a non-market-driven system for the distribution of transplantable organs on the demand side.

The effect of markets on live donors

A second difficult question is whether a prospective system of commerce in transplantable organs should permit payment for use of organs provided by (i.e., sold by) live donors. At least for the present, this ethically serious and troubling issue also can be finessed. Market-oriented reforms can focus, at least at the initial stage, on the use of markets exclusively for the sale of cadaveric organs, preferably by a forward contract.

The ethical concern with live donors is coercion, but the coercion claim may not be as much of a problem as some would argue. While there is an increase in choice, it is coercion only if we equate coercion with hard choices.

We do allow people to choose risk for a price. Life with one kidney is risky. But the question is whether this is a socially acceptable level of risk that should be subject to private choice and decision making or whether the risk should be banned by collective action through paternalistic governmental regulation. Professor Henry Hansmann, for example, has argued that the risk of living with one kidney is quite moderate, equivalent to driving back and forth to work sixteen miles a day.[73] Society tolerates that level of risk in other areas, he argues, why not in the transplant area as well? Clearly there is a benefit for the recipient/purchaser, whose health is improved. Arguably, there are also considerable benefits for the "donor"/seller, who can use the funds received in the transaction for other advantageous purposes.

One must hasten to add that, if any system of commerce is established involving live-"donor" organs, safeguards are necessary to assure voluntarism and to bar other uses of body parts via coerced, not induced sale. Still, despite any safeguards that one might develop, the paternalism concern regarding live-"donor" organ sales is real and pervasive.

Also, there is worry about what some view as organ imperialism— the sale of organs by poor or third-world persons to provide organs for wealthy people. Rationally, the analyst may note that the sellers deem themselves better off, do not consider the risk to be excessive, and deem organ donation to be an avenue of opportunity. The skeptic may even call paternalistic objections to this activity elitist or illustrative of a certain "feel-good" morality. Yet a typical reaction is one, perhaps, of revulsion. And although this may be irrational, non-rational, or exercising a form of symbolic hypocrisy, the objections exist and persist.

The effect of a market for cadaveric organ sale on the "Donor's" family and on society

It is now appropriate to address the issue of cadaveric organ sale. There are essentially two concerns here—the potential effect of a market in cadaveric organs on the family of the "donor" and the potentially dehumanizing effect of organ sales on society.[74]

The family issue is a legitimate concern. By selling his or her organs during life by forward contracting for transplantation at the time of death, an individual takes charge of the disposition of his or her organs at death. In the world of estate planning, this is not unusual, rather it is the norm. By allowing sales and by enforcing these forward contracts

---

73. Hansmann, *supra* note 58, at 72–74.
74. For a forceful statement of this perspective, see Guttmann, *supra* note 58.

for organ transplantation, society validates the autonomy of the individual. At the same time, society takes away the ability of the family to veto the decendent's decision to allow use of his or her organs for transplantation purposes. This undoubtedly detracts from the "silver lining" phenomenon through which family members, in the exercise of altruism, feel good about giving the organs of a loved one to save the life of another human being.

The psychological satisfaction of the family in this circumstance can be considerable, but the autonomy of the patient, if it is to be adequately respected, must outweigh the family's concern. This is, of course, the normal pattern with respect to inheritance, and it is the clear determination of the existing legal regime under the UAGA, which already vests legal authority in the individual to donate his or her organs for transplantation irrespective of the wishes of the family. The family veto recognized in the transplant community is an extralegal custom not validated by existing law. Indeed, the UAGA was expressly drafted to overcome the family veto, giving primacy to the autonomy of the individual donor.[75] Given the existing legal framework, which does not recognize the family veto, the supposed loss of the family's psychological well-being is a weak claim. Ultimately, the autonomy of the donor and the welfare of the beneficiaries who receive the transplantable organs must outweigh the claims of the family.[76] In any event, the establishment of a market for cadaveric organs will take nothing from families to which they are currently legally entitled.[77]

The potentially adverse effect on society of a market in cadaveric organs stems from a concern about the commodification of human body parts (HBPs).[78] This is an abstract, hazy issue. For example, Dr.

---

75. *See supra* notes 18–23 and accompanying text.

76. Rejection of the family veto was one of the recommendations stemming from a joint forum of the American Medical Association, the Annenberg Washington Program of Northwestern University, and the Annenberg Center for Health Sciences at Eisenhower: "An individual's decision to donate should in every case be respected; health care professionals and relatives should act in accordance with that decision, thus, respecting the donor's right and fulfilling the donor's desires." TRANSPLANTATION AND COMMUNICATIONS IN THE '90S AND BEYOND, *supra* note 42, at 2.

77. For individuals who wish to provide this form of psychic satisfaction to members of their family, the option of delegating this choice to family members would continue to exist under the UAGA. The choice of altruism as the basis for an anatomical gift at death would still be available.

78. For a general discussion of the commodification issue, *see* Margaret Jane Radin, *Market-Inalienability*, 100 HARV. L. REV. 1849 (1987).

Leon R. Kass, who objects to the use of markets in transplantable organs, recognizes that his objections "appeal . . . largely to certain hard-to-articulate intuitions and sensibilities that . . . belong intimately to the human experience of our own humanity."[79]

One set of objections to commodification of HBPs focuses on the value of communitarianism. There is the belief that the establishment of a market in cadaveric organs poses a threat to the value of altruism. I just do not see this as a transplant issue. It is an issue that deals with other, broader philosophical issues about how society should be organized and about how people should be motivated to live their lives. Advocates of communitarianism generally are suspicious of what they regard as the atomization of society that stems from reliance on markets for making economic allocation decisions. They are hostile to market transactions, and they worry that commodification of HBPs places yet another set of decisions into an economic context with which they are none-too-pleased to begin with. Again, I view this type of concern to be quite unrelated to organ transplantation issues *per se* but rather related to broader humanitarian concerns that underlie much of how market-based economies function in general.

Significantly, in the context of a market for cadaveric organs, there is no issue of coercion as there could be in the context of live-"donor" organ sales. Similarly, there is no real issue of organ imperialism, there is no concern regarding irreversibility,[80] and there is no problem of exploitation of the poor. Professor Lloyd Cohen, who has written in support of a futures market in transplantable organs, has a wonderful statement regarding the non-risk of exploitation of the poor in the context of a market for cadaveric organs: "[I]n the cadaver market the vendors are neither rich nor poor, merely dead."[81]

The loss of altruism should not in itself be viewed as a problem, except if it results in reduced supply of transplantable organs. Supply

---

79. Kass, *supra* note 42, at 84. Dr. Kass asserts that the sale of body parts comes "perilously close to selling out our souls," *id.* at 83, yet he concedes that "rational calculation" justifies further extension of the lifesaving potential of organ transplantation, presumably by sale of transplantable organs if need be. *Id.* at 86. Dr. Kass laments this conflict, which he sees as posing a painful dilemma. *Id.*

80. When a transaction cannot be undone—e.g., the sale of an organ by a live "donor" or the sale of a human being into slavery—there may be a stronger reason to examine the fairness and the wisdom of allowing exchange transactions.

81. *See* Cohen, *supra* note 58, at 30.

is an empirical not an ethical concern. The issue is not whether or not altruism is a good thing. The question is whether market transactions should be made illegal. Advocates of markets in cadaveric organs have no desire to make altruism a felony. Altruism can coexist peacefully with a flourishing market for cadaver organs. The claim of market proponents is based upon principles of freedom, autonomy, and choice. Indeed, when one carefully examines the argument for preserving altruism by outlawing market transactions, one wonders whether the real fear is that legalization of market transactions will in fact work. That is, given a choice, people would choose to participate in a market and would abandon altruism. Unpacked, the argument to outlaw market exchanges to preserve altruism is in reality an argument to coerce altruism. This surely is a strange way of promoting the supposed good feeling of communitarian solidarity that comes from voluntary donations of the organs of a recently deceased loved one for the benefit of another human being.

To make out the case against market transactions in transplantable organs, advocates for that position must establish the unique features of organs and organ transplantation. Since, in a market economy, market-based transactions are the norm, those seeking to curtail the operation of a market must show that there are special reasons justifying the restriction. I will not argue that organs and their transplantation are not unique in this policy-relevant sense.

There are numerous other lifesaving or life-enhancing therapies for which sales are not prohibited. There is no ban on the sale of alternatives to organ transplantation, such as kidney dialysis. There is no ban on the sale of substitutes for failed body parts, such as artificial organs and other artificial body parts. Thus, we are left with a gnawing concern because the transplantable organ derives from a dead human body. This is not an objection to the use of the organs of a cadaver for transplantation purposes, since a donated organ is acceptable. It is just a question of how we induce donors or families to donate those organs. Does this, as Dr. Kass ominously warns, really "come perilously close to selling out our souls"?[82] The UNOS-sponsored survey, which showed support for compensation for use of transplantable organs, would certainly call that predictive judgment into question.[83]

Analysts must balance the hazy, abstract concern about the effect on society of the mechanism used to motivate individuals to supply their

---

82. *See* Kass, *supra* note 42, at 83.
83. *See* Kittur et al., *supra* note 43.

organs at the time of death for transplantation against other, fundamental values. When life and death are in the balance as far as recipients are concerned and when libertarian values of individual autonomy are involved as far as the "donor" is concerned, I must conclude that there is an insufficient basis to warrant a flat-out prohibition on forward contracting while an individual is alive for the use of that individual's organs for transplantation at the time of death.

IV. CONCLUSION

I have discussed the advantages of allowing commerce in organs in the form of forward contracts for transplantable cadaveric organs.[84] To summarize briefly, some of those advantages are:

- There is a shift in the locus of decision making away from the bedside of the dying family member to an earlier time when an individual can make a determination about organ sale or donation while he or she is healthy and can act coolly and rationally.
- Recognition of market transactions promotes and validates the autonomy of the individual donor/seller.
- Legalization of market exchanges for cadaveric organs creates a legal and public-relations counterforce at the time of a "donor's" death so that the owner/purchaser of the organ and the potential and identified recipient of the transplantable organ can counteract the extralegal influence of the reluctant family of the potential donor and possibly of the attending physician as well.[85]
- Use of financial incentives is likely to induce a greater supply of needed transplantable organs than the current, exclusively altruistic system.

These advantages take on added significance because of the acute need for transplantable organs and the dearth of available organ supply under the current system.[86] This is where the success of organ

---

84. As I have indicated earlier, I am not the first to advocate development of a market in cadaveric organs. *See* sources cited *supra* note 58.

85. An important safeguard would be a requirement that the physician who certifies the death of the organ supplier be independent of the family of the decedent, of the family of the potential recipient, of the owner of the organ, and of any institution that had a stake in the transplant procedure.

86. *See supra* notes 1–6 and accompanying text.

transplantation makes a difference. The squeamishness about markets could be indulged when the stakes were not so high. The lifesaving ability of organ transplantation means that organ supply shortages are costing lives. The claim by organ transplantation experts to mainstream status within the medical community, along with third-party payment for what is now considered to be ordinary and necessary medical treatment, suggest that it is now time to emphasize the similarities between organ transplantation and other forms of lifesaving and quality-of-life-enhancing medical procedures rather than emphasizing the differences. Values regarding organ transplantation fit within the mainstream. They are not unique. We have allowed this ghettoization of organ transplantation policy within the health policy arena to go on for too long. At this point I do not argue for a complete, full-scale market approach. I do not now call for creation of a market for live-"donor" organs. Nor do I now call for experimenting with a market on the demand side for the distribution of transplantable organs. But I do call for a controlled supply-side experiment with the sale of cadaveric organs. Permitting the sale of cadaveric organs in advance through forward contracts, with the concomitant establishment of a computerized donor registry, would represent a reasonable, modest, incremental experiment, one that is well worth trying. This is especially true given the lives at stake.[87] This would allow for a constructive blend of altruism and self-interest and nurture the hope that that combination would help to reduce the existing shortage of transplantable organs. Upon analysis, my reluctant conclusion is that the opposition to a proposal for experimenting with the sale of organs is based upon prejudice not reason.

---

87. *See* Peters, *supra* note 11.

Forcing rescue: the landscape of health care provider obligations to treat patients

Barry R. Furrow

I. INTRODUCTION

A poor citizen living in America suffers a range of indignities—poor housing and diet, limited educational opportunities, a high risk of becoming a crime victim. Restricted access to health care is another such indignity, a fatal one in the wrong circumstances. Between 1975 and 1986 the proportion of low income persons covered by Medicaid fell from 63% to 38%, primarily due to tightened eligibility requirements.[1] During this same period the number of Americans living at or above 125% of the federal poverty level increased by 27%.[2] Hospitals' abilities to subsidize indigent care by cost-shifting to private payers have diminished, as they are forced to negotiate discounts with insurers and employers.[3] Employers now offer fewer and less extensive health care options to their employees, including reduced dependent coverage.

---

1. Michael A. Dowell, *State Insurance Programs for the Uninsured Poor*, Clearinghouse Rev., June 1989, at 141.
2. *Id.*
3. Richard W. Foster, *Cost-Shifting Under Cost Reimbursement and Prospective Payment*, 4 J. HEALTH ECON. 261 (1985).

Justice and Health Care: Comparative. Perspectives Edited by A. Grubb and M.J. Mehlman. © 1995 John Wiley & Sons Ltd.

Those who lack health insurance have trouble finding care.[4] A 1986 study found that nearly 14 million people said they did not even seek health care because they would not be able to afford it.[5] The situation has only deteriorated since 1986. "The uninsured are less likely to get their young children adequately immunized, less likely to receive prenatal care, less likely to have their blood pressure checked, and less likely to see a physician even when they have serious symptoms."[6] When uninsured patients do seek care from hospitals, they are often turned away or superficially treated and transferred to stressed and overburdened public hospitals.[7] When they do receive health care in hospitals, indigent patients experience a higher mortality rate because they do not receive as many high-cost procedures.[8]

The United States has a health care access problem that makes us the embarrassment of modern industrialized societies. Yet, ironically, Americans seem to view access to health care as almost a "right", an egalitarian value that led to political passage of the Medicare and Medicaid programs.[9] These programs consume a significant portion of state and federal budgets, in contrast to housing and food policies characterized mostly by their penuriousness. Access to health care, with

---

4. Emily Friedman, *The Uninsured: From Dilemma to Crisis*, 265 JAMA 2491 (1991).

5. Dowell *supra* note 1 (citing THE ROBERT WOOD JOHNSON FOUNDATION, SPECIAL REPORT—ACCESS TO HEALTH CARE IN THE UNITED STATES: RESULTS OF A 1986 SURVEY (1987)).

6. Dowell, *supra* note 1, at 142. *See generally* Colin McCord & Harold P. Freeman, *Excess Mortality in Harlem*, 322 NEW ENG J. MED. 173 (1990).

7. Andrew B. Bindman et al., *Consequences of Queuing for Care At a Public Hospital Emergency Department*, 266 JAMA 1091 (1991). *See generally* Emily Friedman, *Public Hospitals: Doing What Everyone Wants Done But Few Others Wish to Do*, 257 JAMA 1437 (1987); Andrew B. Bindman et al., *A Public Hospital Closes: Impact on Patients' Access to Care and Health Status*, 264 JAMA 2899 (1990).

8. Jack Hadley et al., *Comparison of Uninsured and Privately Insured Hospital Patients: Condition on Admission, Resource Use, and Outcome*, 265 JAMA 374 (1991). For an excellent survey of research on problems caused by limited access to health care, *see* Karen Davis, *Inequality and Access to Health Care*, 69 MILBANK Q. 253 (1991).

9. The notion of a "right" to health care can mean many different things, from a constitutionally based guarantee like that in the Italian constitution, to a statutory claim based on eligibility thresholds such as Medicare eligibility. For a range of definitions, *see* Mark Kelman, *Health Care Rights: Distinct Claims, Distinct Justifications*, 3 STAN. L. & POL'Y. REV. 90 (1991). *See also* James F. Blumstein, *Financing Uncompensated Care: An Approach to the Issues*, 38 J. LEGAL EDUC. 511 (1988); Sarah H. Carey, *A Constitutional Right to Health Care: An Unlikely Development*, 23 CATH. U. L. REV. 492 (1974).

government help, has become part of American political conscious-ness.[10] A principle of egalitarianism has at times driven national health policy, fueled by public discomfort at the thought of not providing the poor and the elderly with a financial net when they face catastrophic illness and its expense. At the same time, the strong libertarian streak embedded in the American character has often braked the ship of state, diverting impulses toward consistent funding for the poor by suppor-ting a conception of health care as a service best provided by physicians and providers within the parameters of contract and charity.[11] "Trust us," resonate doctors at the frequency of libertarian-ism. "We are professionals, driven by our fiduciary duties to help you." "Grant us respect," chant hospitals, "for we are charities with all that implies." "Leave politics out of health care," the full chorus repeats in a basso ostinato, "for we are nonpolitical."

The realm of "rights" talk offers a useful frame of reference for discussing the current state of access to health care. Judge-made and statutory requirements imposed on health care providers—to rescue patients from a crisis, to fund free care, to mandate benefits—are "rights"-based approach to health care access. Under what circumstan-ces, then, are physicians, health care providers, and insurers compelled to treat patients (or pay for their treatment) at the risk of some legal penalty for failure to comply? What moral vision of health care obligations unifies these obligations imposed on providers by regula-tory schemes, with insurance law obligations imposed by the courts, the handling of "bad debts" by taxing authorities, tax exemptions, and judicially imposed rules? Finally, what more can be done to promote access to necessary health care?

---

10. The best treatment of cultural attitudes of Americans toward welfare and toward health care services can be found in THEODORE R. MARMOR ET AL., AMERICA'S MISUNDERSTOOD WELFARE STATE: PERSISTENT MYTHS, EN-DURING REALITIES (1990).

11. The social legislation of the 1960s and 1970s pushed America toward an egalitarian model of health care delivery.

A uniquely American phenomenon, however, has been the endeavor to extract an *egalitarian* distribution of health care from a delivery system still firmly grounded in *libertarian* principles ... in no other modern society espousing egalitarian principles for the distribution of health care have physicians and hospitals been quite so free as they have in the United States to organize their facilities as they see fit, to practice medicine as they see fit, and to price their services as they see fit.

Uwe E. Reinhardt, *Uncompensated Hospital Care, in* UNCOMPENSATED HOSPITAL CARE: RIGHTS AND RESPONSIBILITIES 8–9 (Frank A. Sloan et al. eds., 1986).

The current debate over national health insurance may lead to broad-based reform of the American system. Or it may not. Comprehensive reform of our expensive, and yet, inadequate, health care system awaits the commitment of a President facing a powerful array of interest groups. Even if some system reform results from the efforts of a new administration, "rescue" obligations will still need to be explored and expanded. This article will pursue a "rights"-based approach, unfashionable in an era of efficiency, scarce resources, and sympathy for constraints on health care providers. The exquisite sensitivity to the world of scarce resources, often displayed by analysts, too readily concedes to providers their desires to retain as much autonomy as possible and to prevent further slippage away from the era of the blank check and the independent provider. Affirmative obligations by courts, tax collectors, and other agents of the state, while certainly inefficient and problematic at times, have advantages. Such obligations tighten the screws on the health care industry, force physicians to better define their professional responsibilities, and stretch the resources of providers and insurers in socially valuable directions. These pressures may speed reform of financial and structural barriers to access. More indigent individuals will ultimately receive more and better care than at present, through expanded obligations of providers to care for patients—to "rescue" them from their distress.[12] Such obligations are not imposed by agents of the state our of thin air; they are grounded in the definition of health professionalism, the images and promises projected by providers, and the concrete expectations created. They are therefore morally justifiable, and as such, not simply conscription without justification.

A. The definition of "rescue"

A duty to rescue is an enforceable legal obligation to help someone out of a situation of peril without a specific prior agreement to do so and without the promise of compensation. Such burdens run the gamut from a doctor treating a stranger in an emergency without the promise of payment, to a hospital providing free care and tolerating a certain level of bad debts, to an insurer paying for health care treatment

---

12. *See* Robert J. Blendon et al., *Uncompensated Care By Hospitals or Public Insurance for the Poor: Does It Make A Difference?*, 314 NEW ENG. J. MED. 1160 (1986) (suggesting that growing reliance on uncompensated care may adversely affect the health care received by the poor).

without a prior agreement to do so. The phrase "uncompensated care" is often used to describe these externally imposed burdens on providers, and "mandated benefits" are those which statutes require employers to provide.[13] These phrases have a clinical sound that obscures the real desperation of individuals presenting in distress, whether to an emergency room or a doctor's office. I prefer to use the phrase "forced rescue" to better capture the desperation of the vulnerable, in need of rescue, and the resistance of providers to such rescue, therefore requiring the coercive power of legal institutions.

A forced rescue context involves a vulnerable person in need, someone who will suffer or die from the denial of an essential health care service,[14] and a provider who is linked to the vulnerable person by one of a number of connections. These links are discovered or constructed by courts and legislatures. Some justifications for forcing rescue on providers include:

- a definition of the provider role, and the duties inherent in that role, that transcends contract limits;
- the creation of reasonable expectations by the provider and reliance by patients;
- a utilitarian justification in "easy" or cost-effective rescue situations;
- recognition of the economic and technological power of providers and the reciprocal burdens such power should properly require.

B. The role of affirmative duties

Is it misguided to cast social and even legal obligations on individual professionals and the medical profession collectively? Skeptics claim providers have obligations bearing on distributive justice only through "specific contractual arrangements when they enter into roles within the social system of health-care institutions."[15] When existing institutional arrangements for the provision of health care fail, these skeptics

---

13. Hawaii mandates benefits as the result of an ERISA (Employee Retirement Income Security Act) waiver. *See generally* BARRY FURROW ET AL., HEALTH LAW: CASES, MATERIALS AND PROBLEMS (2nd ed. 1990).

14. For an earlier treatment of some of these issues, *see* George J. Annas, *Beyond the Good Samaritan: Should Doctors Be Required to Provide Essential Services?*, 8 HASTINGS CENTRE REP., Apr. 1978, at 16.

15. NORMAN DANIELS, JUST HEALTH CARE 118 (1985).

contend that the full extent of provider obligations is to work toward new arrangements to achieve a just distribution of health care.

> Thus, the individual physician or resident does not have an obligation to treat the underserved patients unless he has undertaken such an obligation through prior agreements and decisions. But if such patients exist, then institutional structures, such as incentives which work through reimbursement structures, have to be altered so that some physicians are drawn into undertaking the appropriate obligations.[16]

This is a narrow position: positing obligations created through preexisting contract relations, and expanding obligations to care for needy patients only through voluntarily accepted new distributive structures.

The customary arguments against affirmative obligations to provide care are threefold. First, provision of free health care by providers typically requires an unfair and inefficient cross subsidy from one group of patients to another.[17] However, given the vagaries of hospital pricing structures generally, cross subsidization may not be any less fair than hospital charges to paying patients.[18] If such a subsidy is imposed on all providers, and external payers resist increased charges, the profession will absorb the costs through somewhat lower wages. This is hardly unfair to patients. For example, if a state were to require a certain level of annual pro bono care by each physician as a condition for receiving and retaining a medical license, this would be a subsidy internal to the profession, simply another requirement for the license. It may be objectionable to the medical profession, but it is not unfair to patients and may not be unfair to doctors if the burden is not excessive and is fairly distributed among them.

Second, critics argue that it is preferable to use the power of the government to provide rescue in a systematic way, using the power of taxation to spread the cost fairly. This assumes reducing or eliminating uncompensated care of all kinds. Such a distributional answer through government funding increases may well be preferable, assuring everyone some minimal level of necessary care. But in a world of

---

16. *Id.* at 119.

17. *See* Foster, *supra* note 3, at 261.

18. [I]f the hospital did not treat the poor, its pricing behavior for paying patients would not necessarily be any less irrational or exploitive. It would only make different use of the profits." Mark A. Hall & John D. Colombo, *The Charitable Status of Nonprofit Hospitals: Toward a Donative Theory of Tax Exemption*, 66 WASH L. REV. 307, 363 n. 198 (1991).

deficits and scarce resources, a second best solution will have to suffice. Legal obligations serve a vital gap-filling role in stretching resources in such a world.

Third, libertarian critics object to any affirmative obligation not freely chosen by a provider by claiming that such an obligation is "coercive" and likely to impose excessive enforcement costs. Richard Epstein argues that in the case of moral duties to rescue, "a system of informal norms may influence behavior more effectively than a system of legal coercion."[19] Self-help motivated by benevolence and altruism is preferable, he contends, and intermediate social institutions— charities, social leaders—can do the job.[20] "It is a mistake to think that legal bonds only reinforce social bonds. In many instances, they overpower and destroy them."[21] On this view, altruism is stifled by obligations imposed by the state through its agents—courts and the legislature.[22] Yet, this critique fails to recognize the complex new world of health care systems, professional obligations, and bureaucratic health care. Legal bonds also create social bonds that were nonexistent or weak to start with, and may bolster fading charitable impulses.

The health care industry and medical professionals have extensive affirmative obligations: hospitals as charities exist by legal policy through the tax code, massively subsidized by implicit national policy; physicians are licensed by the state, measured against a role defined by licensing boards and courts, and credentialled by hospital medical staffs in conformity with mandated institutional requirements. An abstract debate about coercion and social versus legal bonds is largely irrelevant to the more complicated issues of providing health care. Health care providers resemble public utilities in some of their characteristics: they provide basic needs, they operate within an environment in which market forces function poorly, and they require external regulation.

Beneficence is not a suitable starting point for questions of access to health care. A system of duties and rights needs to be motivated

---

19. Richard A. Epstein, *Book Review: Rights and "Rights Talk"*, 105 HARV L. REV. 1106, 1118 (1992) (reviewing MARY ANN GLENDON, RIGHTS TALK: THE IMPOVERISHMENT OF POLITICAL DISCOURSE (1991)).

20. *Id.* at 1118.

21. *Id.* at 1119.

22. Ronald M. Green, *Altruism in Health Care, in* BENEFICENCE AND HEALTH CARE 239 (Earl E. Shelp ed., 1982) addresses this concern.

independently of beneficence.[23] An ideal health care system would not have to rely on forced rescue, but surely rescue can be demanded in the absence of the ideal. In an imperfect world where some people experience inadequate health care access all the time, and others some of the time, legal obligations serve to counter the deficiencies of voluntarism, the shortcuts induced by market pressures, and rapidly shrinking insurance coverage for millions of people. We should prefer five hundred thousand points of induced rescue to a thousand points of overburdened voluntarism.

II. PHYSICIANS ALONE

> The poor are poor, and one's sorry for them, but there it is. As civilization moves forward, the shoe is bound to pinch in places, and it's absurd to pretend that anyone is responsible personally. (Mr. Wilcox)[24]

Those in need of necessary medical care are stranded between the world of contracted-for care and government funded care. But is this justifiable? Philosophers considering the obligations of health care providers argue that "in the US at least, an individual provider, and the profession as a whole, have *no legal obligation* to distribute services except to patients to whom they already have contractual obligations."[25] This proposition is so circumscribed by judicial and other restrictions as to be false in practice. A principled framework for legal obligations to treat those in need, prior to any contractual obligation, and expanded obligations to treat them once the nexus is created, will be established below.

A. From contract to covenant

Health care today is most often delivered within institutions—whether hospitals, ambulatory care clinics, or HMO offices—but it is still the individual physician who sees the patient, diagnoses the problem, and prescribes the treatment. This physician also controls the consumption

---

23. JOHN P. REEDER, JR., BENEFICENCE, SUPEREROGATION, AND ROLE DUTY, BENEFICENCE AND HEALTH CARE 83 (Earl E. Shelp ed., 1982).

24. E. M. FORSTER, HOWARD'S END 188 (Vintage Books 1973) (1910).

25. Daniels, *supra* note 15, at 116.

of more than 70% of the health care dollars spent, by directing patients to particular loci of diagnosis and treatment in laboratories and hospitals. The starting point is therefore the obligations on a physician outside an institution.

1. The contract model

Courts often assume the contract model as the starting point for their analysis of tort duties in the doctor–patient relationship.[26] The contract foundations of the doctor–patient relationship are often summarized, hornbook style, in tort decisions. Thus, physicians in private practice may contract their services as they see fit and retain substantial control over the extent of their contact with patients.[27] Physicians may limit their specialty and scope of practice, their geographic area, and the hours and conditions under which they will see patients. There is no obligation to offer services that a patient may require outside the physician's competence and training; or services outside the scope of the original physician–patient agreement, where the physician has limited the contract to a type of procedure, to an office visit, or to consultation only.[28] Physicians may transfer responsibility by referring patients to other specialists. As private practitioners, they may refuse

---

26. Roger D. Masters, *Is Contract An Adequate Basis for Medical Ethics?* 5 HASTINGS CENTER REP., Dec. 1975, at 24.

27. When, for example, a doctor employed by an insurance company examines an individual for the purpose of qualifying him for insurance coverage, most courts considering the issue have held that a doctor owes no duty to the individual to treat or to disclose problems discovered during the examination. The justification is the lack of a doctor–patient relationship, and the rationale that there is a lack of an expectation by the person examined that he is being diagnosed for purposes of treatment. The screening function dominates over the treatment function in the relationship—the doctor is treated like a screening device, purely mechanical in nature. *See* Ervin v. American Guardian Life Assurance Co., 545 A. 2d 354 (Pa. Super. Ct. Law Div. 1988) (holding no duty owed by doctor employed by an insurance company to the plaintiff, where doctor examined the plaintiff for purposes of insurance and failed to discover or disclose his cardiac abnormalities to him; plaintiff died a month after the examination from his heart condition); *accord*, Keene v. Wiggins, 138 Cal. Rptr. 3 (Ca. Ct. App. 1977).

28. When a patient has a reasonable expectation that a physician will disclose all relevant information to him, even though no physician–patient relationship exists, then an examining physician who fails to inform a patient of abnormal test results will be liable for resulting injury. Daly v. U.S., 946 F. 2d 1467 (9th Cir. 1991).

to enter into a contract with a patient, or to treat patients, even under emergency conditions.[29] Both physician and patient can shape the parameters of the relationship.[30] This is the essence of a libertarian definition of professional contracting: the doctor sets the terms and conditions, and no external constraints on bargaining and performance exist. According to this legal summary, doctor and patient are autonomous agents, contracting freely. While the above principles have some support in law and practice *for the physician in private office practice* practicing fee-for-service medicine, they do not begin to define the nature of professional medical obligations as most physicians practice medicine.

2. The limits of the contract model

Physician autonomy claims, as manifested in a pure contract model of health care, are based on little more than historical accident. As Daniels writes, "[i]t is the legacy of the fact, more visible in the U.S. than elsewhere, that physicians have been more independent of institutional settings for the delivery of their skills than many other workers and even than physicians in other countries."[31] The defects of the contract model of the doctor–patient relationship are apparent.

First, the basis of the relationship bears little resemblance to the economic model of arms-length dealings between a buyer and a seller. The patient hardly consents to buy health care in the same way he consents to buy a house or to rent instead, or chooses between a Mercedes and a Ford. He would rather skip the purchase of health care forever, if his body would allow it. The professional has more latitude, since he can find more clients more easily than the patient can find professionals.[32] The patient's interest in a health care service is greater than that of a VCR buyer, for when the need arises it is intense and anxiety-producing. The knowledge disparity between doctor and patient is great, and parity in information may be unattainable, since the purchase of a health care service cannot usually be deferred until a market analysis has been done and comparative shopping completed.

---

29. Hiser v. Randolph, 617 P. 2d 774, 776 (Ariz. 1980) (holding physician on-call at hospital emergency room is obligated to treat all those who come into the emergency room).

30. Clough v. Lively, 387 S.E. 573 (Ga. Ct. App. 1989) (holding patient declined to enter into a physician–patient relationship any broader than necessary to accomplish the drawing of a blood sample).

31. Daniels, *supra* note 15, at 123.

32. MICHAEL D. BAYLES, PROFESSIONAL ETHICS 64 (1981).

Third-party payers dominate the relationship, so that any incentive by either side to bargain based on price sensitivity is diminished or eliminated by the existence of external payers. Finally, the physician is not an independent seller, but sells within social institutions—he is both a citizen of the institution and an agent of the purchaser-patient. He has a monopoly and the patient is neither a mobile nor an independent shopper. As one commentator observed, "[f]rom this point of view, the bargaining situation is more like that between an individual and a public utility."[33]

Second, other social forces and institutions impinge upon and redefine the relationship: third-party payment and utilization review, tort and fiduciary law standards, peer pressure within the institution, and staff privilege constraints.[34] The contract model is hopelessly incomplete in the complex world of health care delivery. The terms of the contract are largely fixed in advance of any bargaining, by standard or customary practices that the physician must follow at the risk of legal penalties. The exact nature of the work to be done by the physician is usually left vaguely defined at best. The relationship is closer to quasi-contract, where we impute standard intentions and reasonable expectations to both the physician and the patient.[35] Professional ethics impose on physicians fiduciary obligations which courts convert into legal obligations. Courts often look outside the parameters of contract law analysis in judging the obligations of a physician to treat a patient, stressing that the physician's obligation to the patient, while having origins in contract, is governed also by fiduciary obligations and other public considerations "inseparable from the nature and exercise of his calling. . . ."[36] Doctors are not viewed as businesspeople, where self-interest is the expected norm.[37] Professionals' ability to

---

33. *Id.* at 66.

34. *Id.* at 26.

35. *See* ROBERT E. GOODIN, PROTECTING the VULNERABLE 63–65 (1985).

36. Norton v. Hamilton, 89 S.E. 2d 809, 812 (Ga. App. 1955) (stating that patient's action was in tort rather than in contract when doctor withdrew from case at time when wife was in premature labor and wife delivered child while husband searched for substitute doctor). *See* Chatman v. Millis, 453 517 S.W.2d 504, 506 (Ark. Sup. Ct. 1975) (malpractice action requires a doctor–patient relationship, a duty owed from doctor to patients, although "[w]e do not flatly state that a cause for malpractice must be predicated upon a contractual agreement between a doctor . . . and patient . . .").

37. It is clear from everyday observation that the behavior expected of sellers of medical care is different from that of business people in general.

withdraw from their contracts is constrained by judicial caselaw defining patient abandonment.[38] Implied abandonment is a negligence-based theory judged by the overall conduct of the physician.[39] Physicians also lose a range of legal protections when they withhold information from patients. Some states deem a doctor's withholding information about his medical error to be fraud, a distinct cause of action.[40] The omission also tolls the statute of limitations in a

---

These expectations are relevant because medical care belongs to the category of commodities for which the product and the activity of production are identical. In all such cases, the customer cannot test the product before consuming it, and there is an element of trust in the relation. But the ethically understood restrictions on the activity of a physician are much more severe than on those of, say, a barber. His behaviour is supposed to be governed by a concern for the customer's welfare which would not be expected of a salesman. In Talcott Parson's terms, there is a "collectivity- orientation," which distinguishes medicine and other professions from business, where self-interest on the part of participants is the accepted norm.

Kenneth Arrow, *Uncertainty and the Welfare Economics of Medical Care*, 53 AM. ECON. REV. 941, 949 n. 15 (1963). *See also* Talcott Parsons, *The Professions and Social Structure and The Motivation of Economic Activities, in* TALCOTT PARSONS, ESSAYS IN SOCIOLOGICAL THEORY 34–68 (Free Press 1964) (1949) (stressing the role of trust in professions as institutions).

38. As discussed *supra*, a doctor who withdraws from the physician–patient relationship before a cure is achieved or the patient is transferred to the care of another may be liable for abandonment. To escape liability, the physician must give the patient time to find alternative care. *See, e.g.*, Norton v. Hamilton, 89 S.E.2d 809 (Ga. Ct. App. 1955) (holding that a cause of action for abandonment exists where a doctor withdrew from a case while a woman was in premature labor and a child was delivered before the husband could find a replacement doctor).

39. *See* Meiselman v. Crown Heights Hosp., 34 N.E.2d 367 (N.Y. 1941); Ascher v. Gutierrez, 533 F.2d 1235 (D.C.Cir. 1976); *See* Leon L. McIntire, *The Action of Abandonment in Medical Malpractice Litigation*, 36 TUL. L. REV. 834 (1962).

40. Negligent spoilation, based on a provider's failure to properly maintain records, or in the extreme cases, active destruction of records, had been recognized by a few state courts. The cause of action requires the existence of a potential civil action, a legal duty by the defendant to preserve evidence relevant to that action, destruction of that evidence, resulting impairment of the plaintiff's ability to prove the lawsuit, a causal relationship between the destruction of the evidence and the impairment of the ability to sue, and damages. Continental Ins. Co. v. Herman, 576 So. 2d 313 (Fla. Dist. Ct. App. 1990) (action recognized as generally valid in Florida, but plaintiff's claim dismissed for failure to show damage). *See generally*, P. Fritz King, *Spoilation: Civil Liability for Destruction of Evidence*, 20 U. RICH. L. REV. 191 (1986).

malpractice suit by the patient against that doctor.[41] An informed consent cause of action is based on failure to disclose information.[42] Some newer cases are also based on a claim for a breach of a physician's fiduciary duty to disclose conflicts of interest.[43] The environment of providers is bounded by legal constraints and specific role requirements.

An express written contract is rarely drafted for specific physician–patient interactions. An implied contract is usually the basis of the relationship between a physician and a patient.[44] A physician who talks

---

The party seeking to take advantage of a defendant's fradulent concealment has the burden of proving that the defendant affirmatively concealed the facts upon which the cause of action is based. As one court noted, however, "The close relationship of trust and confidence between patient and physician gives rise to duties of disclosure which may obviate the need for a patient to prove an affirmative act of concealment." Koppes v. Pearson, 384 N.W.2d 381, 386 (Iowa, 1986).

An action for deceit requires proof that a false representation of a material fact was made, was relied upon by the patient in ignorance, and damage resulted. The representation must be fraudulently made, since an intention to deceive by the physician is needed. *See* Harris v. Penninger, 613 S.W.2d 211, 214 (Mo. App. 1981) (dismissing cause of action based on fraud where plaintiff had failed to assert a claim for damages resulting from the fraud). In Hart v. Browne, 163 Cal. Rptr. 356 (Cal. Ct. App. 1980), a physician was sued for fraud when he advised the lawyer for a surgeon's patient that the surgeon's conduct was not negligent, when the records he had examined in fact showed abundant negligence. *See also* Henry v. Deen, 310 S.E.2d 326 (N.C. 1984) (allowing a theory of civil conspiracy and a punitive damages claim); Kreuger v. St. Joseph's Hosp., 305 N.W.2d 18 (N.D. 1981) (allowing a fraud claim based upon the physician's false representations.)

Some commentators have advocated a major development of these few cases into a new duty to disclose, requiring negligent health care providers to confess their negligence to the patients injured by it. *See* Joan Vogel & Richard Delgado, *To Tell the Truth: Physicians' Duty to Disclose Medical Mistakes*, 28 UCLA L. REV. 52 (1980) (advocating a duty to disclose malpractice to the patient); Theodore R. LeBlang & Jane L. King, *Tort Liability for Nondisclosure: The Physician's Legal Obligations to Disclose Patient Illness and Injury*, 89 DICK. L. REV. 1 (1984) (suggesting the fiduciary relationship creates a duty to disclose information concerning the patient's physical condition).

41. *See, e.g.*, Mastro v. Brodie, 682 P.2d 1162 (Colo. 1984) (defining "discovery of injury" for purposes of tolling statute of limitations).

42. *See generally* Furrow, *supra* note 13 at 338–39 (providing a list of items a physician should consider disclosing: (a) diagnosis; (b) the nature and purpose of the proposed treatment; (c) the risks of treatment; (d) the probability of success; and (e) treatment alternatives).

43. *See* discussion of Moore *infra* section II (B)(3).

44. When a patient goes to a doctor's office with a particular problem, he is offering to enter into a contract with the physician. When the physician

(*cont.*)

with a patient by telephone may be held to have an implied contractual obligation to that patient.[45] Likewise, a physician such as a pathologist, who renders services to a patient but has not contracted with him, is nonetheless bound by certain implied contractual obligations. These implied obligations become part of the professional role, defined by the courts through a variety of rationales. Courts have held that workplace examinations of employees may create physician obligations to the examined person, even though he is not defined as a "patient".[46] These maintenance examinations in the workplace go beyond screening for other purposes, such as insurance, and the courts have found a duty to diagnose and inform.[47] The entanglement of the doctor with a quasi-patient has increased. One explantion could be the expectation of the employee with regard to his employer's obligations to him.[48]

(44, *cont.*) examines the patient, she accepts the offer and an implied contract is created. The physician is free to reject the offer and send the patient away, relieving herself of any duty to that patient. *See, e.g.*, Childs v. Weis, 440 S.W.2d 104 (Tex. Civ. App. 1969) (holding that a physician has no duty to treat where there is no express or implied contract creating a physician–patient relationship). Some courts state as a starting principle that:

[a]s a practical matter, health professionals cannot be required to obtain express consent before each touch or test they perform on a patient. Consent may be express or implied; implied consent may be inferred from the patient's action of seeking treatment or some other act manifesting a willingness to submit to a particular course of treatment.

Jones v. Malloy, 412 N.W.2d 837, 841 (Neb. 1987) *citing* Banks v. Wittenberg, 266 N.W. 2d 788 (Mich Ct. App. 1978).

45. *See* Bienz v. Central Suffolk Hosp., 557 N.Y.S.2d 139 (1990)–(holding that a telephone call for purposes of initiating treatment may create a physician–patient relationship); O'Neill v. Montefiore Hospital, 202 N.Y.S.2d 436 (1960) (holding that a jury question of negligence exists when patient was refused treatment following a telephone conversation with physician).

46. Daly v. Unites States, 946 F.2d 1467 (9th Cir. 1991) (holding that under Washington law, a physician had a duty to disclose abnormal test results even if no physician–patient relationship exists).

47. *See, e.g.*, Cofee v. McDonnell Douglas Corp., 503 P.2d 1366 (1972) Plaintiff applied for a job as a pilot with the defendant aircraft manufacturer; as part of his physical, he was given a blood test, with the results received by a secretary at defendant's medical clinic, time-stamped, and filed. No doctor reviewed the result, which would have led to a diagnosis of cancer of the bone marrow. The court held that the company was negligent in its failure to establish a proper procedure for evaluation of blood test reports.

48. In Green v. Walker, 910 F.2d 291 (5th Cir. 1990), the U.S. Court of Appeals for the Fifth Circuit, interpreting Louisiana law in a diversity action, held that the physician–patient relationship should be expanded to include

Once the physician–patient relationship has been created, physicians are subject to a range of obligations. They must give the patient "continuing attention."[49] Termination of the physician–patient relationship, once created, is subject in some jurisdictions to a "continuous treatment" rule to determine when the statute of limitations is tolled. Treatment obligations cease only if the physician can do nothing more for the patient, or if the physician ceases to attend the patient.[50] A physician who withdraws from the physician–patient relationship before the patient is cured or transferred to another's care may be liable for abandonment.[51] The tort doctrine of abandonment presumes an improper attempt by the physician to extricate herself from this contract, to the patient's detriment. It can be invoked by a patient-plaintiff whenever a treating physician has severed the physician–patient relationship without giving the patient a reasonable time or the opportunity to secure another equally qualified physician, and the patient then suffers injury because of delay in treatment or lack of further treatment.[52] To avoid liability, the physician generally is re-

employees examined by a company physician for employment purposes. The court held that:

> This relationship imposes upon the examining physician a duty to conduct the requested tests and diagnose the results thereof, exercising the level of care consistent with the doctor's professional training and expertise, and to take reasonable steps to make information available timely to the examine of any findings that pose an imminent danger to the examinee's physical or mental well-being.

Id. at 296.

49. *See* Ricks v. Budge, 64 P.2d 208, 211 (Utah 1937) (holding that the obligation of continuing attention may be terminated only when the case no longer requires attention).

50. *See* Jewson v. Mayo Clinic, 691 F.2d 405 (8th Cir. 1982) (stating that treatment ceases when a physician stops attending to the patient). *Cf.*, Wells v. Billars, 391 N.W.2d 668 (S.D. 1986) (holding that an optometrist's duty continued to date when patient visited clinic to take delivery of glasses).

51. *See* Norton v. Hamilton, 89 S.E. 2d 809 (Ga. Ct. App. 1955).

52. *See* Surgical Consultants, P.C. v. Ball, 447 N.W. 2d 676, 682 (Iowa Ct. App. 1989) (stating that "There must be evidence that the physician has terminated the relationship at a critical stage of the patient's treatment, that the termination was done without reason or sufficient notice to enable the patient to procure another physician, and that the patient is injured as a result thereof.") *See also* Lyons v. Grether, 239 S.E. 2d 103 (Va. 1977) (holding that a physician may withdraw from the case only when the patient has reasonable opportunity to acquire needed services from another physician).

quired to give the patient time to find other care.[53] A negligence-based theory, abandonment is judged by the overall conduct of the physician.[54] While contract rules may guide the formation of a physician–patient relationship, termination of that relationship without explicit mutual consent is evaluated by standards of reasonableness.

A duty of "necessary rescue" is imposed by the courts in situations where a person would be left helpless if the professional refuses to help.[55] The physician's right to unilaterally terminate treatment is thus particularly circumscribed in emergency situations, defined as situations where the patient has a "critical need" for that physician's attention. A provider can be "conscripted" to rescue through webs of obligation created by emergency situations. In *Urrutia v. Patino*,[56] the court stated that "a physician is never justified in withdrawing from a case that he has once undertaken *at a critical stage when his replacement cannot be supplied*" (emphasis added). These constraints—critical need for treatment and unavailability or lack of time to secure a replacement—define a situation considerably broader than the normal "emergency" situation.

In a nonemergency situation, the original physician need not physically replace herself with another physician before withdrawing in order to avoid a tort suit for abandonment.[57] Yet the physician must

---

53. *See* Norton v. Hamilton *supra* note 38.

54. Ascher v. Gutierrez, 533 F.2d 1235 (D.C. Cir. 1976) (setting out proper types of evidence for abandonment cases); Meiselman v. Crown Heights Hosp, 34 N.E. 2d 367 (N.Y. 1941) (setting out the types of evidence permissible in cases of physician abandonment); Leon M. McIntire, *The Action of Abandonment in Medical Malpractice Litigation*, 36 TUL. L. REV. 834 (1962) (discussing how the extent and scope of the physician–patient relationship determine duties and obligations).

55. "[A] professional ought to be held morally and professionally (if not necessarily legally) responsible to provide assistance in any situation in which, if he did not, someone would be left helpless. Consider the case of the only doctor in an isolated frontier town. Surely he should not be entitled to withdraw from the case of someone too ill to be moved, no matter how much notice he gives of this intention to do so. Neither should he be entitled to refuse to treat that patient in the first place." Goodin, *supra* note 35, at 67. *See also* Robert Justin Lipkin, *Beyond Good Samaritans and Moral Monsters: An Individualistic Justification of the General Legal Duty to Rescue*, 31 U.C.L.A. L. REV. 252 (1983).

56. 297 S.W. 512, 516 (Tex. Civ. App. 1927).

57. Miller v. Greater Southeast Community Hosp., 508 A.2d 927, 931 (D.C.C.A. 1986). *See also* Wyatt v. Ford, 363 S.E. 2d 866 (Ct. App. Ga. 1987) (trial court had denied physician's motion for summary judgment, court held that the appeal should be dismissed as improvidently granted).

give the patient a list of possible alternative physicians to handle the patient's condition.[58] Suppose, however, that the physician is the only specialist within the relevant geographic area, as measured by the expense or difficulty experienced by a patient when traveling to consult with another specialist. Must the physician continue to treat when the only other available specialist requires the patient to incur large transportation costs, so that the referring physician is essentially unavailable to the patient? The patient may have a critical need for treatment, with alternative care unavailable in any practical sense.

A continuing treatment obligation imposed on physicians against their wishes must withstand several arguments. First, given physician antipathy, forcing a continuation of the physician–patient relationship against the physician's wishes hardly achieves the idealized model of the physician–patient relationship. It is even arguable that the physician might render bad care unconsciously, if not consciously, because of this anger. However, this argument overstates the problem. Physician antipathy must be counterbalanced by patient needs and a realization that the professional role carries with it continuing obligations. Lack of payment by the patient is one area in which there is an analogous body of caselaw that imposes an obligation on physicians even when physicians feel hostile to the patient. The caselaw has consistently declared that the failure of the patient to pay for the physician's services will not justify unilateral termination of the physician–patient relationship so long as the patient still needs medical attendance.[59] These cases often involve emergency situations where the physician has not taken steps in advance to warn the patient of the termination and to find him an alternative provider, and the patient could, therefore, be said to have a legitimate expectancy of a continuing relationship.

Second, it may be argued that such a rule will create perverse obligations for physicians practicing in rural areas. The courts have not faced a situation where substantial travel costs, or even impossibility of access, may result from the remoteness of referral physicians. The rural setting involves a special case of expectations: citizen expectations that a physician who chose to relocate in their area will be available to them

---

58. *Id.* (holding "[w]here a patient is not in need of immediate medical attention, supplying the patient with a list of substitute physicians to replace the attending physician is a reasonable means of severing the professional relationship.") In this regard, direct provision of another colleague to cover the patient is sufficient to relieve the physician of further obligations to the patient.

59. *See* Ricks v. Budge, *supra* note 49.

within reason, and the physician's expectation that he will have to provide care when needed, given the lack of backup in such areas. While a government subsidy or some kind of special program might be useful,[60] it does not seem unreasonable to obligate a physician to treat patients within his realm of expertise, particularlly in emergency situations. Goodin argues for a collective duty on the medical profession to a patient, to be provided by a particular doctor who is "linked"—selected out of the general pool of professionals—by a promise, a contract, or the fiduciary bonds of a health care system.[61] According to Goodin, "it is vulnerability, however engendered, that plays the crucial role in generating special responsibilities."[62]

3. The covenant to serve

The implied contract expectations imposed by the courts suggest a much broader definition of role obligations in forced rescue contexts. May offers the model of a covenant as a basis for health care, rejecting contract, code, and philanthropy as alternatives.[63] Medical codes embody the ideal of philanthropy, that is, dedication to the service of mankind. Such codes succumb to what May calls "the conceit of philanthropy", which assumes "that the professional's commitment to his fellow-man is a gratuitous, rather than a responsive or reciprocal, act."[64] It is a model of a profession owing no duties to patients except

---

60. A special program has existed to subsidize a student's medical education in exchange for a certain number of years of service. The National Health Service Corps Scholarship Program was established by Congress to address the maldistribution of health care manpower in the U.S. 42 U.S.C. § 254d (1988) (National Health Service Corps). Eligible students in professional health degree programs receive scholarships that cover their educational expenses and include a stipend for living expenses. U.S.C. § 2541 (1988) (National Health Service Corps Scholarship Program). In exchange the student agrees to serve "in a health manpower shortage area" to which he is assigned by the Secretary. 42 U.S. § 254d(a) and 254e (1988). *See also* Rendlemen v. Sullivan, 760 F. Supp. 842 (D. Or. 1991) (holding failure to serve in area gives government right to seek repayment, but doctor's actions in starting a homeless clinic should be considered by DHHS as to whether it would make enforcement of his payment obligation unconscionable).

61. Goodin, *supra* note 35, at 126.

62. *Id.*

63. William F. May, *Code, Covenant, Contract, or Philanthropy*, 5 HASTINGS CENTER REP., Dec. 1975, at 29.

64. *Id.* at 32.

those self chosen, much like the contract model. The contract view is also too limited; as May argues, "[t]he kind of minimalism encouraged by a contractualist understanding of the professional relationship produces a professional too gruding, too calculating, too lacking in spontaneity, too quickly exhausted to go the second mile with his patients along the road of their distress."[65]

A covenant, by contrast, is an agreement between parties, a reciprocal relationship based on a gift between partners, and a covenant is a promise based on this original exchange of gifts, labors or services. This historic promissory event then defines future obligations. In medicine, the liberal state defines the obligations of this covenant, since the professions exists with the consent of the state and for its benefit.[66] The physician owes a debt to the community. He owes some group for his education, since the social investment in medicine is large. He was selected for medical school while others were not. He receives an "extraordinary social largess" in exchange for his services.[67] He learned on patients as a beginner, receiving a further subsidy through risk-taking. And he is in the debt of patients treated during his career for his existence and his ability to perform his trade competently. The relationship is therefore marked by elements of exchange and reciprocity. It is bounded by contractual protections, but more is required by the medical covenant and by the social definition of the professional role.[68]

---

65. *Id.* at 35.

66. Bayles, *supra* note 32, at 11–12 (discussing TROYEN BRENNAN, JUST DOCTORING: MEDICAL ETHICS IN THE LIBERAL STATE (1991)). Brennan wants physicians to have a primary role, in contrast to Bayles's view, with medical ethics defined as a set of evolving principles by physicians and other members of the liberal state.

67. May, *supra* note 63, at 32.

68. May writes: "But the contractualist approach to professional behavior falls into the opposite error of minimalism. It reduces everything to tit-for-tat: do no more for your patients than what the contract calls for; perform specified services for certain fees and no more ... But it would be wrong to reduce professional obligation to the specifies of a contract alone ... Professional services in the so called helping professions are directed to subjects who are in the nature of the case rather unpredictable. One deals with the sickness, ills, crimes, needs, and tragedies of humankind. These needs cannot be exhaustively specified in advance for each patient or client. The professions must be ready to cope with the contingent, the unexpected. Calls upon services may be required that exceed those anticipated in a contract or for which compensation may be available in a given case." *Id.* at 34.

B. Affirmative obligations on physicians

A landscape of affirmative obligations, broadly defined, is constructed out of a wide spectrum of legal doctrines. A moral detective finds a legal landscape dotted with eruptions of principles that redefine medical and fiduciary obligations, demanding that providers "rescue" someone in distress. Some doctrines stretch the boundaries of contractual relationships by requiring additional burdens on the provider or creating the fiction of a contract.

1. Rescuing patients from their own ignorance

Basic informed consent doctrine in tort law requires physicians to disclose to patients all information necessary to their health care decision-making.[69] A patient must make an informed choice, that is, must be rescued from his own ignorance about courses of treatment. A physician must disclose to the patient not only the consequences of treatment, but also of inaction. In *Truman v. Thomas,*[70] Dr. Thomas failed to explain to his patient, Rena Truman, the consequences of her persistent refusal to undergo a Pap smear. Dr. Truman saw her as a patient for five years, and often said to her, "You should have a Pap smear."[71] She always declined, either not wanting to pay for it or simply not wanting to undergo any more tests. Dr. Thomas is quoted as saying, "We are not enforcers, we are advisors," in justifying his failure to explain the purpose of the test and the consequences of cervical cancer.[72] The California Supreme Court held that a physician has a duty to disclose to a patient the consequences of a failure to undergo a test or procedure viewed as valuable by a doctor. "If a patient indicates that he or she is going to *decline the risk-free test or treatment, then the doctor has the additional duty of advising of all material risks of which a reasonable person would want to be informed before deciding not to undergo the procedure*" (emphasis added).[73]

---

69. *See* Natanson v. Kline, 354 P.2d 670, 672 (Kan. 1960) (holding doctors owed patient the duty to inform him generally of the possible serious collateral hazards of insulin treatment); and Mitchell v. Robinson, 334 S.W.2d 11, 19 (Mo. 1960) (holding radiologist was obligated to make a reasonable disclosure to patient of nature and probable consequences of radiation treatment).

70. 611 P.2d 902 (S.C. Cal. 1980).

71. *Id.* at 906.

72. *Id.*

73. *Id.*

This "right to an informed refusal" demands that the doctor rescue the patient from her ignorance about choices, in an attempt to ensure that a future bad result is either avoided or the tradeoff is explicitly made by the patient. It requires that the doctor spend a valuable commodity—time—in order to maximize the patient's choices. The doctor controls information otherwise unavailable to patients; from this control flows an obligation to use that information to help patients avoid medical hazards and even to help a patient preserve a tort right to sue the physician.[74]

2. Rescuing third parties from exposure to risks

An example of the extension of physician obligations to those not in a contractual relationship with them is found in caselaw that requires a warning to third parties. What if doctors have information about a patient which, if disclosed, might prevent harm to others? Requirements of confidentiality of the physician–patient relationship militate against disclosure generally, and disclosure may even expose the physician to potential liability. However, physicians and other health professionals have an affirmative obligation to protect third parties against hazards created by their patients. In *DiMarco v. Lynch Homes— Chester County*,[75] the sexual partner of a patient sued the patient's physicians, who had assured her that she would not contract hepatitis. The patient-plaintiff Janet Viscichini, a blood technician, went to the Lynch Home to take a blood sample from one of the residents. During the procedure, her skin was accidentally punctured by the needle she had used to extract blood. When she learned that the patient had hepatitis, she sought treatment from Doctors Giunta and Alwine. They told her that if she remained symptom-free for six weeks, she would not be infected by the hepatitis virus. She was not told to refrain from sexual relations for any period of time following her exposure to the disease, but she practiced sexual abstinence until eight weeks after the exposure. Since she had remained symptom-free during that time, she then resumed sexual relations with the plaintiff. She was later diagnosed as suffering from hepatitis B in September; in December, the plaintiff was similarly diagnosed.

The court cited Restatement (Second) of Torts, Section 324A, which provided, in part, that one who provides services to another may be

---

74. *See* case cited *supra* note 38.
75. 583 A.2d 422 (Pa. 1990).

liable to a third person for harm resulting from his failure to exercise reasonable care, if "the harm is suffered because of reliance of the other or the third person upon the undertaking."[76] The court allowed the action, concluding that the class of persons at risk included any one who is physically intimate with the patient.

> When a physician treats a patient who has been exposed to or who has contracted a communicable and/or contagious disease, it is imperative that the physician give his or her patient the proper advice about preventing the spread of the disease.... Physicians are the first line of defense against the spread of communicable diseases, because physicians know what measures must be taken to prevent the infection of others.[77]

Contagious diseases are thus a consistent example of a physician's duty to disclose risk of real or potential harm or protect others who might be exposed to the risks of disease or infection. Physicians are conscripted into rescue; in the court's words, they "are the first line of defense."[78] Physicians have been held liable for failing to warn the daughter of a patient with scarlet fever, a wife about the danger of infection from a patient's wounds, a neighbor about a patient's smallpox.[79] Family members are foreseeable third parties, as are neighbors.[80] *DiMarco* clearly applies to the risk of contagion from the HIV virus, requiring that physicians be aware of the nature of the HIV virus, its modes of transmission, and the kind of counseling that AIDS necessitates.

---

76. *Id.* at 424.

77. *Id.* at 424. *See also* Shephard v. Redford Community Hospital, 390 N.W. 2d 239 (Mich. Ct. App. 1986) (holding that a duty was owed to child of carrier of contagious disease to properly warn of the danger of transmitting disease to a child).

78. *Id.*

79. Lemmon v. Freese, 210 N.W.2d 576 (Iowa 1973) (epilepsy); and Jones v. Stanko, 160 N.E. 456 (Ohio 1928) (smallpox).

80. Freese v. Lemmon, 210 N.W. 2d 576 (Iowa 1973) (holding physician may be liable for negligence in not diagnosing epilepsy in patient for injury later caused to third party because of patient's epileptic seizure); Jones v. Stanko, 160 N.E. 456 (Ohio 1928) (holding physician liable for failure to warn persons in close proximity to patient that patient has infectious smallpox). *See* Skillings v. Allen, 173 N.W. 663 (N.H. 1919) (physician liable for negligently advising plaintiff's wife that daughter's scarlet fever was not infectious); Edwards v. Lamb, 45 A.480 (1899) (surgeon liable for negligently assuring plaintiff that there was no danger of infection when plaintiff assisted surgeon in addressing plaintiff's husband's wound). *See generally* Bruce A. McDonald, *Ethical Problems for Physicians Raised by AIDS and HIV Infection: Conflicting Legal Obligations of Confidentiality and Disclosure*, 22 U. C. DAVIS L. REV. 557 (1989).

Another line of cases imposes a duty on a physician to protect unknown third parties against medication side-effects that their patients might experience,[81] and to warn third parties of dangers posed by psychiatric patients.[82]

3. Rescuing patients from doctors: disclosing conflicts of interest

The limits of a contract model for the doctor–patient relationship are further revealed by duties imposed by the courts to disclose conflicts of interest between the patient's best interests and a physician's interest in fame and fortune. Patients are vulnerable, and this vulnerability imposes on physicians a "trust", a fiduciary obligation justified by the physician's dominant position in the relationship. Economic conflicts of interest have been the focus of recent cases that use fiduciary concepts to define physician duties to disclose possible conflicts of interest or other information important to a patient in assessing physician motivations.

In *Moore v. Regents of the University of California*,[83] the plaintiff John

---

81. Welke v. Kuzilla, 375 N.W. 2d 403 (Mich. Ct. App. 1985). Welke is part of a line of caselaw requiring physicians to warn third parties about, or take steps to protect them from, patients who are taking medication. These steps might include warning the patient about the effects of medication, or even refusing to prescribe the medication if the patient might still drive. *See* Meyers v. Quesenberry, 193 Cal. Rptr. 733 (Cal. Ct. App. 1983) (physician failed to warn his patient, a diabetic, of the dangers of driving); Gooden v. Tips, 651 S.W.2d 364 (Tex. Ct. App. 1983) (physician failed to warn the patient of the dangers of driving while taking tranquilizers); Watkins v. United States, 589 F.2d 214 (5th Cir. 1979) (negligence to prescribe Valium to mentally ill patient); Freese v. Lemmon, 210 N.W.2d 576 (Iowa 1973) (doctor found liable for failure to warn the patient about the risk of a sudden seizure, and the patient then drove into the plaintiff during a fainting spell); Kaiser v. Suburban Transport. Sys., 398 P.2d 14 (Wash. 1965) *amended*, 401 P.2d 350 (Wash. 1965) (doctor prescribed a drug for a patient, a bus driver, but neglected to tell him that it might make him sleepy; doctor held liable to the bus passengers and other third persons who were harmed when the driver fell asleep at the wheel).

82. Davis v. Lhim, 335 N.W.2d 481 (Mich. Ct. App. 1983), *remanded* 422 Mich. 875 (1985) (held that a psychiatrist owes a professional duty of care to those who could be foreseeably injured by his patient). This obligation has first appeared in the psychiatric context, beginning with Tarasoff v. Regents of the Univ. of Cal., 131 Cal. Rptr. 14, 551 P.2d 334 (1976). *See also* McIntosh v. Milano, 403 A.2d 500 (N.J. Super 1979); Hedlund v. Superior Court of Orange County, 669 P.2d 41 (Cal. 1983); Lipari v. Sears, Roebuck & Co., 497 F. Supp. 185 (D. Neb. 1980).

83. 793 P.2d 479 (Cal. 1990).

Moore (hereinafter Moore) underwent treatment for hairy-cell leukemia at the Medical Center of the University of California at Los Angeles (hereinafter UCLA Medical Center). Moore first visited UCLA Medical Center shortly after he learned that he had hairy-cell leukemia. His physician Dr. Golde hospitalized Moore and withdrew blood and bone marrow aspirate. Dr. Golde failed to disclose his preexisting research and economic interests in the cells before obtaining consent to the medical procedures by which they were extracted. The defendants, including Dr. Golde, were aware that Moore's cell line was of great commercial value.

The court characterized the cause of action as either a breach of fiduciary duty to disclose facts material to a patient's consent, or in the alternative, as the performance of medical procedures without the patient's consent.

> [A] physician who treats a patient in whom he also has a research interest has potentially conflicting loyalties. This is because medical treatment decisions are made on the basis of proportionality—weighing the benefits to the patient against the risks to the patient.... [A] physician who adds his own research interests to this balance may be tempted to order a scientifically useful procedure or test that offers marginal, or no, benefits to the patient. The possibility that an interest extraneous to the patient's health has affected the physician's judgment is something that a reasonable patient would want to know in deciding whether to consent to a proposed course of treatment. It is material to the patient's decision and, thus, a prerequisite to *informed consent*.[84]

In *Moore*, the court explicitly used both fiduciary duty and informed consent doctrine in order to impose an obligation on the physicians to disclose their research and economic interests.[85] The tension in the fiduciary disclosure cases is tangible—a physician must rescue a patient

---

84. *Id.* at 484.

85. Physicians may at times want to try a new or innovative approach to a patient's problems. In Estrada v. Jaques, 321 S.E. 2d 240 (N.C. App. 1984), the plaintiff Estrada's physicians neglected to tell him that the procedure they were trying on him was experimental, an innovation on him that they hoped to study.

The psychology of the doctor–patient relation, and the rewards, financial and professional, attendant upon recognition of experimental success, increase the potential for abuse and strengthen the rationale for uniform disclosure ... Accordingly, we reaffirm our holding that reasonable standards of informed consent to an experimental procedure require disclosure to the patient that the procedure is experimental.

Id. at 255.

from the physician's own mixed motivations and conflicts of interest between the patient's good and his own. The rescuer and the person posing a danger are folded into the same person.

C. Bribed rescue

Physicians often seem to need encouragement to be Good Samaritans. Hesitant to force rescue, state legislatures have enacted Good Samaritan laws to encourage rescue by quieting physician anxiety about lawsuits. Forty-nine states and the District of Columbia have adopted Good Samaritan legislation to protect health care professionals who render emergency aid from civil liability for damages for any injury they cause or enhance in rendering such emergency aid.[86] The statutes take a variety of forms.[87] Some statutes protect health care professionals, while others protect all Good Samaritans, without regard to their profession.[88] Some states grant statutory immunity from suit to

---

See generally on fiduciary obligations, Maxwell J. Mehlman, *Fiduciary Contracting: Limitations on Bargaining Between Patients and Health Care Providers*, 51 U. PITT. L. REV. 365 (1990); Marc. A. Rodwin, *Physicians' Conflicts of Interest: The Limitations of Disclosure*, 321 NEW ENG. J. MED. 1405 (1989); Thomas Boyd, *Cost Containment and the Physician's Fiduciary Duty to the Patient*, 39 DEPAUL L. REV. 131 (1989); EDMUND D. PELLEGRINO & DAVID C. THOMASMA, A PHILOSOPHICAL BASIS OF MEDICAL PRACTICE 260 (1981); Stephen R. Feldman & Thomas M. Ward, *Psychotherapeutic Injury: Reshaping the Implied Contract as an Alternative to Malpractice*, 58 N.C. L. REV. 63 (1979).

Many of the cases use the language of fiduciary obligations in discussing informed consent. *See* Lambert v. Park, 597 F.2d 236 (10th Cir. 1979) (physician's fiduciary duty is to obtain patient's informed consent); Ostojic v. Brueckmann, 405 F.2d 302, 304 (7th Cir. 1968) (existence of physician's fiduciary duty requires full disclosure); Margaret S. v. Edwards, 488 F. Supp. 181, 207 (E.D. La. 1980) (holding "informed consent involves the fiduciary nature of the doctor-patient – relationship . . .").

86. In McCain v. Batson, 760 P.2d 725 (Mont. 1988), a physician on vacation sutured a hiker's wound at his condominium, using limited medical supplies on hand. The court held that this was an "emergency" within the meaning of the statute.

87. CAL. BUS. & PROF. CODE § 2395 (West 1990), for example, states, in relevant part, "No licensee, who in good faith renders emergency care at the scene of an emergency, shall be liable for any civil damages as a result of any acts or omissions by such person in rendering the emergency care."

"The scene of an emergency" as used in this section shall include, but not be limited to, the emergency rooms of hospitals in the event of a medical disaster.

88. *See, e.g.*, FLA. STAT. ANN. § 768.13 (West Supp. 1992) ("Any person
(*cont.*)

emergency medical personnel unless gross negligence is shown.[89] The majority of state statutes exclude medical services rendered in the hospital from the coverage of the statutes, either by excluding emergency services provided in the ordinary course of work or services that doctors render to those with whom they have a doctor–patient relationship or to whom they owe a preexisting duty.[90] Hospital-based emergency assistance by a physician is often protected, however, where the physician is not on duty at the time of the call for help.[91]

The purpose of Good Samaritan statutes is to encourage physicians and other providers to offer emergency aid, by eliminating their largely unfounded fears of malpractice suits for any negligent harm they might cause a victim that they rescue.[92] This reduced standard of care for medical rescuers strikes a balance between penalizing the hasty physician caught in an unexpected treatment setting and promoting risk-free additional rescues.[93] Some states have gone further by providing indigent care immunities, extending Good Samaritan immunity beyond emergencies to the treatment of the indigent generally, especially Medicaid patients.[94] Some

---

(88, *cont.*) . . . who gratuitously and in good faith renders emergency care or treatment . . ."); MASS. GEN. LAWS. ANN. ch. 258A § 9 (West 1988) ("No person who in good faith . . ."), OHIO REV. CODE ANN. § 2305.23 (Anderson 1991) ("No person shall be liable . . . for administering emergency care or treatment . . .").

89. Mallory v. City of Detroit, 449 N.W.2d 115 (1989) (upholding grant of statutory immunity as long as act or omission of emergency medical personnel is not the result of gross negligence or willful misconduct). See generally W.R. Habeeb, Annotation, *Construction of 'Good Samaritan' Statutes Excusing from Civil Liability One Rendering Care in Emergency*, 39 A.L.R. 3d 222 (1971).

90. Guerrero v. Copper Queen Hospital, 537 P.2d 1329, 1331 (Ariz. 1975) (statute not applicable to services in hospital); Colby v. Schwartz, 144 Cal. Rptr. 624 (Cal. Ct. App. 1978) (normal course of practice not protected); Gragg v. Neurological Associates, 263 S.E.2d 496 (Ga. Ct. App. 1979) (crisis during operating procedure is not emergency within meaning of statute).

91. See Gordin v. William Beaumont Hospital, 447 N.W.2d 793 (Mich. Ct. App. 1989).

92. For an interesting discussion of the duty to rescue, see Saul Levmore, *Waiting for Rescue: An Essay on the Evolution and Incentive Structure of the Law of Affirmative Obligations*, 72 VA. L. REV. 879 (1986).

93. MARSHALL SHAPO, THE DUTY TO ACT: TORT LAW, POWER, & PUBLIC POLICY 28 (1977).

94. See American Medical Association, 16 State Health Legislation Report (May 1988). See also ARIZ. REV. STAT. ANN. § 12–571 (1992); FLA. STAT. ANN. § 768.13 (West Supp. 1992); GA. CODE ANN. § 51–1–29 (Michie Supp. 1992); ILL ANN. STAT. ch. 111, § 4404 (Smith-Hurd 1978); ME REV. STAT. ANN. tit. 24, § 2904 (West 1990); S.C. CODE ANN. § 33–55–210 (Law Co-op. 1977); VA. CODE ANN. §§ 8.01–225 to 8.01–225.1 (Michie 1992).

states have considered implementing tort immunity for physicians who treat the indigent.[95]

III. PHYSICIANS IN INSTITUTIONS: THROWING OUT LIFELINES

Ethical and legal discussions tend to focus on the individual physician and her obligations to her patients, whether by agreement or externally expanded by courts and fiduciary concepts. But most health care is delivered by physicians within institutional frameworks—hospitals, managed care organizations (MCOs), group practices. Physicians who practice in institutions, either as employees or members of the medical staff, must provide health care within the limits of the health plan's coverage or their employment contracts with the institution. In this case, the contact between the physician and the patient is preceded by an express contract spelling out the details of the relationship. Physicians who are members of a health maintenance organization have a duty to treat plan members, as part of their contractual obligation to the MCO. The express contracts are between the physician and the MCO, and the subscriber and the MCO, with an implied contract between the subscriber and the treating physician.[96] Members of a

---

95. While the threat that a poor patient will sue a physician is quite low, Molly McNulty, *Are Poor Patients Likely to Sue for Malpractice?*, 262 JAMA 1391 (1980); Sara Rosenbaum & Dana Hughes, *The Medical Malpractice Crisis and Poor Women, in* PRENATAL CARE, REACHING MOTHERS, REACHING INFANTS (1988), the concept of a mandate for free care at some level in exchange for the tort subsidy is a direct step beyond the Good Samaritan statutes, which simply hope for more provider willingness to help someone in distress in exchange for a qualified immunity from suit. The District of Columbia has amended its Good Samaritan Act to provide immunity for volunteer physicians, nurse-mid-wives and nurses providing obstetrical care. 'D.C. CODE ANN. § 2–1345 (Supp. 1992). For a discussion and critique of this act, *see generally* Bridget A. Burke, *Using Good Samaritan Acts to Provide Access to Health Care for the Poor: A Modest Proposal*, 1 ANNALS HEALTH L. 139 (1992). This emphasis on volunteerism in exchange for tort immunity raises troubling questions. It is not particularly fair to force the indigent as a group to trade off their right to sue, with its deterrence potential in exchange for care.

96. A Managed Care Organization is a reimbursement framework combined with a health care delivery system, an approach to the delivery of health care services that contrasts with "fee-for-service" medicine. Managed care is usually distinguished from traditional indemnity plans by the existence of a single

(*cont.*)

hospital staff may also be expressly bound to treat patients, particularly in the emergency room when they are on call.[97] They have waived their rights to refuse to treat particular patients, as a result of their contractual obligations to the hospital. Contractual obligations flow from the employment setting, binding physicians to treat individual subscribers.[98] Professional autonomy is traded for the security of income stability.

The traditional malpractice standard of care applies to hospitals and to individual physicians. Malpractice is usually defined as unskillful practice resulting in injury to the patient, a failure to exercise the "required degree of care, skill and diligence" under the circumstances.[99] A physician is not a guarantor of good results, nor is he required to exercise the highest degree of care possible. However, modern courts grant less leeway to providers than in the past, for example, rejecting "error in judgment" instructions as unduly favorable to defendants.[100]

The standard of care by which the conduct of providers is measured is a national one, requiring the provider to render care consistent with a reasonable level of medical skill and knowledge, based on the adept use of available medical facilities and equipment.[101] Most courts also

---

(96, *cont.*) entity responsible for integrating and coordinating the financing and delivery of services that were once scattered between providers and payers. *See generally* Robert Shouldice, *Introduction to Managed Care: Health Maintenance Organizations, Preferred Provider Organizations, and Competitive Medical Plans* (1991); Jonathan P. Weiner and Gregory de Lissovoy, *Razing a Tower of Babel: A Taxonomy for Managed Care and Health Insurance Plans*, 18 J. HEALTH POL., POL'Y & LAW 75 (1993). Comment, *Contractual Theories of Recovery in the HMO Provider–Subscriber Relationship: Prospective Litigation for Breach of Contract*, 36 BUFF. L. REV. 119, 124–25 (1987).

97. Hiser, *supra* note 29.

98. The traditional scope of the contractual relationship may even include obligations such as completing benefit forms for a patient. *See* Chew v. Meyer, 527 A.2d 828 (Mich App. 1987) (recognizing a cause of action in negligence where a physician's failure to complete plaintiff's insurance form led to plaintiff losing a job).

99. Bardessono v. Michels, 478 P.2d 480, 484 (Cal. 1970) (holding negligence can be found from the fact that the accident itself occurred where an injection renders a patient partially paralyzed).

100. *See* Deyo v. Kinley, 565 A.2d 1286, 1293 (Vt. 1989) (rejecting "error in judgement" instruction in medical malpractice action due to ambiguous language and subjectivity).

101. Hall v. Hilbun, 466 So. 2d 856 (S.C. Miss. 1985) (allowing expert testimony from other localities to be entered into the record to help determine national standard in malpractice action).

allow evidence describing the practice limitations under which the defendant labors.[102]

The law has imposed obligations on physicians, often when they have done something to create reliance or a generalized sense of security.[103] A judicial move from contract to negligence is typically most evident in emergency settings, particularly in hospitals, as courts search for a nexus between doctor and individual in crisis. A case illustrates the point. In *Noble v. Sartori*,[104] two brothers took their third brother, Amel, who was having a "heart attack", to the emergency room at Knox County General. One brother went to Dr. Sartori, who was dressed "like a doctor" in a white coat, with a stethoscope around his neck. He pleaded with the doctor three times to help his brother. Dr. Sartori did not help, but told him to get in line and sign in. They then left and drove to another hospital; the next day Amel died. Dr. Sartori argued that he had not agreed to treat the patient, so no physician–patient relationship existed. The court noted that it was an emergency situation, the physician was obviously a staff physician, and he told the brother to get in line three times. The court, however, went beyond this: "[T]he question here becomes whether the actions of the physician were negligent in the circumstances, and if so, whether the jury could infer what he did was a substantial factor contributing to Noble's death."[105] Dr. Sartori was the only doctor on duty who could have handled the

---

102. *Id.* at 972. Hall's "resource component" allows the trier of fact to consider the facilities, staff and other equipment available to the practitioner in the institution, following the general rule that courts should take into account the locality, proximity of specialists and special facilities for diagnosis and treatment. *See also* Blair v. Eblen, 461 S.W.2d 370, 373 (Ky. Ct. App. 1970) (allowing standard of care to "include elements of locality, availability of facilities, specialization in general practice, proximity of specialist and special facilities as well as other relevant consideration."); Restatement (Second) of Torts, § 299A, Comment g. ("Allowance must be made also for the type of community in which the actor carries on his practice. A country doctor cannot be expected to have the equipment, facilities, experience, knowledge or opportunity to obtain it, afforded him by a large city.")

103. *See* Shapo, *supra* note 93, at pt. 1 (discussing methods by which a power holder may engender reliance on the part of the injured party).
Often the solution for a particular case will depend principally on the fact that a power holder already has done something in a way that engenders reliance on the part of the injured party or has created a generalized sense of security with reference to the latter's physical integrity.
Id. at 4.

104. 799 S.W.2d 8 (Ky. 1990).

105. *Id.* at 4.

problem, and he was available. The court quoted *Rockhill v. Pollard*,[106] to the effect that "a physician who is consulted in an emergency has a duty to respect that interest, at least to the extent of making a good-faith attempt to provide adequate treatment or advice."[107] The court in *Noble* then seemed to define a utilitarian duty to rescue where it was efficient to do so, even if no contract existed or could be constructed: "Thus, although we recognize that in the usual situation a doctor is under no obligation to treat a person, we also recognize [that] the law implies a duty wherever circumstances put parties in a relationship to each other where when one acts negligently and it causes injury to the other."[108] This sounds like a judicial summary of a vulnerable plaintiff, susceptible to a physician's failure to act.[109] It was an emergency rescue, and the physician's refusal to act breached his legal obligation to rescue the vulnerable plaintiff. The plaintiffs had expectations as to the doctor's treatment of the ill brother; by agreeing to serve in the hospital emergency room the physician had traded some autonomy for income. The web of obligations entangled Dr. Sartori fairly.

The myth of the independent and freely contracting physician has thus been undermined in many ways. The courts have been willing to stretch contract and fiduciary principles to snag physicians and impose obligations on them. Courts have also imposed duties on physicians to "rescue" patients and third parties—from their own ignorance, from external risks, from the physician's own conflicts of interest.

The complexity of reimbursement under Medicare and Medicaid and the multiple sources of funding for patient care have pushed courts toward imposing new duties to rescue on providers. As physicians increasingly practice within managed care frameworks and under utilization review constraints in hospitals, they have an emerging duty to learn how the reimbursement mechanisms work.

One emerging duty to rescue is the obligation to throw a financial lifeline to a patient. A physician may have a duty to assist patients in obtaining payment for health care.[110] This is an obligation of financial

106. 485 P.2d 28 (Or. 1971) (holding that in order to ensure physician liability, plaintiff must show physician's conduct was outrageous in the extreme and that he suffered emotional distress as a result).

107. *Id.* at 63.

108. *Noble*, 799 S.W.2d 8, 9–10.

109. *See also* Richard v. Adair Hospital Foundation Corp., 566 S.W.2d 791 (1978) (examining what constitutes an emergency situation which may render a physician or hospital liable for failing to treat a patient); and RESTATEMENT (SECOND) OF TORTS § 323 (1965).

110. *See* discussion of *Wickline, Wilson,* and other case *infra*.

rescue, using insider information to open channels of reimbursement for a patient in a crisis. At a minimum, this means that the doctor must be aware of reimbursement constraints so that he can promptly advise the patient or direct him to an appropriate institutional office for further information. Federal and state payment systems are designed to control health care cost inflation. Medicare's prospective payment system, the Diagnosis-Related Groups (DRG) system, approved in 1982 by Congress, creates a complex administered price system for hospital services.[111] Many states also have implemented prospective payment hospital reimbursement systems,[112] and private insurers are also piggy-backing on the system.[113] Such approaches, aimed at controlling escalating health care costs, create tensions between cost control and quality of care. The pressure is to reduce diagnostic tests, control lengths of stay in hospitals, and trim the fat out of medical practice.[114]

Physicians have affirmative obligations to treat their patients in conformity with recognized standards of care, to inform them of the risks of treatments, and to advise them of conflicts of interest. But must a physician actively assist a patient in obtaining funding for a procedure that the physician feels is necessary? No court would require a physician to pay out of his own pocket for a treatment that a patient needs—there is no "duty to rescue" in the sense of a physician's financial obligation to support his patient.[115] However, *Wickline* and other cases may support the argument that a physician operating within

---

111. *See* Tax Equity and Fiscal Responsibility Act of 1982, Pub. L. No. 97–248, § 101, 96 Stat. 324, 331 (codified as amended at 26 U.S.C. § 1 (1986)).

112. *See generally* Furrow, *supra* note 13 at 694–95.

113. Barry R. Furrow, *The Ethics of Cost Containment: Bureaucratic Medicine & the Doctor as Patient Advocate*, NOTRE DAME J. L., ETHICS, & PUB. POL'Y 189 (1988).

114. *See* William R. Roper, *Balancing Efficiency and Quality—Toward Market-Based Health Care*, 3 NOTRE DAME J. L., ETHICS & PUB. POL'Y 169 (1988) (analyzing the past and future course for Medicare and its effects on health care cost and quality). *See generally* Barry R. Furrow, *Medical Malpractice and Cost Containment: Tightening the Screws*, 36 CASE W. RES. L. REV. 985 (1986) (proposing four strategies for physician advocacy in refining the beneficence principle in the world of cost containment); Furrow, *The Ethics of Cost-Containment, supra* note 113 at 216–17 (1988) (examining the role and benefit of interacting health care cost containment with traditional tort law doctrine).

115. One could argue on this point that the abandonment cases require a direct subsidy by the doctor, in cases where the doctor must continue to treat even though the patient owes the doctor money on a past bill. *See* Ricks v. Budge, *supra* note 49 (holding that it is a question for the jury whether plaintiff suffered damages by a physician's refusal to continue treatment of plaintiff unless plaintiff satisfied an old account).

a reimbursement structure and bureaucracy is expected to be familiar with the mechanisms of payment.

A. The duty to understand reimbursement: *Wickline*

Wickline v. State[116] considered physician obligations to use their special position to rescue patients from reimbursement limits. The case involved the release of a patient from the hospital post-operatively in less time than the treating physician thought ideal (four days instead of eight). The physician had applied for an extension of hospitalization time from Medi-Cal (California's Medicaid program), had been refused, and had not filed an appeal. Dicta in the case suggests that the court expected treating physicians to be aware of the reimbursement structure and to engage in bureaucratic infighting when necessary, exhausting procedural rights when the utilization review process has rejected a recommendation.

> The patient who requires treatment and who is harmed when care which should have been provided is not provided should recover for the injuries suffered from all those responsible for the deprivation of such care, including, when appropriate, health care payors . . . [The] physician who complies without protest with the limitations imposed by a third-party payor, when his medical judgment dictates otherwise, cannot avoid his ultimate responsibility for his patient's care. He cannot point to the health care payor as the liability scapegoat when the consequences of his own determinative medical decisions go sour.[117]

If further payment was available dependent upon following an appeals procedure, and the provider was ignorant of this procedure, he might be liable for patient harm attributable to his ignorance. If a patient is discharged against the better judgment of a treating physician when reimbursement is denied, he risks liability for malpractice. He has not made a good faith effort to "rescue" the patient from further bad outcomes.

B. Joint liability for treatment denied: *Wilson I*

The case of *Wilson v. Blue Cross of Southern California*[118] qualified and limited *Wickline* but also expanded potential liability of outside re-

---

116. 228 Cal. Rptr. 661 (Cal. App. Ct. 1986), *published at* 741 P.2d 613 (Cal. 1987) (debating whether the physician or health care payer bears responsibility for allowing a patient to be discharged prematurely).

117. *Id.* at 670–71.

118. 222 Cal. App. 3d 660 (1990).

viewers. It held that a physician could be jointly and severally liable with a utilization review body for a patient's bad outcome.

Howard Wilson suffered from major depression, drug dependency, and anorexia. He entered College Hospital on March 1, 1983. An Alabama Blue Cross policy which covered Wilson had no provision for concurrent utilization review. In 1983, Alabama Blue Cross had delegated authority to California Blue Cross to do reviews. In 1983 California Blue Cross contracted with Western Medical, a third-party utilization review organization, to make determinations of medical necessity. Western applied federal Medicare utilization review standards to private insurance patients. On March 11, Western Medical decided that Wilson's hospital stay was not justified or approved. Although Dr. Taff, the treating physician, felt that Wilson would require three to four weeks of care. Dr. Taff did not appeal against the utilization review determination made by Western Medical. Wilson was discharged, and on March 31 he killed himself. Dr. Taff felt that Wilson would have lived if he had remained in hospital. The court refused to follow the *Wickline* dicta, which had suggested that civil liability for a discharge decision rested solely within the responsibility of a treating physician.[119] The court instead applied the test of joint liability for tortious conduct, Restatement (Second) of Torts Section 431: "[An] actor's negligent conduct is legal cause of harm to another if (a) his conduct is a substantial factor in bringing about the harm, and (b) there is no rule of law relieving the actor from liability because of the manner in which his negligence has resulted in harm."[120] The court concluded that it was a triable issue of material fact as to whether Western's conduct was a substantial factor in causing the suicide.

The relevant points of *Wilson* from the perspective of a duty to rescue analysis are that (1) after denying further payment, the payer or utilization reviewer cannot pass the buck to the treating physician for a discharge decision: they may be jointly liable for a "bad" decision; (2) a doctor does not have to pursue appeal channels if they are not clearly spelled out or well understood; the negative implication is a doctor must appeal if the appeals process is clear.[121]

Wilson means that a physician may be held to affirmative obligations to demand further reimbursement for a ready patient.

---

119. Wickline, *supra* note 116, at 672.
120. RESTATEMENT (SECOND) OF TORTS § 431 (1965).
121. The jury in *Wilson II* (*see* footnote 122) used a clear and convincing standard to reject liability for the utilization review body.

C. The duty to coordinate financing: *Wilson II*

One ongoing case based in part on an expansive view of physician obligations is *Wilson v. Chesapeake Health Plan, Inc.*[122] The plaintiff Hugh Wilson, a 31-year-old black employee of the city of Baltimore, developed liver disease. He was a member of a prepaid health plan, the Chesapeake Health Plan, Inc. (Chesapeake). Dr. Cooper, a specialist to whom Wilson was referred by his primary care physician, repeatedly reassured Wilson that a liver transplant would be covered under his HMO plan.

Dr. Cooper made arrangements with Presbyterian Hospital in Pittsburgh, Pennsylvania, to put him on the list of donor liver recipients and to perform the transplant. In August 1985 Wilson arrived at Presbyterian Hospital. At that time Chesapeake advised the hospital that they were not certain that the plan would cover the transplant. Wilson's admission was delayed, and a demand for full payment was made. Wilson's wife Joyce worked to obtain financing. On August 28, a suitable liver was available but because Mr. Wilson lacked evidence of financial coverage of the procedure, the hospital threw the liver away. Between August 29 and September 4 Wilson deteriorated further. His wife returned to Baltimore to work further on the financing problem, and learned that the Maryland Medical Assistance Program would pay for the procedure once the Wilsons had spent down their savings. During this period a second liver became available, but it was also thrown away. By September 4, Wilson had deteriorated further. On September 5 Joyce Wilson returned to find Wilson in a coma. He died on September 6.

The plaintiffs pleaded a variety of theories. Count 16, Negligence, alleged that Dr. Cooper and the health plan

> knew or should have known that staff and resources existed . . . to assist the Wilsons in determining the scope of coverage provided by their HMO, other insurers, and alternative funding sources, but they failed to utilize such resources, alert plaintiffs to the existence of such resources or advise them of the need to identify a funding source.[123]

The *Wilson II* duty means that providers, including outside specialists,

---

122. Plaintiff's amended complaint, Wilson v. Chesapeake Health Plan, Inc., (4th Cir.) (No. 88019032/CL76201) (complaint is in the possession of the author).

123. *Id.* at 33. This count in the complaint withstood both a motion to dismiss and a motion for summary judgment.

should at a minimum know enough to refer patients to experts with a managed care organization or hospital when they need information as to possible sources of funding for a medically necessary procedure. The bundle of services offered by the health care provider, in these times of limited resources, now includes not only medically correct diagnosis and treatment that complies with the standard of care, but also information as to how to fund such care.

IV. INSTITUTIONAL CARE: EXPANDED ACCOUNTABILITY

Hospitals began as the doctor's workshop, little more than a shell within which health care services were provided.[124] As they have grown in complexity, their obligations to patients have also grown. The health care institution provides support, equipment, and administration to physicians, and is, therefore, responsible for sloppy or careful practice within its walls. The notion of a covenant is central to the role of the institution as well as the physician; the covenant reminds the professional community that it is not good enough for the individual doctor to be a good friend or parent to the patient; that it is important also for whole institutions—the hospital, the clinic, the professional group—to keep covenant with those who seek their assistance and sanctuary. Thus the concept permits a certain broadening of accountability beyond personal agency.[125]

A. The Expansion of Tort Duties

Hospitals have a duty to provide adequate staff and services to deal with expected medical problems.[126] Hospitals, like physicians, are expected to keep up with with an evolving standard of medical practice. In *Washington v. Washington Hospital Center*,[127] the court considered

---

124. ROSEMARY STEVENS, IN SICKNESS AND IN WEALTH: AMERICAN HOSPITALS IN THE TWENTIETH CENTURY (1989); PAUL STARR, THE SOCIAL TRANSFORMATION OF AMERICAN MEDICINE (1982); CHARLES E. ROSENBERG, THE CARE OF STRANGERS: THE RISE OF AMERICA's HOSPITAL SYSTEM (1987).

125. May, *supra* note 63, at 36.

126. Douglas v. Freeman, 814 P.2d 1160 (Wash. 1991) (recognizing hospital has duty to provide necessary medical hospital assistance to a doctor and to supervise all those who practice medicine within its facilities).

127. 579 A.2d 177 (D.C. Cir. 1990).

whether the defendant hospital should have had end-tidal carbon dioxide monitors in place in 1987. This was a new technology that many hospitals had installed by 1986. The defendant hospital argued that use by teaching hospitals was not a fair standard of care, since "[i]nstitutions with significantly enhanced financial resources and/or government grants which accelerate their testing and implementation of new and improved technologies would naturally have available to them items which, inherently, were not yet required for the general populace of hospitals."[128] The court rejected the argument, noting the effectiveness of the new technology and its relatively low cost.

The failure of a hospital to maintain adequate services to deal with medical emergencies can create liability.[129] Hospital responsibility goes beyond supplying up-to-date equipment. The power of the institution in managing hundreds of personnel and setting up systems for smooth operation has led to judicial recognition of a duty to design proper systems. For example, institutional providers are increasingly expected to implement protocols that address difficult treatment and ethical issues.[130] Doctors have often used such protocols to guide nurses in decision making in their absence,[131] and such protocols are used to guide physician performance.[132] Standardized approaches to a particular clinical or treatment problem or approach are manifested in a health care institution through written policies, bylaws, personnel directives,

---

128. *Id.* at 183, n. 5.

129. *See* Herrington v. Miller, 883 F.2d 411 (5th Cir. 1989) (failure to provide adequate 24-hour anesthesia service).

130. An algorithm or protocol is "a set of instructions that describes how a patient who comes with a given set of signs or symptoms should be managed, step by step, so that the findings at each step influence which next step is to be taken, until the patient is successfully diagnosed and treated." AVEDIS DONABEDIAN, THE METHODS AND FINDINGS OF QUALITY ASSESSMENT AND MONITORING 38 (1985) (Vol. III of AVEDIS DONABEDIAN, EXPLORATIONS IN QUALITY ASSESSMENT AND MONITORING).

131. *See* Hall v. Hilbun, 466 So. 2d 856 (Miss. 1985) (stating the real negligence of Dr. Hilbun, according to the plaintiff's expert from the Cleveland Clinic, was that he failed to leave detailed protocols for the nursing staff describing what danger signs to watch out for post-operatively).

132. Clinical algorithms have been converted to protocol charts and computerized algorithms that both define clearly how the clinician should make a decision and provide him with appropriate feedback. Margolis, *Uses of Clinical Algorithms*, 249 JAMA, 627, 629 (1983).

or educational programs.[133] Internal manuals, including emergency room policy and procedure manuals, are admissible at trial when they contain information concerning general industry standards or evidence that an institutional defendant violated its own policy. Liability will result from institutional failure to study and take action, rather than from action that, although reasonable when implemented, later proves to be ineffective. Florida, for example, has incorporated by statute "institutional liability" or "corporate negligence" in its regulation of hospitals. Hospitals and other providers will be liable for injuries caused by inadequacies in the internal programs that are mandated by the statute.[134]

A hospital and its contracting physicians may be liable for damages caused by defects in systems they develop and implement. In the Florida case of *Marks v. Mandel*,[135] the plaintiff brought a wrongful death action against the hospital, alleging negligence and failure of the on-call system to produce a thoracic surgeon and failure of the hospital staff to send the patient to a hospital with a trauma center. The Florida Supreme Court held that the trial court erred in excluding from evidence the hospital's emergency room policy and procedure manual. This manual set out in detail how the on-call system should operate and itemized procedures for responding to calls made from ambulances. The court held that evidence was sufficient to go to the jury on the issue of liability of the hospital and the emergency room supervisor for the failure of the on-call system to produce a thoracic surgeon in a timely fashion.

Support systems must also be adequate to handle the range of problems the hospital purports to treat. Short staffing has thus been rejected as a defense where the available staff could have been juggled to achieve closer supervision of a problem patient.[136] Courts are less

---

133. For a study of unjustifiable costs using such algorithmic criteria as a quality audit, *see* Michael P. Corder et al., *A Financial Analysis of Hodgkin Lymphoma Staging*, 71 AM J. R. PUB. HEALTH 376 (1981). For a lawyer's discussion of protocols in the hospital, *see* Barbara R. Pankau, *AIDS: Responding to the Issues*, 3 HEALTH LAW 1, 10 (1987).

134. FLA. STAT. ANN. § 768.60 (West 1986).

135. 477 So. 2d 1036 (Fla. 1985).

136. Horton v. Niagara Falls Memorial Medical Ctr., 51 A.D.2d 152 (N.Y. Sup. Ct. 1976) (holding hospital guilty of negligence in connection with a patient's fall from window where hospital could have but failed to provide continuous supervision for the short time before patient's mother-in-law arrived).

tolerant of excuses for failures by institutions when patient injury results. Institutions must run a well-managed system of care.

The fundamental principle of agency law is vicarious liability, i.e., the master (employer) is responsible for the torts of his servant (employee) even though the master was not negligent. It is a nonfault rule of liability. In the medical setting, physicians have traditionally been treated as independent contractors rather than employees; as a result, the hospital is relieved of any agency-based liability for their negligent acts. As the courts have considered the range of situations in which physicians provide care in the hospital setting, they have extended agency principles to limit the independent contractor defense and thereby circumvent vicarious liability limitations.[137] An expanded notion of accountability is apparent in the judicial treatment of agency law and independent contractor defenses.

The control test was first used by the courts to test whether the doctor was an employee or subject to the control of the hospital. The courts apply a number of standard criteria for evaluating the existence of a master–servant relationship. If the contract gives the hospital substantial control over the doctor's choice of patients or if the hospital furnishes equipment, then a master–servant relationship can be found.[138] The control test looks to the terms of the contract and the actual relationship between the hospital and the physician.

The inherent function test takes the inquiry one step further, looking at those functions of a hospital which are essential to its operation. Radiology labs and emergency rooms are two such functions.[139] This notion of "inherent function" overlaps substantially with the "non-delegable duty" rule in agency law, as expressed in corporate negligence cases. Where a function is considered to be an inherent part of the functioning

---

137. See *generally* ARTHUR F. SOUTHWICK, THE LAW OF HOSPITAL AND HEALTH CARE ADMINISTRATION, ch. XIV (2d ed. 1988); Note, *Theories for Imposing Liability Upon Hospitals for Medical Malpractice: Ostensible Agency and Corporate Liability*, 11 WM. MITCHELL L. REV. 561 (1985).

138. The caselaw reflects divergent applications of the "control" test, because of the breadth of the factors involved. *See* Mduba v. Benedictine Hospital, 52 A.D.2d 450 (N.Y. 1976) (doctor failed to give blood to patient, resulting in his death; hospital in the contract between doctor and hospital had guaranteed doctor's salary and controlled his activities. Court held doctor to be an employee); Kober v. Stewart, 417 P.2d 476 (Mont. 1966) (finding contract establishes the method by which hospital hired a doctor as supervisor).

139. *See, e.g.*, Adamski v. Tacoma Gen. Hosp., 579 P.2d 970 (Wash. Ct. App. 1978).

of the health care institution, the courts have held that the institution cannot escape liability because of the status of the physician. Vicarious liability applies in spite of a physician's independent contractor status.

The ostensible agency or apparent authority test is also commonly used to channel liability from the negligent physician to the health care institution. In some settings, such as the emergency room or the radiology laboratory, the institution is held to offer services to the patient through a doctor, even though the doctor who renders the service is not an employee. The ostensible agency or apparent authority test then looks to the patient and his expectations as to treatment.[140] Several jurisdictions have allowed cases to proceed past summary judgment motions, or to go to the jury, on agency-based theories of ostensible agency or apparent authority. The courts use agency principles to hold a hospital liable for negligent acts of independent contractors such as radiologists or emergency room physicians. Hospitals have thus been held liable for the acts of radiologists, residents, emergency room physicians, and surgeons, even though these persons were not hospital employees.[141] Courts hold hospitals liable for the malpractice of their

---

140. *See, e.g.*, Porter v. Sisters of St. Mary, 756 F.2d 669 (8th Cir. 1985) (holding the plaintiff failed to prove, under RESTATEMENT (SECOND) OF AGENCY § 267, that he relied upon representations that the physician was an agent of the hospital). When the plaintiff entered the emergency room with a collapsed lung, an employee of the hospital said that he had called Dr. Schneider, "... and he's our best person for the job." The court held that statement was insufficient to satisfy the requirements to prove apparent authority because plaintiff had then deliberated for several days before selecting Dr. Schneider to perform further surgery which gave rise to his injuries.

Apparent authority is governed by two alternative Restatement Sections. RESTATEMENT (SECOND) OF AGENCY § 267 provides:

One who represents that another is his servant or other agent and thereby causes a third person justifiably to rely upon the care or skill of such apparent agent is subject to liability to the third person for harm caused by the lack of care or skill of the one appearing to be a servant or other agent as if he were such.

RESTATEMENT (SECOND) OF TORTS § 429 (1965) provides:

One who employs an independent contractor to perform services for another which are accepted in the reasonable belief that the services are being rendered by the employer or by his servants, is subject to liability for physical harm caused by the negligence of the contractor in supplying such services, to the same extent as though the employer were supplying them himself or by his servants.

141. The number of courts that have adopted exceptions to vicarious
(*cont.*)

independent contractor physicians where there is evidence that the hospital allowed or encouraged patients to believe that the physicians were authorized agents of the hospital.

Other institutional forms have developed over the past decade. Managed care networks are one example. Squeezed by reimbursement limitations and rising health care costs, employers and medical providers have turned to managed care to control costs. The Director of the Federation of American Health Systems, Michael Bromberg, describes managed care as "the hottest growth area in health care delivery today."[142] In one decade, the change from feefor-service care to managed care has become a stampede.[143] Health care is increasingly delivered through large managed care systems, with health maintenance organizations and preferred provider organizations (PPOs) growing rapidly. About 60% of the 160 million Americans with employer-sponsored health insurance were enrolled in a managed care plan in 1987;

(141, *cont.*) liability, including ostensible agency, include Shepard v. Sisters of Providence, 750 P.2d 500 (Or. Ct. App. 1988) (resident clothed in ostensible authority when he assisted private surgeon in an operation with a private patient, in the hospital); Pamperin v. Trinity Memorial Hospital, 423 N.W. 2d 848 (Wisc. 1988) (radiologists); Thompson v. Nason Hospital, 535 A.2d 1177 (Pa. Super Ct. 1988) (surgeons); Richmond County Hospital Authority v. Brown, 361 S.E.2d 164 (Ga. 1987) (holding hospital liable for emergency room physicians under doctrine of ostensible or apparent authority); Martell v. St. Charles Hospital, 523 N.Y.S. 2d 342 (N.Y. Sup. Ct.) (holding hospital vicariously liable for emergency room physician's actions even if hospital emergency room where actions occurred was run by an independent contractor); Strach v. St. John Hospital Assoc., 408 N.W.2d 441 (Mich. Ct. App. 1987) (physicians referred to surgery unit as part of hospital's team and surgery team doctors exercised direct authority over hospital employees); Barrett v. Samaritan Health Services, Inc., 735 P.2d 460 (Ariz. Ct. App. 1987) (physician's organization vicariously liable for physician's actions).

142. Michael D. Bromberg, *Managed Care—Who Reviews the Reviewers?* 21 FED'N AM. HEALTH SYS. REV., July/Aug. 1988, at 6; *see also* Glenn Kramon, *'Managed Care' is Top Plan Now*, N.Y. TIMES, June 14, 1988, at D2, c.1.

143. The escalation in medical spending by both the Medicare program and private health insurers has led to an intensified focus on managing health care costs. Traditional fee-for-service insurance, which pays medical charges without question, has declined sharply over the past few years. For example, Aetna Life and Casualty Company now covers only 22% of the 11 million people covered for health benefits, compared with 64% in 1988. Employees are offered the chance to join an HMO or other discount network more and more frequently. Milt Frudenheim, *Health Insurers' Changing Role*, N.Y. TIMES, Jan. 16, 1990, at D2, c.1.

in 1980 only 5 to 10% were enrolled in such plans.[144] HMOs and PPOs (excluding managed fee-for-service plans) enrolled over 27% of employees with group health insurance in 1987. This contrasts with 1981 figures of 4% enrollment.[145]

Managed care organizations (MCOs) create a new set of relationships between payers, subscribers and providers. These new relationships create new liability risks. The subscriber typically pays his fee to the MCO rather than the provider, giving up control over his treatment and choice of his treating physician. The payer, in turn, shifts some of its financial risk to its approved providers, who must also accept certain controls over their practice. The physician, traditionally the patient's agent and advocate, as a quid pro quo, now receives many patients from the payer.[146]

---

144. Jon Gabel et al., *The Changing World of Group Health Insurance*, 7 HEALTH AFF., Summer 1988, at 48, 53.

145. *Id.* at 52. Managed care organizations (MCOs) are most commonly represented by health maintenance organizations (HMOs), which include group models, network models, and IPAs (HMO contracts with an association of independent practitioners). *See* Gary Scott Davis, *Introduction* to *Managed Health Care Primer, in The Insider's Guide to Managed Care: A Legal and Operational Roadmap* 1 National Health Lawyers Association (1990). Other organizations include Preferred Provider Organizations (PPOs), Exclusive Provider Organizations (EPOs), utilization review organizations, and even hospitals. While a staff model HMO will have a central location for practice, other models involve physicians and dentists in their own offices, providing care to subscribers under contract to the MCO. A Health Maintenance Organization (HMO) is an entity that provides comprehensive health care services to an enrolled membership for a fixed per capita fee. HMOs are thus both insurers and providers of medical care. HMOs are usually classified into four categories based on their relationship with medical care providers: staff model HMOs directly employ physicians to provide medical care; group model HMOs contract with an independent, multi-specialty corporation or partnership of physicians to delivery care; network HMOs contract with a number of groups of physicians who also may serve patients not belonging to the HMO; and individual practice association (IPA) and HMOs contract, the IPA in turn contracts with individual physicians to provide care in their own offices.

146. Ernest W. Saward & E.K. Gallagher, *Reflections on Change in Medical Practice: The Current Trend To Large-Scale Medical Organizations*, 250 JAMA 2820 (1983); Starr, *supra* note 124.

Young doctors want to work in these new settings, to gain the advantages of free time and control over work load. One survey found that more than 50% of the young doctors polled preferred a guaranteed salary to traditional fee-for-service compensation, and 81% preferred a group practice or HMO, while just 11% favored solo practice. Physicians want more time for families

(*cont.*)

Medical practice is therefore firmly embedded within a variety of health care delivery structures. Doctors are affiliated with PPOs or group practices with staff privileges at least at one hospital. The physician without institutional linkages is a fading breed. The logic of institutional responsibility has been readily extended to managed care organizations. The relationship of the MCO to its member physicians is more varied than that of the hospital with its medical staff, and this relationship will determine the source of liability. Staff model HMOs, employing physicians on a salaried basis in its own medical facilities, satisfy the master–servant requirements of agency law. In *Sloan v. Metropolitan Health Council of Indianapolis, Inc.*,[147] the Sloans sued Metro, a health maintenance organization, alleging a negligent failure to diagnose. Metro claimed that its physicians were independent in their practice of medicine, and that Metro did not control their judgment in diagnosis or treatment decisions. It therefore invoked the "corporate practice of medicine" doctrine, which makes it unlawful for a corporation to practice medicine. The defendant argued that a physician may not accept directions in diagnosing and treating ailments from a corporation, and is therefore an independent contractor. The court rejected this defense, finding it to be a "non sequitur to conclude that because a hospital cannot practice medicine or psychiatry, it cannot be liable for the actions of its employed agents and servants who may be so licensed."[148] An HMO, likewise, should not be insulated from liability. The court noted that Metro's staff physicians were under the control of its medical director, a physician, and "[t]he circumstances establish an employment relationship where the employee performed acts within the scope of his employment."[149] Independent practice

---

(146, *cont.*) and personal interests. Ron Winslow, *Debt-Burdened Doctors Seek Financial Security*, WALL ST. J., Oct. 10, 1989, at B1.

147. 516 N.E.2d 1104 (Ind. Ct. App. 1987).

148. *Id.* at 1108.

149. *Id.* at 1109. In Schleier v. Kaiser Found. Health Plan, 876 F.2d 174 (D.C. Cir. 1989) a staff model HMO was held vicariously liable for physician malpractice, not of its employee-physician, but of an independent consulting physician. The court found grounds to hold the HMO vicariously liable: (1) the consultant physician had been engaged by an HMO-employed physician, (2) the HMO had the right to discharge the consultant, (3) services provided by the consultant were part of the regular business of the HMO, and (4) the HMO had some ability to control the consultant's behavior, since he answered to an HMO doctor, the plaintiff's primary care physician. This judicial willingness to impose respondeat superior liability for the negligence of a consulting, non-employee physician clearly applies to the IPA model HMOs

association (IPA) model HMOs that become "the institution", "hold out" the independent contractor as an employee, and restrict provider selection, are vulnerable to ostensible agency arguments. The development of complex cost and quality controls, which strengthen the supervisory role of the HMO, together with the managed care industry's preference for the capitation method of physician compensation, are likely to lead the courts to hold the IPA model HMO–physician relationship to respondeat superior liability.

Malpractice cases have also extended the non-delegable duty doctrine of agency law to impose obligations on hospitals as quasi-utilities to maintain responsibility for emergency rooms.[150] In *Jackson v. Power*,[151] the Alaska Supreme Court held that a hospital had a "non-delegable duty to provide non-negligent physician care in its emergency room." It could not shift liability onto independent contractors, once it determined that it had a duty to provide that emergency room care. The hospital, licensed as a "general acute care hospital," was required to comply with state regulations designed to promote "safe and adequate treatment of individuals in hospitals in the interest of public health, safety and welfare," including the provision of a physician at all times to respond to emergencies.[152] It had also voluntarily assumed a broader duty, as a result of its accreditation by the Joint Committee on the Accreditation of Health-care Organizations (JCAHO).

The *Jackson* court analogized hospital emergency services to the operation of an airline. Patients, like passengers, deserve protection. The court then noted the pervasive regulation of the hospital industry in Alaska, as in other states, and the "close parallel between the

---

and even PPOs. In Boyd v. Albert Einstein Medical Ctr., 547 A.2d 1229 (Pa. Super. Ct. 1988) another ostensible agency case involving an HMO, the court asked whether the HMO through its agents created the appearance that an agency relationship existed between the HMO and the negligent physician; and whether the patient reasonably relied upon the appearance to his detriment or injury.

150. A non-delegable duty is an exception to the rule that an employer is not liable for the negligence of an independent contractor. W. PAGE KEETON ET AL., PROSSER AND KEETON ON THE LAW OF TORTS, § 71, at 511–12 (5th ed. 1984). The court in Jackson v. Power, 743 P.2d 1376, 1383 (Alaska 1987) observed that a non-delegable duty analysis is based upon a judicial assessment that "... *the responsibility is so important to the community that the employer should not be permitted to transfer it to another.*" Id. at 512 (emphasis added). *Accord*, Alaska Airlines v. Sweat, 568 P.2d 916, 925–26 (Alaska 1977).

151. 743 P.2d 1376, 1377 (Alaska 1987).

152. *Id.* at 1382.

regulatory scheme of airlines and hospitals. Undoubtedly, the operation of a hospital is one of the most regulated activities in this state." The court gave a number of justifications for its quasi-utility analysis: the implication from pervasive legislative regulation that the hospital is the ultimate repository of responsibility; public expectations of hospitals as responsible for the quality of care rendered by physicians and finally, the commercialization of medicine.[153]

A hospital as a public utility may capture the reality of today's health care system. The health care industry is pervasively regulated, particularly by the federal government. Health care generally is viewed as an inappropriate industry for free market principles. Health care at least in the emergency room in a crisis is considered a necessity by most people, an expectation created by hospitals over the years.[154] The halo effect of nonprofit status, and the willingness of hospital administrators to draw on this line of credit in their marketing, supports obligations derived from public expectations as to emergency care.[155] Given the extent of government regulation and the special status of health care, the argument that hospitals approach the status of public utilities is a

---

153. Jackson, *supra* note 151. Not all courts have found the *Jackson* position compatible. The application of the non-delegable duty doctrine to hospitals was rejected in Estates of Milliron v. Francke, 793 P.2d 824, 827–28 (Mo. 1990) (distinguishing *Jackson* since it involved radiology, not emergency room practice) and Albain *v.* Flower Hosp., 553 N.E.2d 1038 (Ohio 1990) (noting that the normal application of non-delegable duty doctrine is premised on peculiar risks and special precautions attendant to the work itself, "The practice of medicine in a hospital by an independent physician with staff privileges does not involve the type of risks and precautions required . . .") *Id.* at 1048.

154. For an intriguing discussion of the role of expectations in generating claims, *see* Leslie Pickering Francis, *Consumer Expectations and Access to Health Care,* 140 U. Pa. L. Rev. 1881 (1992). Francis argues that expectations are based on beliefs about the future. The more unreasonable the beliefs, the less moral weight they carry, and context determines the reasonableness of the beliefs.

Francis proposes "encouragement" as a second feature of expectations that deserve moral weight. "Without the acknowledgement that it is sometimes reasonable to rely on assurances that expectations will be fulfilled, much planning would be undercut." *Id.* at 1892.

155. The mission of a hospital, and its projection to the community at large, creates expectations. "Voluntarism, community, and cooperation are potent values for hospitals, which *deliver* care. Hospitals sit in one place and render intimate, caring human services to people who often feel a personal identification with the institutions' histories, staffs, and corporate identities. None of this applies to health *insurance,* whose tasks are actuarial, technical, impersonal,

supportable position.[156] It justifies imposing rescue obligations on institutions, and requires that they meet a heavy burden of proof to avoid responsibility for such care.

B. Hospitals and indigent care: from charity to obligation

Hospitals and other institutions have extensive obligations to treat their patients properly, once they enter the hospital. But what are the obligations of institutions to "rescue" distressed individuals who present themselves at the hospital door? Emergency rooms are a visible combat zone in the American health care system—overburdened, understaffed and underfinanced. They have become the gateway to the health care system for the uninsured and the indigent, a safety net of last resort to replace the shrinking government net.[157] Yet trauma centers and emergency rooms have been eliminated in the past few years to stem financial losses.[158] From the hospital's viewpoint, undesirable patients enter through the emergency room, stressing hospital budgets.[159]

---

and bureaucratic." Laurence D. Brown, *Capture and Culture: Organizational Identity in New York Blue Cross*, 16 J. HEALTH POL. POL'Y & L. 651, 669 (1991).

156. *See* William F. Corley, *Hospitals as a Public Utility: or "Work with Us Now or Work for Us Later*, 2 J. HEALTH POL. POL'Y & L. 304 (1978); A.J. Priest, *Possible Adaptation of Public Utility Concepts in the Health Care Field*, 35 L. & CONTEMP. PROB. 839 (1970).

157. Robert Stern et al., *The Emergency Department as a Pathway to Admission for Poor and High-Cost Patients*, 266 JAMA 2238, 2243 (1991):

In summary, our study has shown that certain patient groups often thought to be disadvantaged—the elderly, nonwhites, the poor—are more likely than other patient groups to be admitted through the emergency department, and admission through the emergency department is associated with higher costs of care. . . . Some system to compensate hospitals for these additional costs may be worthwhile to preserve access to care for disadvantaged patients and to ensure the financial viability of institutions that serve the disadvantaged.

158. Melinda Bech et al., *State of Emergency: Hospitals are seeking radical solutions to ease walk-in patient overload*, NEWSWEEK, Oct. 14, 1991 at 52 (discussing the means hospitals have pursued to deal with the walk-in overload).

159. James M. Perrin, *High Technology and Uncompensated Hospital Care, in* UNCOMPENSATED HOSPITAL CARE: RIGHTS AND RESPONSIBILITIES (Frank Sloan et al. eds., 1986).

Much uncompensated hospital care does not involve high-technology services. Nevertheless, a sizeable proportion does arise from the intensive care of sick and premature newborns, accident victims, and people suffering from certain malignancies. In one private academic teaching hospital, newborn care accounts for almost 25 percent of uncompensated care.

Id. at 70.

The goal has often been to transfer them as soon as possible to public hospitals. Where treatment is given, hospitals tend to undertreat patients if their insurance coverage is inadequate.[160] A 1988 study of a publicly subsidized hospital in Memphis found that during one 92-day study, private hospitals made 190 requests to transfer patients to the public facility. Almost all patients transferred (91%) were sent for primarily economic reasons. One-fourth of these patients were unstable, according to explicit clinical criteria, upon arrival at the public hospital.[161] But most hospitals are still trying to reduce bad debts by avoiding nonpaying patients.[162]

1. Sources of obligations to render care

The sources and limits of obligations on hospitals to render emergency care have been well described by other commentators.[163] The Joint Commission on Accreditation of Healthcare Organizations' *Accredita-*

---

160. Paula A. Braveman et al., *Differences in Hospital Resource Allocation Among Sick Newborns According to Insurance Coverage*, 266 JAMA 3300 (1991). The study examined the relationship between health insurance coverage and utilization of hospital inpatient services by sick newborns. It concluded that similar pressures were found on providers across all hospital ownership types.

The observed pattern of hospital resource suggests strongly that allocation of hospital services to sick newborns was influenced significantly by expected reimbursement rather than determined strictly by medical need. *Id.* at 3307.

Comparisons between newborns without insurance and those with prepaid private coverage also contribute to the ability of this study to indicate the far greater likelihood of too little care for some groups than too much care for others. It is known that care provided in the first days of life can have a significant impact on a highrisk newborn's chances for long-term survival and optimal health and development. The concept of equity suggests that treatment provided to sick newborns should be based on clinical criteria alone. *The finding of allocation of fewer hospital services to vulnerable groups likely to be at higher risk during the first days of life constitutes prima facie evidence of serious inequity and suggests the need for intensive and systematic public surveillance of the pressures on institutions, providers, and patients under current health care financing systems.* (emphasis added) *Id.* at 3308.

161. *See* Arthur L. Kellerman & Bela B. Hackman, *Emergency Department Patient 'Dumping': An Analysis of Interhospital Transfers to the Regional Medical Center at Memphis, Tennessee*, 78 AM. J. PUB. HEALTH 1287 (1988). *See also* Robert L. Schiff et al., *Transfer to a Public Hospital: A Prospective Study of 467 Patients*, 314 NEW ENG. J. MED. 552 (1986).

162. *See* George J. Annas, *Your Money or Your Life: 'Dumping' Uninsure Patients from Hospital Emergency Wards*, 76 AM. J. PUB. HEALTH 74 (1986).

163. Karen H. Rothenberg, *Who Cares?: The Evolution of the Legal Duty to Provide Emergency Care*, 26 HOUS. L. REV. 21 (1989).

tion Manual for Hospitals states: "Unless extenuating circumstances are documented in the patient's record, no patient is arbitrarily transferred to another hospital if the hospital where he is initially seen has the means for providing adequate care."[164]

State courts have developed common law doctrinal bases for a duty on hospitals to care for patients who could not pay, but the duty has not been contagious.[165] A hospital's emergency department is presumed to have a duty to provide care to all who seek it.[166] Courts have adopted a number of different strategies to this end. They have stretched the facts to find an admission, so that the doctor–patient relationship exists.[167] A nurse who examines a patient and calls a doctor has thus created a provider–patient relationship with a facility.[168] A second strategy has been to find a duty to treat based on public reliance or established custom.[169] This approach has not found much support, and raises difficult issues regarding the definition of "emergency" and the nature and extent of care to be provided.[170] A third approach, one that the Alaska Supreme Court in *Jackson* articulated in its vicarious

---

164. JOINT COMMISSION ON ACCREDIDATION OF HEALTHCARE ORGANIZATIONS, AMH ACCREDITATION MANUAL FOR HOSPITALS § 1.33 (1990).

165. Wilmington Gen. Hospital v. Manlove, 174 A.2d 135 (Del. 1961) (finding that where a hospital refuses service to a patient in case of an unmistakable emergency, liability is on the hospital if the patient has relied on a well-established custom of the hospital to render aid in such a case).

166. J. Koeze, *Access to Treatment, in* HEALTHCARE FACILITIES LAW: CRITICAL ISSUES FOR HOSPITALS, HMOs, AND EXTENDED CARE FACILITIES § 6.2.1, 424 (Anne M. Dellinger ed., 1991).

167. *See* discussion of Noble v. Sartori, text at § II.

168. O'Neill v. Montefiore Hosp., (N.Y. App. Div. 1960) (reversing a lower court decision to dismiss the case in favor of the hospital where the plaintiff's proof was sufficient to permit the inference that the nurse in charge of the emergency ward undertook to provide medical attention for the deceased).

169. Wilmington Gen. Hosp. v. Manlove, 174 A.2d 135 (Del. 1961) (holding private hospital may be liable for refusal of service to a patient in case of emergency if the patient has relied upon a well-established custom of the hospital to render care in such a case) is the leading case for a reliance approach. *See also* Williams v. Hospital Auth. of Hall County, 168 S.E.2d 336 (Ga. Ct. App. 1969) (holding public hospital which assumes the duty of furnishing emergency first-aid facilities to injured persons cannot arbitrarily refuse its facilities to a member of the public in need of such treatment); Mercy Medical Ctr. of Oshkosh v. Winnebago County, 206 N.W.2d 198 (Wis. 1973) (discussing the social policy that private hospitals with emergency rooms have a duty to admit those in need of such service because the public expects such service).

170. *Supra*, note 139, at 425–27.

liability analysis, is to hold hospitals to be public utilities, with a fiduciary duty owed to the public for emergency care.[171]

State and federal legislation has reduced the significance of common law duties by offering explicit mandates for emergency care.[172] The most powerful current statutory source of obligations is The Consolidated Omnibus Budget Reconciliation Act (COBRA),[173] the Emergency Medical Treatment and Women in Active Labor Act, enacted to counter the emerging scandal of patient dumping. It mandates that patients be medically stable for transfer, imposes stiff penalties for inappropriate transfers, and creates a civil cause of action for damages. COBRA has been used to impose sanctions on physicians and hospitals,[174] although it provides statutory escape clauses for providers who

---

171. *See, e.g.*, Doe v. Bridgeton Hosp. Assn., 366 A.2d 641, 644–646 (N.J. 1976) (holding private, non-profit hospitals could not refuse to permit their facilities to be used for elective abortions during first trimester pregnancy where hospitals had facilities for such abortions and permitted use of facilities for therapeutic abortions), *cert. denied*, 433 U.S. 914 (1977); Jeffrey E. Fine, *Opening the Closed Doors: The Duty of Hospitals to Treat Emergency Patients*, 24 WASH. U. J. URB. & CONTEMP. L. 123 (1983).

172. Over twenty states have some kind of regulation or statute that prohibits facilities from denying emergency care based on ability to pay, although remedies are often deficient. *See* Koeze, *supra* note 166, at 428. *See also* Dowell, *supra* note 1.

173. Consolidated Omnibus Budget Reconciliation Act, 42 USC § 1395dd (1988) (examination and treatment for emergency medical conditions and women in labor).

174. Owens v. Nacogdoches County Hospital District, 741 F. Supp. 1269 (E.D. Tex. 1990):

Plaintiff's [a 16 year old pregnant woman] evidence demonstrates a long-standing pattern of patient dumping, caused by staffing policies that in the opinion of a series of medical experts would inevitably lead to standards of care at Memorial Hospital that patently did not meet state or federal statutory requirements. Bluntly stated, Memorial Hospital has callously and negligently allowed a situation to develop in which all emergency obstetric and gynecological services to indigent patients—an enormous and ever-increasing load—have been left to on-call private physicians like Dr. Thompson, and the dumping of pregnant women has been the inevitable result.

Id. at 1280.

Abercrombie v. Osteopathic Hosp. Founders Ass'n, 950 F.2d 676 (10th Cir. 1991) (sixty-eight-year-old woman with chest pains, went to an Osteopathic, court held that either of the following violations is sufficient because hospital has a strict liability standard to provide screening: (1) hospital must provide a proper screening examination, and/or (2) patient may not be discharged if the emergency medical condition has not stabilized).

want to avoid caring for indigents who enter through the emergency room.[175] COBRA has attracted much analysis and worry on the part of providers, given its explicit demand for forced rescue under the specific circumstances of the Act. It is the most recent expression of our political willingness to conscript hospitals to rescue patients they would otherwise try to avoid.

2. The tax collector

Prior to 1950, most nonprofit institutions were supported by donations, providing services that served the public good—they were traditional charities, easily distinguishable from business firms. By 1950, however, hospitals had evolved from donative institutions to commercial nonprofits.[176] With the growth of technological medicine and of health care financing through the Medicare and Medicaid programs,

> hospitals have become mainstream service institutions providing medical care on a fee-for-service basis to the public at large, while performing little or no role in subsidizing care for the poor. Nevertheless, seventy-five percent of general hospitals remain nonprofit today, presumably in large part as a consequence of institutional inertia. They are anachronistic and perhaps also a bit opportunistic, continuing to trade on whatever goodwill attaches to the image of a nonprofit organization, and enjoying as well the benefits of tax exemption and other fiscal and regulatory privileges that nonprofit status continues to bring.[177]

Courts split over whether indigency must be established. *See* Nichols v. Estabrook, M.D., 741 F. Supp. 325 (D.N.H. 1989) (holding liability cannot be based on COBRA, absent allegation by plaintiffs that their financial condition or lack of health insurance contributed to defendant's decision not to treat their son and to send him to another hospital, where family pediatrician would be in attendance). *Contra*, Gatewood v. Washington Healthcare Corp., 933 F.2d 1037 (D.C. Cir. 1991) (holding act draws no distinction between patients with and without health insurance yet it does not create simply another malpractice cause of action). *Accord*, Cleland v. Bronson Health Care Group, Inc., 917 F.2d 266 (6th Cir. 1990) (holding act is not limited to indigent or uninsured persons who seek treatment or examination at hospital emergency rooms and hospital met its duty to stabilize patient in emergency room and thus did not violate the act even though patient was misdiagnosed).

175. *See* Rothenberg, *supra* note 163.
176. Henry Hansmann, *The Evolving Law of Nonprofit Organizations: Do Current Trends Make Good Policy?* 39 CASE W. RES. L. REV. 807, 813 (1988–89).
177. *Id.* at 813–14.

The tax exemption granted to nonprofit hospitals by the federal, state, and local governments has been a continuing and massive subsidy.[178] Comprising less than 3% of all nonprofit organizations, hospitals account for more than half of nonprofit sector expenditures.[179] But charitable giving to hospitals has dropped considerably since 1968.[180]

The federal government, through Internal Revenue Service (IRS) tax exemptions for hospitals and other providers, has made health policy by indirection since 1969.[181] In that year the IRS ruled that hospitals do not have to provide free or below-cost care to those unable to pay in order to retain their federal charitable tax exemption.[182] This ruling removed an important barrier to "dumping" indigent patients by allowing voluntary nonprofit hospitals to refuse to treat uninsured patients.[183] The ruling described a hospital which "limits admissions to those who can pay the cost of their hospitalization, either themselves or through private health insurance, or with the aid of the public programs such as Medicare." A hospital is charitable, since "by providing hospital

---

178. Hall & Colombo, *supra* note 18, at 314 n.18.

179. JAMES T. BENNETT & THOMAS J. DiLORENZO, UNFAIR COMPETITION: THE PROFITS OF NONPROFITS 73 (1989).

180. The nonprofits have become similar, and one commentator writes that "[b]y the mid-1960s ... the notion of an institution closely connected to its community seemed like a romantic remnant of a 'pre-scientific' era." David Rosner, *Heterogeneity and Uniformity: Historical Perspectives on the Voluntary Hospital,* *in* SICKNESS AND IN HEALTH: THE MISSION OF VOLUNTARY HEALTH CARE INSTITUTIONS 122 (1988).

181. Daniel M. Fox & Daniel C. Schaffer, *Tax Administration as Health Policy: Hospitals, the Internal Revenue Service, and the Courts,* 16 J. HEALTH POL. POL'Y & L. 251 (1991).

182. Rev. Rul. 69–545, 1969–2 C.B. 117, also released as T.I.R. 1022, dated Oct. 28, 1969.

183. Fox and Schaffer, *supra* note 181, argue that the IRS made policy without admitting it.

> In our interpretation of events, the Internal Revenue Service, thinking that it was merely reasoning from legal principles, in effect accepted the hospital industry's view of the history and purpose of hospitals ... The Internal Revenue Service accepted the hospital industry's argument, to a large extent, as the result of research by a junior member of its staff ... They accepted without verification that hospitals are primarily places where sophisticated medical procedures are carried out for the benefit of entire communities, most of whose residents had or would shortly have an insurer or public agency willing to pay their bills. In this formulation, an appropriate use of any surplus revenue of nonprofit hospitals would be to purchase new technology rather than to subsidize the cost of care.

Id. at 252–53.

care for all those persons in the community able to pay the cost thereof either directly or through third-party reimbursement, [the] hospital . . . is promoting the health of a class of persons that is broad enough to benefit the community." This explanation left open the argument that a hospital that accepted Medicare and Medicaid patients and had an emergency room open to all was one way to get the exemption, but not the only way. The IRS position, based on a staffer's research, was that Medicare and Medicaid had eliminated the need for free care for patients, and the demand for such care was disappearing.[184]

For the next twenty years, the IRS neither clarified nor enforced its rulings.[185] "There is no record of a nonprofit hospital losing its charitable status for turning away patients from its emergency room for inability to pay, for transferring such a patient to a public hospital even though the transfer was medically sound, or for refusing patients enrolled in Medicaid."[186]

The current IRS stance is intensified scrutiny of not-for-profit hospitals' operations. Hospital audits have stepped up, and the IRS is exploring a "Closing Agreement" policy with facilities, allowing hospitals to keep tax-exempt status while correcting problems.[187]

Some states have taken a more aggressive position, administering the exemption on a hospital-specific, annual basis, requiring each hospital to demonstrate yearly its delivery of free care in an increment sufficient to earn the subsidy.[188] Other state taxing authorities have moved aggressively to compel uncompensated care in exchange for tax exemptions of health care providers. The most famous of these actions, in *Utah County v. Intermountain Health Care, Inc.*,[189] required a level of free care beyond that provided by Intermountain, leading to the revocation of their tax-exempt status. Most other states have been

---

184. *Id.* at 260.

185. UNITED STATES, INTERNAL REVENUE SERVICE, EXEMPT ORGANIZA-TION HANDBOOK, § 349.2 (May 18, 1988).

186. Fox & Schaffer, *supra* note 181, at 273.

187. Jeffrey M. Green, *IRS to explore closing agreement with hospitals*, AHA NEWS, May 4, 1992, at 1; Ron Winslow, *IRS Reviews Nonprofit Hospitals For Abuses of Tax-Exempt Status*, Wall St. J., Apr. 3, 1992, at B1.

188. Hall and Colombo, *supra* note 18, at 325–36. Alabama allows a tax exemption only if the hospital demonstrates that 15% of its business con-stitutes treatment of charity patients, or free care. Each hospital must certify annually to the tax commissioner that this test is met. ALA. CODE ANN. § 40–9–1(2) to -1(3) (Supp. 1992).

189. 709 P.2d 265 (Utah 1985) (holding that hospital was not exempt from property tax because it did not meet the definition of a charity).

satisfied with mere availability of indigent care, without more, while others simply presume that provision of health care is a charitable purpose.[190] Pennsylvania and a few other states have been pockets of aggressive scrutiny of hospitals.[191] As the IRS position toughens, the states are more likely to follow suit, in search of revenue, with increased skepticism toward the claims of charity so readily accepted by taxing authorities from hospitals in the past.[192]

V. INSURER RESPONSIBILITIES

Experimental treatments that promise rescue from certain death for desperate individuals are often at the heart of insurance litigation. Third-party payers often refuse reimbursement of "experimental" treatment under insurance policies covering only "accepted" medical treatments. These disputes raise two issues: (1) Is the treatment in fact experimental? (2) Is it excludable under the policy language?[193] Distinguishing experimental from accepted treatments is difficult, since medical professionals often disagree. The need to control costs and

---

190. *See, e.g.,* Medical Center Hosp. of Vermont v. City of Burlington, 566 A.2d 1352 (Vt. 1989) (hospital was not required to prove it dispensed free care; fact that it made health care available was sufficient to allow tax-exempt status).

191. Terese Hudson, *Not-for-profit Hospitals Fight Tax-Exempt Challenges,* HOSPITALS, Oct. 20, 1990, at 32–37.

192. *See* Evangelical Lutheran Good Samaritan Soc'y Board of Equalization of Latah County, 804 P.2d 299 (Idaho 1990) (denying tax-exempt status to independent living facility division of multi-level care facility while granting tax-exempt status to skilled nursing division); Chicago Health Servs. v. Commissioner of Revenue, 462 N.W.2d 386 (Minn. 1990) (holding that hospital's auxiliary outpatient facility did not meet the definition of institution of public charity and was not entitled to property tax exemption); Hospital Utilization Project v. Commonwealth, 507 Pa. 1, 487 A.2d 1306 (1985) (holding that organization which is a provider of statistical analysis of patient treatment and cost date to hospitals was not a charitable organization and was not exempt from sales and use tax); Cape Retirement Community, Inc. v. Kuehle, 798 S.W.2d 201 (Mo. Ct.App. 1990) (holding retirement home was not exempt from taxes because its application procedure did not provide equal access to both rich and poor).

193. Paul J. Molino, *Reimbursement Disputes Involving Experimental Medical Treatment,* 24 J. HEALTH & HOSP. L. 329 (1991); Jennifer Belk, *Undefined Experimental Treatment Exclusions in Health Insurance Contracts: A Proposal for Judicial Response,* 66 WASH. L. REV. 809 (1991); Lee N. Newcomer, *Defining Experimental Therapy—A Third party Payer's Dilemma,* 323 NEW ENG. J. MED. 1702 (1990).

avoid quack remedies justifies payer sensitivity to wasting resources on useless rescue attempts by providers and patients.[194] However, the history of insurance regulation suggests the need to tip the balance toward subscribers and patients when the therapy has some admitted efficacy.[195] Mandated rescue by insurers through compelled payment of treatment has been achieved by the courts in several cases, where the insurer could not justify its refusals except on the basis of saving money.

Courts interpret ambiguity in favor of subscribers in close cases, demanding coverage exclusions that leave no room for doubt, recognizing the imbalance of power between insurer and insured.[196] Courts require that contracts disclose relevant information and use clear language that the layman can understand. Courts construe coverage clauses broadly and exclusions narrowly.[197] Insurers bemoan the difficulty in drafting adequate exclusions for experimental therapy, since courts subject any restrictive attempts to careful scrutiny. Their concerns may be legitimate, but the courts still demand a fair evaluation of the usefulness of treatments and full disclosure to subscribers

---

194. Grace P. Monaco & Rebecca L. Burke, *Insurer as Gatekeeper—Part Two: Policy Obstacles in Unproven Methods Litigation*, 20 FORUM 400 (1985).

195. *See* Reilly v. Blue Cross & Blue Shield United of Wis., 846 F.2d 416 (7th Cir. 1988) (holding the coverage denial based on a treatment's success rate of less than 50% may be an unreasonable application of an experimental treatment exclusion); Dozsa v. Crum & Forster Ins. Co., 716 F. Supp. 131 (D. N.J. 1989) (stating insurer abused its discretion in evaluating a treatment with criteria used to assess whether a treatment was investigational when the contract excluded experimental treatment), *cert. denied*, 488 U.S. 856 (1988).

196. Baucci v. Blue Cross-Blue Shield of Conn., Inc., 764 F. Supp. 728 (D. Conn. 1991) (chemotherapy with autologous bone marrow transplant covered for treatment of breast cancer); Adams v. Blue Cross/Blue Shield of Md., Inc., 757 F. Supp. 661 (D. Md. 1991) (holding if treatment not experimental for other forms of cancer, it is not experimental for breast cancer); Pirozzi v. Blue Cross-Blue Shield of Va., 741 F. Supp. 586 (E.D. Va. 1990) (holding high dose chemotherapy with autologous bone marrow transplant was covered under the specific language of the policy); Fasio v. Montana Physicians' Serv., 553 P.2d 998 (Mont. 1976) (holding treatment prescribed by a licensed physician was covered notwithstanding insured's contention that services performed were "experimental" and "unacceptable medical practice"; also holding that failure to notify plaintiff's of policy change excluding certain types of treatment bars insurer from taking advantage of the exclusion).

197. McLaughlin v. Connecticut Gen. Life Ins. Co., 565 F. Supp. 434, 440 (N. D. Cal. 1983) (holding the proper interpretation of the insurance policy clauses is broad for coverage clauses and narrow for exclusion clauses).

of any exclusions. Otherwise, a duty to rescue through reimbursement will be enforced. "Say what you mean, or you pay" is the maxim of contract interpretation in the courts. Contracts, health care advertising, and a past history of insurance coverage create expectations in the public, so insurers cannot get a free ride on those expectations while avoiding responsibility when the bill comes due.[198]

The pressure from the courts, through application of rules of contract interpretation in favor of subscribers, has motivated insurers to fund definitive experiments to resolve the issues over accepted versus experimental therapies. Blue Cross and Blue Shield's support for a clinical trial of the drug HDCT-ABMT in the treatment of advanced staged breast cancer is a recent example.[199] The incentive effect of the courts' interpretive rules is evident, driving insurers toward a form of rescue of subscribers by covering experimental therapies that may prolong life, until a clinical resolution of efficacy is established. Insurers are caught in a web of equity issues and can only extricate themselves by proving that the evidence does not justify payment.

VI. PROFESSIONAL GROUPINGS AND OBLIGATIONS: MANDATING COORDINATION OF CARE

Physicians as part of a professional group may have an obligation to coordinate care in some fashion for discrete groups of patients in distress. Ethicists often articulate this as a moral obligation, which does not bind any one physician.[200] But can it be a binding legal obligation at the group level, without penalizing any one physician? Patients may be too poor to pay for care, may refuse to comply with a prescribed course of treatment, may have a contagious disease that terrifies the

---

198. *See* Kenneth S. Abraham, *Judge-Made Law and Judge-Made Insurance: Honoring the Reasonable Expectations of the Insured*, 67 VA. L. REV. 1151, 1192 (1981) (creation by insurers of a misleading impression about coverage explains use by courts of equitable principles to find for insureds).

199. Ron Winslow, *Blue Cross to Help Pay for Clinical Test on Controversial Breast Cancer Therapy*, WALL ST. J., Oct. 30, 1990, at B4, c.1.

200. "[P]rofessionals recognize a responsibility to establish equal opportunity for or equal access to their services ... This obligation belongs to professions as a whole and cannot be directly reduced to a similar obligation on the part of individual professionals." Bayles, *supra* note 32, at 27. *See also* Michael D. Bayles, *A Problem of Clean Hands: Refusal to Provide Professional Services*, 5 SOC. THEORY & PRAC. 165–81 (1979).

provider,[201] or may interfere with a provider's care of other patients. Yet they all are patients needing treatment and demanding a Good Samaritan for their rescue. Consider the problem of Brenda Payton. In *Payton v. Weaver*,[202] Brenda Payton, a black woman with end-stage renal disease, sued her physician to force him to continue treating her. She needed hemodialysis two or three times a week to stay alive. She was a poor woman living on Social Security in a housing project, addicted to heroin and barbiturates for over 15 years, overweight, with emotional, and alcohol problems. Reluctantly, Dr. Weaver finally decided to stop giving her dialysis in his outpatient clinic, since she had failed to abide by the treatment regimen and was sometimes abusive during dialysis when several patients were hooked up to the single dialysis machine. Dr. Weaver finally told Brenda that he could no longer treat her. However, he did supply her with a list of the names and telephone numbers of all dialysis providers in San Francisco and the East Bay.

The court focused on the ability of the patient to control her disruptive conduct. "Absent such control or modification her conduct was of such a nature as to justify respondent hospitals in refusing to permit her access to their facilities. Whatever collective responsibility may exist . . . it is clearly not absolute, or independent of the patients' responsibility."[203]

Physicians who refuse to treat a difficult patient can create severe financial and treatment problems for that patient. In another case, a patient, Jeanie Joshua, suffered from kidney dysfunction. She suffered further injury when a home dialysis unit malfunctioned. She then sued the physician in charge of her care, the maker of the machine, the home nurse, and others. She was forced to seek conventional dialysis. None of the kidney specialists nor six kidney centers in Santa Barbara and Ventura Counties would accept her for dialysis. She was, therefore, required to

---

201. Oscar W. Clarke & Robert B. Conley, *in The Duty to 'Attend Upon the Sick'*, 266 JAMA 2876 (1991), express concern about the willingness of doctors to care for patients with AIDS. The First Code of Ethics adopted by the AMA in 1847 defined an ethical duty to treat patients in "times of pestilence". In 1912, the AMA asserted that doctors have the freedom to choose which patients they will serve. In the 1957 Code of Ethics, the duty to treat patients described in 1847 was eliminated. *See* Walter J. Friedlander, *On the Obligation of Physicians to Treat AIDS: Is There a Historical Basis?* 12 REV. INFECTIOUS DISEASES 191 (1990). *See* WIS. STAT. ANN. § 146.024 (Supp. 1992) (prohibiting individual health care providers from refusing to treat patients because they have AIDS).
202. 182 Cal. Rptr. 225 (Cal. Ct. App. 1982).
203. *Id.* at 231.

drive three times a week to Los Angeles, a round trip of 150 miles.[204] The physicians who refused to treat her maintained simply that she was a difficult, noncompliant patient.[205]

The court in *Payton v. Weaver* noted that health care providers might have to find a way to share the responsibility for difficult patients:

> [W]hile disruptive conduct on the part of a patient may constitute good cause for an individual hospital to refuse continued treatment, since it would be unfair to impose serious inconvenience upon a hospital simply because such a patient selected it, it may be that there exists a *collective* responsibility on the part of the providers of scarce health resources in a community, *enforceable through equity* [italics added], to *share* the burden of difficult patients over time, through an appropriately devised contingency plan.[206]

This novel suggestion rests on a judicial assumption of a legal obligation for providers to treat a patient, thereby sharing the burden. The courts are capable of developing principles of group responsibility, using existing powers in equity. Where a group of providers has a special responsibility to persons with a concrete need for coordinated care, these providers should be able to be obligated to work out among themselves a method for providing that care.[207]

The government is the best coordinator of any rescue situation involving large numbers. But if the government, i.e., the legislature or the administrative agencies with authority, does not act, can a court exercising its equitable powers, so called "public action" powers, force providers collectively (if they are subject to the courts' powers jurisdictionally) to find a way to treat indigents? Why not derive individual

---

204. Ms. Joshua was quoted as saying, "The tragedy is that I am forced to make this my total preoccupation. When you are left without life support in the area where you live, it takes over your whole life. So granted I'm a big pain in the butt. What's that got to do with denying me life support?" Robert Reinhold, *When Doctors Shun Difficult Patients*, N.Y. Times, Nov. 14, 1988, at A16.

205. *Id.*

206. Payton, *supra* note 202, at 230.

207. If A's interests are vulnerable to the actions and choices of a group of individuals, either disjunctively or conjunctively, then that group has a special responsibility, to (a) organize (formally or informally) and (b) implement a scheme for coordinated action by members of the group such that A's interests will be protected as well as they can be by that group, consistently with the group's other responsibilities. Goodin, *supra* note 35, at 136. Goodin further observes that "[t]he more realistic the case, the greater the need for coordination." *Id.* at 137.

duties from collective duties imposed by the courts, legislature, ethics of professional organizations?

One collective duty that can be found in caselaw is a duty of institutions and groups within institutions to monitor the workings of the scheme to make sure that everyone who is vulnerable is protected. Such groups and their members are occasionally assigned responsibility in cases of failure to rescue. Suppose a patient is left paralyzed through some failure during surgery and no one claims to be able to reconstruct the causal factors that led to the injury. Tort doctrines such as res ipsa loquitur reconstruct negligence by dispensing with a plaintiff's need to prove fault of any one particular defendant with specificity.[208] This relaxation is based in some situations on assumptions of group responsibility.[209] The doctrine of joint and several liability then imposes the obligation to pay the injured patient upon each health care provider causally implicated in the patient's injury.[210] Hospital corporate negligence has likewise imposed a new burden on hospitals to account for the behavior of physicians and other staff who are purportedly independent contractors.[211] Hospitals have been held to a duty to supervise the medical care given to patients by staff physicians. Providers must detect physician incompetence or take steps to correct problems upon learning information raising concerns of patient risk. Hospitals must have proper procedures developed to detect impostors.[212] They should also properly restrict the

---

208. *See generally* DAN B. DOBBS, TORTS AND COMPENSATION: PERSONAL ACCOUNTABILITY AND SOCIAL RESPONSIBILITY FOR INJURY 173–74 (1985).

209. The classic case recognizing the team practice of medicine in a hospital, and the need for collective responsbility to prevent patient injury is Ybarra v. Spangard, 154 P.2d 687 (Cal. 1944) (holding all members of operating room liable for negligence during surgery); *see also* Anderson v. Somberg, 338 A.2d 1 (N.J. 1975) (holding defendant must prove lack of liability in case where foreign object left in patient's body after surgery).

210. As to joint and several liability generally, *see* W. Prosser & P. Keeton, Torts § 50 (5th ed. 1984).

211. For a good description of the justification for corporate negligence on hospitals, with a full citation of cases, see Pedroza v. Bryant, 677 P.2d 166 (Wash. 1984).

212. *See, e.g.*, Insinga v. LaBella, 543 So. 2d 209 (Fla. 1989) (holding non-physician fraudulently obtained an appointment to the medical staff, after having assumed the name of a deceased Italian physician; the court applied corporate negligence, noting that at least seventeen jurisdictions had adopted the doctrine.); Hendrickson v. Hodkin, 11 N.E.2d 899 (N.Y. 1937) (hospital held liable for allowing a quack to treat a patient on its premises).

clinical privileges of staff physicians who are incompetent to handle certain procedures; they also need methods to divine a staff doctor's concealment of medical errors.[213] A failure to implement proper procedures to detect physician problems leads to direct liability for patient injury.

The obligation of a health care institution to protect patients has been considerably expanded by both courts and legislatures. The next step should be to impose upon professional groups a duty to rescue individuals in desperate situations. The AIDS epidemic is one recent example of a crisis that has left many patients without access to health care, as dentists and physicians in some communities have refused patients, or have set up waiting lists to indirectly avoid treating such patients.[214] Dental and medical associations in such situations have sometimes been slow to react to patient need, in spite of their self-proclaimed ethical obligations. Should not a legal duty be imposed at the professional group level, to find professionals to provide care? Such a duty could be tort- or fiduciary-based, derived from standards set forth in the ethical rules of that association. Ideally, injunctive relief beyond damages would be desirable to motivate proper rescue in such distress circumstances. Or it could be made a condition of licensure, with a system set up that would allow buying out of such service in special cases, so long as coverage was available.

---

213. *See* Cronic v. Doud, 523 N.E.2d 176 (Ill. App. Ct. 1988) (holding hospital can be liable for breaching duty to know qualifications and standard of performance of the physicians who practice on its premises); Corleto v. Shore Memorial Hospital, 350 A.2d 535 (N.J. Super. Ct. Law Div. 1975) (holding hospital could be held liable to patient for permitting known incompetent physician to perform abdominal surgery and in allowing him to remain on the case when the situation was obviously beyond his control).

Under the Health Care Quality Improvement Act of 1986 (HCQIA), hospitals must check a central registry, a national database maintained by the Unisys Corporation under contract with the Department of Health and Human Services, before a new staff appointment is made. This database contains information on individual physicians who have been disciplined, had malpractice claims filed against them, or had privileges revoked or limited. If the hospital fails to check the registry, it is held constructively to have knowledge of any information it might have gotten from the inquiry.

214. In Wilmington, Delaware, in 1986 and 1987, for example, persons with AIDS (PWAs) were unable to get dental care. Local dentists were unwilling to treat such patients, in spite of the rhetoric of professional dental ethics. Moralsuasion was at first unsuccessful, and a legally enforceable duty upon the professional group, to come up with an access solution, would have been extremely valuable.

VII. REDRAWING THE MAP

[I]deals of private charity and voluntarism...act as the opiate of the American public, deluding a basically decent people into believing that . . . deeply troubling social problems requiring whole dollars for their solution [can] be adequately addressed with just two bits' worth of trickle-down generosity...."[215]

A. The ideal: redistribution in the liberal state

State and federal governments provide direct subsidies through Medicaid, as do some counties and municipalities, for indigent health care. In all but three states, state or local governments are obligated by statute or constitution to provide some medically indigent health care.[216] The cost totaled 3.9 billion dollars in 1982. Rate regulation at the state level also allows for subsidies for the provision of indigent care. State or county hospitals provided 11.6 billion dollars worth of indigent care in 1988. In other states, general assistance or general relief covers some care, as do Aid to Medically Indigent programs.[217] Some states have adopted catastrophic illness programs, or risk-sharing pools. For example, Hawaii has required employers to provide employees with insurance. Other states have focused on helping institutions that provide uncompensated care. States with all-payer rate setting systems have managed to permit charge-shifting, or setting up special pools of uncompensated care funds. Other states have tried revenue pools. These efforts are not enough—they are scattered, uncoordinated, unrelated to the distribution of the worst cases, and grossly inefficient.[218]

Mandated care of the indigent has been criticized as inefficient and inequitable. Critics note that choice and access depend upon proximity

215. Uwe E. Reinhardt, *Charity at a Price*, N.Y. TIMES BOOK REV., Aug 20, 1989, at 14.

216. *See* Blendon, *supra* note 12, at 1160. For an example of how such a statute functions, see Sioux Valley Hosp. Ass'n v. Yankton County, 424 N.W.2d 379 (S.D. 1988) (county pays for emergency hospitalization of indigent).

217. State and county hospitals contributed up to $11.6 billion in 1988. In other states, state general assistance or general relief covers some care, as do Aid to Medically Indigent programs. Michael Dowell, *State and Local Government Legal Responsibilities to Provide Medical Care for the Poor*, 3 J.L. & HEALTH 1 (1988–89). *See also* Hall & Colombo, *supra* note 18, at 307; Blendon, *supra* note 12.

218. Peter H. Schuck, *Designing Hospital Care Subsidies for the Poor*, *in* UNCOMPENSATED HOSPITAL CARE: RIGHTS AND RESPONSIBILITIES 69 (Frank A. Sloan et al. eds., 1986).

to providers that offer such care and upon accessing it before the provider has offered all it is required to for that year. If emergency room care is the only way to gain access, patients will use it although ambulatory care would be far more efficient and cost-effective. Mandated care may also impose perverse incentives on providers to simply meet a quota of care, regardless of which patients are in fact the neediest.[219] Such forced rescue may be attractive to government, allowing it to dodge responsibility, since its cost does not appear as a line item in the budget, and leaves both the revenue side and the expenditure side unaffected.[220] Population mobility and competition between states for low tax rates to attract businesses may also have perverse effects upon state level efforts to subsidize the poor.

A national solution to the problem of forced rescue is undoubtedly the best approach, particularly to subsidizing hospital care. Government is a superior mechanism to private charity for collecting and redistributing income to the poor, achieving economies of scale, and lowering overhead.[221] Several social programs—Medicare, even Medicaid with its minimum coverage requirements—demonstrate some evidence of a political desire to provide a uniform minimum with respect to health care for the poor.[222] But that desire does not translate into adequate access for many citizens.

B. The hybrid ideal: government plus collective responsibility

A national solution to problems of indigent care in cases of emergency or traumatic injury, while ideal, may come only in a piecemeal fashion. The law should continue to articulate and expand affirmative obliga-

---

219. *Id.* at 77–78.

220. *Id.* at 78. "Especially in times of budgetary stringency, the temptation to achieve important social objectives such as subsidization of hospital care for the poor through mandated private expenditures rather than by raising taxes may prove nearly irresistible." *Id.*

221. It's a fine thing that our elected leaders have decided to use the bully pulpit to encourage private charity. As a taxpayer, I don't even mind seeing a few of my dollars going to pay for the propaganda. The trouble is that these same elected leaders have used the same bully pulpit to poison the minds of citizens against the mechanism of selflessness and social generosity that is at these leaders' actual disposal: the government. A free society deciding to tax itself to make itself a better society—that's the real united way.

Michael Kinsley, *Charity Begins With Government*, TIME, Apr. 6, 1992, at 74.

222. *Id.* at 80.

tions on health care professionals and their institutions. These role or collective obligations flow from the special power and expertise of health care professionals. Such duties plug the holes in the social net left by deficient social programs and a lack of national or state political will.

Principled justifications for imposing affirmative duties to treat can be derived from many sources. Health care institutions receive large sums of federal money for treating Medicare and Medicaid patients. These sums are conditioned on compliance with a variety of federal obligations. Private parties such as employers, insurers, and other providers also impose contractual demands through their reimbursement agreements.[223] History plays a part, since hospitals have taken on burdens of care that now can be dropped only with the greatest effort. This is so because of public expectations, created in part by institutions and used by them to their advantage. A concept of stabilized expectations is at the heart of many such affirmative duties. Such expectations as to the availability of rescue allow individuals to exist on a day-to-day basis free of the overriding anxiety that if they are hit by a car, or struck by a catastrophic illness, they are doomed by lack of access to health care. For the poor, a lack of access to health care can reduce life to a desperate Hobbesian terror that the liberal state promised to banish from our conception of a moral Republic.

Expectations evolve as the capabilities of the health care system evolve, so that what was unrealistic, or simply not even contemplated in 1950, is now within the range of the possible. The power of technology can mandate efficient rescue. Given the high costs of accidents, a general legal duty to rescue would save lives and reduce the cost of rescue operations.[224] Relationships also create duties, both through explicit contract terms and implied obligations.[225]

Finally, the fundamental nature of powerful institutions with unique access to technologies, personnel, and information creates obligations to treat all patients consistently.[226] In cases involving hospitals the language of the courts is full of the language of power and responsibility,

---

223. It is well accepted that the government may condition the receipt of federal moneys upon reasonable conditions, so long as such conditions are clearly expressed. *See* Pennhurst State Sch. & Hosp. v. Halderman, 451 U.S. 1, 17 (1981) ("...if Congress intends to impose a condition on the grant of federal moneys, it must do so unambiguously.")

224. *See* generally Lipkin, *supra* note 55.

225. *See* Shapo, *supra* note 93, at pt. I and pt. II.

226. *Id.*

showing a judicial recognition of the resources now commanded by modern health care institutions.[227]

The affirmative obligations that this article has either discovered in the legal landscape or argued as desirable can be summed up in four propositions:

1. *Nexus demands rescue.* Individual providers face strong claims by patients for care under difficult, quasi- or actual emergency circumstances. When a provider says, "Why me? Why should I be forced to help?", we respond, "You are here and therefore in a position to help this victim. Is there a stronger claim upon you now?"[228] Has the role of physician created a covenant with expectations legitimately felt by the public at large? Is there a nexus between provider and patient created by the facts of the specific situation?

2. *Institutions owe rescue.* Institutional providers are visible emblems of rescue in trauma crises, not easily disengaged once a life in peril presents. As nonprofits are forced into competition to survive with for-profits, outpatient clinics, and franchised operations, they have in many cases narrowed or dropped their traditional offerings of service, while expanding into money-making ventures. The demands of taxing authorities, the mandates of COBRA, and the duties of the common law are useful counterpressures to competitive pressures on hospitals to cut back on indigent care. At the institutional level, the pressures of competition are likely to limit indigent care unless countervailing pressures are created. Institutions are constructs, and the state, through its agents the courts and the legislatures, may reconstitute these constructs in more productive ways.

3. *Coordination of rescue should be fostered.* Collegial and professional groupings have a duty to share and distribute burdens where people are in need of rescue. The covenant binds the group as well as the physician to figure out ways to provide care for those in distress, those who are unpleasant or contagious, those too poor to gain easy access. Hospital collaboration can sometimes be found in sharing emergency cases and providing backups when centers are overloaded. Other institutions have set up primary care clinics to provide alternative

---

227. *See* Pedroza v. Bryant, 677 P. 2d 166, 169 (Wash. 1984) (adopting the doctrine of hospital corporate negligence justified by hospitals superior position to control physicians and public's perception of hospital as a "multifaceted health care facility responsible for the quality of medical care and treatment rendered").

228. Goodin, *supra* note 35, at 126, asks this question.

services and systems of care,[229] or screening and treatment programs for the homeless.[230] Local professional groups have struggled to find "volunteers" to deal with risky patients. Cooperative efforts occur, but all too rarely. The development of affirmative obligations is a worthwhile project for courts or legislatures, to extract from the professional group a level of rescue that their ethical codes promise but often fail to deliver.

4. *The liberal state owes the vulnerable access to necessary care.* The rights and privileges of citizenship support a strong argument that government should protect the vulnerable by setting a threshold point of deserved care and funding it fairly.[231] Regional planning or state resource reallocation, such as the Oregon Medicaid experiment, might distribute certain health care more fairly;[232] access to emergency care, to prenatal and obstetric care, in situations where emergencies can be real and life-threatening, should be assured.[233] The liberal state has an obligation at a minimum to protect vulnerable citizens from medical emergencies.[234] Rights-based

---

229. *Id.*

230. Frank Cerne, *California hospital hits the road to care for the homeless*, AHA *News*, May 4, 1992, at 5.

231. I leave for another discussion the problem of defined "deserved care" and the arguments for and against treating health care as a "right". However, at the level of emergency care, for vulnerable and distressed individuals, a rights-based analysis is easily justifiable.

232. The attempts by the states to better allocate their scarce health resources is chronicled in John J. Kitzhaber & Mark M. Gibson, *The Crisis in Health Care—The Oregon Health Plan as a Strategy for Change*, 3 STAN. L. & POL'Y REV. 64 (1991).

233. For a discussion of the role of the non-poor in welfare and redistribution, with benefits also usually accruing to them, *see* ROBERT E. GOODIN ET AL., NOT ONLY THE POOR: THE MIDDLE CLASSES AND THE WELFARE STATE (1987); ROBERT HAVEMAN, STARTING EVEN: AN EQUAL OPPORTUNITY PROGRAM TO COMBAT THE NATION'S NEW POVERTY (1988).

234. *See generally* ROBERT E. GOODIN, REASONS FOR WELFARE: THE POLITICAL THEORY OF THE WELFARE STATE, (1988). Goodin makes a powerful argument for the welfare state.

We individually and collectively have a strong moral responsibility to protect those whose interests are especially vulnerable to our actions and choices. [It is an adjunct to a market economy.] Both the market and the welfare state aim at essentially the same end, after all. Both are basically mechanisms for promoting public welfare.

Id. at 153–54. He rejects the position that the function of the welfare state is to coordinate people's charitable impulses, that it is primarily "a means of eliminating those individual acts of charity which are designed to mitigate poverty, by centralizing them in the hands of the state." *Id.* at 155, *quoting* ANDREW SHONFIELD, MODERN CAPITALISM 93 (1965). He notes that charity

(cont.)

obligations to rescue vulnerable patients in need of care will always be needed in a world of scarce resources. In fairness we can demand that our health care providers fill in the gaps in the reimbursement net where a person will suffer serious harm without rescue.

(234, *cont.*) is not generally susceptible to problems of free-riding, nor does it require public intervention. *Id.* at 157.

The problem that the welfare state is designed to answer, according to Goodin, is the problem of dependency.

The Americans with Disabilities Act and the corpus of anti-discrimination law: a force for change in the future of public health regulation*

Lawrence O. Gostin

Legal controls over the unfettered exercise of public health powers have long been regarded as ineffective and idiosyncratic.[1] Public health statutes (many written before the sciences of virology, bacteriology and

---

*This work is an expansion of ideas previously explored in Lawrence O. Gostin, *The Americans with Disabilities Act and the U.S. Health Care System*, 11 HEALTH AFF. 248 (1992) and Lawrence O. Gostin, *Public Health Powers: the Imminence of Radical Change*, 69 MILBANK Q. 268 (1991).

1. *See* Scott Burris, *Rationality Review and the Politics of Public Health*, 34 VILL. L. REV. 933, 933–82 (1989). Scott Burris, *Fear Itself: AIDS, Herpes, and Public Health Decisions*, 3 YALE L. & POL'Y REV. 479 (1985); Deborah Jones Merritt, *Communicable Disease and Constitutional Law: Controlling AIDS*, 61 N.Y.U. L. REV. 739 (1986); Wendy Parmet, *AIDS and Quarantine: The Revival of an Archaic Doctrine*, 14 HOFSTRA L. REV. 53 (1985); Wendy Parmet, *Health Care and the Constitution: Public Health and the Role of the State in the Framing Era*, 20 HASTINGS CONST. L. Q. 267 (1993).

Justice and Health Care: Comparative Perspectives. Edited by A. Grubb and M.J. Mehlman. © 1995 John Wiley & Sons Ltd.

epidemiology had fully come of age) delegate wide ranging powers to officials.[2] The major check on the exercise of these powers has been constitutional review by the judiciary. The courts, however, are reluctant to interfere in public health decision making, and have not yet developed a cogent set of criteria for establishing effective boundaries around the proper exercise of public health authority.

This paper argues that constitutional review—long the standard bearer for judicial activity in the public health realm—is quietly, but effectively, being replaced with a more cogent statutory review. That review is provided by disability law. The advent of disability law is remarkably recent. The first comprehensive federal disability statute was not enacted until the Rehabilitation Act of 1973. The Rehabilitation Act was followed by perfecting amendments (e.g., the Civil Rights Restoration Act of 1988) and new statutes (e.g., the Fair Housing Amendments of 1988), culminating in the landmark Americans with Disabilities Act of 1990 (ADA).

The ADA and the corpus of disability law are regarded as highly effective mechanisms to redress discrimination and remove physical barriers for people with disabilities. Remarkably, the legislative history of the Rehabilitation Act shows that Congress gave only the scantiest attention to the possibility that the law might apply to communicable disease. Indeed, the definitive affirmation of the role of disability law to protect persons with infectious conditions did not occur until the Supreme Court's *Arline* decision in 1987.[3]

Even in the Congressional deliberations on the ADA, confusion reigned as to whether and how the ADA might control the exercise of public health powers, and whether the ADA should prempt state communicable disease laws. The Congress viewed this question in a most narrow and uninstructive way during the debates on the distracting question of food handlers.

The judicial and congressional inattention to the broader public health impact of the ADA is ill-conceived. I will argue that this landmark legislation will unleash a powerful review mechanism that will set effective boundaries on the historic exercise of public health powers. This statutory review will, moreover, gradually supplant much, but not all, of the constitutional analyses in the public health sphere. Ultimately, the ADA will provide a much needed impetus for states to

---

2. Lawrence Gostin, *The Future of Public Health Law*, 12 AM. J.L. & MED. 461 (1986).

3. School Bd. of Nassaw County, Fla. v. Arline, 480 U.S. 273 (1987) (Rehnquist, J., dissenting).

reform fundamentally outdated statutes relevant to communicable and sexually transmitted disease. This reformation will bring state statutes into conformity with the letter and spirit of the ADA.[4]

First, this paper will review the constitutional history of the courts' attempts to check the powers of the public health department. Such a review will demonstrate how ineffective and inconsistent constitutional review has been, and suggest that adequate review criteria have not emerged. This section will show that, whether the courts are applying First, Fourth, or Fourteenth Amendment standards, ultimately they are highly deferential to public health officials. Second, this paper will carefully examine the key concepts in the ADA as they apply to communicable disease. This section will reveal Congress's clear intention to include communicable disease, even asymptomatic infection, as a disability. It will also define and analyze the new "direct threat" standard in the ADA, particularly its application to exercise of public health powers under Title II (public services) of the Act. Finally, the paper will propose a standard of review under the ADA for the future regulation of public health powers.

I. CONSTITUTIONAL PARAMETERS OF PUBLIC HEALTH POWERS: A DECIDEDLY DEFERENTIAL APPROACH

Constitutional review of the exercise of public health powers is plagued by a continuing sense of doctrinal uncertainty. The early courts were highly deferential to state public health regulation under the police powers. To some courts, the Constitution had "no application to this class of case."[5] "Where the police power is set in motion in its proper sphere, the courts have no jurisdiction to stay the arm of the legislative branch."[6] One court went so far as to declare the universality of the judicial rule that "constitutional guaranties must yield ... to promote the public health."[7] Even as late as 1966, a court held that "drastic

---

4. The Milbank Memorial Fund and the US Centers for Disease Control have sponsored a project on the future of communicable disease law chaired by the author.

5. *In re* Caselli, 204 P. 364, 364 (1922).

6. Arizona *ex rel.* Conway v. Southern Pacific Co., 145 P.2d 530, 532 (1943) (quoting State *ex rel.* McBride v. Superior Court, 174 P. 973, 976 (1918)).

7. People *ex rel.* Baker v. Strauz, 54 N.E.2d 441, 444 (Ill. 1944).

measures for the elimination of disease are not affected by constitutional provisions, either of the state or national government."[8]

Most courts have not totally abdicated their responsibility to set limits on the authority of public health departments. Certainly a set of minimalist principles can be ascertained. In the seminal case of *Jacobson v. Massachusetts*, the Supreme Court held that a vaccination requirement must have a "real or substantial relation" to public health objectives and could not be a "plain, palpable invasion of rights." The state "must refrain from acting in an arbitrary, unreasonable manner," or "going so far beyond what [is] reasonably required for the safety of the public."[9]

The "arbitrary, oppressive and unreasonable" standard is highly deferential. States need only show a good faith intention to promote the public health, as well as some medical evidence that the restriction of individual rights may be beneficial to the health of the community. Since *Jacobson*, no uniform and coherent set of criteria have emerged from the courts in reviewing public health powers.[10]

We like to believe that modern constitutional doctrine goes much further in setting rational boundaries around the exercise of public health powers. However, modern constitutional review is remarkably similar in approach to *Jacobson*. Although courts have occasionally engaged in more focused scrutiny, modern constitutional law in the public health sphere is drawn to be highly mechanistic. It places overly burdensome restrictions on some public health measures while placing virtually no restriction on others. It is difficult to predict the outcome of cases and so provides little guidance to legislators and public health officials. The courts have failed to establish clear criteria on the critical

---

8. *In re* Halko, 246 Cal. App. 2d 553, 566, 54 Cal. Rptr. 661, 663 (1966) *citing* Larsen v. Board of Supervisors, 214 N.W. 682, 684 (Iowa 1927), *in* Deborah June Merritt, *Communicable Disease and Constitutional Law: Controlling AIDS*, 61 N.Y.U. L. REV. 739 (1986).

9. Jacobson v. Massachusetts, 197 U.S. 11, 28–31 (1905).

10. At various times, however, courts have required three conditions for upholding public health regulation. *See* City of Cleburne, Tex. v. Cleburne Living Ctr., Inc., 473 U.S. 432 (1985) (requiring the true purpose of the power must be for the preservation of health and not some ulterior motive); *In re* Martin, 83 Cal. App. 2d 164, 188 P. 2d 287, 291 (1948) (requiring that the subject of compulsory power actually be infectious before the control measure could be imposed); *ex parte* Shepard, 51 Cal. App. 49, 195 P. 1077 (1921) (requiring more than mere suspicion before invoking health regulation). *See also* Jew Ho v. Williamson, 103 F. 10, 22 (C.C.N.D. Cal. 1900) (great discretion is given to a state to decide which measures are necessary to protect the public health but the measure in itself should not pose a health risk to the subject).

balance between restrictions on individual rights, level of risk to the public, and efficacy of the control measure. Courts have based their review of public health powers on either the Fourteenth Amendment, the Fourth Amendment, or the First Amendment, but a deferential balancing test, reminiscent of *Jacobson*, is evident irrespective of the constitutional vehicle.

A. Substantive due process and equal protection under the Fourteenth Amendment

Constitutional theorists point to a highly mechanistic two-tiered[11] approach to judicial decision making which emerged during the last several decades.[12] The lowest level of scrutiny (the "rational basis" test) validates state conduct which does not impinge upon a fundamental right or "suspect" class so long as it is reasonably related to a valid government purpose.[13] Since public health represents a highly beneficial purpose, courts afford the state "maximum deference"[14] under this standard of review. Courts often uphold the public health decisions of the state without a careful examination of benefits and risks in contexts ranging from classifying and reporting infectious disease,[15] to the control of sexually transmitted and needle-borne infections in bathhouses,[16] theaters,[17] bookstores,[18] and prisons.[19] In all of these cases the

---

11. A third tier, intermediate scrutiny, most often applied in instances of gender discrimination, is inapplicable in this analysis. *See* Craig v. Boren, 429 U.S. 190 (1976).

12. LAWRENCE TRIBE, AMERICAN CONSTITUTIONAL LAW, § 16 (2d. ed. 1988).

13. *See, e.g.*, Kardmas v. Dickinson Public Schools, 108 S.Ct. 2481, 2489–90 (1988).

14. James A. Kushnar, *Substantive Equal Protection: The Rehnquist Court and the Fourth Tier of Judicial Review*, 53 MO. L. REV. 423, 449–50 (1988).

15. *See* New York State Society of Surgeons v. Axelrod, 157 A.D.2d 54 (N.Y. App. Div. 1990) (holding that nothing positive would be gained by designation of HIV infection as a communicable or sexually transmissible disease).

16. City of N.Y. v. New St. Mark's Baths, 130 Misc. 2d 911 (N.Y. Sup. 1986), *aff'd*, 122 A.D. 2d 747 (1986); People v. 3Mc S, AIDS LIT. RPTR., Sept. 9, 1988; Los Angeles v. Benson, AIDS LIT. RPTR., May 13, 1988.

17. *Public Health: Theatre Closure*, AIDS LIT. RPTR., Oct. 28, 1988, at 1640.

18. *E.g.*, Movie & Video World, Inc. v. Board. of Comm'rs of Palm Beach, 723 F. Supp. 695 (S.D. Fla. 1989).

19. *E.g.*, Muhammad v. Carlson, 845 F. 2d 175 (8th Cir. 1988), *cert. denied*, Muhammad v. Quinlan, 489 U.S. 1068 (1989); *see also* Doe v. Coughlin, 518 N.E. 2d 536, 523 N.Y.S.2d 782 (1987), *cert. denied*, 488 U.S. 879 (1988).

courts readily yield to the discretion of state officials. Issues critical to public health analysis barely surface under the lowest level of judicial review: whether the action is overly burdensome of individual rights, whether it comports with the clear weight of scientific opinion, and whether there are less restrictive ways of accomplishing the public health objective.

The highest level of judicial scrutiny occurs when states impinge on "fundamental" rights such as travel,[20] marriage,[21] and certain privacy interests associated with reproduction.[22] Strict scrutiny is also triggered if the state burdens certain "suspect" classes such as race[23] or national alienage.[24] Such measures must be narrowly tailored to serve a compelling objective, and must be the least restrictive alternative for achieving that objective.[25]

These two traditional tiers of constitutional review are outcome determinative. Once the standard of review is decided upon, it is highly predictive of the decision of the court. Thus, public health measures which burden personal freedom (e.g., isolation or quarantine), marriage (e.g., a ban on marriage of persons with sexually transmitted infections), or define a class based upon race (e.g., strict limitations on sickle cell disease) theoretically ought to be subject to intensive review.[26] The public health justification would have to overwhelm the human rights concerns. If, however, the public health measure did not directly

---

20. Shapiro v. Thompson, 394 U.S. 618, 629–31 (1969).

21. Loving v. Virginia, 388 U.S. 1, 12 (1966); Zablocki v. Redhail, 434 U.S. 374, 383–84 (1978).

22. See Griswold v. Connecticut, 381 U.S. 479, 485–86 (1965).

23. See, e.g., Regents of the University of California v. Bakke, 438 U.S. 265 (1978).

24. See, e.g., Graham v. Richardson, 403 U.S. 365 (1971).

25. E.g., Kramer v. Union Free School District, 395 U.S. 621, 627 (1969); Cf., Addington v. Texas, 441 U.S. 418, 427 (1979) (state must justify confinement by proof more substantial than a mere preponderance of the evidence).

26. As late as the 1960s, however, courts were treating public health decisions offering liberty as if they did not require serious scrutiny at all. See In re Halko, 246 Cal. App. 2d 553, 54 Cal. Rptr. 661 (2d Dist. 1966) (upholding isolation of persons with pulmonary tuberculosis without any inquiry as to whether it was essential to the public health; only question asked by the court was whether the health officer had probable cause to believe the person had an infectious disease). "The Legislature is vested with broad discretion in determining what are contagious and infectious diseases and in adopting means for preventing the spread thereof." 246 Cal. App. 2d at 557; See also Moore v. Armstrong, 149 So. 2d 36 (S.Ct. Fla. 1963) (upholding detention of person in a tuberculosis hospital).

burden these almost arbitrary touchstones of constitutional juris-prudence, they might receive a perfunctory examination, where the courts almost obsequiously yield to public health judgments. In either case, there is little room for clear and cogent review criteria which carefully measure risk, efficacy, alternatives, and human rights burdens.

While the Supreme Court is slowly moving from this rigid tiered approach to constitutional review, the Court's new decision making process is still largely uninstructive and unpredictable. The *Cleburne*[27] doctrine, often referred to as a third tier of constitutional review, does not take the inquiry much further than the post-*Jacobson* "true purpose" test.[28] The *Cleburne* court invalidated a zoning ordinance excluding group homes for mentally handicapped people. The Court did not raise its standard of review, but nevertheless searched into the record to conclude that no rational basis existed to warrant a legislative finding that mentally handicapped people posed a threat. What the legislature may not do is base its decision on "vague, undifferentiated fears" or "irrational prejudice."[29]

Recently, the Court has refrained from finding new "fundamental" rights, particularly in medically related fields. Rather, courts have referred to a series of "liberty interests" to refuse psychotropic medication,[30] avoid admission to mental hospitals,[31] or to withdraw life sustaining treatment.[32] The right to be left alone by public health officials or doctors, is, however, only one interest to be balanced against a series of competing state interests. Notably, in each of these cases, the state interests prevailed over the liberty interest of the individual. In essence, the Court's notion of a "liberty interest" is so weak that it begins to resemble a rational basis test—the medical activity is upheld so long as the state can point to some legitimate justification. The Court certainly has not yet enunciated how collective and personal interests will be balanced or reconciled in particular cases.

27. City of Cleburne, Tex. v. Cleburne Living Center, Inc., 473 U.S. 432 (1985).

28. *See* Loving v. Virginia, 388 U.S. 1,12 (1966); Zablocki v. Redhail, 434 U.S. 374, 383–84 (1978).

29. City of Cleburne, 473 U.S. at 449,450. *See also* Brennan v. Stewart, 834 F.2d 1248, 1258 (5th Cir. 1988) (decisions based on physical and mental disabilities should be reviewed "somewhat closer than usual").

30. Washington v. Harper, 494 U.S. 210, 221 (1990).

31. Parham v. J.R., 442 U.S. 584 (1979).

32. Cruzan v. Director, Missouri Dept. of Health, 497 U.S. 261 (1990).

B. Search and seizure: blood and urine tests, screening, and the Fourth Amendment

The Fourth Amendment's prohibition on unreasonable searches and seizures has long been construed to apply to blood and urine tests. Under the Warren Court's *Schmerber* doctrine, probable cause, or at least individual suspicion, must exist before testing without consent: "warrants are ordinarily required for searches of dwellings and absent an emergency, no less could be required where intrusions into the human body are concerned."[33] The courts recognize that "the integrity of an individual's person is a cherished value ... which is protected from unreasonable searches and seizures."[34]

The *Schmerber* doctrine ought not to be susceptible to the same vacuous balancing test that occurs under the Fourteenth Amendment, but that is exactly where it is leading.

The Supreme Court assigns a privacy value to be free from forced medical testing. But it balances that privacy value against the intrusiveness of the bodily search and the public interest it is designed to effectuate. The Court has recognized state interests such as "national security"[35] and "public safety"[36] in drug testing without any careful examination of whether testing will achieve the stated objective.

The Court is quietly abandoning each of the key principles of the *Schmerber* doctrine including the requirement of a warrant, individualized suspicion or probable cause, and a clear nexus to achievable public health goals. For example, courts have used the "special needs" doctrine to justify nonconsensual testing of sexual offenders conducted without the procedural safeguards of a warrant or individualized suspicion.[37] Courts have also declared that the judiciary may use equitable authority to compel testing in the absence of statutory

---

33. Schmerber v. California, 384 U.S. 757, 770 (1966).

34. People v. Bracamonte, 540 P.2d 624, 632 (S.Ct. Cal. 1975) *quoting* Schmerber v. California, 384 U.S. 757, 772 (1966).

35. National Treasury Employees Union v. Von Raab, 489 U.S. 656, 674 (1989).

36. Skinner v. Railway Labor Executives' Ass'n, 489 U.S. 602, 615 (1989) ("permissibility of a particular practice is judged by balancing its intrusion on the individual's Fourth Amendment interests against its promotion of legitimate governmental interests").

37. In the Matter of Juveniles A, B, C, D, and E, 847 P.2d 455 (Wash. 1993) (holding that a statute requiring mandatory HIV testing of convicted sex offenders applied to juveniles under the "special needs" doctrine where the

authority.[38] The result of this disintegration of the *Schmerber* doctrine is a pure balancing test where little guidance is provided on which interests weigh more heavily, and where public health discretion is generally upheld.

Courts have been highly deferential in reviewing federal and state screening programs. Federal courts have upheld HIV screening in the Departments of State[39] and Defense,[40] and cases are pending challenging screening of Job Corps applicants[41] as well as immigrants and temporary visitors to the United States.[42] Since HIV is not transmitted casually, and there is little risk of transmission by any known modality in these settings, it is difficult to conceive how large-scale indiscriminate screening achieves rigorous public health objectives.[43]

In *Leckelt*[44] the court rejected a Fourth Amendment claim by a nurse who was required to be tested for HIV against his will. The hospital argued that the test was necessary to protect the health of patients, even though there was not a single case of health care professional-to-patient transmission of HIV at the time.[45] Kevin Leckelt's medical

---

state's interest in testing high risk groups and protecting society from the spread of HIV outweighed the privacy interests of the offenders, the statute was narrowly-tailored to the purpose, and the testing was not conducted for law enforcement purposes).

38. Syring v. Tucker, 498 N.W.2d 370 (Wis. 1993) (holding that the circuit court, despite the absence of statutory authority, had authority in equity to compel HIV testing of a woman who bit a social worker).

39. Local 1812, Am. Fed'n of Gov't Employees v. U.S. Dept. of State, 662 F. Supp. 50 (D.D.C. 1987).

40. Batten v. Lehman, U.S.D.C. Cal., No. 85–4108, Jan. 18, 1986.

41. Dorsey v. U.S. Dept. of Labor, U.S.D.C. No. 88–1898.

42. *See* Larry Gostin et al., *Screening Immigrants and International Travelers for the Human Immunodeficiency Virus*, 322 NEW ENG. J. MED. 1743, 1743–46 (1990). With regard to recent HIV testing of Haitian immigrants seeking refuge in the United States, the United States District Court found that subjecting HIV positive detainees to a second screening, conducted without an attorney present, violated the Refuge Act and the Due Process rights of the detainees. Haitian Centers Council, Inc. v. Sale, 823 F.Supp. 1028 (E.D.N.Y. 1993).

43. Gostin, *supra* note 42, at 1743–46; *see also* Larry Gostin et al., *The Case Against Compulsory Casefinding in Controlling AIDS: Testing, Screening, and Reporting*, 12 AM. J.L. & MED. 7, 19–20 (1986).

44. Leckelt v. Board of Comm'rs of Hosp. Dist. No. 1, 909 F.2d 820, 832–33 (5th Cir. 1990).

45. There is one instance of believed transmission of HIV infection from a health care professional to patients, that of the dentist, Dr. David Acer, in Florida. Dr. Acer may have transmitted the virus to as many as five patients,

(*cont.*)

condition (infection with the hepatitis B virus), apparent homosexuality, and long-term relationship with a partner with AIDS meant that the hospital had individualized suspicion. The court, without any fiiding that Leckelt posed a significant risk to patients or staff, upheld the testing because of the generalized need to protect the health of employees and prevent the spread of infectious disease.

Curiously, another federal Court of Appeals found that indiscriminate HIV screening of all hospital staff violated the Fourth Amendment because the "risk was low, approaching zero."[46] Certainly, these cases can be distinguished because one involved individualized suspicion and the other a broader screening program. Still, the public health justifications were similar, and no data could be offered showing even an elevated risk to patients.

C. Freedoms of expression and Religion: does the First Amendment effectively impede public health officials in the exercise of their authority?

At the heart of the conflict between public health and individual rights is the claim by citizens that they possess fundamental freedoms which public health officials cannot diminish. Many public health cases have been adjudicated under the First Amendment because the subjects of regulation claim that it interferes with their freedom of expression, association, or religion. Two paradigmatic cases emerge: first, the right

---

(45, *cont.*) including Kimberly Bergalis, who later testified before Congress regarding health care professional-to-patient transmission. The Centers for Disease Control has promulgated guidelines to prevent this type of transmission, calling for the use of universal precautions in the care of all patients, especially in procedures involving blood and other bodily fluids such as semen, vaginal secretions and amniotic fluid. Some specifications of universal precautions include (1) use of barrier protection such as gloves and goggles, (2) immediate washing of hands after performing procedures, (3) careful use of sharp instruments to prevent injury, and (4) prohibition of health care professionals with exudative lesions or weeping dermatitis from direct patient care. Centers for Disease Control, *Update: Universal Precautions for Prevention of Transmission of the Human Immunodeficiency Virus, Hepatitis B Virus and Other Bloodborn Pathogens in Health-Care Settings*, 37 MORBIDITY & MORTALITY WEEKLY REP. 277 (1988); *see also* Larry Gostin, *Hospitals, Health Care Professionals, and AIDS: The "Right to Know" the Health Status of Professionals and Patients*, 48 MD. L. REV. 12, 24 (1989).

46. Glover v. Eastern Neb. Community Office of Retardation, 867 F.2d 461, 463 (8th Cir. 1989), *cert. denied*, 493 U.S. 932 (1989).

of persons to refuse compulsory vaccination[47] or treatment[48] because it is contrary to their religious beliefs[49] and, second, the rights of persons to frequent bathhouses, video stores, theaters, and other public places in the exercise of their freedoms of expression and association. Despite the absolutist language of the First Amendment (Congress shall pass "no law" abridging these freedoms), the courts have resorted to a familiar balancing test where state interests are afforded great weight and deference.

1. Compulsory vaccination cases

A great majority of states have enacted compulsory or local option vaccination statutes. These statutes were the subject of frequent constitutional attack and were almost universally upheld.[50] While freedom of religion was not a central concern in all cases,[51] many courts upheld compulsory vaccination in the face of First Amendment

---

47. *See, e.g.,* Brown v. Stone, 378 So. 2d 218 (Miss. 1979) (holding that interests of school children prevail over parents' religious beliefs) *cert. denied,* 449 U.S. 887 (1980).

48. State *ex rel.* Holcomb v. Armstrong, 239 P.2d 545 (Wash. 1952) (upholding chest x-ray requirement as condition for university registration against religious challenge).

49. Maricopa County Health Dept. v. Hammon, 750 P.2d 1364 (Ariz. Ct. App. 1987) (holding that policy of the state is "to balance the individuals' rights to education against the state's need to protect against the spread of infectious and contagious disease).

50. Itz v. Penick, 493 S.W.2d 506 (Tex. 1973) (holding that except in certain religious and medical exemptions, mandatory immunization before admission into school does not interfere with parents' rights, equal protection, due process, delegation of power, or access to education). *But see* Davis v. Maryland, 451 A.2d 107 (Md. 1982) (holding that the legislature's religious exemption from compulsory immunization must not violate the Establishment clause).

51. Several courts have upheld the statute on grounds other than the First Amendment. *See, e.g.,* Heard v. Payne, 665 S.W.2d 865, 867 (Ark. 1984) (holding that a chiropractor who believes children are allergic to vaccine is not permitted to exempt them from immunization) *reh'g denied* (1984); State *ex rel.* Mack v. Board of Educ., 204 N.E.2d 86, 89 (Ohio Ct. App. 1963) (holding that a child does not have an absolute right to enter school without immunization solely based on parent's objection) *reh'g denied* (1963); Pierce v. Board of Educ. of Fulton, 219 N.Y.S.2d 519, 520 (N.Y. 1961) (upholding statute despite parents' belief that vaccination would be detrimental to their children); Stull v. Reber, 64 A. 419, 419 (Pa. 1906) (holding that lack of consent to vaccination is not trespass on individual's rights).

claims.[52] Freedom of religion does "not import an absolute right in each person to be, at all times and in all circumstances, wholly freed from restraint. There are manifold restraints to which every person is necessarily subject for the common good."[53] Indeed, compulsory vaccination need not even be triggered by the existence of an epidemic;[54] nor must a grave or immediate health risk exist to outweigh religious liberty.[55] However, one court has refused to intervene when the urgency previously created by an epidemic had passed.[56]

Courts, however, do not allow public health officials completely free reign to immunize the community from preventable disease. While the state may vest broad discretion in its officials,[57] they must regulate fairly.[58] Public health officials have broad discretion under many state

---

52. Many courts have used the rationale that public health takes precedence over religious freedom. *See, e.g.*, Brown v. Stone, 378 So.2d 218, 220 (Miss. 1979) *reh'g denied* (1980), *and cert. denied*, 449 U.S. 887 (1980); Wright v. DeWitt Sch. Dist., 385 S.W.2d 644, 646 (Ark. 1965); Cude v. State, 377 S.W.2d 816, 819 (Ark. 1964) *reh'g denied* (1964); Sadlock v. Board of Educ. of Carlstadt, 58 A.2d 218, 220 (N.J. 1948). Moreover, the Supreme Court has made plain its view that public health imperatives in vaccination programs override religious freedoms and that a state need not provide a religious exemption for its immunization program in dictum. *See* Prince v. Mass., 321 U.S. 158, 166–67 (1944), *cert. denied*, 321 U.S. 804. A New York court has required a demonstration that opposition to inoculation stem from sincerely held religious convictions and not merely be framed in terms of religious belief in order to gain the exemption required. *In the Matter of Christine* M., 595 N.Y.S.2d 606 (1992).

53. Syska v. Montgomery County Bd. of Educ., 415 A.2d 301, 304 (Md. Ct. Spec. App. 1980) *citing* Jacobson v. Massachusetts, 197 U.S. 11, 26 (1905) (holding that compulsory rubella immunization for school admission did not violate mother's constitutional right).

54. *See In re* Elwell, 284 N.Y.S.2d 924, 930 (N.Y. Fam. Ct. 1967) (holding that compulsory vaccination for school admission is valid exercise of the state police power to prevent against disease). *See also* Board of Educ. v. Maas, 152 A.2d 394 (N.J. Super. Ct. App. Div. 1959) *cert. denied*, 363 U.S. 843 (1960) (holding that vaccinations are an effective health measure and are within the power of the legislature).

55. Wright v. DeWitt Sch. Dist., 385 S.W.2d 644 (Ark. 1965) (holding that mandatory vaccination outweighs religious liberty even when there is no grave or immediate health risk).

56. *In the Matter of Christine M.*, 595 N.Y.S.2d 606 (1992).

57. *See* Zucht v. King, 260 U.S. 174 (1922) (holding that it is constitutional for public officials to be vested with the authority to enforce compulsory school vaccinations for the protection of public health).

58. Raper v. Lucey, 488 F.2d 748, 753 (1st Cir. 1973). *See* Avard v. Dupuis, 376 F. Supp. 479, 482 (D.N.H. 1974) (holding the religious exemption standardless and unconstitutional).

statutes to provide a religious exemption to vaccination, but they cannot exercise this discretion arbitrarily.[59]

2. The bathhouses and adult video shop cases

Government action to impede the spread of sexually transmitted infection has often focused on the closure or regulation of public places such as bathhouses, adult video shops, theaters, and bookstores.[60] Regulation of public places, particularly where literature, films, or live theater is presented, implicates the First Amendment freedoms of expression, press, and association. Theoretically, these freedoms cannot be abridged absent a "substantial governmental interest."[61] Nonetheless, courts have shown little hesitation in upholding regulation, even closure, of such establishments in the name of public health.[62] To these courts, the preservation of public health is an

---

59. Brown v. Stone, 378 So.2d 218 (Miss. 1979) (holding that provisions of a compulsory vaccination statute providing religious exceptions violated the Equal Protection Clause); Kolbeck v. Rutgers, the State Univ., 202 A.2d 889, 893 (N.J. Super. Ct. App. Div. 1964) (holding that the state cannot show a preference for one religion over another when creating exemptions for mandatory vaccinations); Davis v. Maryland, 451 A.2d 107, 113 (Md. 1982) (holding that a student vaccine exemption which recognizes that parents are members of a recognized church or religious denomination violates the Establishment Clause of the First Amendment).

60. E.g., City of New York v. New Saint Mark's Bath, 497 N.Y.S.2d 979, 983 (N.Y. App. Div. 1986) (holding that closure of bathhouse would not violate First Amendment rights of association and privacy); Mitchell & Bob's Discount Adult Bookstore, Inc. v. Commissioner of the Comm'n on Adult Entertainment Establishments of the State of Delaware, 802 F. Supp. 112 (D.Del. 1992) (holding that ordinance amendments regulating hours of adult book stores and prohibiting closed booths are Constitutional as means to further state interest of curbing the spread of AIDS).

61. United States v. O'Brien, 391 U.S. 367, 377 (1968) (laying down a four part test: (1) the regulation must be within the constitutional power of the government; (2) it must further an important or substantial government interest; (3) the government interest must be unrelated to the suppression of free expression; and (4) the incidental restriction on First Amendment freedoms must be no greater than is essential to the furtherance of that interest).

62. See generally Stephen L. Collier, Comment, Preventing the Spread of AIDS by Restricting Sexual Conduct in Gay Bathhouses: A Constitutional Analysis, 15 GOLDEN GATE U.L. REV. 301 (1985); Note, The Constitutional Rights of AIDS Carriers, 99 HARV. L. REV. 1274 (1986).

overriding state purpose.[63] Because of the presence of a compelling public health objective, courts have not always required that the state prove the restriction on First Amendment rights is strictly necessary. Governments have broad latitude in experimenting with possible solutions to public health problems.[64] Thus, courts faced with free expression or association claims require only some reasonable scientific evidence of a public health necessity, even if there is an equally respected scientific view that the restriction is not essential to the public health.[65]

The bathhouse cases emerge as powerful examples of scientific uncertainty about the best public health approach.[66] To some, the health risk represented by sexual activity with anonymous partners in bathhouses is unmistakable. To others, however, closure only means that sexual activity will move to another venue, and an opportunity for targeted health promotion would be lost. In upholding the closure of bathhouses,[67] courts reasoned that they need not choose among reasonable scientific alternatives: "The judicial function is exhausted with the discovery that the relation between means and end is not wholly vain and fanciful, and illusory pretense."[68] Even when operating under the First Amendment, therefore, the courts will not gauge the scientific merits of decisions to close public places.[69]

---

63. *E.g.*, State v. Mountain Timber Co., 135 P. 645, 647 (Wash. 1913), *aff'd*, 243 U.S. 219 (1916) (holding that the police power of the state permits interference with individual liberty whenever public interest demands it).

64. *E.g.*, Whalen v. Roe, 429 U.S. 589 (1977) (holding that state legislation which affects individual liberty or privacy may not be held unconstitutional simply because the court found it unnecessary); *see also*, Paris Adult Theater I v. Slaton, 413 U.S. 499 (1973) (holding that the state can regulate obscene material although there is a lack of definite proof of a nexus between anti-social behavior and obscene material).

65. *See generally* Burris, *Rationality Review and the Politics of Public Health*, 34 VILL. L. REV. 933, 969 (1989).

66. *See generally* RONALD BAYER, PRIVATE ACTS, SOCIAL CONSEQUENCES: AIDS AND THE POLITICS OF PUBLIC HEALTH (1989).

67. California v. Three 3MCS, Inc. No. C685816 slip op (Cal. Sup. Ct. Aug. 30, 1988); Los Angeles v. Benson, Super. Ct. LA City, Cal. AIDS Lit. Rptr.; May 13, 1988. *See also* City of New York v. Big Apple Spa, 130 Misc. 2d 920, 497 N.Y.S.2d 988 (N.Y. Sup. Ct. 1986) (court used same rationale with regard to heterosexual conduct).

68. City of New York v. New Saint Mark's Bath, 497 N.Y.S.2d 979, 983 (N.Y. App. Div. 1986) (holding that closure of bathhouse would not violate First Amendment rights of association and privacy).

69. California v. Three 3MCS, Inc., No. C685816, slip op at 8–9 (Cal. Sup.

Still less clear is the impact of adult video stores, theaters, or bookstores in contributing to the spread of sexually transmitted infections. Federal[70] and state[71] courts have almost universally upheld

Ct. Aug. 30, 1988) ("it is not the function of the courts to determine which scientific view is correct"). One notable exception occurred in San Francisco where a less restrictive alternative was required so that bathhouses could remain open subject to strict regulation designed to decrease unprotected sexual activities. California *ex rel.* Agnost v. Owen, No. 830 321 (Cal. Super. Ct. Nov. 30, 1984).

70. *E.g.*, Mitchell & Bob's Discount Adult Bookstore, Inc. v. Commissioner of the Comm'n on Adult Entertainment Establishments of the State of Delaware, 802 F.Supp. 112 (D.Del. 1992) (holding that ordinance amendments regulating hours of adult book stores and prohibiting closed booths are constitutional as means to further state interest of curbing the spread of AIDS); Bamon Corp. v. City of Dayton, 923 F.2d 470 (6th Cir. 1991) (affirming summary judgment in favor of city ordinance regulating open doors in adult book stores); Postscript Enterprises v. City of Bridgeton, 905 F.2d 223 (8th Cir. 1990) (affirming summary judgment in favor of ordinance requiring open doors for viewing areas in adult book store); Wall Distrib., Inc. v. City of Newport News, 782 F.2d 1165, 1168 (4th Cir. 1986) (holding that ordinances making it a criminal offense to exhibit films in enclosed booths was valid restriction on manner of speech); *see also* Ellwest Stereo Theaters, Inc. v. Wenner, 681 F.2d 1243, 1246 (9th Cir. 1982) (holding that city ordinance requiring that viewing areas of booth in which coin-operated viewing devices are located be visible from main aisle is reasonable regulation of manner in which films may be viewed); Movie & Video World v. Board of County Comm'rs, 723 F. Supp. 695, 701 (S.D. Fla. 1989) (upholding regulation that all doors be removed from booths showing sexually explicit films); Doe v. City of Minneapolis, 898 F.2d 612 (8th Cir. 1990) (upholding constitutionality of ordinance requiring removal of doors to booths in adult book stores); Suburban Video v. City of Delafield, 694 F. Supp. 585, 587 (E.D. Wis. 1988) (holding that open door requirement of booths did not violate First Amendment rights); Berg v. Health & Hosp. Corp., 667 F. Supp. 639, 641 (S.D. Ind. 1987) (upholding constitutionality of open door requirement), *aff'd*, 865 F.2d 797 (7th Cir. 1989); Broadway Books v. Roberts, 642 F. Supp. 486, 492 (E.D. Tenn. 1986) (upholding validity of open booth requirement).

71. City News & Novelty, Inc. v. City of Waukesha, 487 N.W.2d 316 (Wis.Ct.App. 1992) (affirming summary judgment for city ordinance requiring viewing booths to be viewable from public points in adult oriented establishments as a means to control the spread of communicable diseases like AIDS); City of Lincoln, Neb. v. ABC Books, Inc., 470 N.W.2d 760 (Neb. 1991) (denying injunctive relief from ordinance that required visibility of booths in an adult book store); Centaur, Inc. v. Richland County, S.C., 392 S.E.2d 165 (S.C. 1990) (upholding constitutionality of ordinance requiring unobstructed view of every area in interior of sexually oriented businesses); Adult Entertainment Ctr., Inc. v. Pierce County, 788 P.2d 1102, 1106 (Wash.

(cont.)

the constitutionality of local ordinances that require viewing booths to be open to the public. Courts have validated the delegation of authority to local governing bodies such as county health departments and Boards of Supervisors, declaring such ordinances akin to those passed by the legislature itself.[72] Again, courts do not require the risk to public health to be proven.[73] The government is entitled to "infer" a health threat from evidence that more than one person sometimes occupies a booth at the same time.[74] Equal protection and undue burden arguments regarding open viewing booths have also been rejected by the courts.[75]

The goal of regulation is to prevent sexual activity, including masturbation, "and its related unsanitary conditions and other activities offensive to decency that demonstrably accompany furtive viewings of sexually explicit materials."[76] Courts have viewed regulation of bookstores and video shops for public health purposes as "time, place, and manner" restrictions.[77] Regulation of these shops was upheld

---

(71, *cont.*) Ct. App. 1990) (holding that open booth requirement of ordinance providing for licensing of businesses providing booths for their customers to view sexually explicit material was reasonable time, place, and manner restriction); *See also* Rahmani v. State, 748 S.W.2d 618, 621 (Tex. Ct. App. 1988) (holding that permit requirements did not constitute impermissible prior restraint on free speech), *cert. denied*, 490 U.S. 1081 (1989); Lopex v. State, 756 S.W.2d 49, 51 (Tex. Ct. App. 1988) (upholding validity of local ordinance requiring a permit as proof of interior design compliance to discourage the use of an adult arcade as a place for sexual encounters); EWAP Inc. v. City of Los Angeles, 97 Cal. App. 3d 179, 182 (1979) (upholding ordinance denying permits for the operation of picture shows if any person involved knowingly allowed any sexual acts or solicitations for such acts in the picture arcade).

72. Marsoner v. Pima County, 803 P.2d 897 (Ariz. 1991) (reversing appellate court decision that Board of Supervisors lacked authority to enact ordinance requiring licensing of adult amusement establishments).

73. Adult Entertainment Ctr. v. Pierce County, 788 P.2d at 1105 (when holding the open booth requirement as constitutional, the court noted that the necessity for the legislation need not be proven absolutely).

74. *Id.* at 1105–06 (requiring the testimony of only one person in booth as sufficient to claim health risk).

75. Doe v. City of Minneapolis, 898 F.2d at 620–22 (holding that ordinance requiring removal of doors to booths in adult book stores treated similarly situated commercial establishments the same; economic effect on book stores not controlling in First Amendment analysis).

76. Adult Entertainment Ctr. v. Pierce County, 788 P.2d at 1106 (citing Wall Distrib. Inc. v. City of Newport News, 782 F.2d 1165 (4th Cir. 1986)).

77. *E.g.*, City of Renton v. Playtime Theaters, 475 U.S. 1132 (1986) *reh'g denied*, 475 U.S. 1132 (1986).

because it was content-neutral and narrowly tailored to serve a public health purpose, and left ample alternative channels of communication.[78] Local officials, however, may not impose onerous licensing requirements such as demanding a high moral character from the proprietor or an inordinately expensive license fee.[79]

The lack of clear standards of constitutional review results in inconsistent and unpredictable decision making, and gives little guidance as to the lawfulness of an array of public health powers. The Americans with Disabilities Act and the corpus of anti-discrimination law should close that doctrinal gap in the public health sphere.

II. THE AMERICANS WITH DISABILITIES ACT AND THE CORPUS OF ANTI-DISCRIMINATION LEGISLATION

The Americans with Disabilities Act of 1990[80] (ADA) and the corpus of anti-discrimination legislation[81] appear to be unlikely sources of law to fill the doctrinal void left by deferential constitutional standards.

---

78. *See* Ward v. Rock Against Racism, 491 U.S. 781 (1989).

79. Suburban Video v. City of Delafield, 694 F. Supp. 585, 592 (E.D. Wis. 1988) (holding that licensing requirements that do not further substantial government interest contravene constitutional rights); Broadway Books v. Roberts, 642 F. Supp. 486, 494–95 (E.D. Tenn. 1986) (holding unconstitutional a 30 day residence requirement that does not demonstrate a compelling state interest and a good moral character requirement which permits unguided discretion to licensing authority); *but see* Centaur, Inc. v. Richland County, S.C., 392 S.E.2d 165 (S.C. 1990) (upholding constitutionality of licensing requirement, but permitting denial of license under enumerated circumstances such as failure to provide "reasonably necessary information").

80. The Americans with Disabilities Act of 1990, 42 U.S.C. § 12101–12201 (1992) (established a clear and comprehensive prohibition of discrimination on the basis of disability).

81. The ADA does not repeal the body of anti-discrimination legislation that preceded it. The Federal Rehabilitation Act of 1973 proscribes discrimination of persons with "handicaps" (defined almost identically to "disability") by entities which are in receipt of federal financial assistance and does not reach into the purely private sector. The principal application of the Rehabilitation Act in the post-ADA era will be to protect disabled employees of the federal government, since they are not covered by the ADA (§ 101(5)(B)(i)).

Discrimination against persons with disabilities in housing is dealt with under the Federal Fair Housing Amendments of 1988. *See* Baxter v. Belleville, 1989 U.S.D.C. LEXIS 10298 (S.D. I 11.1989).

(cont.)

Anti-discrimination law, on its face, is concerned with what I will refer to as "pure discrimination." Pure discrimination occurs when a public or private entity treats a person unfairly, not because she lacks adequate skill, qualifications, or experience, but because of her disability. The primary goal of the ADA, then, is to assure equality of opportunity, full participation, equal living and self-sufficiency to allow people with disabilities to compete on an equal basis.[82]

Public health regulation of communicable disease does not fit comfortably within the ADA's rubric of pure discrimination. Certainly, the annals of public health are replete with examples of pure discrimination against "discrete and insular" minorities such as prostitutes,[83] drug dependent people,[84] gays,[85] and racial minorities.[86] The exercise of public health powers such as testing, screening, reporting, vaccination, treatment, isolation and quarantine are, however, qualitatively different than the ADA's paradigm of pure discrimination: the state is regulating public health, not withdrawing jobs, benefits or services because of a disability; here, the motive is health related, not grounded in prejudice; and the usual qualification standards of education, skill, or experience are not pertinent. Persons are treated unequally in public health regulation because of communicable medical conditions, not as a direct result of pure prejudice.

When a health department exercises public health powers, the pivotal issue is whether it must comply with the standards of the ADA. Despite the qualitative differences between a communicable disease (e.g., tuberculosis, syphilis, or hepatitis B), and a physical disability

---

(81, *cont.*)   The Education for All Handicapped Children Act, 20 U.S.C. para. 1400 *et seq.*, gives all school aged handicapped children the right to a free public education in the least restrictive environment appropriate to their needs. See Martinez v. Sch. Bd. of Hillsburough Cty, Fla. 861 F.2d 1502 (11th Cir. 1988), reversing, 711 F. Supp. 1293 (M D Fla. 1989); Community High School Dist. v. Denz, 124 Ill. App. 3d 1291, 463 N.E. 2d 998 (2d Dist. Ill, 1984) (legislation and the judicial decisions construing them are referred to as the corpus of anti- discrimination law).

82. PL 101–336, § 2(a)(8), (9).

83. *See* ALLAN M. BRANDT, NO MAGIC BULLET: A SOCIAL HISTORY OF VENEREAL DISEASE IN THE UNITED STATES SINCE 1880 (1985).

84. *See generally* DONALD F. MUSTO, M.D., THE AMERICAN DISEASE: ORIGINS OF NARCOTIC CONTROL (1973).

85. RONALD BAYER, PRIVATE ACTS; SOCIAL CONSEQUENCES: AIDS AND THE POLITICS OF PUBLIC HEALTH (Rutgers Univ. Press, New Brunswick, New Jersey, 1989).

86. *See* Jew Ho v. Williamson, 103 F. 10 (C.C.N.D. Cal. 1900).

(e.g., sight, hearing, or mobility impairments), the ADA applies to each equally. Certainly, the actions of health departments that directly affect the opportunities of persons with communicable diseases in employment and in public accommodations are covered under Titles I and III respectively. If a health department required testing for disease or exclusion from a job in schools, hospitals, food service establishment or day care, it would undoubtedly have to comply with the standards in Title I of the ADA; the private entity in testing or excluding workers would be simply enforcing a state requirement. Similarly, if the health department required testing or exclusion of workers or residents in a public accommodation, it would have to comply with the standards in Title III of the ADA. Since public accommodation is defined to include health care providers, hospitals, day care centers, social services establishments, schools, and other entities traditionally regulated by health departments,[87] it is clear that ADA standards would apply.

It could be argued, however, that the ADA does not apply to health department regulations that do not directly affect opportunities in employment and public accommodations. The exercise of traditional public health powers such as screening, vaccination, reporting, contact tracing, and isolation are not specifically mentioned in the ADA. Title II (public services) does not refer to the exercise of police powers; exercising the authority of the state to protect public health, it can be argued, is not a "public service."

There are several reasons for the assertion in this essay that Title II does govern the exercise of traditional public health powers. Generally speaking, the exercise of traditional public health powers is a service provided to the public by health departments. The service is designed to protect the public and that protection is achieved both by voluntary and involuntary participation in public health programs. Any time a health department exercises compulsory powers it also expends resources, provides services, and protects the community. For example, the state buys and distributes vaccines and provides treatment and care for persons in isolation.

Moreover, it would be a bizarre reading of the ADA to make rigid distinctions among the various activities of government. When the state provides a service or benefit to a person, such as Medicare or food stamps, it undoubtedly has to do so in a non-discriminatory manner. The most striking example of this requirement was the recent denial of a Medicaid waiver to the State of Oregon when its proposed

---

87. *See* 42 U.S.C. § 12181(7) (1992).

health plan discriminated against persons with disabilities. The original plan consistently rated the quality of life of persons with disabilities lower than that of non-disabled persons. Consequently, services provided to persons with disabilities were systematically placed in low (unlikely to be covered) positions on the priority list. The plan was found to violate the ADA.[88] Following revision to reflect ADA concerns, Oregon received its waiver.

Likewise, when a state exercises coercive powers with the potential to seriously affect a person's liberty, autonomy, or privacy, it should have the same obligation to follow the non-discrimination principles in the ADA. The exercise of public health powers is a substantial part of the functions of health departments. If Congress had intended to carve out, or exclude, these functions from the coverage of the ADA, it would have done so expressly and clearly.

Principles of parallel construction in the legislation also militate towards inclusion of public health powers. If a government department deprives an infected health care worker of a job, excludes a child from school, or refuses a medical license based upon a person's disease status, it clearly is covered. It seems inconceivable that the ADA does not apply if the same or another government agency coerces the individual, or even deprives the person of liberty on the basis of a disease status. Such a tortuous construction would have to posit that Congress required health departments to act in a non-discriminatory manner when it withheld a small benefit or service, but not when it deprived a person of liberty.

Indeed, a great deal of evidence exists in Title II to suggest that its provisions apply to the exercise of traditional public health powers. The definition of "public entity" at 42 U.S.C. § 12131 expressly includes state and local governments. The definition squarely includes health department activities. Further, this section defines "qualified individual with a disability" to include eligibility to participate in programs or activities provided by a public entity. The "activities" of a health department assuredly include disease control.

Finally, 42 U.S.C. § 12132 contemplates coverage for persons who are subjected to the "activities" of a public entity, or "discrimination

---

88. Letter from Louis W. Sullivan, Secretary, U.S. Department of Health and Human Services, to Barbara Roberts, Governor of Oregon (Aug. 7, 1992); Richard A. Knox, *U.S. Rejects Oregon Health Care Plan*, Boston Globe, Sept. 4, 1992, at 3. The Oregon plan, following revision to comply with the ADA, received its waiver.

by any such entity." Discrimination by a health department would certainly include the exercise of compulsion against a person with a communicable disease without sufficient justification based upon a significant risk to the public. A public health department ought to be held to the same standard in exercising public health powers as it is in employment or accommodations—grounding policies in facts and not in irrational fears about persons with disabilities.

The Department of Justice (DOJ) regulations relating to state and local government services also appear to cover the exercise of public health powers.[89] The DOJ sees its jurisdiction within the context of the "ADA's expanded coverage of state and local government operations."[90] It will exercise complaints against agencies and other governmental components carrying out their "functions," including state medical boards. The DOJ's jurisdiction extends expressly to "all programs, services, and regulatory activities" relating to "public safety" and "all other government functions not assigned to other designated agencies."[91] Title II, therefore, covers "all actions of state and local governments"[92] which squarely include the exercise of their compulsory powers.

DOJ regulations under Title II liberally discuss individualized assessment and "direct threat standards" for tuberculosis and other communicable diseases.[93] To demonstrate the applicability of the ADA to communicable disease, the relevant definitions, legislative history, and standards are analyzed.[94]

A. Communicable disease as a disability

1. *"Physical or mental impairment"*

Disability is defined broadly in the ADA to mean "a physical or mental impairment that substantially[95] limits one or more of the major life

---

89. Dept. of Justice Nondiscrimination on the Basis of Disability in State and Local Government Services Final Rule, 56 Fed. Reg. 35,694 (1991) (codified at 28 C.F.R. pt. 35).

90. 28 C.F.R. pt 35, subpt. G (1993).

91. *Id.*

92. *Id.* at subpt. A.

93. *Id.*

94. As above.

95. The physical or mental impairment must substantially limit a major life activity. Persons with minor or trivial impairments such as a simple infected finger are not disabled within the meaning of the Act. *See* SENATE COMMITTEE ON LABOR AND HUMAN RESOURCES, S. DOC. NO. 116, 101st Cong., 2d Sess. 22 (1989).

activities,[96] a record of such impairment, or being regarded as having such an impairment."[97] "Physical or mental impairment" includes: (1) any physiological disorder or condition, disfigurement or anatomical loss affecting any of the major bodily systems; or (2) any mental or physiological disorder such as mental retardation or mental illness. The legislative history[98] as well as the prior case law,[99] make clear that "disability" includes diseases and infections which are communicable (e.g., tuberculosis,[100] hepatitis,[101] and HIV[102]) as well as those which

---

96. *Id.* (The term "physical or mental impairment" does not include simple physical characteristics, such as blue eyes or black hair. Nor does it include environmental, cultural, and economic disadvantages in and of themselves. Thus age and homosexuality are not characterized as disabilities under the Act.)

97. *See* 42 U.S.C. § 12111 (1992). The definition of disability in the ADA is comparable to the term "handicap" in section 7(8)(B) of the Rehabilitation Act of 1973 and § 802(h) of the Fair Housing Act. The Congress intended that regulations implementing the Rehabilitation Act and the Fair Housing Amendments apply to the term disability in the ADA. The use of the term "disability" instead of "handicap" represents currently acceptable terminology. *See also* THE AMERICANS WITH DISABILITIES ACT OF 1989: REPORT OF THE COMMITTEE ON LABOR AND HUMAN SERVICES, S. Rep. No. 116, 101st Cong., 2d Sess. 21 (1992).

98. *Id.* at 22. Indeed, the House Energy and Commerce Committee rejected an amendment offered by Congressman Dannemeyer that would have expressly excluded currently contagious and sexually transmitted diseases or infections from the definitions of "disability." *See* HOUSE COMMITTEE ON ENERGY AND COMMERCE, H.R. REP. No. 485, 101st Cong., Sess. 4 (1990) (to accompany H.R. 2273).

99. *See, e.g.,* Strathie v. Dep't of Transp., 716 F.2d 227, 232–34 (3d Cir. 1983) (holding that hearing impairment problems are to be treated as disabilites); Doe v. N.Y. Univ., 666 F.2d 761, 775 (2d Cir. 1981) (arguing that psychiatric problems are majority life activities which are properly classified as handicaps).

100. *See* School Bd. v. Arline, 480 U.S. 273 (1987) (school teacher with tuberculosis was handicapped within the meaning of § 504 of the Rehabilitation Act of 1973).

101. New York State Ass'n for Retarded Children v. Carey, 612 F.2d 644 (2d Cir. 1979) (mentally retarded children who are carriers of serum hepatitis B could not be excluded from public school because they were handicapped and did not pose a health hazard); Jeffrey S, a minor by Ernest S., his father v. State Bd. of Educ. of Georgia, 896 F.2d 661 (11th Cir. 1990) (Civil Rights Restoration Act of 1987 applied respectively to corrections officer who alleged discrimination because he had infectious hepatitis disease); Kohl v. Woodhaven Learning Center, 865 F.2d 930 (8th Cir. 1989), *reversing in part*, 672 F. Supp. 1221 (W.D. M.O. 1987) (inoculation of school staff for hepatitis not a "reasonable accommodation.")

102. *See, e.g.,* Doe v. Centinela Hosp., 57 U.S.L.W. 2034 (C.D. Cal. 1988); Chalk v. U.S. Dist. Ct., 840 F.2d 701 (9th Cir. 1988).

103. EEOC v. AIC Security Investigations, Ltd., 823 F. Supp. 571 (N.D.Ill.

are not (e.g., cancer,[103] heart disease,[104] arthritis,[105] diabetes, and epilepsy[106]).

The legislative history of the Rehabilitation Act barely mentions infectious disease.[107] In *Arline*, the question arose for the first time in the Supreme Court whether discrimination on the basis of contagiousness constitutes discrimination "by reason of...handicap."[108] The Court held that a teacher who had been hospitalized with tuberculosis that affected her respiratory system had a "record" of substantial physical impairment. The fact that a person with a record of impairment is also contagious does not remove her from protection as a handicapped person.

The *Arline* Court observed that, in defining a handicapped person, the contagious effects of a disease cannot be meaningfully distinguished from the disease's physical effects. "It would be unfair to allow an employer to seize upon the distinction between the effects of a disease on others and the effects of a disease on a patient and use that distinction to justify discriminatory treatment."[109] Citing the example of cosmetic disfigurement, the Court argued that Congress was as

---

1993) (awarding a security company executive $272,000 in damages, reflecting judicial reduction to statutory cap, when employer terminated him following diagnosis of brain cancer that did not affect his job performance).

104. *See* Bey v. Bolger, 540 F. Supp. 910 (E.D. Pa. 1982) (post office employee sought reinstatement but was denied because of his hypertension).

105. School Bd. of Nassau County, Fla. v. Arline, 480 U.S. 273, 283 (1987) *citing* 118 Cong. Rec. 36761 (1972) (statement of Sen. Mondale) ("a woman 'crippled by arthritis' was denied a job not because she could not do the work but because college trustees [thought] normal students shouldn't see her").

106. The Senate Labor and Human Resources Committee Report on the ADA cited examples of individuals with controlled diabetes or epilepsy who were "often denied jobs for which they are qualified." Such denials are the result of negative attitudes and misinformation. *See* S. REP. No. 116, 101st Cong., 2d Sess. 24 (1990). In addition, in an appendix to the regulations on the Rehabilitation Act, the Department of Health and Human Services specifically listed a number of diseases to which the Act applied, including epilepsy, cerebral palsy, muscular dystrophy, multiple sclerosis, cancer, heart disease, and diabetes. 45 C.F.R. 84, App. A at 377 (1985).

107. School Board of Nassau County, Fla. v. Arline, 480 U.S. 273, 297 (1987) (Rehnquist, J., dissenting).

108. *See, e.g.*, Lower Courts had already found that contagious diseases were handicaps. *See, e.g.*, New York State Ass'n of Retarded Children v. Carey, 612 F.2d 644 (2d Cir. 1979).

109. School Bd. v. Arline, 480 U.S. at 282 (1987).

concerned about the effects of impairment on others as it was about its effects on the individual.[110]

The inclusion of contagious conditions in the definition of handicap was, according to *Arline*, consistent with the basic purpose of disability law to protect people against the prejudiced attitudes and ignorance of others. "Society's accumulated myths and fears about disability and disease are as handicapping as are the physical limitations that flow from ... impairment. Few aspects of ... a handicap give rise to the same level of public fear and misapprehension as contagiousness."[111]

2. *"Record" of or "regarded" as being impaired*

A person is disabled if he or she has a "record" of or is "regarded" as being disabled or is perceived to be disabled, even if there is no actual incapacity.[112] A "record" indicates that the person has had a history of impairment, or has been misclassified as having had an impairment. This provision is designed to protect persons who have recovered from a disability or disease which previously impaired their life activities.[113] By including those who have a record of impairment, Congress acknowledged that people who have recovered from disease such as epilepsy or cancer face discrimination based upon prejudice and irrational fear.[114]

The term "regarded" as being impaired includes individuals who do not have limitations in their major life functions, but are treated as if they did. This concept protects people who are discriminated against in the false belief that they are disabled. It would be inequitable for a defendant who intended to discriminate on the basis of disability to successfully raise the defense that the person was not, in fact, disabled. This provision is particularly important for individuals who are perceived to have stigmatic conditions that are viewed negatively by society. It is the reaction of society, rather than the disability itself, which deprives the person of equal enjoyment of rights and services. Persons with infectious diseases are particularly prone to irrational

---

110. *Id.* at 283.

111. *Id.* at 284.

112. This concept derives from Southeastern Community College v. Davis, 442 U.S. 397 (1979).

113. Senate Report (Labor and Human Resources Committee) No. 101–116, Aug. 30, 1989 (to accompany S. 933), p. 23.

114. School Bd. v. Arline, 480 U.S. at 284 (1987).

fears by those who are misinformed about the modes and relative risks of transmission. Persons with disfiguring conditions such as leprosy or severe burns may also suffer from negative attitudes and misinformation because they are perceived to be disabled.[115]

3. Asymptomatic infection as a disability

The fact that a record or perception of disability is included within the ADA is vitally important in determining whether pure asymptomatic infection can be regarded as a disability. The abiding interest at the time of *Arline* was whether an asymptomatic carrier of a contagious infection such as HIV could be regarded as handicapped. A Justice Department memorandum in June 1986 concluded that while the disabling effects of AIDS may constitute a handicap, contagiousness—the ability to transmit infection to others—is not a potential characteristic.[116] The *Arline* court in its widely studied footnote 7 claimed that the facts of the case "do not present, and we therefore do not reach, the question whether a carrier of a contagious disease such as AIDS could be considered to have a physical impairment."[117]

On July 29, 1988, C. Everett Koop, the Surgeon General, wrote to the Justice Department seeking a fresh opinion in light of *Arline* and the growing scientific understanding that HIV infection is the starting point of a single disease process.[118] In response, the Justice Department withdrew its previous opinion, concluding that "section 504 protects symptomatic as well as asymptomatic HIV-infected individuals against discrimination." The person is protected only if he or she "is able to perform the duties of the job and does not constitute a direct threat to the health or safety of others."[119]

---

115. Senate Report (Labor and Human Resources Committee) No. 101–116, Aug. 30, 1989 (to accompany S. 933, p. 24).

116. Opinion of Charles J. Cooper, Assistant Attorney General, Office of Legal Counsel, for Ronald E. Robertson, General Counsel, Department of Health and Human Services, June 23, 1986.

117. *Id.* at 282, n. 7.

118. Letter from C. Everett Koop to Douglas Kamiec, Acting Assistant Attorney General, July 29, 1988.

119. Memorandum for Arthur B. Culvahouse, Jr., Counsel to the President, from Douglas W. Kamiec, Acting Assistant Attorney General, Office of the Legal Counsel, re Application of Section 504 of the Rehabilitation Act to HIV-Infected Individuals, Sept. 27, 1988. The concept of "direct threat" as a qualification standard is discussed below.

The applicability of asymptomatic infection to handicapped status had already been clarified in amendments to the Rehabilitation Act. The Civil Rights Restoration Act of 1987,[120] intended as a codification of *Arline*, states that a person with a contagious disease or infection is handicapped if he or she does not "constitute a direct threat to health or safety" and is able to "perform the duties of the job."[121] Since *Arline*, the courts have consistently held that HIV-related diseases, including asymptomatic HIV infection, are covered handicaps.[122]

B. Direct threat: an evolving qualification standard

1. *Applicability of the "direct threat" standard to all parts of the ADA*

The anti-discrimination principle in the ADA applies only to "qualified individuals."[123] A "qualified" person must be capable of meeting all of the performance or eligibility criteria for the particular position, service or benefit.[124] There is, moreover, an affirmative obligation to provide "reasonable accommodations"[125] or "reasonable modifications"[126] if they would enable the person to meet the performance or eligibility criteria. Employers are not required to provide reasonable accommodations if it would impose an undue hardship on the operation of the business.[127]

The key concepts of "qualification" and "reasonable accommodations" or "modifications", on their face, apply only to a person's ability

---

120. Civil Rights Restoration Act of 1987, Pub. L. No. 100–259, 102 Stat. 28 (codified as amended in scattered sections of the U.S.C).

121. *Id.* at § 9(c).

122. *See, e.g.*, Centinela Hosp., 57 U.S.L.W. 2034 (D.C. Cal. 1988). *See also* Lawrence Gostin, *The AIDS Litigation Project: A National Review of Court and Human Rights Commission Decisions, Part II: Discrimination*, 263 JAMA 2086–93 (1990).

123. 42 U.S.C. §§ 12112, 12133 (1992).

124. *Id.* § 12112 (requiring qualification standards, employment tests, or other selection criteria to be "job-related" and "consistent with business necessity"). *See also Id.* at § 12133 (requiring the disabled person to meet the "essential eligibility requirements" for the receipt of services or the participation in programs or activities).

125. *Id.* § 12111(b)(5).

126. *Id.* § 12111(2).

127. *Id.* at § 102(b)(5)(A). *See also* Southeastern Community College v. Davis, 442 U.S. 397, 410–12 (1979) (holding that "unique financial and administrative burdens" or requirements which call for "fundamental alteration in the nature of the program" impose undue hardships on businesses).

to do a job or participate in public programs, with or without adaptations or modifications by the employer or public entity. A specific ban against discrimination of disabled people who are "qualified," without better established limits, might require covered entities to integrate persons in jobs, accommodations, and services, even if they posed a risk of transmission of disease. This prospect led some Congressmen to ask whether employers could be required to employ persons with AIDS if they risked "exposing others to tuberculosis, cytomegalovirus, and other AIDS-associated illness?"[128]

AIDS-related conditions provide poor examples because of the low risk of transmission. It does, however, defy established public health practice to suggest that persons with readily transmissible air-borne conditions could not be excluded from a particular job or enclosed public spaces such as cinemas; that persons with food-borne diseases could not be prevented from working as waiters in restaurants or kitchens; or that public health departments could not set reasonable rules for the control of sexually transmitted disease in bathhouses. In short, the essence of public health regulation is that persons may be treated differently based upon a rigorous scientific assessment of the risk of transmission.

Congress anticipated this problem in relation to employment and public accommodations. Titles I and IV of the ADA state expressly that qualification standards can include a requirement that a person with a disability "not pose a direct threat to the health or safety of others"[129] if reasonable accommodations or modifications will not eliminate that direct threat. The ADA clearly provides a right to take action to protect the health and safety of all persons in employment and public accommodations.[130]

The question arises as to whether the same standard is similarly applicable to Title II, since the concept of "direct threat" is not expressly extended to public services. Title II is of seminal importance in the regulation of public health since it is concerned with activities of state and local government. If taken at face value, Title II could

---

128. William Dannemeyer, Joseph Barton, & Donald Ritter, House Report (Energy and Commerce Committee) No. 101–485 (IV), May 15, 1990 (to accompany H.R. 2273), p. 126.

129. 42 U.S.C. §§ 12113(b), 12182(b)(3).

130. *See* H.R. REP. No. 596, 101st Cong., 2d Sess. 11 (1990) (allowing drug testing of employees in safety-sensitive positions in order to protect lawful exercises of businesses).

appear to undermine rules, regulations and practices of public health departments which exclude persons from services, programs, or activities because of a communicable disease. A defense of direct threat is not expressly available under Title II. As Congress likely did not intend such a result, future regulations should specifically apply the "direct threat" standard to Title II.

Title II applies only to "qualified" individuals. Although that term is not defined in Title II, it can reasonably be taken to have the same meaning as in Title I. Indeed, in discussing the qualification standards for public services, the House Committee on Energy and Commerce referred to the long-standing section 504 principle that a person must meet the basic eligibility requirements of the program, and could not pose "a significant risk . . . [to the health or safety of others] that . . . [cannot] be eliminated by reasonable accommodation."[131]

2. Defining "direct threat": how significant must health risks be?

By utilizing the Supreme Court's term "direct threat," Congress intended to codify *Arline*.[132] Although the "direct threat" criterion was limited to persons with contagious disease in the Senate bill, it was extended in Conference to all individuals with disabilities.[133] The ADA defines "direct threat" consistently with the *Arline* decision: "a significant risk to the health or safety of others" that cannot be eliminated by reasonable accommodation in employment,[134] or reasonable modification of policies, practices, or procedures, or by the provision of auxiliary aids or devices in public accommodations.[135]

"Significant risk" therefore, becomes the standard against which public health regulation must now be measured. The question now becomes which risks are significant? It is possible to arrive at a rather

---

131. H.R. REP. No. 485, 101st Cong., 2d Sess. 37 (1990).

132. *See Id.* at 26,51–52 (1990), *Id.* at pt. 2, 121. (The term "direct threat" is also found in the Civil Rights Restoration Act of 1988 and the Fair Housing Amendments of 1988).

133. H.R. CONF. REP. NO. 596, 101st Cong., 2d Sess. 11 (1990); H.R. REP. NO. 485, 101st Cong., 2d Sess., pt. 3, 51 (indicating that in the House, the standard of "direct threat" was extended by the Judiciary Committee to all individuals with disabilities, and not simply to those with contagious diseases or infection).

134. 42 U.S.C. § 12111(3). *See also* H.R. REP. NO. 116, 101st Cong., 2d Sess. 27 (1989) (suggesting that direct threat to property may also be sufficient).

135. 42 U.S.C. § 12182(b)(3) (1992).

sophisticated jurisprudential and public health understanding of the concept of significant risk by piecing together the language in *Arline* and the ADA's rich legislative history.

First, determination of significant risk becomes a public health inquiry.[136] Relevant evidence must be provided by the multiple disciplines of public health, including medicine, virology, bacteriology, and epidemiology. The science of public health provides the sole grounding for determinations of modes of transmission, probability levels for transmission, efficacy of policies and practices for interrupting transmission, and the likelihood and severity of risk. Disability law has been thoughtfully crafted to replace reflexive actions based upon irrational fears, speculation, stereotypes, or pernicious mythologies,[137] with carefully reasoned judgments based upon well established scientific information.[138]

Second, significant risk must be determined on a case-by-case basis, and not under any type of blanket rule, generalization about a class of disabled persons, or assumptions about the nature of disease. This requires a fact-specific individualized inquiry resulting in a "well-informed judgement grounded in a careful and open-minded weighing of risks and alternatives."[139] A specific determination must be made that the person is in fact a carrier of a communicable disease and that the disease is readily transmissible in the environment in which he or she

---

136. *See, e.g.,* H.R. Rep. NO. 485, 101st Cong., 2d Sess. 51 (1990) (to accompany H.R. 2273) (House Judiciary Committee indicating that direct threat must be based on objective and accepted public health guidelines).

137. The legislative history is replete with statements that rejecting decision making based upon ignorance, misperceptions, and patronizing attitudes. *See* LABOR AND HUMAN RESOURCES COMMITTEE REPORT, S. REP. No. 116, 101st Cong., 2d Sess. 27 (1989) (accompanying S. 933); H.R. Rep. No. 485, 101st Cong., 2d Sess. 52, 153 (1990) (accompanying H.R. 2273); pp. 52, 153; HOUSE COMMITTEE ON ENERGY AND COMMERCE, H.R. REP. NO. 485, at 38; House Committee on Education and Labor, H.R. REP. NO.485 (II) at 77, 121. For historical works of excellence which chronicle the invidious discrimination and prejudiced attitudes toward illness and disease *see, e.g.,* SUSAN SONTAG, ILLNESS AS A METAPHOR (1986); ALLAN BRANDT, NO MAGIC BULLET: A SOCIAL HISTORY OF VENEREAL DISEASE IN THE UNITED STATES SINCE 1880 (1985); Dell, *Social Dimensions of Epilepsy: Stigma and Response, in* PSYCHOPATHOLOGY IN EPILEPSY 185–210 (S. Whitman & B. Hermann eds., 1986).

138. School Bd. v. Arline, 480 U.S. 273, 285 (1987).

139. Hall v. U.S. Postal Service, 857 F.2d 1073, 1079 (6th Cir. 1988) *quoting* Arline, 480 U.S. 273 (1977). *See also* Mantolete v. Bolger, 757 F.2d 1416 (9th Cir. 1985); Strathe v. Dept. of Transp., 716 F.2d 227 (3d Cir. 1983).

will be situated. In the context of behavioral risks, the specific conduct must be identified and credible evidence must be provided to the effect that the person is likely to engage in the dangerous behavior. For example, if a mentally ill or mentally retarded person were to be excluded from school or a job because he or she posed a "direct threat," objective evidence must be presented from the commission of recent dangerous acts.[140] If a person with a needle-borne or sexually transmitted infection were to be denied equal employment or housing opportunities, evidence of a likelihood that the person would share needles or engage in sexual activity in that setting must be offered.

Third, the risk must be "significant," not speculative, theoretical, or remote. The ADA sets a "clear, defined standard which requires actual proof of significant risk to others."[141] This is derived from the highly regarded footnote 16 in *Arline*:[142] "A person who poses a significant risk of communicating an infectious disease to others in the workplace will not be otherwise qualified for his or her job if reasonable accommodation will not eliminate that risk." The Court illustrated its point by observing that a school board would not be required to place a teacher with active, contagious tuberculosis with elementary school children.

Several distinct issues emerge from the concept of significant risk: what is the standard of proof, who bears the burden of proof, and what level of risk is required? Court cases and legislative history do not provide definitive answers, but some guidance can be offered. The *standard of proof* goes to the issue of the probative value of evidence required. The standard of proof ought to be based upon clear and convincing evidence. The public health position taken should be consistent with the clear weight of scientific evidence. Restrictions on liberty ought not be based upon a minority medical opinion. A single physician's view, for example, that HIV might be transmitted casually or from a bite is not sufficiently persuasive when compared with all the accumulated scientific evidence data.[143] The proof of risk, on the other hand, need not be conclusive or decisive. "Little in science can be

---

140. H.R. REP. NO. 485 at 52; S. REP. NO. 116 at 27.77.
141. H.R. REP. NO. 485 at 53.
142. School Bd. v. Arline, 480 U.S. at 287.
143. A Maryland court has demonstrated increasing reliance on scientific data, holding that information on AIDS transmission from reputable scientific journals and institutions constituted a proper object for judicial notice. Faya v. Almarez, 629 A.2d 327 (Md. 1993).

proved with complete certainty, and section 504 does not require such a test."[144]

The *burden of proof* should fall on the entity seeking to demonstrate significant risk. This is consistent with the fact that "direct threat" is a defense in Title I.[145] Thus, an employer, public health department, or public accommodation must be able to offer evidence substantiating its decision to treat disabled people inequitably because they pose a threat to others. It would be difficult, if not impossible, for a person with a communicable disease to prove that transmission cannot occur or is unlikely to occur.

The *level of risk* required is an imponderable because the concept of "significant" is elastic and may vary depending upon the circumstances and severity of the outcome. For example, minor or inconsequential infections might require a higher risk of transmission than lethal or fatal infections. Significant risk is not a remote risk, possibly not even an "elevated risk."[146] There must be a material, real, or substantial possibility that the disease can be transmitted.

The factors to be used in determining significant risk are increasingly well understood.[147] The decision maker must determine significant risk based upon reasonable medical judgments and the current state of scientific understanding concerning:

(a) Mode of transmission.

The mechanism of transmission of most diseases is well established by epidemiologic research. A significant risk should be based upon a primary mode of transmission, not a mode which is unestablished or highly inefficient. A blood-borne disease, for example, could conceiv-

---

144. Chalk v. US District Court, 840 F.2d 701 (9th Cir. 1988).

145. While the "direct threat" standard is not framed as a defense in Title III, it is reasonable to conclude that Congress intended that the public accommodation should bear the burden of substantiating a direct threat.

146. H.R. Rep. No. 485 at 53 (stating that the decision to exclude cannot be based on merely "an elevated risk of injury").

147. The following discussion is based upon the amicus curiae brief of the American Medical Association in *Arline*, and the discussions in several of my previous works. *See* Larry Gostin, *The Politics of AIDS: Compulsory State Powers, Public Health and Civil Liberties*, 49 OHIO ST. L.J. 1017, 1020–26 (1989); Larry Gostin, *Hospitals, Health Care Professionals and AIDS: The "Right to Know" the Health Status of Professionals and Patients*, 48 MD. L. REV. 12, 15–24 (1989); Larry Gostin, *The Case Against Compulsory Casefinding in Controlling AIDS Testing, Screening and Reporting*, 12 AM. J.L. & MED. 7, 21–24 (1986).

ably be transmitted through a bite,[148] through rough play among children,[149] or by bleeding into food.[150] Yet, the "significant risk" test would not be met if personal restrictions were based upon such speculative mechanisms of transmission.

(b) Duration of risk.

A person can be subject to compulsory public health powers only if he or she is actually contagious, and only for the period of time of contagiousness. A fundamental principle of public health law,[151] often breached in early cases,[152] is the requirement that the subject must be proven by medical examination or testing to be carrying an infectious agent. "The mere possibility that persons may have been exposed [to a disease] is not sufficient . . . They must have been exposed to it, and the conditions actually exist for a communication of contagion."[153] The person must also be actively infectious. The key factual determination in *Arline* was whether a teacher was actively contagious and currently capable of transmitting tuberculosis through casual contact.[154]

(c) Probability of risk.

The authority of the public health department to impose restrictions grows as the probability of the risk of transmission increases. The

---

148. *See, e.g.*, United States v. Moore, 846 F.2d 1163 (8th Cir. 1988), *affirming*, 669 F. Supp. 289 (D. Minn. 1987) (holding that the mouth and teeth of an HIV infected person could be regarded as a "dangerous" or "deadly weapon"); Indiana v. Haines, 545 N.E. 2d 834 (Ind. App. 2d Dist. 1989) (reinstating a conviction for "attempted murder" for splattering emergency workers with HIV-contaminated blood).

149. *See, e.g.*, Thomas v. Atascadero Unif. School Dist., 662 F. Supp. 376 (C.D. Cal. 1986) (holding it unlawful to exclude an HIV-infected kindergartner who bit another child and was labelled "aggressive").

150. *See, e.g.*, People v. Dunn, Florida Crim. Case, Assoc. Press release, Sept. 28, 1987 *reported* in Larry Gostin et al., THE AIDS LITIGATION PROJECT, U.S. Govt. Printing Office: Washington D.C. (1990) (convicting prisoner of introducing "contraband" into a state facility by lacing guards' coffee with HIV-contaminated blood). See further discussion of food workers *infra* section II B4. 4).

151. *See* Lawrence Gostin, *The Future of Public Health Law*, 12 AM. J.L. & MED. 461, 467 (1986) (discussing a series of cases with regard to this principle).

152. *Id.* at 480–83; *ex parte* Company, 139 N.E. 204 (1922).

153. Smith v. Emery, 11 A.D. 10, 42 N.Y.S. 258 (1896).

154. Arline, 480 U.S. at 287, n. 16.

probability that a person will transmit disease is a scientific calculation that can be made with relative degrees of confidence. The range of probability that a person will contract hepatitis B virus or HIV from a percutaneous exposure (e.g., a needle stick or cut), for example, is well established by prospective studies.[155] The level of risk from a single sexual relationship is much more difficult to calculate. Substantial probabilities of transmission based upon firm scientific calculations provide the best justification for public health powers.

(d) Severity of harm.
The seriousness of harm to third parties represents an important calculation in public health regulations. In assessing the validity of public health powers, a rough inverse correlation exists between the seriousness of harm and the probability of it occurring. As the seriousness of potential harm to the community rises, the level of risk needed to justify the public health power decreases.

Central to the understanding of the "significant risk" criterion is the fact that even the most serious potential for harm does not justify public health regulation in the absence of a reasonable probability that it will occur. Parents of school children, for example, have difficulty comprehending why courts would uphold the exclusion of children from school who are infested with lice, but not those infected with HIV. The reason is that a very high probability exists that other children will become infested with lice, but that the risk of contracting HIV in that setting is highly remote.

The interaction between probability and severity of risk emerges as a pointedly unresolved issue at the interface of disability law and public health regulation. Consider the application of the "direct threat" standard to an HIV infected health care professional.[156] While the risk of transmitting infection to the professional's patients is highly remote, the consequence to any patient infected is grave. Courts are simply unprepared to respond to this dilemma by the application of a rational set of standards.

The *Leckelt* case showed a fundamental misunderstanding of the

---

155. The range of risk for HIV transmission following a needle stick is between 0.03 and 0.9%, compared with 12–17% for HBV transmission. *See* Lawrence Gostin, *Hospitals, Health Care Professionals, and AIDS: The "Right to Know" the Health Status of Professionals and Patients*, 12 MD. L. REV. at 17.

156. *See generally,* Larry Gostin, *HIV-infected Physicians and the Practice of Secondary Invasive Procedures*, 19 HASTINGS CTR. REP. 32, 32–39 (1989).

relationship between probability and severity of risk by concluding that even though the probability of HIV transmission "may be extremely low . . . there is no cure for HIV or AIDS at this time, and the potential harm of HIV infection is extremely high."[157] If the seriousness of harm were dispositive it would require courts to uphold almost any restriction on a person with AIDS even if the risk were "low, approaching zero."[158]

Again in *Behringer* the court concluded that "(w)here the ultimate harm is death, even the presence of a low risk of transmission justifies the adoption of a policy which precludes invasive procedures when there is 'any' risk of transmission."[159] There, an otolaryngologist was diagnosed with AIDS at the hospital where he enjoyed surgical privileges. The hospital failed to maintain confidentiality of the diagnosis and employees and other members of the community learned of the surgeon's condition. The hospital, recognizing the risk, imposed informed consent requirements on the surgeon, and suspended then barred surgical privileges for the surgeon.[160]

The court held that, under the informed consent doctrine, disclosure of the risk from procedures performed by a surgeon with AIDS was required, as "the ultimate arbiter of whether the patient is to be treated invasively by an AIDS-positive surgeon . . . will be the fully-informed patient."[161] The court found that the hospital, while breaching its duty of confidentiality to the surgeon, acted properly in imposing conditions on the surgeon, practice of medicine at the institution given the "materially enhanced risk" posed by the surgeon and the hospital's legitimate public health purpose of preventing the spread of infection.[162]

---

157. Leckelt v. Board of Comm'ns of Hosp. Dist. No. 1, 909 F2d 820, 1990 U.S. App. LEXIS 14852, at 28–29 (5th Cir. 1990). The court relied more on the fact that Kevin Leckelt refused to follow infection control policy by reporting his contagious conditions and submitting to HIV testing. This led the court to conclude that the reason for his dismissal was not *solely* his handicap. Query, would the court's decision be affected by the ADA language which does not use the word "solely" by reason of his or her disability?

158. Glover v. Eastern Neb. Office of Retardation, 867 F.2d. 461 (8th Cir. 1989) *cert. denied*, 110 S.Ct. 321 (1989) (finding HIV screening of staff in mental retardation facility was unconstitutional because of the exceedingly low risk).

159. Behringer Est. v. Medical Ctr. at Princeton, 592 A.2d 1251, 1283 (1991).

160. *Id.* at 1254.

161. *Id.*

162. *Id.* at 1276.

Likewise, in the more recent *Almarez* case, the court went a step further, permitting recovery for two patients' fear of acquiring AIDS from an HIV-positive surgeon for the period between when the two patients learned of the surgeon's illness and received their own HIV-negative test results. There, the two patients were operated on by a prominent breast cancer surgeon, and later learned through news accounts that the surgeon was HIV-positive.[163]

The court acknowledged that the patients' complaints failed to identify any actual channel of transmission for the AIDS virus, but permitted recovery for fear (and its manifestations in headaches and sleeplessness) nonetheless. The court, however, cut-off recovery for the patients' *continued* fear, reasoning that current, credible scientific evidence indicates that 95% of individuals exposed to HIV will test positive for the antibodies to the virus within six months. The court also found that the HIV-infected surgeon had a duty to warn patients of the risk, and that the hospital might also be liable, under the doctrine of agency, for its failure to control risk.[164]

(e) Human rights burdens.

While human rights burdens are often missing from public health calculations,[165] they are of central importance. The nature, severity, and duration of the personal restrictions must be weighed against the efficacy of the public health power. Substantial public benefit would be required to justify restrictions of great severity and/or duration. A requirement to report an infectious condition to a public health department which maintained strict confidentiality would not impose significant human burdens. A short period of exclusion from school due to infectious measles might similarly be reasonable. On the other hand, isolation for a disease without a finite period of infectiousness would be burdensome both in the degree and the duration of human deprivation. Courts must first determine if the health risk is significant. This ought to be followed by a weighing of efficacy (will the public health power reduce a serious health threat?) and burdens (at what human, social, and economic cost will the public health benefit be achieved?).[166]

---

163. *Id.* at 329.

164. Faya v. Almarez, 620 A. 2d 327 (Md. 1993).

165. The American Medical Association amicus curiae brief in *Arline* is silent as to the impact of public health regulation on individual rights.

166. This balancing of benefits and burdens is further explained in Allan Brandt et al., *Routine Hospital Testing for HIV: Health Policy Considerations, in* LAWRENCE GOSTIN, AIDS AND THE HEALTH CARE SYSTEM, 125–42 (1990).

3. Medical examination and testing: pre- and post-test medical inquiries

The ADA specifies that the prohibition of discrimination against persons with disabilities applies to medical examinations and inquiries.[167] Historically, employers gathered information concerning the applicant's physical and mental condition through application forms, interviews, and medical examinations. This information was often used to exclude persons with disabilities from employment—particularly applicants with hidden disabilities such as epilepsy, emotional illness, cancer, or HIV infection.[168]

Employers used pre-employment medical information to avoid hiring persons with disabilities because of bias or misconceptions about their ability to do the job. As employee health insurance and benefit costs rose to substantial proportions of their annual operating costs, employers were driven to screen out persons who might generate substantial medical bills. Thus, many employers aggressively screened job applicants to avoid paying the health care costs of persons with potentially expensive medical conditions.

These forms of discrimination, although sometimes understandable, have been technically unlawful since the Rehabilitation Act of 1973. Enforcement, however, was exceedingly difficult, since an employer did not have to disclose that the person's disability was the sole reason for the failure to hire. So long as employers were able to conduct extensive medical examinations before offering a job, they could effectively hide the true reason for the employment decision.

The ADA's most radical departure from the Rehabilitation Act is its proscription against pre-offer medical inquiries.[169] Under 42 U.S.C. § 12112(c)(2), employers are prohibited from conducting medical examinations or inquiries into whether a job applicant is disabled. Pre-employment inquiries must be limited to assessing the applicant's ability to perform job-related functions.[170] Thus, employers may not require job applicants to undergo extensive medical examinations and screenings, including testing for communicable diseases such as tuberculosis, AIDS, or hepatitis. This will strictly limit the employer's ability

---

167. 42 U.S.C. § 12112(c)(2)(B) (1992).

168. *See* S. REP. No. 116, *supra* note 113, at 39.

169. For the purposes of the ADA, drug testing is not considered a medical examination, and employers are not prohibited from taking action against a person who is currently engaging in the alleged use of drugs. 42 U.S.C. §§ 12114, 12210 (1992).

170. *Id.* § 12112(c)(2)(B).

to obtain information about a person's current and future illness, diseases, or genetic pre-conditions before a job is offered. From an employer's perspective, it will mean that he or she will be severely limited in holding down health insurance costs by seeking to foresee the future health status of applicants.

The ADA permits an employer to require an entrance examination only after an offer of employment has been made. All entering employees must be subjected to the same examination and the medical information must be kept strictly confidential.[171] Employers also have very limited rights to conduct medical examinations or inquiries after a person is hired. The employer cannot compel an employee to take a medical examination or inquire whether the employee is disabled unless the examination or inquiry is job related and consistent with business necessity.[172]

Congress, in enacting the ADA, recognized that a medical examination or inquiry that is not job related serves no legitimate employment purpose, but simply stigmatizes persons with disabilities.[173] The ADA will significantly impede the growing use of medical testing and information gathering by employers across America, transforming the way the business community makes hiring decisions.

Even though the ADA does not significantly restrict the rights of insurers (including self-insurers) or companies administering benefit plans from underwriting risks, employers are not permitted to deny health insurance or other benefits coverage completely based on a person's diagnosis, prognosis, or disability. All people with disabilities must have equal access to the health insurance coverage provided to all employees. Employers, however, may circumvent testing restrictions by placing a cap or other limit on coverage for certain procedures or treatments for conditions such as AIDS. They may also exclude pre-existing conditions.[174]

While employers are permitted to establish or change plans based upon insurance underwriting principles, they are not allowed to use "subterfuge" to evade the purposes of the ADA (§ 501(c)).[175] In June of 1993, the Equal Opportunity Employment Commission (EEOC)

---

171. *Id.* § 12112(c)(3).

172. *Id.* § 12112(c)(4).

173. S. REP. No. 116, *supra* note 142, at 39, 40.

174. *Id.* at 29.

175. For a more detailed discussion of the antidiscrimination principles that are applicable to health insurance and health benefits packages, *see* Lawrence Gostin & Alan Widiss, *What's Wrong with the ERISA Vacuum? The Case Against*

(*cont.*)

issued interim guidance for enforcement of the ADA in cases of disability-based distinctions in the terms or provisions of employer-provided health insurance plans. The Guidance identifies four requirements under the ADA in the area of health insurance:

> 1. disability-based insurance distinctions are permitted only if the plan is bona fide and if the distinctions are not being used as a subterfuge for purposes of evading the ADA,
> 2. decisions about the employment of an individual with a disability may not be motivated by concerns about the impact of the individual's disability on the employer's health plan,
> 3. employees with disabilities must be accorded equal access to whatever health insurance the employer provides to employees without disabilities, and
> 4. an employer may not make an employment decision about any person, whether or not that person has a disability, because of concerns about the impact on the health plan of the disability of someone with whom that person has a relationship.[176]

The Guidance instructs EEOC investigators to determine whether insurance terms or provisions single out particular disabilities, discrete groups of disabilities, disability in general, or specific procedures or treatments of particular disabilities or groups of disabilities. The burden of proof is placed on the employer to justify the disability-based distinction, as the employer has control of the data relied on to make the disability-based distinction decision. The employer must prove both that the plan is bona fide and that the disability-based distinction is not being used as a subterfuge to evade the purposes of the ADA. Such proof may include actuarial data supporting the employer's decision and rationale, or evidence demonstrating why non-disability-based options were considered and rejected.[177]

(175, *cont.*) *Total Freedom for Employers to Decide What Coverage Is to be Provided When Risk Retention Plans are Established for Health Care*, 19 JAMA 269 (1993).

176. EQUAL OPPORTUNITY EMPLOYMENT COMMISSION, EEOC ISSUES INTERIM ENFORCEMENT GUIDANCE ON THE APPLICATION OF THE ADA TO DISABILITY-BASED PROVISIONS OF EMPLOYER-PROVIDED HEALTH INSURANCE, (June 8, 1993).

177. *Id.* The EEOC's Guidance standards are being tested in a recent case filed by the EEOC against Mason Tenders District Council Trust Fund charging that an amendment to the Fund's health insurance plan violates the ADA by excluding coverage of AIDS-related conditions. Terence Donaghey, a plan participant of the multi-employer trust fund, was denied coverage for his AIDS-related illnesses. The Fund failed to provide any actuarial basis for the AIDS exclusion amendment. Under the EEOC's Guidance, disability-

4. The food handlers controversy and the preemption clause: a federalist approach

A dissenting view in the House Judiciary Committee expressed the concern that a person with AIDS could not be transferred out of a food handling position even if the employer continued to pay the same wages. This would be the "ultimate undue hardship." "Unfortunately, there are many Americans who panic at the mention of the AIDS and would refuse to patronize any food establishment if an employee were known to have the virus." This policy will "translate to no customers and no business at all."[178]

The House Amendment (the "Chapman Amendment"), but not the Senate bill, specified that it shall not be a violation of the ADA for an employer to refuse to assign or continue to assign any employee with an infectious or communicable disease of public health significance to a job involving food handling, provided the employer makes reasonable accommodation to offer a comparable alternative employment opportunity.[179] The House receded to the Senate with the following amendment: The Secretary of Health and Human Services must publish a list of infectious and communicable diseases which are transmitted through handling of the food supply, specifying the methods by which such diseases are transmitted, and widely disseminating the information about the dangers and their modes of transmission.[180]

The ADA authorizes employers to refuse to assign individuals to a job involving food handling if they have a presently infectious condition that is listed as transmissible through the food supply.[181]

---

based exclusions may be found to be subterfuges used to evade the ADA when they are not justified by legitimate risk classification and underwriting procedures. The Fund has filed a motion for summary judgment claiming that ERISA exempts it from the purview of the ADA. The suit is pending in District Court in New York. Equal Opportunity Employment Commission, EEOC FILES LAWSUIT AGAINST INSURANCE PLAN THAT EXCLUDES COVERAGE FOR INDIVIDUAL WITH AIDS, (June 9, 1993). The EEOC won its first judgment under the ADA in June of 1993 (EEOC v. AIC Security Investigations, Ltd., 823 F. Supp. 571 (N.D. Ill. 1993)), and filed two more cases in addition *to Mason Tenders* in Sept., 1993 (EEOC v. H. Hirschfield Sons Co. and EEOC v. Allied Services Division). EEOC ADA Litigation List (Oct., 1993).

178. H.R. REP. No. 485(III), 101st Cong., 2d Sess. 146–47 (1990), *reprinted in* 1990 U.S.C.C.A.N. 445.

179. H.R. CONF. REP. No. 596, 101st Cong., 2d Sess. 12–13 (1990), *reprinted* in 1990 U.S.C.C.A.N. 565.

180. 42 U.S.C. § 12113(d)(1) (1992).

181. *Id.* § 12113(d)(2).

The Chapman Amendment contained the fundamental misconception of disability law that it is permissible to fire an employee if the reason for the discrimination is not the employer's biases, but to protect the business from the irrational fears of patrons. The courts do not allow employers to succumb to wholly unsubstantiated fears of customers as a justification for discrimination, even if this involves picketing of the establishment.[182] Exclusion of HIV-infected food handlers was not condoned under the Rehabilitation Act and state handicap law because of the absence of any evidence that infection could be transmitted through food.[183]

The purpose of the food handlers compromise was to ensure the American public that "valid scientific and medical analysis, using accepted public health methodologies and statistical practices regarding risk of transmission" will be brought to bear in analyzing food-borne transmission of disease.[184] This is the same standard that ought to be applied to future public health decision making.

The food handlers controversy was a largely irrelevant Congressional pandering to the unsubstantiated fears of the public about AIDS. What emerged as a problem of significant import, however, was the interaction between the ADA, and state or municipal public health statutes. Federal laws, unless they specify otherwise, preempt state and local statutes with comparable coverage. The ADA specifies that state or local law which creates "*greater* protection for the rights of individuals with disabilities" is not preempted.[185] The question arises whether public health laws which *restrict* a disabled person's rights more than the ADA allows are preempted. The simple answer is that all state and local public health law which restricts the rights of persons with communicable diseases in ways which are inconsistent with the ADA will be invalidated by federal courts. Although the preemption provision in 42 U.S.C. § 12113(c) applies only to food handlers, it illustrates clearly the interaction of the entire ADA with public health law. That section specifies that state, county, or local law or regulation designed to protect the public health from individuals who pose a significant risk

---

182. Mosby v. Joe's Westlake Restaurant, Cal. Super. Ct., San Francisco County, No. 865045, *reported in* Larry Gostin, *The AIDS Litigation Project: A National Review of Court and Human Rights Commission Decisions; Part II: Discrimination*, 286 JAMA 2086, 2086–93 (1990).

183. *See, e.g.*, Little v. Bryce & Randall's Food Market, 733 F.2d 937 (Tex. App. Hous. 1st Dist. 1987).

184. H.R. Conf. Rep. No. 596, 101st Cong., 2d Sess. 14 (1990).

185. 42 U.S.C. § 12201(b) (1992) (emphasis added).

of contamination of the food supply is not overruled or modified by the ADA.

The House Conference Report emphasizes that section 103(c)(3) "clearly defines certain types of existing and prospective state and local public health laws that are not pre-empted by the ADA."[186] The public health law must be designed to protect the community from significant public health risks which cannot be eliminated by reasonable accommodation. This pre-emption strategy supports legitimate state and local laws and regulations designed to protect the public from communicable disease, thus carrying out "both the letter and the spirit" of the ADA.[187]

The ADA appears to interfere with the classic constitutional principle that the state has sole police power authority to preserve the public health. True federalism, however, provides states with ample authority to regulate public health, but only within national guidelines ensuring that decisions are based upon rigorous public health evidence, rather than on false perception, unsubstantiated fears or pure prejudice. Properly understood, the ADA strikes a constitutional balance that can only generate better and more consistent public health decision making.

III. CONCLUSION: A STANDARD OF PUBLIC HEALTH REVIEW BASED UPON ANTI-DISCRIMINATION PRINCIPLES

The Americans with Disabilities Act emerges as far more effective in reviewing public health powers than deferential constitutional analysis. The standard of review proposed in this paper would place the burden of proof on public health authorities to demonstrate by rigorous scientific assessment: the mode of transmission is well established; the person is currently contagious and is likely to remain so for the duration of the control measure; a reasonable likelihood exists that the person will actually transmit the disease if the control measures are not applied; the transmission of disease may result in serious harm; and the costs and human rights burdens are not disproportionate to the public health benefit to be achieved.

This standard is exacting and requires the public health department to have a clear basis for the exercise of its powers. The reason for the

---

186. H.R. CONF. REP. No. 596, 101st Cong., 2d Sess. 17–18 (1990).
187. Id.

more focused review is that the ADA restates the fundamental question that courts must ask of public health regulators. No longer must the courts ask what risks an uninformed, perhaps prejudiced, public is prepared to tolerate. Instead, courts should inquire whether there is sufficiently convincing evidence of harm to the public to justify discrimination against a person with disabilities. Once the issue is framed as coming within the corpus of anti-discrimination law, rather than the vague and undifferentiated traditions of the police powers, a whole new way of thinking about public health law becomes possible.

Racist health care: reforming an unjust health care system to meet the needs of African-Americans*

Vernellia R. Randall

"Racist" and "racism" are provocative words in American society. To some, these words have reached the level of curse words in their offensiveness. Yet, "racist" and "racism" are descriptive words of a reality that cannot be denied.[1] Ethnic Americans[2] live daily with the

---

*Nothing is ever done in isolation. The success of this project is due in large measure to the unwavering support of many individuals. I am thankful to Maxwell J. Mehlman, Director, Law-Medicine Center, Case Western Reserve University School of Law, and Dean Francis Conte, University of Dayton for financial support needed to complete this project. I am grateful to my colleagues Professors Vincene Verdun, Patricia Rousseau, Sean Murray and Teri Geiger for their thoughtful comments on a draft manuscript. I especially want to acknowledge the prompt and untiring research, comments, and help of research assistants Joy Walker and Lisa Feelings. I must acknowledge my sons, Tshaka Civunje and Issa Lateef, whose support and confidence kept me going.

1. *See generally* STOKELY CARMICHAEL & CHARLES E. HAMILTON, BLACK POWER: THE POLITICS OF LIBERATION IN AMERICA 2–32 (1967) (detailing the effect of race relations on African-Americans politically, socially, and economically in the United States. "[Racism] has represented daily reality to millions of black people for centuries, yet it is rarely defined perhaps just because that reality has been such commonplace." *Id.* at 3.)

2. The remainder of this paper will refer primarily to African-Americans because my academic research focuses on African-Americans. However, it is important to

(cont.)

Justice and Health Care: Comparative Perspectives. Edited by A. Grubb and M.J. Mehlman. © 1995 John Wiley & Sons Ltd.

effects of both institutional and individual racism. Race issues are so fundamental in American society that they seem almost an integral component. Some Americans believe that race is the primary determinant of human abilities and capacities.[3] Some Americans behave as if racial differences produce inherent superiority in European-Americans.[4] In fact, such individuals respond to African-Americans[5] and European-

---

(2, *cont.*) note that other ethnic Americans (Native-Americans, Latino-Americans, Asian-Americans) have similar or greater health care access problems and are similarly plagued by the effects of institutional racism in the health care system.

3. *See generally* R. J. Hernstein, *Still An American Dilemma*, 98 PUB. INTEREST 3–17 (1990) (criticizing the methods and conclusions of A COMMON DESTINY: BLACKS AND AMERICAN SOCIETY (1989) for ignoring the possibility that different outcomes, between African-Americans and European-Americans may be the product of psychological and intelligence differences between the two races. The author argues that costs to society of attempting to benefit African-American disproportionately may outweigh the benefits); RONALD TAKAKI, BRAINS OVER MUSCLES: THE MEANING OF INTELLIGENCE AND RACE IN AMERICAN HISTORY (1984) (explaining how intelligence has been viewed historically in the United States, and how the "idea of intelligence" has "influenced and been influenced by the idea of race in American history."); *See also* PAUL R. EHRLICH & SHIRLEY FELDMAN, THE RACE BOMB: SKIN COLOR, PREJUDICE, & INTELLIGENCE (1977); ANDRE JOSEPH, INTELLIGENCE, IQ & RACE: WHEN, HOW & WHY THEY BECOME ASSOCIATED (1977); DANIEL LAWRENCE, RACE, INTELLIGENCE AND CULTURE (1975) (reviewing critical books published between 1969 and 1974 in Great Britain and the United States that support the idea of racial differences in intelligence); ELIZABETH WATTS, RACIAL DIFFERENCES IN INTELLIGENCE: AN ANTHROPOLOGICAL APPROACH, HUMAN MOSAIC 47–53 (1973–1974) (discussing controversial views concerning the existence of population differences in mental ability); Josephine Schuyler, *Race, Diet and Intelligence*, 76 CRISIS 207–10 (1969) (criticizing Arthur R. Jensen of the University of California who holds that intelligence is determined by heredity).

4. In a national poll, when asked, "What are your personal feelings about ... people who believe whites are racially superior to all other races" 1% were extremely favorable, 4% were favorable and 23% were neither favorable or unfavorable. *National Opinion Research Center* February, 1990 *available* in Westlaw, Poll (Sept. 1993).

5. For purposes of this Article, I use the term "African-American" as a synonym for the terms "colored," "Negro," "Afro- American," and "Black."

The predicament of African-Americans cannot be overstated. We arrived as *"Africans"* and were slaves to be sold. We were given Anglo names and became their *"negroes"*—their property. After Reconstruction there was a push by African-American leaders to give dignity to the name by capitalizing it. So *"negroes"* became *"Negroes"*. Even still, in the 1900 *"Colored"* competed with *"Negroes"*. Many thought that *"colored"* showed that we were no longer possessions. *"Afro-American"* was first proposed in 1880, but it never caught on. Through the social unrest of the 1960s we became *"Blacks"*. We wanted

Americans[6] differently merely of race.[7] As a consequence, many African-Americans are injured by judgments or actions that are directly or
indirectly racist.

respect. We wanted opportunity. We wanted to be proud of our heritage. The
change to "*African-American*" denotes double consciousness and dual cultural
heritage. It comes close to describing who we are as a people. *See generally*,
Jewell Holmes Guinn, *From African to Black, An American Evolution*, PHOENIX
GAZETTE, Feb. 27, 1989.

Each change in label represents a change in attitudes of African-Americans
toward ourselves and toward others. Ultimately, the changing names of descend-
ants of African slaves represent a continuing struggle by us to gain the power
to define ourself. It represents a struggle to gain social and political power.
While powerful groups do not appear to care about how they are labeled (i.e.
Americans of British descent and Jews), powerless groups frequently try to
relabel themselves. Powerful groups who are unwilling to give up power often
meet these efforts with ridicule and hostility. "The power to name is frequently
also the power to define. The power to name a group can be the power to
position it socially and politically". Charles Paul Freud, *Rhetorical Questions: The
Power of, and Behind, a Name*, WASH. POST, Feb. 7, 1989, at A23.

6. I use the term "European-Americans" to denote individuals usually called
"white". Historically, ethnic Americans have been designated in a hyphenated
name: "Black-Americans", "Asian-Americans", "Native-Americans", "Hispanic-Americans". Presumption seeming to be that you would know that these
individuals would not be recognized as Americans unless we designate them
as such. On the other hand, "white" persons need no designation because they
are presumed to be Americans. Consequently, linguistically "white" persons
maintain a position of power.

White people didn't bother to define themselves racially in any particular way
until rather recently. According to usage historian Stuart Berg Flexner, general
references to 'white men' entered the language only in the 1830s, and didn't
gain wide usage until the Civil War. What did whites call themselves until then?
They called themselves "people" or "citizens." In other words, they occupied,
unchallenged, the center of their racial universe, and needed no further
definition of the sort assigned to such outsiders as Indian "savages" or black
slaves. "White" became an important term at the time of Emancipation; a
reaction to the power threat presented by another racial group.

See, e.g., Freud, *supra* note 5, at A23.

Similarly, I reject the designation of "minorities" because of its connotation
of subordination. It would be "nice" if no designations at all were needed, but
the reality of the situation requires us to discuss the needs of specific ethnic
groups. I used the term European-American rather than Anglo-Saxon to
provide balance with the other designations; that is, designations which
identify the geographic region from which the original ancestors migrated.

7. *See generally* Andy Dabilis, *Racial episodes decried in Medford, Winchester*,
BOSTON GLOBE, Jan. 16, 1993, at 34 (maintaining "We're for the white race.
We believe in separation because mixing doesn't work, We are miles apart in
(cont.)

Much of the attention of the last 20 years has focused on individual racist behavior.[8] However, just as individuals can act in racist ways, so

---

(7, *cont.*) culture and intelligence. They are a couple of notches below us."); MICHAEL KRONENWETTER, UNITED THEY HATE: WHITE SUPREMACISTS IN AMERICA (1992); Jill Hodges, *A Surge of Hate: Number of Racist Incidents on rise* STAR TRIB., Feb. 2, 1992, at 1B; John Carmody, *Is U.S. Racist?*, LOS ANGELES TIMES, Feb. 12, 1990, at P7, P8, C6 (surveying 204 stories about race relations that were aired on the three major networks shows that one out of three sources interviewed said America is racist); *The Doug Wilder Solution*, WASH. TIMES, Jan. 11, 1990, at F2 (asserting that the United States has gotten itself into a first- class race-relations mess because many otherwise intelligent, decent, good-hearted people have dedicated their lives to giving moral and legal force to racial stereotypes); Jonathan Kaufman, *The Color Line*, BOSTON GLOBE, June 18, 1989, at 16 (maintaining that whites have become disillusioned with blacks and lack interest in race relation); KEVIN FLYNN & GARY GERHARDT, THE SILENT BROTHERHOOD: INSIDE AMERICA'S RACIST UNDERGROUND (1989) (asserting that the movement has gathered a large majority of ordinary people. They see the underground's survivalist creed as the way whites can protect their race from "living off of welfare"); Mary Katherine Joeckel, *A Critical Study of Ideologies of Women in Contemporary White Supremacy*, Dissertation, The University of Nebraska—Lincoln (1989) (maintaining that white supremacy is enjoying a new era of appeal in the United States. Today's white supremacists differ from their ancestors in that they agitate for demolition of rather than changes in the existing social order); C. N. Hallman, L. F. Lister, *White Supremacy and its Associated Groups: An Associated Bibliography*, 17 REFERENCE SERVICES REV. 7–18 (1989) (reviewing recent scholarly and popular periodical literature, as well as recent books, reports, and curriculum guides about white supremacy and white supremacist groups in the U.S. Included are reports on the Ku Klux Klan, and neo-Nazi groups like Aryan Nation, and skinheads); Courtland Mulley, *Racism Alive, Thriving*, WASH. POST, May 23, 1985, at D1 (maintaining that race relations, is a matter of overwhelming concern among these African-Americans. The students raised questions about reports they had heard about the Aryan Nation and the rise of white supremacist groups and racial violence).

In a national poll, when asked "In general, how do you think people in the United States feel about people of other races?", 35% indicated that many white persons disliked blacks and 2% indicated that almost all white persons disliked blacks. *Gallup Poll*, May 10, 1992. On another question, when told that "on the average (negroes/blacks) have worse jobs, income, and housing than white people" and asked if they thought these differences were due to discrimination 40% said yes. *National Opinion Research Center*, April 1991.

8. *See generally*, John T. Harvey, *Institutions and the Economic Welfare of Black Americans in the 1980s*, 25 J. ECON. ISSUES 115–35 (1991) (explaining that the overall system that has developed since the civil rights movement has taken racism underground. The growing black underclass is still trapped in a circle of discrimination); Darnell F. Hawkins, *The "Discovery" of Institutional Racism: An*

can institutions. Institutions can behave in ways that are overtly racist (i.e., specifically excluding African-Americans from services) or inherently racist (i.e., adopting policies that while not specifically directed at excluding African-Americans, nevertheless result in their exclusion). Therefore, institutions can respond to African-Americans and European-Americans differently. Institutional behavior can injure African-Americans; and, when it does, it is nonetheless racist in outcome if not in intent.

I. INTRODUCTION

Health care reform is a major initiative in the United States today. The concern regarding health care is widely discussed and recorded in literature that includes books, articles, and editorials.[9] Most of the

---

Example of *the Interaction Between Law and Social Science*, 6 RES IN. RACE & ETHNIC REL. 167–82 (1991) (discussing public policy implications of the distinction between individual and institutionalized forms of racial bias in the 1990s); Richard Lowy, *Yuppie Racism: Race Relations in the 1980's*, 21 J. BLACK STUDIES 445–64 (1991) (maintaining that Yuppie racism refers to the assumption by young urban professionals that the civil rights movement of the 1960s has corrected racial injustice in the US. The author argues that racism remains a major problem because young adults are ignorant of history and perpetuate the structural inequalities in American society); Benjamin P. Bowser, *Race Relations in the 1980s: The Case of the United States*, 15 J. BLACK STUDIES 307–24 (1985) (asserting that contrary to many social scientists' assumptions, ending overt prejudice and legislated segregation has not assured racial equality in the United States. Studies show how discrimination serves white self-interest as elite white groups protect their historic privilege through institutional racism and internal colonialism); Jenny Williams, *Redefining Institutional Racism, in* ETHNIC AND RACIAL STUDIES 323–48 (1985) (arguing that the historical use of the term "institutional racism" is a simplistic and misleading label for a complex situation); Eugene Victor Wolfenstein, *Race, Racism and Racial Liberation*, 30 W. POL. Q. 163–82 (1977) (maintaining that institutional racism results when the charismatic group effect is routinized. Racial conflict of this sort prevents black and white workers from uniting); Charles S. Bullock, Harrell R. Rodgers Jr., *Institutional Racism: Prerequisites, Freezing and Mapping* 37(3) PHYLON 212–23 (1976) (arguing that even though blatant forms of discrimination have been banned by law, subtle forms continue to exist. Discrimination still persists especially through the use of institutional subordination); Terry Jones, *Institutional Racism in the United States*, 19 SOC. WORK 218–25 (1974) (examining the concept of institutional racism and some of the ways that these systems develop and maintain themselves).

9. For instance, according to the computerized legal search program Nexis, between January 1, 1990 and August 30, 1991 there was more than 6000 articles which discuss health care reform.

discussion focuses on reforming health care to control cost or to provide better access. Very little of that discussion observes the needs of persons of color, in general, and African-Americans, in particular.[10]

The need to focus specific attention on African-American health care and health care reform is overwhelming. Not only are African-Americans sicker than European-Americans, they are dying at a significantly higher rate.[11] These are undisputed facts. This disparity in health care has the effect of precluding African-Americans from gaining full access to the economic system. Decent health is a precursor to getting the other attributes, such as money, education, contacts, know-how, necessary to exploit the American system to full advantage. When people are sick and poor, they are just as enslaved as if the law made them so.[12]

Factors affecting health include socioeconomic status, biology, and environment. Yet, in a racist society such as ours, the effect of race is all-encompassing. Race not only affects socioeconomic status, biology, and physical environment; it also affects the way health care institutions function to provide services. Independent of economics, race affects access to care. Independent of economics, race affects the type and quality of health care treatment received. Consequently, to improve the health of African-Americans, it is not sufficient merely to remove economic barriers to access. To improve the health of African-Americans, health care institutions must be more than affordable. They must be just.[13] If we want justice in health care for African-Americans, then

---

10. During the same period mentioned *infra*, only forty articles mention minority interests and its relationship to health care reform.

11. *See* text *infra* section II.F and notes accompanying footnotes.

12. *See generally* NORMAN DANIELS, JUST HEALTH CARE (1985) (arguing that health care is of special moral importance because it affects an individual's share of the range of opportunities normal for his society).

13. Distributive justice involves the dissemination of social goods or ills. To have distributive justice, not only should like cases be treated the same but unlike cases should be treated differently. However, there must be a morally relevant reason for treating people differently. A "just" society is one in which, at a minimum, a person can take advantage of the "normal" range of lifetime opportunities in that society. Since individuals must have "normal species-typical functioning" to avail themselves of that normal range of opportunities. A just society would assure access to some basic level of services and assure that those services are provided in a culturally sensitive non-discriminatory manner. *See, e.g.*, NORMAN DANIELS, *supra* note 12, at 1–17 (arguing that health care should be distributed more equally than other social goods); P. MENZEL, MED. COSTS, MORAL CHOICES: A PHILOSOPHY OF HEALTH CARE ECONOMICS IN

every effort must be made to design a system that provides needed health care by assuring complete access and by eliminating institutional racism. Consequently, a just health care system will focus on eliminating the disparity in health care between African-Americans and European-Americans. Several policy approaches can be taken to deal with this issue: (1) expanding insurance coverage, (2) targeting special health services to African-Americans, and/or (3) using Title VI of the Civil Rights Act of 1964[14] to eliminate racist practices in health care delivery and health care education.

This paper evaluates these policy options and the feasibility of reforming an unjust health care system to meet the needs of African-Americans. Part II explores the disparity between the health status of African-Americans and European-Americans Part III discusses the health care system and the manifestations of institutional racism. Part IV analyzes selected policy options for making the health care system more just.

II. DISPARITY IN AFRICAN-AMERICAN AND EUROPEAN-AMERICAN HEALTH STATUS

Negroes (or African-Americans) have been subject to victimization in the sense that a system of social relations operates in such a way as to deprive them of a chance to share in the more desirable material and nonmaterial products of a society which is dependent, in part, upon their labor and loyalty. They are 'victimized' also, because they do not have the same degree of access which others have to the attributes needed for rising in the general class system—money, education, contacts, know-how [and Health].[15]

AMERICA 85 (1983) (emphasizing that if health care is a necessity, it should be realistically accessible to all, including those who cannot easily afford it); Buchanan, *The Right to a Decent Minimum of Health Care*, 13 PHIL. & PUB. AFF. 55, 55 (1984) (maintaining that there is at least a right to a decent minimum of health care); Norman Daniels, *Health Care Needs and Distributive Justice, in* IN SEARCH OF EQUITY: HEALTH NEEDS AND THE HEALTH CARE SYSTEM 1 (1983), *reprinted in* 10 PHIL. & PUB. AFF. 146, 146 (1981) (recognizing a generally held belief that health care is "special", and should be treated differently from other social goods).

14. Civil Rights Act of 1964, Title VI, Pub. L. No. 99–352, 378 252 (codified at 42 U.S.C. §§ 2000d–200d–4 (1982).

15. LOUIS L. KNOWLES & KENNETH PREWITT, INSTITUTIONAL RACISM IN AMERICA 1 (1969) (*quoting* ST. CLAIR DRAKE).

Full participation in a society requires money, education, contacts, know-how and health.[16] Health is not only significant in itself, but it also affects availability of and decisions regarding choices throughout one's life.[17]

> For example, lack of prenatal care leads to greater likelihood of infant death, neurological damage, or developmental impairment; childhood illnesses and unhealthy conditions can reduce learning potential; adolescent childbearing, substance abuse and injuries cause enormous personal, social and health effects; impaired health or chronic disability in adults contributes to low earning capacity and unemployment; chronic poor health among older adults can lead to premature retirement and loss of ability for self-care and independent living.[18]

Thus, health status is an important ingredient in a person's "social position,... present and future well-being,"[19] and a critical one for African-Americans. When one is born poor, with limited opportunity for quality education and with the burden of racism, one's "good" health becomes the only fungible asset. Understanding the nature of African-Americans, health, is critical to appreciating the racist nature of health care institutions.

Health is a complex concept that is difficult to measure.[20] The difficulty in assessing one's health may result, in part, from a general inability to conceptualize good health. In addition, widespread professional disagreement over the meaning of health contributes to the difficulty in measuring it.[21]

The World Health Organization defines health as "... a state of complete physical, mental, and social well-being and not merely the absence of disease or infirmity."[22] However, for African-Americans

---

16. See *infra* text accompanying notes 20–30.

17. NATIONAL RESEARCH COUNCIL, A COMMON DESTINY: BLACKS AND AMERICAN SOCIETY 393 (Gerald D. Jaynes & Robin M. Williams eds., 1989).

18. *Id.*

19. *Id.*

20. See US DEPT. OF HEALTH & HUMAN SERVICES, HEALTH STATUS OF MINORITIES AND LOW INCOME GROUPS: THIRD EDITION 5–8 (1991) (exploring different facets of health care that affect the overall health of minorities and low income groups).

21. One reason the definition presents a problem is that the professionals tend to use such subjective measures to define health.

22. Woodrow Jones, Jr. & Mitchell F. Rice, *Black Health Care: An Overview,* in HEALTH CARE ISSUES IN BLACK AMERICA: POLICIES, PROBLEMS AND PROSPECTS 3, 4 (Woodrow Jones, Jr. & Mitchell F. Rice eds., 1987) (*quoting*

that definition has little validity. Given the fact that the pervasive nature of racism in American society affects African-Americans at all economic levels, there cannot be "complete...mental and social well-being"[23] for African-Americans until the problem of racism in society is addressed and resolved.

Health is also defined as a "lifestyle in which an individual attempts to maintain balance and to remain free from physical incapacity while maximizing social capacity."[24] That definition currently has more validity for African-Americans because it recognizes that an individual's life style impacts health and that life style is influenced by social class. It recognizes that African-Americans, surrounded by racism, cannot strive for complete mental well-being, but can strive to maintain a balance. The definition recognizes that what the African-American must do to maintain balance and remain free from physical incapacity will be different from what is required of the European-American. For instance, recent discussions regarding hypertension among African-Americans hypothesize that the ongoing continued stress of living in a racist society may be a significant factor in the development of hypertension. If this is true, then a life style of dieting and exercise (recommended preventive activity for hypertension) would not be sufficient to prevent hypertension in African-Americans although it might suffice for European-Americans.

Whatever the definition of health, generally speaking, "health" refers to the presence or absence of disease. Using that definition of health, there are several ways to determine health: by direct observations, records, and self-report.[25] Each of these ways of measuring health presents its own measurement problems. First, inaccuracies can occur in direct observations because medical practices and diagnostic labeling may vary. That variation may be not only by geographic area but by physician and hospital.[26] Second, interpretation errors can result if researchers misinterpret symptoms and results, or when researchers

---

John Romano, *Basic Orientation and Education of the Medical Student*, 143 JAMA 411 (1950))

23. *Id.*

24. *Id.*

25. Ronald M. Andersen et al. *Black-White Differences in Health Status: Methods or Substance?, in* HEALTH POLICIES AND BLACK AMERICANS 72, 75 (D. Willis ed., 1989).

26. *Id.* at 75–76. *See generally* RONALD M. ANDERSON ET AL., TOTAL SURVEY ERROR: APPLICATIONS TO IMPROVE HEALTH SURVEYS (1979).

inappropriately generalize based on a condition of another time or a more general population group.[27] Finally, failure to consider intra-ethnic diversity[28] may lead to erroneous conclusions about African-American health.[29]

Whatever the difficulty in measuring health status, understanding the full extent of differences in health between African-Americans and European-Americans is essential to appreciate fully the need for reform in the health care system and to understand inadequacies in current reform approaches that ignore, dismiss, or do not recognize these difference. To describe the health status of African-American, this paper presents research on the amount of dissatisfaction, discomfort, disability, disease, low birth weight, and death that occurs in the African-American population as compared to the European-American population.[30]

A. Health status: African-Americans' dissatisfaction

Dissatisfaction is the degree of discontentment a person has with his or her health.[31] As a measure of health, it is assumed that a person who has poor health will be more dissatisfied overall than a person with

---

27. Andersen et al., *supra* note 25, at 76.

28. Differences among African-Americans.

29. *Id.*; *see also* J.J. Jackson, *Urban Black Americans, in* ETHNICITY AND MEDICAL CARE 37–129 (A. Harewood eds., 1981) (noting that studies need to account for potentially large differences between northern and southern blacks, urban and rural blacks, native and foreign-born blacks).

30. D.L. Patrick and J. Elinson, *Methods of Sociomedical Research, in* HANDBOOK OF MED. SOC. 437–59 (H. Freeman et al. eds., 1979). Articles discussing health status of African-Americans often only utilize death rates. I attempt to utilize a broad range of health status measurements to give the reader a more thorough view of African-American health status and a broader basis for assessments. Although more complete, such an approach raises some conflicts. Some of the more subjective measurements don't always support a position that African-Americans have "poorer" health status than European-Americans. While it is the position of this paper that African-Americans suffer from a "poorer" health status, the contradictory results of subjective measurements do not disprove the thesis of this paper. In fact these apparent discrepancies are important in that they show subjective reporting differences and the problem institutions will face if they rely only on subjective data for health status analysis.

31. Dissatisfaction information is collected by means of population surveys, individual and household surveys, and surveys of hospitalized patients. Andersen et al., *supra* note 25, at 81.

good health. Because it relies on this self-evaluation, dissatisfaction is the *most* subjective of the health measurements. In fact, the reasons for dissatisfaction with health vary not only based on an individual's situation, but also on ethnicity, race, and culture. Consequently, it is subject to many potential interpretive errors.[32]

Nevertheless, 17% of African-Americans report their health as fair or poor compared to 9% of European-Americans.[33] That is, 88.8% more African-Americans than European-Americans reported their health as fair or poor.[34] Similarly, 50% more African-Americans than European-Americans report themselves as having some, little, or no satisfaction with their health and physical condition.[35] Notwithstanding interpretive errors, these figures reflect a significant difference between African-Americans' and European-Americans' dissatisfaction with their health.

B. Health status: African-Americans' discomfort

Discomfort is the level of such feelings as aches and pains, tiredness, and sadness experienced by an individual.[36] As for dissatisfaction, this information is obtained through self-reporting and is subject to

---

32. *Id.*

33. *Id.* at 82–83.

34. The excess percentage is calculated by dividing the European-American rate into the African-American rate multiplying by 100 and substracting 100. For example, to obtain the 1987 excess death rate for both sexes you divide the European-American death rate (511.1 per 100,000) into the African-American death rate (778.6 per 100,000) to obtain 1.5234. You multiply 1.5234 by 100 to obtain 152.34%; and you subtract 100 to obtain the excess death rate of 52.34%.

The disparity in perception of health status is present in all age groups. To illustrate this point consider that the percentage of African-Americans between the age of five and seventeen who assessed their health status as fair or poor was 4.2%, while the percentage of European-Americans in that same age range and making the same assessment was only 2.1%. IRENE JILLSON-BOOSTROM, SHATTERED HOPES, ENDANGERED LIVES: THE HEALTH AND WELL-BEING OF ADOLESCENT MINORITY MALES IN THE UNITED STATES. A REPORT PREPARED FOR THE OFFICE OF MINORITY HEALTH (Sept. 30, 1990).

35. Andersen et al., *supra* note 25, at 83 (*quoting* National Opinion Research Center, 1985). Twelve percent of African Americans compared to 8% of European-Americans report "some, little, or no satisfaction" with their health and physical condition. *Id.*

36. *Id.* at 80.

considerable measurement error.[37] Surveyors asked individuals to check fifteen symptoms that were (or were not) experienced in the last year. Some symptoms related to the various body systems representing both acute and chronic problems. Some symptoms were common experiences such as sore throat or runny nose. Other symptoms were infrequent and often associated with serious problems such as the loss of more than ten pounds in weight. The mean number of symptoms reported represents the score for a population group.[38]

Measuring health status by the results of reported discomfort surveys presented some interesting results. One such result is that African-Americans under 45 years of age actually reported *fewer* symptoms than European-Americans.[39] There are several ways to interpret this result. The most obvious is that the African-American age group, in fact, has fewer and less severe symptoms. However, that interpretation would be at variance with results of studies based on more objective measurements, i.e., death rates.[40] A second interpretation of this interesting result is that there is considerable underreporting among African-Americans, particularly of the more serious symptoms.[41] That

---

37. *Id.*

38. *Id.* at 81.

39. *Id.* at 83 (*quoting* Center for Health Administration Studies, University of Chicago, unpublished data study described in ANDERSEN ET AL., AMBULATORY CARE AND INSURANCE COVERAGE IN AN ERA OF CONSTRAINT, Ch. 6 and app. A (1987)). During 1985, African-Americans in the age group under 18 reported 0.4 symptoms per person per year while European-Americans reported 0.6 symptoms resulting in a –33.3% excess discomfort. *Id.* In the age group 18–44, African-Americans reported 1.1 symptoms per person per year while European-Americans reported 1.3 symptoms resulting in a –15.4% excess discomfort for African-Americans. *Id.* African-Americans 45–64 years old reported 1.9 symptoms per person per year while European-Americans reported 1.7 symptoms resulting in a 11.8% excess discomfort for African-Americans. *Id.* Finally, African-Americans over 65 reported 2.1 symptoms per person per year while European-Americans reported 2.0 symptoms resulting in a 5% excess discomfort for African-Americans. *Id.*

40. Death rates include homicide rates since death by means of violence is considered a public health issue. *See infra* note 71.

41. There are a number of reasons why African-Americans might under-report symptoms. First, in a culture that has limited access to health care, it might be viewed as futile to complain about "aches and pains." Second, African-Americans may actually expect some "aches and pains" as normal and not a sign of illness. Third, African-Americans may be reluctant to complain to a stranger about their health. While all these reasons can be articulated by other populations subgroups, it may be that given the impact of racism, African-Americans are more reluctant than others to complain about their health and/or to seek help.

interpretation is strengthened by a finding that once African-Americans with symptoms are in the health care system, they require more visits than their European-American counterparts.[42] Thus, it is more likely that the underreporting of symptoms contributes to an inaccurate reflection of health status.

C. Health status: African-Americans' disability

Health status based on disability can be defined as the inability to engage in gainful employment; or as the temporary or long-term reduction of a person's activities because of a health condition.[43] Health researchers generally use three measurements of disabilities: restricted activity days, work loss days and bed disability days.[44] This paper uses restricted activity days as a measure of health status since restricted activity days is a broader measurement than work loss days, and work loss days would not necessarily include unemployed individuals. It is also broader than bed disability days, since an individual could be sick enough to have many activities restricted without necessarily being confined to bed.

As in the other measurements, using restricted activity days to represent health status can lead to significant interpretive error. First, there are a number of reasons a person may lose workdays. Employees may take sick days to stay home with a sick child; children may miss school for physician appointments; and, people may falsely claim disability to collect insurance money.[45] Second, instead of being a measure of disease, disability may be more a measure of morale and conformity.[46] Despite the risk of interpretive error, restricted activity days are accepted as a general measure of health status.

Using the number of days of restricted activity per year, African-Americans under age five have no extraordinary disability. This outcome is entirely predictable since a child under five is involved in

---

42. Andersen et al., *supra* note 25, at 95; Joanna Kravitis & John Schneider, *Health Care Need and Actual Use by Age, Race and Income, in* EQUITY IN HEALTH SERVICES, 186 (R. Andersen et al., 975).

43. Andersen et al., *supra* note 25, at 80.

44. *Id.*

45. *Id.*; *See generally,* Patrick & Elinson, *supra* note 30, at 437–59 (H. Freeman et al. eds., 1979).

46. Andersen et al., *supra* note 25, at 80 *citing* D.L. Patrick & J. Elinson, *Methods of Sociomedical Research, in* HANDBOOK OF MEDICAL SOCIOLOGY 437–59 (H. Freeman et al. eds., 1979).

neither school nor work. What is not predictable is the 22.8% fewer restricted activity days for African-Americans in the age group 5–17.[47] Given the higher death rate[48] and disease rate[49] of African-Americans to that of European-Americans in this age group, it is likely that this difference is either an interpretation[50] or reporting error. This assessment of error would seem particularly true since African-Americans in the 18-and-over age group reported 37.5% more days of activity restriction per year than European-Americans.[51]

D. Health status: African-Americans' disease rate

Health status may also be based on the presence of which disease can be divided into acute conditions[52] and chronic conditions.[53] The most

---

47. *Id.* at 83, *quoting* National Health Statistics 1985, Table 69.

48. African-Americans have higher death rates for every age group except 85 years and older. The African-American to European-American death ratio for 1–4 years old is 1.80, for 5–9 years it is 1.62, for 10–14 years it is 1.25 and for 15–19 years it is 1.04 *See* U.S. DEPT. OF HEALTH & HUMAN SERVICES, *supra* note 20, Table 16 at 30.

49. It is interesting to note that when looking at the number of school-loss days associated with acute conditions per 100 youths aged 5–17, African-Americans had 427.2 days whereas European-Americans had 322 days. National Center for Health Statistics, CURRENT ESTIMATES FROM THE NATIONAL HEALTH INTERVIEW SURVEY, 1988D.

50. For example, the 5–17 year old age group could in fact have more illness but fewer restricted days because of cultural differences. African-American culture tends to encourage individuals to continue activity despite illness. This is especially true for children since families may not afford to take the child to the doctor or to take off work to stay at home with a sick child. Thus, it could be that African-American children are actually encouraged to continue activities despite illness.

51. Andersen et al., *supra* note 25, at 83 *quoting* National Center for Health Statistics, 1985, Table 69. African-Americans under 5 had the same number of days of restricted activity (9 days) as European-Americans. *Id.* African-Americans between the age of 5 and 17 reported fewer (7 days) of restricted activity than European-Americans (9 days) resulting in an excess disability for African-Americans of −22.2%. *Id.* Finally, African-Americans over 18 reported more (22 days) of restricted activity than European-Americans (16 days) resulting in an excess disability for African-Americans of 37.5%. *Id.*

52. Acute conditions are those diseases or injuries that last less than two weeks. Commonly, those diseases reported as acute conditions are respiratory problems such as colds and minor injuries. Andersen et al., *supra* note 25, at 85.

53. Chronic conditions are those conditions that have lasted two weeks or longer. Chronic conditions include diseases or impairments that are likely to be irreversible. These diseases range from the major killers such as heart

common method of determining the presence of disease in a population is by reviewing hospital medical records.[54] When measuring
African-American health based on reported acute conditions,[55] it would
appear that African-American health is better than that of European-
Americans. For the age group under 18, 36.3% fewer African-Americans
than European-Americans reported acute health conditions; for the
18–44 age group, 15.9% fewer African-Americans than European-
Americans reported acute conditions; and, for ages 45 and above,
10.1% reported fewer conditions.[56] Interestingly, despite the seemingly
lower incidence of acute diseases among African-Americans, they have
a higher mortality rate from acute conditions than European-Americans have.[57]

The percentage calculated for limitations in activity due to chronic
diseases is higher in African-Americans than in European-Americans
for all age groups.[58] For instance, for the under-18 age group, 20%
more African-Americans than European-Americans reported limitations in activity because of chronic disease; for the 18–44 age group,

---

disease to others less likely to kill but which can result in considerable
debilitation such as arthritis. Andersen et al., *supra* note 25, at 84.

54. Like other records, hospital medical record also have their deficiencies.
For example, because not all illnesses are covered in medical records, the
records may present a biased picture of the illnesses of a population due to
non-coverage of all illnesses. *Id.* at 79. *See generally* Kravitis & Schneider, *supra*
note 42, at 169–87.

55. Andersen et al., *supra* note 25, at 83 *quoting* National Center for Health
Statistics, 1985, table 3. CURRENT ESTIMATES FROM THE NATIONAL HEALTH
INTERVIEW SURVEY, 1985, series 10, no. 160. African-Americans under 18 had
fewer acute conditions (183 per 100 persons per year) than European-Americans (283 per 100 persons per year) resulting in an excess disease-acute
conditions of –36.3%. *Id.* African-Americans 18–44 had fewer acute conditions
(130 per 100 persons per year) than European-Americans (174 per 100 persons
per year) resulting in an excess disease-acute conditions of –15.9%. *Id.*
African-Americans 18–44 had fewer acute conditions (98 per 100 persons per
year) than European-Americans (109 per 100 persons per year) resulting in an
excess disease-acute conditions of –10.1%. *Id.*

56. *Id.*

57. *See* US DEPT OF HEALTH & HUMAN SERVICES, *supra* note 20, at 154–57.
For instance, African-American males have 58% more deaths from pneumonia
than European-American males. African-American females have 26% more
deaths from pneumonia than European-American females. *Id.* at 155–56
(Tables 23 and 24).

58. Chronic diseases can be divided into those which limit activities and
those that do not. As a measurement of severity, those chronic diseases that
limit activity are more severe.

22.5% more African-Americans than European-Americans reported limitations; in the 45–64 age group, 34.8% more African-Americans than European-Americans reported limitations; and in the 65–69 age group, 31.6% more African-Americans reported limitations than European-Americans. Finally, in the 70-and-over age group, 23.8% more African-Americans than European-Americans reported limitations.[59] Therefore, while African-Americans report fewer acute conditions, they tend to report more limitations based on chronic conditions.

E. Health status: African-Americans' low birth weight rate

Low birth weight is a common measurement of the health of infants. Low birth weight is defined as weight of less than 2500 grams. Prior to the 1960s, low birth weight infants had a very low chance of survival. As survival rates improved, low birth weight babies were often found to suffer extensive handicaps, including severe and moderate mental retardation, cerebral palsy, seizure disorder, blindness, hearing defects, and behavioral, learning, and language disorders.[60] Therefore, low birth weight can be an objective measurement of future health status.

In 1980, European-Americans had a low birth weight rate of 5.7%, while African-Americans had a low birth weight rate of 12.5%. The evidence indicates that while low birth weight is holding steady at 5.7% for European-Americans, it has actually risen over the last 12 years to 12.7% for African-Americans.[61] Therefore, African-American infants

---

59. Andersen et al., *supra* note 25, at 83 (*quoting* National Center for Health Statistics, 1985, Table 67). In the age group under 18, 20% more African-Americans (6%) reported limitation in activity than European-Americans (5%). *Id.* In the age group 18–44, 12.5% more African-Americans (9%) reported limitation in activity than European-Americans (8%). *Id.* In the age group 45–64, 34.8% more African-Americans (31%) reported limitation in activity than European-Americans (23%). *Id.* In the age group 65–69, 31.6% more African-Americans (50%) reported limitation in activity than European-Americans (38%). *Id.* Finally, in the age group 70 and over, 23.1% more African-Americans (48%) reported limitation in activity than European-Americans (39%). *Id.*

60. US DEPT OF HEALTH & HUMAN SERVICES, *supra* note 20, at 90.

61. *Id.* at 107–08. In fact, when compared to other countries, the percentage of African-American low birth weight babies (12.5%) fall behind Hungary (11.79%) and Israel (7.16%). While European-Americans' percentage of low birth weight babies (5.7%) is comparable to Japan (5.18%), New Zealand (5.27%) and Austria (5.68%). *Id.*

are 222.81% more likely to suffer from low birth weight and its accompanying handicaps.[62]

F. Health status: African-Americans' death rate

The most objective measure of health is the death rate.[63] Despite some subjective self-reporting (dissatisfaction, discomfort and acute disease), which might suggest equal, if not better, well-being among the African-American population, the objective statistics based on death show just the opposite.

> Wounded, [racism] retreated to more subtle expressions from its most deeply entrenched bunker ... [F]orms of sophisticated racism attached to economic opportunities unfortunately can still be found today.
> ... NOWHERE IS THAT BETTER EXEMPLIFIED THAN IN THE RATE OF EXCESS DEATH AMONG BLACK AMERICANS.[64] (emphasis added).

---

62. US Department of Health and Human Services, HEALTH STATUS OF MINORITIES AND LOW-INCOME GROUPS: THIRD EDITION 108.

63. While health, illness and morbidity are poorly defined and the transition can be gradual, death is a clearly defined event. Consequently, it is the single most reliable indicator of the health status of a population. However, because mortality rates increase so sharply with increasing age, comparisons among populations over time must be adjusted for differing age distribution. Thus mortality rates are adjusted in accordance with the weights in the age distribution of a standard population. U.S. DEPARTMENT OF HEALTH AND HUMAN SERVICES HEALTH STATUS OF MINORITIES AND LOW-INCOME GROUPS: THIRD EDITION.
However, even this information presents measurement problems. The number and causes of deaths for African-Americans and European-Americans are usually obtained from death certificates and autopsy reports. However, the amount and quality of data on deaths varies and depends on a number of factors including: the extent to which the deceased were medically studied before death, the degree of familiarity that certifying physicians had with them, changes in diagnostic and demographic terminology, frequency of misclassifications and the accuracy and completeness of the information. Andersen et al., *supra* note 25, at 78–79. Furthermore, comparisons of deaths for African-Americans to European-Americans may reflect "survivor effects as well as selection by competing causes which can lead to interpretive errors". *Id.* at 79. *See also* Richard Cooper & Brian E. Simmons, *Cigarette Smoking and Ill Health among Black Americans*, 83(7) N.Y. ST. J. MED. 344, 349 (1985).

64. Joe Fegain, *Slavery Unwilling to Die: the Background of Black Oppression in the 1980s*, 17 J. Black Studies 173, 200 (1986) (arguing that the theory of *internal colonialism* views blacks as slaves of society. The history of blacks in the US is traced, beginning with the introduction of slavery during the 1600s. The

(cont.)

"Excess death" is the number of deaths actually observed prior to the age of 70 years, minus the number of deaths that would be predicted when age-and sex-specific death rates of the US European-American population are applied to the African-American population.[65] African-American women have 53.12% excess deaths and African-American men have 52.67% excess deaths.[66] In fact, African-Americans experience 60,000 excess deaths a year compared to mortality rates of European-Americans.[67]

When death rate statistics are broken down by causes of death, the data are striking. For instance, African-American women had 324.1% more deaths due to homicides,[68] 163% more deaths due to diabetes,

---

(64, *cont.*) features of slavery—legal until the passage of the Thirteenth Amendment in 1865—persisted as a form of semi-slavery until 1960 and as a different form of institutionalized racism later). *See also* Lonnie R. Bristow, *Mine Eyes Have Seen*, 261 JAMA 284, 284–85 (1989). Since the civil rights and voting rights laws of the early 1960s the United States has seen significant changes in the status of African- Americans. However, it is arguable whether "apartheid-U.S. . . . or whether economic segregation and the perpetuation of our essentially feudal status amount to its continuation, in fact, if not in law." Romona Hoage Edelin, *Toward An African-American Agenda: An Inward Look, in* THE STATE OF BLACK AMERICA 173, 177–79 (Janet Dewart ed., 1990). Death rate statistics seem to suggest that the feudal status of African-Americans has continued in fact.

65. Bristow, *supra* note 64, at 284.

66. European-American males had age adjusted death rates of 668.2. African-American males had age adjusted death rates of 1023.2. The excess death rate for African-American males was 53.13%. European-American females had aged adjusted death rates of 384.1. African-American females had age adjusted death rates of 586.2. The excess death rate for African-American females was 52.62%. European-American (both sexes) had age adjusted death rates of 511.1. African-American females had age adjusted death rates of 778.6. The excess death rate for African-American females was 52.34%. Department of Health and Human Services, *supra* note 20, at Table 13, pp. 26–27, and Table 3, p. 143.

67. H.R. REP. No. 804, 101st Cong., 2nd Sess. 19 (1990) *reprinted in* U.S.C.C.A.N. 3296, 3297.

68. Health status includes not only physical health but mental health as well. Thus, in a racist, oppressive society, homicide is as much as indication of mental health and public health as suicide. *See generally* Beth Alexander, *Violence: a public health problem. (Editorial)*, 8 PEDIATRICS FOR PARENTS, 1 (1992); Laurie Jones, *Gun violence as Public Health Issue* 35 AM. MED. NEWS 3 (1992); C. EVÉRETT KOOP & GEORGE LUNDBERG, *Violence in America: a Public Health Emergency*, 267 JAMA 3075 (1992); Antonia C. Novello et al., *A Medical Response to Violence*, 267 JAMA 3007 (1992). Violence takes a high toll in mortality, morbidity, quality of life, and use of health care resources. Belloni et al., *Application of Principles of Community Intervention*, 106 PUBLIC HEALTH

77.6% more deaths due to cerebrovascular disorders, 78.4% more deaths due to cirrhosis of the liver, and 78.4% more deaths due to heart disease than European-American women.[69] Furthermore, African-American women have a 178.43% excess maternal rate.[70] African-American men had 598.7% more deaths due to homicides,[71] 100% more deaths due to diabetes, 92.6% more deaths due to cerebrovascular disorders, 88.4% more deaths from cirrhosis of the liver, and 81.8% more deaths due to pulmonary infectious disease than European-American men.[72]

Deaths in the first year of life have consistently been used as an objective determination of health of a population. Therefore, it is significant that in the first year of life, 108.14% more African-American infants die than do European-American infants.[73] Finally, not only is infant mortality used as an objective determination of the health of a population, but it is also used as a measure of the health of a nation. Generally, the United States infant mortality rate is reported as one general rate: 8.6 which places the United States 22nd among nations.[74]

REP. 244, 244–47 (1991). It has been a community problem from early American history. "Before there was professional law enforcement, everyone in a community was involved in crime prevention." *Id.* at 245–46. Thus, recognizing homicide as a health issue is a return to deep rooted ideas of community. *Id.* at 245. *See generally* D.E. Beauchamp, *Community: The Neglected Tradition of Public Health*, HASTINGS CTR. REP. 28, 28–36 (1985).

69. Andersen et al., *supra* note 25, at 84 (*quoting* National Center for Health Statistics 1986a, Table 21).

70. This is the rate of death per 100,000 live births from deliveries and complications of pregnancy, childbirth and the immediate period after childbirth (the puerperium). Department of Health and Human Services, *supra* note 20, at 100 Table 1.

71. The homicide rate for African-American males living within Standard Metropolitan Statistical Areas (SMSAs) is more than twice that for young African-American males residing outside SMSAs. Belloni et al., *Community Intervention, supra* note 68, at 245–46. *Homicide Among Young Black Males—United States, 1970–1982*, 34 MORBIDITY & MORTALITY WKLY. REV. 629–33 (Oct. 18, 1985).

72. Andersen et al., *supra* note 25, at 84 *quoting* National Center for Health Statistics 1986a, Table 21.

73. *See also* U.S. DEPT. OF HEALTH & HUMAN SERVICES, *supra* note 20, at 113 (Table 14); Antonio A. Rene, *Racial Differences in Mortality: Blacks and Whites*, in Jones & Rice, *supra* note 22, at 21. African-Americans had more infant deaths (17.9 per 1000 live births) than European-Americans (8.6 per 1000 live births). *Id.* Thus, the excess infant mortality for African-Americans was 108.2%

74. US Department of Health and Human Services, *supra* note 25, at 104, Table 5.

However, as indicated, that rate is misleading. When compared to the infant mortality of other nations, African-Americans rank 32nd among countries compared to European-Americans' 12th-place ranking.[75]

G. Summary

The picture that is clearly painted by these health measurements is one of significant disparity between two races.[76] While there are some age group variations in the more subjective health measurements (e.g., dissatisfaction), the most objective health measurement (death) clearly indicates that African-Americans are sicker than European-Americans.[77]

If African-Americans are sicker as a result of disparate treatment in the health care system, then they are victims of unequal access to health care.[78] Without decent health, it becomes nearly impossible for African-Americans to gain the other attributes (money, education, contacts, know-how) necessary to gain access to the American economic system. Therefore, when African-Americans are sick and poor, they are just as enslaved as if the law made them so.

II. INSTITUTIONAL RACISM AND AFRICAN-AMERICAN HEALTH STATUS

Racism is both overt and covert, it takes two closely-related forms: individual whites acting against individual blacks, and acts by the total white community against the black community. We called these 'individ-

---

75. NATIONAL RESEARCH COUNCIL, *supra* note 17, at 398. On an international level African-Americans ranked 32nd after Portugal (17.8) and Cuba (16.5). European-Americans ranked 12th after Spain (8.5) and France (8.3). Japan Ranked 1st with only 5.5 infant deaths per 1000 live births. U.S. DEPARTMENT OF HEALTH AND HUMAN SERVICES, HEALTH STATUS OF MINORITIES AND LOW- INCOME GROUPS: THIRD EDITION, 104, Table 5: Infant Mortality Rates: 36 Selected Countries, 1980–1985.

76. *See generally* H.R. REP. NO. 804, 101st Cong., 2nd Sess. 1990, 1990 U.S.C.C.A.N. 3296 (finding that African-Americans are disproportionately represented among individuals from disadvantaged backgrounds and that the health status of individuals from disadvantaged backgrounds, including racial and ethnic minorities, in the United States is significantly lower than the health status of the general population of the United States).

77. Andersen et al., *supra* note 25, at 82.

78. *See* KNOWLES & PREWITT, *supra* note 15, at 1 (inferring from others' quotes that African-Americans have been denied opportunities that they have helped develop).

ual racism and institutional racism'. The first consists of overt acts by individuals, which causes death, injury or the violent destruction of property. The second type is less overt, or more subtle, less identifiable in terms of specific individuals committing the acts. But, it is no less destructive of human life. The second type originates in the operation of established and respected forces in the society, and thus receives far less public condemnation than the first type.
When white terrorists bombed a black church and killed 5 black children, that is an act of individual racism, widely deplored by most segments of the society. But,...[when] black babies die each year because of the lack of proper food, shelter, and medical facilities, and thousands more are destroyed and maimed physically, emotionally, and intellectually because of conditions of poverty and discrimination in the black community, that is the function of institutional racism.[79]

African-Americans are sicker than European-Americans.[80] Knowing that African-Americans are sicker than European-Americans does not explain why. It certainly does not indicate the presence of institutional racism. To understand the role of institutional racism in health status requires an understanding of how health status is determined.

Many things affect health status. An individual's personal life style choices affect health status because they affect an individual's personal behavior and psycho-social health, which affect his or her physical health. Physical environment and biology also affect health status. Health care institutions affect health status because both personal behavior and human biology are affected by an individual's access to health care, and by the quality of health care the individual receives from health care institutions.[81]

Class theory maintains that the primary factor affecting differences in health care status between racial groups is socioeconomic.[82] According to the class theory, socioeconomic class affects life style, psycho-social behavior, personal behavior, human biology, physical environment, access to health care, and the behavior of the system and its institutions

79. CARMICHAEL & HAMILTON, *supra* note 1, at 4.

80. *See supra* text and accompanying notes 15–78.

81. Trevor Hancock, *Beyond Health Care: From Public Health Policy to Healthy Public Policy*, 76 CAN. J. PUB. HEALTH 9, 11 (Supp. 1985).

82. When individuals are separated into different racial population groups, there is general recognition of a health disparity between them. The explanation usually given for this disparity is that differences exist in socioeconomic status or class.

toward the individual.[83] According to the class theory, it is lack of money, not racism, that explains the disparity in health.

Certainly, access to health care services is related to ability to pay, and ability to pay is related to access to health insurance. It is estimated that 37 million Americans are uninsured.[84] The spiraling costs of health care and health insurance make it impossible for many individuals to afford to purchase either privately. And yet, only about half of the poor meet government assistance programs' eligibility requirements.[85] Many African-Americans are unemployed or employed in jobs that do not provide health care insurance. Many African-Americans are above the poverty line, disqualifying them for government assistance programs. Other African-Americans, approximately 25%, fall between the cracks, uninsured, without government assistance and without equitable access to health care. Consequently, many policy makers are suggesting health care reform proposals designed to minimize the effect ability (or inability) to pay has as a barrier to health care.[86]

Even if any of the health care reform proposals are successful, the effect of socioeconomic class on health status will not be eliminated. In fact, its major effect will still exist, since socioeconomic class will continue to affect personal behavior and psycho-social health, physical environment, and human biology. Nevertheless, theoretically, access to health care will no longer be based on economics and ability to pay. If one accepts the class theory, then one must believe that establishing a universal health insurance will minimize the impact of class on health care access and should result in improved health for African-Americans.

The class theory, however, oversimplifies the issue and completely ignores the independent role of race in American society.[87] Race

---

83. Certainly, poverty is a major factor in health. The poor are unable to afford the food, housing, clothing and education which would allow them to be equal participants in American society. Notwithstanding the role of poverty in health, in America, race has a separate and independent role which has never fully been addressed.

84. *See generally*, Lawrence D. Brown, *The Medically Uninsured: Problems, Policies and Politics*, 15 J. HEALTH POL'Y & L. 315, 318 (1990); Karen Davis, *Closing the Gap* in *Health Insurance Coverage for African-Americans* (unpublished paper on file at Case Western Reserve, Health Matrix); Jack Hadely et al., *Comparison of Uninsured and Privately Insured Hospital Patients*, 265 JAMA 374, 376 (1991) (suggesting that the amount of care an individual receives is related to whether the individual has health insurance).

85. *See infra* note 206 and accompanying text.

86. *See infra* notes 204–27 and accompanying text.

87. R.M. Cooper et al., *Improved Mortality Among U.S. Blacks, 1968–1978, The*

influences not only life style, personal behavior, psycho-social behavior, physical environment, and biology, but also socioeconomic status. Thus, race has a double influence.

Racism in America establishes separate and independent barriers to health care institutions and to medical care. Those who advocate for the class theory ignore the fact that removing economic barriers does not remove racial barriers. Racial barriers to health care are exhibited in two areas. First, institutional policies based on race establish barriers to access to health care to African-Americans. Second, practitioners provide disparate medical treatment to African-Americans based on their race which is not related to their socioeconomic class.

A. Racial barriers to access

> It is hard to separate the effects of discrimination from those of concentration of Negroes in those areas where medical facilities are not easily accessible and in those income brackets that do not permit the purchase of medical facilities in the competitive market. Discrimination increases Negro sickness and death both directly and indirectly and manifests itself both consciously and unconsciously. Discrimination is involved when hospitals will not take in Negro patients; or when—if they do permit Negro patients—they restrict their numbers, give them the poorest quarters, and refuse to hire Negro doctors and nurses to attend them. . . . Ill health reduces the chance of economic advancement, which in turn operates to reduce the chance of getting adequate medical facilities or knowledge necessary for personal care.[88]

Discrimination in health care has its foundation in the historical relationship between African-Americans and southern medical institutions. As slaves, African-Americans were perceived as property.[89] While slave owners attempted to protect their own economic interests by

---

Role of Anti-Racist Struggle, 11 INT'L J. HEALTH SERVICES 511, 511–22 (1981); NATIONAL RESEARCH COUNCIL, *supra* note 17, at 428–29; S. Woodlander et al., *Medical Care and Mortality: Racial differences in preventable deaths*, 15 INT'L J. HEALTH SERVICES 1, 1–22 (1985); *cf.* J.L. Haywood, *Coronary Heart Disease Mortality/Morbidity and Risk in Blacks. II Access to medical Care*, 3 AM. HEART J. 794, 794–96 (1984) (explaining that African-Americans with hypertension at all social levels report less frequent use of medical care, more difficulties in getting into the health care system and greater dissatisfaction with medical care).

88. GUNNAR MYRDAL, AN AMERICAN DILEMMA 174 (1944).

89. Slavery in North America was one of the "harshest form of social relations ever to exist." ALPHONSO PINKNEY, BLACK AMERICANS 2 (1969).

(*cont.*)

providing minimal health care, most left the slaves to live or die as fate might befall them.[90]

After the Civil War, the Bureau of Refugees, Freedmen and Abandoned Lands (Freedman Bureau) was instituted to "furnish supplies and medical services" to the former slaves.[91] However, the Freedman Bureau had very limited effect in providing services to former slaves. In fact, the Compromise of 1877 effectively ended the period of Radical Reconstruction which had been an attempt by the nation to make affirmative efforts in helping African-Americans.[92]

During the Post-Reconstruction era, African-Americans were excluded from health care either by prohibition or discrimination.[93]

> [Even] where segregation and discrimination [were] not required by law

---

(89, *cont.*) The slave had no rights and received no protection from society. The slave owner had absolute power over the slave. *Id.*

90. PINKNEY, *supra* note 89, at 6. Jones & Rice, *supra* note 22, at 6; *see also* Mitchell Rice, *On Assessing Black Health*, 9 URB. LEAGUE REV. 6, 6–12 (Winter 1985–1986). The dual status of slaves as valuable property and as persons with human rights may have encouraged some slave owners to provide at least minimal health care. *See generally* J. Thomas Wren, A. *Two-Fold Character: The Slave as Person and Property in Virginia Court Cases, 1800–1860*, 24 S. STUD. 417–31 (1985) (maintaining that although slaves were perceived as property in the antebellum South, Virginia courts often recognized their humanity as well. By 1860, the Southern legal system had begun to accept an implicit duality in the status of the slaves as both property and person); Arthur Howington, *A Property of Special and Peculiar Value: The Tennessee Supreme Court and the Law of Manumission*, 44 TENNESSEE HIST. Q. 302–17 (1985); Winstanley Briggs, *Slavery in French Colonial Illinois*, 18 CHI. HIST. 66–81 (1989–90) (arguing that the high cost of slaves and the risk of offending tribal neighbors led the settlers to treat their slaves as subordinate, but valuable property).

91. PINKNEY, *supra* note 89, at 24 (*citing* JOHN H. FRANKLIN, RECONSTRUCTION AFTER THE CIVIL WAR 36–37) (1961)).

92. Throughout the period of Reconstruction, attempts were made to obstruct the progress toward "racial democracy." PINKNEY, *supra* note 89, at 26. The 1876 election was in dispute between Rutherford B. Hayes (Republican) and Samuel Tilden (Democrat). Hayes was declared winner with the understanding the remaining troops in the South would be withdrawn, the South would be accorded home rule, and with the assurance that the "dominant whites [would have] political autonomy and nonintervention in matters of race policy." PINKNEY, *supra* note 89, at 26 (citing WOODWARD, REUNION AND REACTION 246 (1966)). Thus, the Republican Party "abandon[ed] the Negro to former slave holders [and] the compromise signaled a return toward slavery." PINKNEY, *supra* note 89, at 26.

93. Jones & Rice, *supra* note 22, at 6.

they became deeply ingrained in the mores. Such behavior became part of the American Way of Life'....[94]

This "way of life" remained visible until the Civil Rights Movement of the 1960s.[95] After the 1960s, health care institutions either fled predominant African-American communities or instituted policies which resulted in limited access for African-Americans.[96]

Discrimination can take two forms. It can be based on racist conduct that is intentional or it can be based on conduct which, although not intentional, nevertheless results in a disproportionate disparate impact on African-Americans. Much of the institutional racism has historically

---

94. For instance, in 1875 Congress passed the Civil Rights Act which made it a crime for a person to deny any citizen equal access to accommodation in inns, public conveyances, theaters, and other places of amusement. Civil Rights Act of 1875, 18 St. 335. In 1883, the Supreme Court declared the Civil Rights Act of 1875 unconstitutional. *The Civil Rights Cases*, 109 U.S. 3 (1883). In 1896 the Court ruled that separate (segregated) facilities for African-Americans and European-Americans did not violate the Thirteenth or Fourteenth Amendment. Setting the pattern for race relations for more than three decades, the ruling declared that "If one race be inferior to the other socially, the Constitution of the United States cannot put them on the same plane." Plessy v. Ferguson, 163 U.S. 538 (1896).

95. In 1954, the court questioned the "separate but equal" doctrine of *Plessy v. Ferguson*. In particular, in a unanimous decision, the court found that legally sanctioned racial segregation is usually interpreted as connoting the inferiority of blacks, which adversely affects the educational development of black children. "Any language in *Plessy v. Ferguson* contrary to this finding is rejected." Brown v. Board of Education, 347 U.S. 483, 494–95 (1954).

Brown v. Board of Education was a significant milestone in civil rights. However, it was the civil rights movement of the 1960s which culminated in the Civil Rights Act of 1964 and the Voting Rights Act of 1965, which resulted in many of the overt signs of discrimination being eliminated.

In particular, the Civil Rights Act of 1964 (Public Law 88–352) prohibited the denial of the right to vote in national elections because of race and made a sixth grade education a presumption of literacy (Title I). Title II prohibited discrimination in places of public accommodation. Title III authorized the Justice Department to file suits to desegregate public facilities. Title IV authorized the Justice Department to file suit to desegregate public schools or colleges. Title V established the Commission on Civil Rights. Title VI prohibited discrimination in federally-financed programs. Title VII prohibited discrimination in employment. Title VIII authorized the gathering of registration and voting statistics based on race. Title IX allowed for federal appeals court intervention in civil rights cases to be remanded to state courts. Title X established the Community Relations Service in the Department of Commerce.

96. *See infra* notes 97–182 and accompanying text.

moved from intentional conduct to unintentional. While this classification may offer a distinction when assigning fault or culpability, the
classification makes little difference to the African-American feeling the
adverse affects of discrimination.

This legacy of a racist health care system persists today in African-
Americans who are sicker than European-Americans and who continue
to experience racial barriers to access. These barriers to can be divided
into three major groups: barriers to hospitals, barriers to nursing
homes, and barriers to physicians and other providers.

1. Barriers to hospitals

The institutional racism that exists in many hospitals manifests itself
in a number of ways including the adoption, administration and
implementation of policies that restrict admission;[97] the closure, relo-
cation or privatization of hospitals that serve the African-American
community;[98] and the transfer of unwanted patients (known as "patient
dumping") by hospitals and institutions.[99]

Admission Restrictions.

Many hospitals discriminate by using patient referral and acceptance
practice standards that limit access. These practices restrict the admission of African-Americans to hospitals.[100] Discriminatory admission
practices include:

- Layoffs of recently hired African-American physicians—where
  those African-American physicians admit most of the African-
  American patients served by the hospital.[101]

---

97. Jones & Rice, *supra* note 22, at 6.

98. Alan Sager, *The Closure of Hospitals that Serve the Poor: Implications for
Health Planning*, A Statement to the Subcommittee on Health and the Environ-
ment, Committee on Energy and Commerce, US House of Representatives, 2
(April 30, 1982); Mark Schlesinger, *Paying the Price: Medical Care, Minorities, and
the Newly Competitive Health Care System, in* HEALTH POLICIES AND BLACK
AMERICANS 275–76 (David Willis ed., 1989).

99. *Equal Access to Health Care: Patient Dumping, Hearing before a Subcommittee
of the Committee on Government Operations* 100 Cong, 1st Sess. 270–87 (July 22,
1987); Robert L. Schiff et al., *Transfers to a Public Hospital: A Prospective Study of
467 Patients*, 314 NEW ENGL. J. MED. 552–57 (1986).

100. Stan Dorn et al., *Anti-Discrimination Provisions and Health Care Access: New Slants
on Old Approaches*, CLEARINGHOUSE REV. 439, 441 (Special Issue, Summer 1986).

101. *Id.*

- Not having physicians on staff who can accept Medicaid patients.[102]
- Requiring pre-admission deposits as a condition of obtaining care.[103]
- Refusing to participate in programs to finance care for low-income patients not eligible for Medicaid.[104]
- Accepting only patients of physicians with staff privileges when the patients of such physicians do not reflect the racial composition of the local community.[105]

Such practices may have a devastating effect on African-Americans. The practices may banish African-Americans to distinctly substandard institutions treating mostly minority groups. They may completely prevent care where African-Americans have no access to other sources of care.

Community availability.

Racial barriers to health care access are based, in large part, on the unavailability of services in a community. Increasingly, hospitals that serve the African-American community are either closing, relocating or becoming private. In a study of the years between 1937 and 1977, researchers showed that the likelihood of a hospital's closing was directly related to the percentage of African-Americans in the population.[106] Throughout the 1980s many hospitals relocated from heavily African-American communities to predominantly European-American suburban communities.[107]

This loss of services to the community resulted in reduced access to African-Americans. Geographic availability and proximity are important determinants to seeking health care services early. If African-Americans fail to seek early health care, they are more likely to be sicker when they do enter the system; and the cost for the patient to

---

102. *Id.*
103. *Id.*
104. *Id.*
105. *Id.*
106. Sager, *supra* note 98, at 2. A total of 210 hospitals either closed or relocated during the period studied. A disproportionate number of the hospitals that closed or relocated were originally located in communities where the population was predominately African-American.
107. *See generally* NAACP v. Wilmington Medical Ctr., Inc., 657 F.2d 1322 (1981) (proposal to reduce urban facility which served predominantly minorities and to construct a new suburban facility); Byran v. Koch, 627 F.2d 612 (1980) (closure of a New York City hospital whose patients were 98% minorities).

receive service and for the system to provide services at that point is likely to be greater than at an earlier stage. Therefore, not only does the loss of services significantly increase health care costs to African-Americans, but also, it increases health care costs to the society in general.[108]

Another devastating trend that affects the access of African-Americans to health care is the privatization of public hospitals. Quite a few hospitals (public and non-profit) have elected to restructure as private, for-profit corporations. As public hospitals, many were obligated to provide uncompensated care under the Hill-Burton Act.[109] As private hospitals, these institutions are most likely to discontinue providing general health services to the indigent populations,[110] and essential primary health care services to serve African-American communities.[111]

---

108. Sager, *supra* note 98, at 2–3; *see also* Roger Wilkins, *Loss of Hospitals in Central City Said to Cause Array of Problems*, N.Y. TIMES, Sept. 17, 1979, at D4.

109. In 1946 Congress passed the Hospital Survey and Construction Act, presently codified as Title VI of the Public Health Service Act, 42 U.S.C. § 291. One goal of the Hill-Burton Act was to assure that hospitals would provide medical services to the residents in their communities, including those who were indigent. GEORGE ANNAS ET AL., AMERICAN HEALTH CARE LAW 80–81 (1990).

Specifically, hospitals which receive funds under the Hill-Burton Act are obligated to perform a community service requirement. *Id.* at 75. In order to comply with the community service requirement, subpart G of the regulations requires that recipient health facilities be made available to all residents and prohibits exclusion of anyone in the area served by the hospital on the basis of any factor unrelated to need. *Id.* at 77.

The Hill-Burton community services requirement was completely ignored for 30 years. Privately initiated lawsuits during the 1970s gave rise to the 1972 regulation changes. *Id.* These regulations outlined a program for monitoring compliance by Hill- Burton facilities relying on state agencies for implementation. *Id.* Unfortunately, the 1972 regulations did not amend or specify the meaning of community service. Kenneth R. Wing. *The Community Service Obligation of Hill-Burton Health Facilities*, 23 B.C.L. REV. 577, 613–14 (1982). It was not until 1974 that HEW, under court order, finally issued regulations interpreting the community service requirement. *Id.* at 614–15.

Community service now included the requirement that recipient facilities must participate in Medicare and Medicaid and take "such steps as necessary" to insure that Medicare and Medicaid patients were admitted without discrimination. *Id.* at 615. These regulations stopped short of imposing explicit standards for assessing compliance with the substantive requirement. In addition, evaluation and enforcement of the community service obligation was primarily on state Hill-Burton agencies, and a twenty year limitation was placed on the community service obligation. *Id.* at 615–16. This limitation has subsequently been invalidated.

The problem of limited resources is not new and has plagued the African-American community since slavery. Historically, African-American communities attempted to address the problem by establishing African-American hospitals. At one point there were more than 200 African-American hospitals in the United States. African-Americans relied on these institutions to "heal and save their lives."[112]

Now, these institutions are fighting for their own survival. By the 1960s, only 90 African-American hospitals remained. Between 1961 and 1988, 57 African-American hospitals closed and 14 others either merged, converted or consolidated. By 1991, only 12 hospitals continued to "struggle daily just to keep their doors open."[113] As a result of closures, relocations, and privatization, many African-Americans are left with limited, if any, access to hospitals.

Patient dumping.

An African-American seeking care at a private hospital faces the possibility of being "dumped", that is, the hospital may transfer an "undesirable" patient to a different facility.[114] The transfer is medically appropriate only when the care required is not available at the transferring hospital. However, many transfers are for economic reasons,

---

In 1978, HEW proposed new charity care regulations. *Id.* at 616. These new regulations were intended to give more specific meaning to the community service obligation and to federalize the enforcement and monitoring of responsibilities. *Id* at 616–17. The result was the 1979 regulations. The 1979 regulations explicitly preclude exclusion of anyone who is in need of services offered by the facility and who is able to make some manner of payment. *Id.* at 620. These regulations explicitly clarify the obligation of Hill-Burton recipients with regard to people who rely on Medicare or Medicaid. *Id.* at 621. The 1979 regulations also prohibited the pre-admission deposits and the required referrals to staff physicians, both of which effectively excluded otherwise eligible patients. *Id.* at 622.

110. Under Hill-Burton, a hospital is released from the uncompensated care requirement under the statute buy-out provision. 42 U.S.C. § 291a(1).

111. *Cf.*, N.A.A.C.P v. Medical Ctr., 657 F.2d 1322 (medical center proposing to close high-risk obstetrical care, inpatient pediatric care and gerontology services).

112. *The Crisis of the Disappearing Black Hospitals*, EBONY, March 1992, at 23–28.

113. *Id.*

114. *See generally* Judith Waxman & Molly McNulty, *Access to Emergency Medical Care: Patients' Rights and Remedies*, 22 CLEARINGHOUSE REV. 21–27 (Nov. 1991); Geralding Dallek and Judith Waxman, *Patient Dumping: A Crisis in Emergency Medical Care for the Indigent*, 19 CLEARINGHOUSE REV. 1413 (1986).

i.e., the patient was either uninsured or unable to make admission deposits.[115] African-Americans are disproportionately affected by these practices.[116]

In 1986, Congress passed the Emergency Medical Treatment and Active Labor Act which became effective as Section 9121 of the Consolidated Omnibus Reconciliation Act (COBRA).[117] The Act provides a cause of action against hospitals that "dump" patients with emergency conditions from their emergency rooms, or who "dump" pregnant patients in active labor.[118] Several states have made "patient dumping" illegal.[119]

However, limited enforcement of these legislative enactments makes

---

115. *Equal Access to Health Care: Patient Dumping, supra* note 99, at 270–87.

116. A study of transfers among 467 medical transfers to Cook County Hospital showed that 89% were African-Americans or Hispanic-Americans. The study concluded that most of the patients were transferred for economic reasons and without their consent. Schiff, *supra* note 99, at 552–57.

117. 42 U.S.C.A. §§ 1395 dd(a) (West Supp. 1992).

118. Under COBRA, hospitals are required to provide appropriate medical screening examinations within the capabilities of the hospital. If a person has an emergency or is in active labor, the hospital must stabilize the medical condition or provide treatment for labor or transfer under certain conditions. In particular, there can be no transfer until stabilized except at the request of patient or if it is medically necessary and another facility is more appropriate. A transfer is appropriate if: the receiving facility has available space and qualified personnel and has agreed to accept the transfer. The transferring facility must provide appropriate medical records. The transfer must be made using qualified personnel and equipment. Enforcement is through termination of Medicare provider agreement, civil monetary penalties, and civil action for personal injury or financial loss. 42 U.S.C.A. §§ 1395 dd(a)-(d) (West Supp. 1992).

119. *See generally* ARIZ. REV. STAT. ANN. § 11–297.01 1–3d (1956) (providing for transfers in three situations: where no hospital exists, where the existing hospital is over-crowded, or where the necessary services are not provided at the transferring hospital.); CAL. HEALTH & SAFETY CODE § 1317.2 (West 1990) (providing for various conditions to be met prior to the transfer of a patient such as exams, evaluations, emergency treatment. The transfer may not create a medical hazard, the hospital receiving the patient must have an appropriate bed, personnel and equipment necessary for treatment; relevant transfer information must be given to the receiving hospital.); FLA. STAT. ANN. § 401.45 1 (West 1943) (providing that no person shall be denied emergency medical treatment); IDAHO CODE § 39–1391 (1947) (providing for emergency treatment to persons appearing seriously sick or injured without admission of that person. This can have the effect of requiring stabilization prior to transfer. However, since the patient is never actually admitted, the hospital can realistically transfer the patient at any time); ILL. ANN. STAT. ch.

patient dumping an ongoing problem. For instance, as of October 30, 1990, only 530 facilities had been investigated;[120] only 139 facilities were found in violation of the statute;[121] and only five facilities actually lost their Medicare contracts.[122] A high percentage of African-Americans are uninsured or under-insured.[123] Consequently, patient dumping continues to be an issue that plagues African-Americans. Furthermore, hospitals have developed methods to dump the patient without invoking the statute. For instance. the statute provides that hospitals receiving federal funding must accept any patient who "comes to an

---

111 1/2, para 6151 (Smith-Hurd 1934) (providing that no health care provider can refuse needed emergency treatment to a person whose life would be threatened in the absence of such treatment due to an inability to pay.); MASS. GEN. LAWS ANN. ch. 111 § 70E (West 1958) (providing for prompt lifesaving treatment in an emergency without discrimination or delay. There is an exception stating that a delay may not impose a material risk.); N.C. GEN. STAT. § 131E–117 15 (1943) (providing for no transfers or discharges but allows many exceptions including consideration of the patient's own or other patients' welfare, and nonpayment for the stay. The effect of the exceptions is that patients are not protected from nonmedical transfers.); PA. STAT. ANN. tit. 35, § 449.8 (1930) (providing that transfers may only occur in instances where the facility lacks the staff or facilities to properly render definitive treatment.); TENN. CODE ANN. § 68–11–701 (1955) (requiring stabilization prior to transfer and such efforts necessary to sustain the patient during the transfer.); TEX. CODE ANN. § 241.027 b (West 1986 & Supp. 1992) (providing for medically appropriate transfers from physician to physician and from hospital to hospital by providing the following: notification to the receiving hospital prior to the transfer, stabilizing prior to and during the transfer, provisions for the appropriate personnel and equipment for the transfer, necessary records. Transfers may not be based on discrimination or economic status.) *But see* COLO. REV. STAT. ANN. § 26–15–106 8b (West 1989) (providing for transfers of indigent patients without any restrictions except for a prior agreement to the transfer by the receiving contract provider.) DEL. CODE ANN. tit 16 § 1121 18 (allowing transfers for the patient's own welfare or the welfare of other patients, and for nonpayment); WASH. REV, CODE ANN. § 70.168.100 e (West 1961 & Supp 1992) (requiring only that prior to transfer, agreements with providers outside the region are established to facilitate the transfer); *See also* Dorn & Waxman, *States Take the Lead in Preventing Patient Dumping*, 22 CLEARING HOUSE REV. 136 (1988).

120. Waxman & McNulty, *Access to Emergency Medical Care*, *supra* note 114, at 21–27.

121. *Id.*

122. *Id.*

123. *See infra* notes 207–09 and accompanying text.

emergency room." If hospitals reroute the patient before the patient arrives then the statute will not apply.[124]

In *Johnson*, a parent called the paramedics after her baby went into cardiac arrest.[125] The paramedics contacted University of Chicago hospital.[126] The hospital told the paramedics to take the child to another hospital even though it was only five blocks away.[127] The child was taken to a hospital without a pediatric intensive care unit and had to be transferred to another hospital.[128] The child died after admission to the second hospital.[129] The plaintiff sued on common law claims and for violation of COBRA. The district court dismissed and the Seventh Circuit upheld the dismissal of the COBRA claim.[130] The Seventh Circuit noted that "In accordance with the plain meaning of the statutory language, we do not believe that the infant ever 'came to' the hospital or its emergency department. For purposes of COBRA, a hospital-operated telemetry system is distinct from that same hospital's emergency room."[131] The court went on to acknowledge that a ". . . hospital could conceivably use a telemetry system to dump patients"; nevertheless, the court held that the "statute does not expressly address the question of liability in such a situation."[132] Thus, the Seventh Circuit leaves the door open for other hospitals to continue dumping patients, most of whom will be African-Americans.

2. Barriers to nursing homes

Nursing homes[133] are the most segregated publicly licensed health care

---

124. Johnson v. University of Chicago Hosps., 982 F.2d 230 (1992).
125. *Id.* at 231.
126. *Id.*
127. *Id.*
128. *Id.*
129. *Id.*
130. *Id.*
131. *Id.* at 232.
132. *Id.*
133. "Nursing homes" is a generic term used to describe two types of facilities: intermediate care facilities (ICF) and skilled nursing-care facilities (SNF). Intermediate care facilities provide institutional, health-related services above the level of room and board, but at a level of care below that of hospital or SNF care. See 42 U.S.C. §§ 1396c(d) (1988); *see also* 42 C.F.R. § 440.150 (1991). Skilled nursing facilities provide institutional care above the level of ICF services but below the level of a hospital. See 42 U.S.C. § 1396d(i) (1988); 42 C.F.R. § 440.40 (1991).

facilities in the United States. Smith, in his study, concludes that racial discrimination is the major factor explaining that type of segregation.[134] It has been suggested that any difference in African-American use of nursing homes can be explained by cultural biases against using nursing homes as care source for disabled or aged family members.[135] However, in some areas (such as Delaware and Detroit Metropolitan) African-Americans make up a higher portion of nursing home residents than European-Americans. This suggests that African-Americans do not consistently decide against nursing homes.[136]

Furthermore, even where racially neutral policies exist, institutional racism is still a factor. For instance, evidence about the use of nursing homes under Medicaid demonstrates that institutional racism has an impact even without regard to economic class.[137] For instance, although

---

134. Cassandra Butts, *The Color of Money: Barriers of Access to Private Health care Facilities for African-Americans* (Unpublished manuscript on file at Case Western Reserve, Health Matrix Office) (*citing* David A. Smith, *Discrimination in Access to Nursing Homes in Pennsylvania* (1991)).

135. *But see* Linton v. Carney, 779 F. Supp 925, 933 (M.D. Tenn 1990) (rejecting defendants' assertion that "self-selection preferences" of the minorities, based upon the minorities' reliance upon the extended family, lack of transportation, and fear of institutional care, adequately explain the disparate impact).

136. Butts, *supra* note 134, at 5–7. For instances, although African-Americans rely on family and friends for long- term care, the rate of use of nursing homes is rising faster for African-Americans than for European-Americans. SENIOR HEALTH DIGEST, No. 91–17 (Sept. 16, 1991).

137. An individual's eligibility for Medicaid is based on certain personal characteristics relating to need, such as old age, disability or blindness, and on the basis of the person's indigence. Indigence is measured by certain state and federal financial standards. To obtain Medicaid coverage for nursing home care, the patient must first establish financial eligibility and then meet additional medical need requirements demonstrating eligibility for ICF or SNF services. The medical requirements are established by the state to guard against unnecessary treatment.

In order to determine a patient's medical eligibility, states generally require that each Medicaid recipient's need for admission to a nursing home be evaluated prior to the recipient's admission to the institution or, if the patient has already been admitted, prior to an authorization of Medicaid reimbursement for his or her care. *See* 42 C.F.R. §§ 456.271 and 456.372. This process is referred to as the pre-admission evaluation (PAE) process.

Once a patient has been admitted to a nursing home, his or her continued need for ICF or SNF care is annually reviewed by state Medicaid officials pursuant to a process referred to as utilization review. 42 U.S.C. § 1396a(a) (30).

African-Americans constitute only 12% of the nation's total population, the African-American poverty rate (31%) is three times
greater than the European-American poverty rate (10%).[138] However,
African-Americans constitute only 29% of the Medicaid population
and 23% of the elderly poor.[139] Medicaid expenditures for African-
Americans are only 18% of total expenditures.[140] If, indeed, African-
Americans are sicker, then Medicaid expenditures for African-Americans
should at least be equal to, if not greater than, the percentage of
Medicaid's African-American population. It is this combination of
under-representation and under-spending in Medicaid that suggests
racism.

In part, this disparity in expenditure is based on the limited access
that African-Americans on Medicaid have to nursing homes, both
intermediate and skilled nursing facilities.[141] Only 10% of Medicaid
intermediate care patients are African-Americans.[142] Similarly, only 9%
of Medicaid skilled nursing care facilities' patients are African-Americans.[143] This disparity may be due in part to a policy allowing limited
bed certification. Under limited bed certification, nursing homes determine the number of beds that are certified to participate in Medicaid.
Federal regulations permit a distinct part of intermediate care facilities

---

138. BUREAU OF THE CENSUS, U.S. DEPT. OF COMMERCE SERIES P60, NO.
168 CURRENT POPULATION REPORTS, CONSUMER ICOME: MONEY AND POV-
ERTY STATUS IN THE UNITED STATES 1989 (Nov. 1990).

139. NAACP Legal Defense & Educ. Fund, Inc. An African American
Health Care Agenda: Strategies for Reforming an Unjust System, *Racial
Disparities in Medicaid Coverage for Nursing Home Care* (1991) (unpublished
proceedings, on file at Case Western Reserve University School of Law, *Health
Matrix: Journal of Law-Medicine* office).

140. *Id.*

141. In part, this limited access is caused by the rules that the government
generates. For instance, federal law authorizes state agencies who perform
review and certification functions to certify facilities for either SNF or ICF
reimbursement. Such certification may be of a "distinct part of an institution."
See 42 U.S.C. § 1395x and 42 U.S.C. § 1396a(a)(28). A "distinct part" SNF or
ICF must be an entire separately identifiable unit consisting of all the beds
within that unit (such as a separate building, floor, wing, or corridor). A
distinct part SNF or ICF unit is paid as an entity separate from the rest of the
institution. Medicare Program; Swing-Bed Program, 54 Fed. Reg. 37, 270 (Sept.
7, 1989). Consequently, facilities allowed to limit the number of beds that they
have available by certifying only part of their facility.

142. *Racial Disparities in Medicaid Coverage for Nursing Home Care* (1991)
(unpublished data located at the University of Dayton School of Law).

143. *Id.*

to be certified.[144] Some states will certify a limited number of beds.[145] Thus, the certified portion of a facility need not contain all intermediate care residents.[146] Furthermore, some states will certify beds which are not in a separately administered unit of a facility, but are instead part of a wing or ward that also contains non-certified beds.[147]

Limited bed certification programs allow nursing home operators to give preference to private pay patients by reserving for their exclusive use beds which are unavailable to Medicaid patients.[148] It also allows the nursing home operators to change the bed certification, resulting in disruption of the care of Medicaid patients by displacing them after they have been admitted to a nursing home.[149]

Displacement can occur in several ways. It occurs when a patient exhausts his or her financial resources. The patient needs to make a transition from private pay to Medicaid.[150] At that point, a patient may be told that his or her bed is no longer available.[151] Furthermore, displacement occurs when a patient with insurance (private, Medicaid or Medicare) is transferred from a skilled nursing facility to an intermediate care facility. If the insurance will not cover intermediate care, the patient may not have financial resources to continue obtaining nursing home care.[152] Similarly, displacement can occur when a patient already on Medicaid and authorized to receive skilled nursing care is reclassified for intermediate care only.[153]

A nursing home can manipulate the availability of nursing home beds by certifying (and decertifying) beds. This certification and decertification process limits access to minorities. *Linton v. Carney*[154] effectively challenged the practice.

---

144. 42 U.S.C. § 1395 (federal Medicare statute recognizing "distinct part" certification); 42 U.S.C. § 1396a(a)(28) (applying "distinct part" certification to Medicaid SNF certification).

145. *See* Linton v. Carney, 779 F. Supp. 926, 931. ("Tennessee, at the provider's instructions, certified a limited component of beds in a facility which provides the same ICF level of care in all beds.")

146. *Id.*

147. *Id.*

148. *Id.* at 932.

149. *Id.*

150. *Id.*

151. *Id.*

152. *Id.*

153. *Id.*

154. Linton v. Tenn. Community Health & Environmental, 779 F. Supp. 925, *aff'd* 923 F.2d 855 (6th Cir. 1981).

In *Linton*, Mrs. Linton was threatened with an involuntary transfer from the facility she occupied. The threatened transfer was due to a change in her classification status by the Tennessee Medicaid program.[155] Although Mrs. Linton occupied a bed in the nursing home certified for her new classification, the nursing home threatened to decertify her bed.[156] No other beds were available in the facility.[157] Joining Mrs. Linton (as a plaintiff-intervenor) was Mrs. Carney, an 89-year-old African-American who could not find an available nursing home in the state of Tennessee.[158] The District Court found the limited bed certification policy to violate both Title VI of Civil Rights Act and the Medicaid statute.[159]

The *Linton* court recognized that Title VI prohibits policies and practices with adverse disparate impact on ethnic and racial minorities.[160] According to the court, the plaintiffs showed that the defendants' limited bed certification policy had a disparate impact on racial minorities.[161] While the defendants argued the "self-selection preferences" of the minorities adequately explained the disparate impact,[162] the court rejected that interpretation as "sufficient justifica-

---

155. *Id.* at 928–30.

156. *Id.* at 928.

157. *Id.*

158. The policy of decertification particularly affected African-Americans. Despite representing 39.4% of the Tennessee's Medicaid recipients, African-Americans comprised only 15.4% of the Medicaid recipients in nursing homes. *Id.* at 932. Furthermore, the court noted that the health of African-Americans was generally poorer than that of European-American resulting a in correspondingly greater need for nursing home services. Despite this "greater need", the system of licensed nursing homes served European-Americans "[relegating African-Americans] to substandard boarding homes which receive no Medicaid subsidies. *Id.*

159. *Id.* at 933–34.

160. In particular the court cited to Guardians Ass'n v. Civil Service Comm'n, 463 U.S. 582 (1983), which recognized that Title VI extends to unintentional disparate impact discrimination as well as deliberate discrimination. Further, *Linton* acknowledged that in Alexander v. Choate, 469 U.S. 287, 292–94 (1985), the Supreme Court delegated to agencies responsibility to determine "what sorts of disparate impacts upon minorities constituted sufficiently significant social problems, and were readily enough remediable, to warrant altering the practices of the federal grantees that had produced those impacts." *Id.* at 934.

161. *Id.* at 935.

162. According to the defendants, such self-selection preferences were based on minorities reliance on the extended family, on the lack of transportation, and on the fear of institutional care. *Id.* at 935.

tion for minority under-representation in nursing homes."[163] Therefore, the defendants did not meet their burden of proof.[164]

Linton demonstrates that health care programs can operate in a racist way despite the appearance of racial neutrality. Any reform to the health care system that does not specifically address race has the potential of being racist and discriminatory.

3. Barriers to physicians and other providers

Another important aspect of access to care is the availability of health care providers who serve the African-American communities.[165] It should go without saying that proximity increases utilization. At this point, data on the actual numbers of white physicians who have offices in the African-American community are not available. There are probably very few. Consequently, African-American physicians have been an important aspect of filling the availability gap. Without physicians and providers in their communities, African-Americans are likely to delay seeking health care. That delay can result in more severe illness, increased health care cost, increased mortality and increased costs to society.

Given the increased morbidity and mortality among African-Americans logically one would expect more health care providers in their communities not fewer, and more African-Americans in health care fields. Scrutiny of the physicians heading in the Yellow Pages of any major city, clearly indicates that many physicians do not physically serve the African-American community.

Furthermore, despite being 12% of the population, African-Americans are seriously under-represented in health care professions. Only 3% of the physicians in the United States are African-Americans;[166]

---

163. *Id.*

164. *Id.*

165. Providers include physicians, nurses, pharmacists, dentists as well as the many other health care professionals who serve a community.

166. Jones & Rice, *supra* note 22, at 10–13. Lack of African-American representation in medicine is traceable to segregation in medical schools. *Id.* at 11. For instance, an African-American did not receive a degree in an American school until 1847. While some white schools (nine) admitted African-Americans prior to the Civil War, most schools did not. In fact, even in 1971, 21 medical schools out of 85 still had no African-American students. *Id.* Even with the admission of African-Americans to predominantly white schools, the African-American medical schools, Howard University and Meharry Medical

(cont.)

only 2.5% of the dentists in the United States are African-Americans;[167] and only 3.6% of the United States pharmacists are African-Americans.[168] While this lack of representation is particularly significant for African-American communities which rely on African-American physicians for care,[169] it also impacts the entire community. Shortage of adequate care results in sicker individuals and an increase in overall health care costs. If African-Americans are sicker, they need more physicians, not fewer. Yet, we see the same limited availability of providers, as of hospitals, to service African-American communities.[170]

The shortage of African-American professionals further affects health care availability by limiting African-American input into the

---

(166, *cont.*) School, still train 75% of African-American physicians. Donald Wilson, *Minorities and the Medical Profession: A Historical Perspective and Analysis of Current and Future Trends*, 78 J. NAT'L MED. ASSN. 177, 178 (1986); Jones & Rice, *supra* note 22, at 10–13; *see generally* Max Seham, M.D., BLACKS AND AMERICAN MEDICAL CARE 20–21 (1973); U.S. DEPT. OF HEALTH & HUMAN SERVICES, MINORITIES & WOMEN IN THE HEALTH FIELDS Table 3 (1990).

167. Jones & Rice, *supra* note 22, at 10–13; U.S. DEPT. OF HEALTH & HUMAN SERVICES, *supra* note 130, Table 3 (1990). *See also*, Amanda Husted, *Shortage of Black Dentists has Ill Effect in Community*, ATLANTA J. & CONST., Aug. 19, 1991, at B3 (discussing effect of shortage of African-American dentists on community).

168. Jones & Rice, *supra* note 22, at 10–13; U.S. DEPT. OF HEALTH & HUMAN SERVICES, *supra* note 166, Table 3 (1990).

169. *See* Kenneth Reich, *Panel Hears Horrors of Health Care Crisis*, L.A. TIMES, Jan. 12, 1992, at B1 (reporting that witnesses at public hearing tell of long waits at county-run facilities in minority communities). In fact, 75% of African-American physicians practice in or near African-American communities, 90% had patient loads that were at least 50% African-American or minority, 2/3 had 70% African-American or minority patient loads, and 1/3 had 90% African-American or minority patient loads. H.R. REP. No. 804, *supra* note 76, at 20, *reprinted in* 1990 U.S.C.C.A.N. 3299.

170. In addition, even programs (i.e., Medicaid) do not necessarily expand access since many primary care providers either do not accept Medicaid patients or limit the number of such patients they will accept. Karen Davis et al., *Health Care for Black Americans: The Public Sector, in* HEALTH POLICIES AND BLACK AMERICANS, *supra* note 98, at 225–26. It is only natural to look to the African-American physician to "fill" this gap. *See generally*, H.R. Rep. No. 804, *supra* note 76, at 20, *reprinted in* 1990 U.S.C.C.A.N. 3299 (finding that minority health professionals historically tended to practice in low-income areas and to serve minorities; that minority health professionals tended to engage in the general practice of medicine and specialities providing primary care; and that access to health care among minorities can be substantially improved by increasing the number of minority health professionals).

health care system.[171] While the control of health care distribution is ultimately in the hands of the individual physician, that control is influenced and limited by law, hospital practices and policies, and the medical organization of the physician's practice. With so few African-American health care professionals, the control of the health care system lies almost exclusively in European-American hands.

The result is an inadequate, if not ineffective, voice on African-American health care issues. This lack of African-American voice leads to increased ignorance on the part of European-Americans regarding issues pertaining to African-American health. When health care issues are defined, the policy makers' ignorance results in their overlooking African-Americans' health concerns.

B. Racial disparities in medical treatment

Racial barriers to access are only one aspect of institutional racism. Another aspect is the occurrence of racial disparities in type of services ordered and in the provision of medical treatment itself,[172] well-documented in studies done in cardiology, cardiac surgery, kidney disease, organ transplantation, internal medicine and obstetrics.

Cardiology and cardiac surgery.
African-Americans and European-Americans have similar rates of hospitalization for circulatory system disease. Yet, studies have found that European-Americans are one-third more likely to undergo coronary angiography[173] and two to three times more likely to undergo bypass surgery.[174]

---

171. *See* H.R. REP. NO. 804, *supra* note 76, at 20, *reprinted in* 1990 U.S.C.C.A.N. 3299 (finding that the number of individuals who are from disadvantaged backgrounds [including racial minorities] in health professions should be increased for the purpose of improving the access of other such individuals to health services).

172. One wonders how much of the disparity in treatment is a legacy in medical practice from slavery when "... doctors frequently complained that they were unable to administer treatment because the slaves were not amenable to the same medical treatment as white patients." PINKNEY, *supra* note 89, at 6.

173. Council on Ethical and Judicial Affairs, *Black-White Disparities in Health Care*, 263 JAMA 2344 (1990); *see also* Mark B. Wenneker & Arnold M. Epstein, *Racial Inequalities in the use of Procedures for Patients with Ischemic Heart Disease in Massachusetts*, 261 JAMA 253, 253–57 (1989).

174. Council on Ethical and Judicial Affairs, *Black-White Disparities in Health*
(*cont.*)

Kidney disease and kidney transplantation.

The aggressive treatment of long-term kidney disease is based in part on race. Studies indicate that European-Americans are 5% to 15% more likely to receive aggressive treatment.[175] In fact, the most favored patient for long-term hemodialysis is a European-American male between the ages of 25 and 44.[176] A European-American on dialysis is two-thirds more likely to receive a kidney transplant than a non-European-American.[177] While the likelihood of receiving a kidney transplant is related to income, the effects of income and race are independent from each other,[178] meaning that middle-income African-Americans are less likely to receive a kidney transplant than middle-income European-Americans.

Internal medical treatment.

The patient's race has been correlated with the intensity of medical treatment. For example, when hospitalized with pneumonia, African-Americans were less likely than European-Americans to receive intens-

---

(174, *cont.*) *Care, supra* note 173, at 2344–45; *see also* Albert Oberman & Gary Cutter, *Issues in the Natural History and Treatment of Coronary Heart Disease in Black Populations: Surgical Treatment*, 108 AM. HEART J. 688, 688–94 (1984) (discussing results of study showing a preferential selection of whites for coronary artery bypass grafting). *Cf.*, Charles Maynard et al., *Blacks in the Coronary Artery Surgery Study: Race and Clinical Decision Making*, 76 AM. J. PUB. HEALTH 1446, 1446–48 (1986) (finding that rate of by-pass surgery could not be explained by differences in clinical or angiographic characteristics).

175. Council on Ethical and Judicial Affairs, *Black-White Disparities in Health Care, supra* note 173, at 2345; *see generally* C.M. Kjellstrand & George M. Logan, *Racial, Sexual and Age Inequalities in Chronic Dialysis*, 45 NEPHRON 257, 25763 (1987) ("[I]n three of four categories, blacks received less dialysis than whites").

176. *See also* Council on Ethical and Judicial Affairs, *Black-White Disparities in Health Care, supra* note 173, at 2345; Kjellstrand & Logan, *supra* note 175.

177. *Id.; see also* C.M. Kjellstrand, *Age, Sex and Race Inequality in Renal Transplantation*, 148 ARCHIVES INTERNAL MED. 1305, 1305–09 (1988); P.W. Eggers, *Effect of Transplantation on the Medicare End-Stage Renal Disease Program*, 318 NEW ENG. J. MED. 223–29 (1988) (reporting that while African-Americans accounted for 33% of patients with end-stage renal problems, they were only 21% of the patients who received kidney transplants).

178. *Black-White Disparities, supra* note 173, at 2345; *see also* P.J. Held et al., *Access to kidney transplantation: Has the United States Eliminated Income and Racial Differences?* 148 ARCHIVES INTERNAL MED. 2594, 2594–00 (1988).

ive care.[179] This disparity in medical treatment persisted even after controlling for clinical characteristics and income.[180]

Obstetrical treatment.
African-Americans were more likely to be classified as "clinic" patients despite comparable ability to pay for care. Private patients were more likely than clinic patients to have caesarean sections.[181] This is true even though clinic patients were in poorer health and were more likely to have low birth weight babies.[182]

These studies all raise the issue that African-Americans receive health care treatment different from the "preferred" patient the European-American male. Whether this difference is based on individual prejudices or medical school training, it is evidence of institutional racism that cannot be tolerated. Any patient seeking care from a physician should be able to be assured of the most appropriate medical treatment available. Irrespective of race, each of us should be assured that the physician will act in our best interest. Every person should be assured that the physician will not let personal prejudice or medical prejudice influence our medical treatment. As the situation exists, an African-American does not have those assurances.

C. Summary

Race affects *access to care* independent of socioeconomic class. Race also affects *medical treatment* independent of socioeconomic class. While the disparities in treatment decisions reflect clinical characteristics, income, medical or biological differences, they also reflect racial bias.[183] To improve the health of African-Americans, it is not sufficient merely to remove barriers to access based on socioeconomic class. Health care institutions must rid themselves of institutional racism.

---

179. *Black-White Disparities, supra* note 173, at 2345; *see also,* John Yergan et al., *Relationship between Patient Race and the Intensity of Hospital Services,* 25 MED. CARE 592, 600, 603 (1987) (suggesting that nonwhite pneumonic patients receive fewer services, especially with regard to intensive care).

180. *Black-White Disparities, supra* note 173, at 2345; John Yergan et al., *supra* note 179.

181. *Id.; see also* R.H. de Regt et al., *Relation of Private or Clinic Care to the Cesarean Birth Rate,* 315 NEW ENG. J. MED. 619, 619–24 (1986).

182. *Black-White Disparities, supra* note 173, at 2344; de Regt et al., *supra* note 181.

183. *Black-White Disparities, supra* note 173.

Medicine has found cures and controls for many afflictions, improving the health of all Americans—African-Americans, Asian-Americans, Hispanic-Americans, Native-Americans and European-Americans.[184] However, the health institutions have failed to extend the same magnitude of improvement in health among European-Americans to African-Americans and other minority populations.[185] Health institutions have failed to eliminate the racial distribution of health care.[186] They also continue to perpetuate distinctions. Such a situation is intolerable. Of all the influences on African-Americans' health, the influence of health care institutions, though relatively small, should nevertheless be free of racial prejudice and discrimination.

IV. HEALTH POLICY AND ELIMINATING THE HEALTH DISPARITY

> This the American black man knows: his fight here is a fight to the finish. Either he dies or wins. If he wins, it will be by no subterfuge or evasion of amalgamation. He will enter modern civilization here in America as black man on terms of perfect and unlimited equality with any white man, or he will enter not at all. Either exterminate root and branch, or absolute equality. There can be no compromise. This is the last great battle of the West.[187]

Institutional racism is a term that describes practices in the United States nearly as old as the nation itself. Institutional racism comprises those policies, practices, and activities which injure or damage an individual or group based on race. Like individual racism, the effects of institutional racism can derive from intentional or unintentional conduct. For African-Americans who face disproportionate morbidity and mortality, whether the conduct was intentional or not is irrelevant. When medical institutions' behavior sets up racial barriers to access and provides racially disparate treatment of African-Americans, and thereby injures those the institutions purport to help, the institutions are institutionally racist.

African-Americans have not profited as much as European-Ameri-

---

184. KNOWLES & PREWITT, *supra* note 15, at 99.

185. *Id.* at 98 (implicating health institutions for the failure to carry on medical advances and treatment to the black community).

186. *Id.* at 99.

187. W.E.B. DUBOIS, BLACK RECONSTRUCTION 703 (1962).

cans by the early advances of health care. In fact, the gap between African-American health and European-American health has widened over the last ten years.[188] Racism has adversely affected African-American health independently of other factors contributing to excess African-American morbidity and mortality. We have much to lose by its persistence.

In 1992, the presence of institutional racism in a system dedicated to improving the life of all Americans is a powerful indictment of a system that offers part of its population what some consider the best health care in the world.[189] Despite having ultimate responsibility for providing health care for all Americans, despite a belief in this country that all persons have certain rights to life, liberty and health, the American health care institution has contributed to and perpetuated racism.

> What white Americans have never fully understood—but what the Negro can never forget—is that white society is deeply [racist]. White institutions created it, white institutions maintained it and white societies condone it.[190]

---

188. U.S. DEP'T. OF HEALTH & HUMAN SERVICES, *Secretary's Taskforce Report on Minority Health.*

189. Scott, *Lawmakers Differ on Measures to Reform Health care*, MEMPHIS BUS. J., June 1, 1992, 41 (stating that lawmakers agree America has the best health care service in the world); Storer H. Rowley, *Prescription from Canada: Would Universal Health Care Work in the Country?*, CHI. TRIB., May 31, 1992 (reporting that "[m]any Americans still boast that they have the best health care money can buy and that it's there on demand, without Canada's occasionally lengthy waiting lines"); Joel Havemann, *A Safety Net Snags on Its Cost; Western Europe's Prized Welfare Programs Follow Citizens From Cradle to Grave. But Tax Rates are Astronomical by U.S. Standards, and Critics Are Gingerly Making Changes*, Los Angeles Times, April 21, 1992, at A1 (reporting that "[t]he U.S. medical profession insists that it delivers the best health care in the world, that most medical breakthroughs bear a Made-in-the-USA label"); John Lucadamo, *Porter, Sullivan Clash at Debate Over Everything But Pensions*, CHI. TRIB., March 10, 1992 (reporting that "Porter said the United States has the best health care in the world 'for those in the system'"); George Will, *Revision of Our Health-Care System Should be High on Nation's Agenda*, ATLANTA J. & CONST., Mar. 9, 1992 (stating that "America can provide the world's best health care—if you can afford it"); President George Bush, *Remarks of President Bush to the San Diego Rotary Club* (Feb. 7, 1992) FED. NEWS SERV., (reporting that "[t]his country has the best health care system in the world—the best. And the quality of health care in America is unrivaled").

190. Tom Wicker, Introduction to REPORT OF THE NATIONAL ADVISORY COMMISSION ON CIVIL DISORDERS, at vii (1968).

For health care institutions to remove the blemish of racism, they must develop specific solutions. To bring African-American health on par with European-American health, we must design and implement a delivery system to effectively address the health issues of African-Americans. There are four policy/legislative positions that can be adopted (singly or in some combination).[191]

First, the health care system, legislature or court can do nothing. The legislature (and courts) could continue to rely on the present system without specifically addressing issues relevant to African-American health. This position denies that the health care system perpetuates disparity among African-Americans and European-Americans. However, this position does provide a base measure against which other policy alternatives can be evaluated. Second, insurance coverage could be expanded. Expanding insurance coverage would theoretically remove economic barriers to health care. Third, based on those facts that suggest severe treatment disparity between African-Americans and European-Americans, special health services could be targeted to African-Americans. Finally, Title VI of the Civil Rights Act could be used to eliminate racist practices in health care delivery systems.

Policy options are neither right nor wrong and can only be evaluated in the context of how well the policy satisfies other criteria. These policy alternatives can be evaluated using seven criteria: horizontal equity, vertical equity, economic efficiency, preference satisfaction, privacy, avoidance of stigma, and political feasibility. Horizontal equity seeks to treat equals as equals. For example, a policy proposal that targets services to all diabetic patients residing in the United States satisfies the criterion of horizontal equity, whereas a policy targeting all African-American diabetic patients does not.[192] Vertical equity is unequal treatment of unequals, trying to make them more equal. Vertical equity suggests that a good policy proposal is one that favors the have-nots over the haves in the distribution of benefits.[193] Economic efficiency is the use of resources to produce the maximum benefit for

---

191. Dorothy Howze, *Closing the Gap Between Black and White Infant Mortality Rates: An Analysis of Policy Options, in* HEALTH CARE ISSUES IN BLACK AMERICA: POLICIES, PROBLEMS AND PROSPECTS (Woodrow Jones, Jr. & Mitchell F. Rice eds., 1987).

192. Duncan MacRae, Jr. & Ron Haskins, *Combining the Roles of Scholar and Citizen, in* MODELS FOR ANALYSIS OF SOCIAL POLICY 119–22 (Ron Haskins & James J. Gallagher eds., 1981).

193. *Id.*

the smallest expenditure.[194] Preference satisfaction requires that a policy produce the most happiness for the greatest number of people, usually by creating options and allowing individuals to maximize their own preferences. Therefore, in selecting between alternative policy options, the policy which is consistent with people's preferences is favored.[195] One problem with preference measurement is that human preferences do change as a result of education and advertising. Therefore, weight given to preference satisfaction should be considered against the likelihood of the preference being changed. The privacy criterion stipulates that a policy should not allow intrusion into the life of the individual.[196] Avoidance of stigma means that individuals are not negatively labeled as different from other citizens not affected by the policy.[197] Political feasibility is the possibility that the particular alternatives have a chance of being adopted and implemented by the courts and legislature.[198]

A. "Do nothing" policy option[199]

Horizontal equity.
In evaluating the different policy options, the "do nothing" option serves as a baseline. The existent system does not provide African-Americans who are ill with the same access as sick European-Americans; nor

---

194. Ron Haskins, *Social Policy Analysis: A Partial Agenda, in* MODELS FOR ANALYSIS OF SOCIAL POLICY 204 (Ron Haskins & James J. Gallagher eds., 1981).

195. Duncan MacRae, Jr. & Ron Haskins, *Models for Policy Analysis, in* MODELS FOR ANALYSIS OF SOCIAL POLICY 19–20 (Ron Haskins & James J. Gallagher eds., 1981).

196. Robert M. Moroney, *Policy Analysis within a Value Theoretical Framework, in* MODELS FOR ANALYSIS OF SOCIAL POLICY 87–88 (Ron Haskins & James J. Gallagher eds., 1981).

197. MacRae, *supra* note 192, at 121–23. The debate that has raged around the stigma that can be attached to selective programs is centered in the idea that the poor are responsible for their situation.

198. MacRae & Haskins, *supra* note 195, at 2.

199. The chart below is a visual representation of how well "doing nothing" meets the various criteria. A minus sign (−) means that the criterion is not met. A plus sign (+) means that the criterion is met. A question mark (?) means that it is uncertain as to how well the criterion will be met.

Horizontal equity	Vertical equity	Economic efficiency	Preference satisfaction	Privacy	Stigma	Political feasibility
−	−	−	−	+	−	+

do African-Americans receive the same treatment once in the health care system. Consequently, sick African-Americans are not treated the same as sick European-Americans. The current system lacks horizontal equity.

Vertical equity.

Doing noting maintains the status quo and does not attempt to improve access or treatment services for African-Americans. African-American communities have fewer providers and medical institutions. African-Americans have disproportionate morbidity and mortality. Doing nothing does not address the unique needs of African-Americans. Doing nothing does not close the gap in health between African-Americans and European-Americans. Given the unequal access and unequal medical treatment, doing nothing makes no changes which, by treating African-Americans differently, would lead to equal health care. Therefore, vertical equity does not exist.

Economic efficiency.

To the extent that the United States is already spending enough to bring every citizen high quality, high-technology care, economic efficiency is not met. Of the $817 billion that is spent each year on health care, it is estimated that $200 billion is spent on unnecessary medical care, overpriced procedures and inefficient administration.[200] Apparently,

---

200. *Wasted Health Care Dollars*, 57(7) CONSUMERS REPS 435 (1992); *see generally* George Lundberg, *National Health Care Reform: The Aura of Inevitability Intensifies*, 267 JAMA 2521–24 (1992) (The costs of malpractice coverage and defensive medicine are unknown but very large—perhaps in excess of $20 billion per year. Defensive medicine probably benefits no one except these with the health care jobs that are generated . . . The current system is rife with administrative waste, inefficiency, and a ubiquitous "hassle factor."); D.U. Himmelstein & S. Woolhandler, *Cost Without Benefit: Administrative Waste in U.S. Health Care*, 314 NEW ENG. J. MED. 441–45 (1986) ("With the institution of a national health plan, $30 billion in administrative costs could be saved."); Jasjit Ahluwalis, *Health Care in the United States: Our Dynamic Jigsaw Puzzle*, 150 ARCHIVES INTERNAL MED. 256, 256–258 (1990) ("Up to 20% of every dollar spent on the administrative aspects of health care is wasted. If the system were streamlined, then $15 billion of the $78 billion spent in administration could be saved."); Eli Ginzberg, *Commentary: US Health Policy—Expectations and Realities*, 260 JAMA 3647, 3647–50 (1988) ("The 'waste' in the system of medical care exemplified in physicians' doing too much and, worse still, often performing diagnostic and therapeutic procedures that are contrain-

the current system is not economically efficient. Reforming the health care system to meet the needs of African-Americans will not be any more economically inefficient than the current system.[201] On the other hand, failure to reform the system will mean continued costs in African-American lives. This cost is one which will not only affect individual lives and the African-American community, but also the general society in lost productivity and additional health care expenses.

Preference satisfaction.

Preference satisfaction requires that a policy produce the most happiness for the greatest number of people, usually by creating options and allowing individuals to maximize their own preferences. Whether preference satisfaction exists depends on whose perspective one considers. Certainly, for those who have access to the health care system and adequate treatment, doing nothing might allow them to maximize their own preferences. However, for African-Americans whose access to health care is limited and whose treatment is below standard, doing nothing would not create options or allow them to maximize their preferences.

---

dicated"); *cf.*, State of North Carolina *ex rel.* Rufus L. Edmisten v. P.I.A. Asheville, Inc, 740 F.2d 274 (1984) (indicating that the legislative histories of both the National Health Planning and Resource Development Act of 1974 and of the 1979 amendments and North Carolina's certificate of need legislation show that Congress and the North Carolina legislature were concerned about "the unrelenting rise in the cost of health care, and about wasteful, duplicative major acquisitions by health care providers"); Alabama Renal Stone Institute, Inc. v. State Health Planning Agency, 594 So. 2d 106 (Ala. Civ. App. 1991) (explaining that to allow the hospitals to use the Medstone device to perform kidney lithotripsy without first obtaining a certificate of need would be contrary to the intent of the legislature to avoid oversupply and the substantial waste that will occur); *but see* Maxwell J. Mehlman, *Health Care Cost Containment and Medical Technology: A Critique of Waste Theory*, 36 CASE W. RES. L. REV. 778 (1985/1986) (stating that the high cost of health care has led to proposals to reduce wasteful medical technology under Medicare and other payment systems. Achieving this objective is problematic because of the difficulties of defining, detecting and eliminating technology waste).

201. There is no system imaginable "that's more dysfunction[al] than the one we have now, more expensive, not doing the job with more waste." *Wasted Health Care Dollars, supra* note 200 (*quoting* Dr. Philip Caper, an internist and medical policy analyst at Dartmouth Medical School).

Privacy.

The privacy criterion stipulates that a policy does not allow intrusion into the life of the individual. The current system maximizes an individual's privacy. Theoretically, the free-choice, fee-for-service, retrospective payment system, currently serving much of the population, neither limits from whom an individual can seek services nor limits the services that a provider can render. Those enjoying limitless services are not required to disclose information to receive care. In this way, doing nothing maximizes the privacy of those with access to health care services; while those without access to services have no privacy issues, because they are excluded from participation.

Stigma.

Avoidance of stigma means that individuals are not negatively labeled as different from other citizens not affected by the policy. To the extent that doing nothing allows the gap in health between African-Americans and European-Americans to continue, it may cause some stigma. Individuals who believe that a major cause of illness and death is behavior may view reports of poorer health among African-Americans as evidence of poor health behavior. To some extent they are correct.[202] However, if European-Americans fail to acknowledge the

---

202. *See supra* text accompanying notes 82–86; *see generally* E. Richard Brown, *Health USA; A National Health Program for the United States*, 267 JAMA 552, 552–58 (1992) (explaining that state programs must designate funds for a prevention account, to be used for community-based disease prevention and health promotion programs targeted to population groups with the greatest unmet needs); Harold Freeman, *Race, Poverty, and Cancer*, 83 J. NAT'L CANCER INST. 526, 526–27 (1991) (showing that shared elements lead to common life style, attitudes, and behavior. Such cultural factors deeply influence health, and any successful intervention must necessarily take these powerful cultural realities into account); Antonia C. Novello et al., *Hispanic Health: Time for Data, Time for Action*, 265 JAMA 235, 253–55 (1991) (explaining that differences in health behaviors and health exist between US-born and foreign-born members of the same ancestral group; in general, recent arrivals tend to be of better health); J. Michael McGinnis, *Communication for Better Health*, 105 PUB. HEALTH REP. 217–18 (1990) (stating that better control of behavioral risk factors alone could prevent between 40% and 70% of premature deaths); Council on Scientific Affairs, *Education for Health; A Role for Physicians and the Efficacy of Health Education Efforts*, 263 JAMA 1816, 1816–19 (1990) (suggesting that many health problems are caused or exacerbated by individuals' life styles, and that a result has been efforts to avert health problems of all kinds leading

role of the health care system, doing nothing results in a failure of the health care system to accept responsibility for its role in the health of African-Americans. It also leads to indirect blaming and negative labelling of African-Americans.

Political feasibility.
Political feasibility is the possibility that the particular alternatives have a chance of being adopted and implemented by the courts and legislature. Maintaining the status quo is generally easier than making substantial changes. The likelihood that specific actions will be taken to improve the health of African-Americans seems slim, since little attention is being given to the problem.

Summary.
The do nothing option allows for the social, economic, and health care disparity to continue to exist between African-Americans and European-Americans. Racial and economic barriers to access experienced by African-Americans would persist. Racial and economic barriers to entering the health care professions would remain. Doing nothing would be to insist on ignoring the racial disparities in medical treatment. This situation is untenable. The health of African-Americans clearly indicates that something needs to be done.

B. Expanded insurance coverage

1. *Background*

The United States and South Africa are the only major industrialized nations without a universal health insurance system that guarantees access to health care for all of their citizens. What the United States has instead of universal health care is a scheme of employer-financed insurance and government programs[203] that still leaves more than 37

---

to the development of programs designed to promote healthful behavior and improve health).

203. In 1965, Congress responded to the medical insurance problems by creating Medicare and Medicaid. Congress established Medicare to provide medical care to the elderly. Their ability to pay was irrelevant. *See generally* Social Security Amendments of 1965, PUB. L. NO. 89–97, 79 Stat. 286 (codified as amended in scattered sections of 42 U.S.C.) Medicaid, a cooperative
(*cont.*)

million Americans without the financial resources to pay for health care.[204]

The lack of health insurance is a particular issue for African-Americans who are less likely to have employer-financed insurance.[205] While public programs, such as Medicaid and Medicare, are important sources of health care coverage for many low-income and African-Americans, they do not reach all of the uninsured poor.[206] In fact, one-fourth (25%) of African-Americans have no source of health coverage.[207]

Even more disturbing is that the number of uninsured African-Americans is increasing. In 1977, only 18% of African-Americans had no health coverage.[208] Furthermore, the gap between African-American uninsured and European-American uninsured is widening. For instance, while the proportion of uninsured non-elderly European-Americans increased only 3% from 1977 to 1987 (from 12% to 15%), the proportion of uninsured non-elderly African-Americans increased 7% (from 18% to 25%) during the same period.[209]

(203, *cont.*) federal program, provides health insurance to eligible individuals and families. 42 U.S.C. § 1396 (1992).

Since 1965, Medicare and Medicaid have grown significantly. Medicare currently accounts for approximately 35% of national health care expenditures and 40% of hospital revenues. *See generally* OFFICE OF TECHNOLOGY ASSESSMENT, MEDICAL TECHNOLOGY AND COSTS OF THE MEDICARE PROGRAM 45–61 (1984) (hereinafter OTA MEDICARE). *Medical Technology Assessment: Hearings on H.R. 5496 before the Subcommittee on Health and the Environment of the Committee on Energy and Commerce*, 98th Cong., 2d Sess. 544 (1984) [hereinafter cited as *Hearings on H.R. 5496*] (statement of Raymond Dross, M.D., on behalf of Health Insurance Association of America).

Yet, Medicare's impact extends well beyond the program. For example, other institutional purchasers of health care, such as private insurers, typically follow Medicare's lead with regard to medical technology and payment schedules. OTA MEDICARE, *supra* note 203, at 23.

204. Pamela Short et al., *Health Insurance of Minorities in the United States*, 1(2) J. HEALTH CARE FOR POOR & UNDERSERVED 9–24 (1990).

205. In 1985 only 47% of African-Americans had employment related insurance compared to 62% of non-African-Americans. Stephen Long, *Public Versus Employment-related Health Insurance: Experience and Implications for Black and NonBlack Americans, in* HEALTH POLICIES AND BLACK AMERICANS 200–12, at 203 (David P. Willis ed., 1989); *see also* Davis, *supra* note 170.

206. Only 28% of African-Americans had public insurance.; Long, *supra* note 205, at 203; *see also* Davis, *supra* note 63, at 1.

207. Short et al., *supra* note 204; *see also* Long, *supra* note 205, at 203; Davis, *supra* note 170, at 1.

208. Short et al., *supra* note 204.

209. *Id.*; Davis, *supra* note 170, at 3–6.

Since private health insurance coverage is linked to employment, racial barriers to employment are one explanation for the significant difference in insurance coverage. For example, in 1990 the African-American unemployment rate was 240% more than the European-American unemployment rate.[210] Even where employed, the African-American is more likely to be in a lower paying job which does not provide employer-based health insurance.[211] Another factor affecting insurance coverage is the higher percentage of African-American families with only one adult.[212] Families with two working adults are more likely to have at least one adult with employer-based insurance.[213]

However, while the absence of health insurance is much more likely with lower income, race is an independent factor affecting whether an individual will be insured. In fact, the racial difference in proportion of uninsured is most marked at higher incomes.[214] For example, poor/low-income African-Americans are uninsured at about the same rate as poor/low-income European-Americans; however, middle/high-income African-Americans are almost twice as likely to be uninsured than higher-income European-Americans.[215]

---

210. Davis, *supra* note 170, at 5.

211. *Id.* (reporting that as of 1988, the mean earnings for European-American males was 36% higher than African-American males).

212. In 1990, 61% of African-American families with children under the age of 18 were single caregivers, (i.e. single parent, single foster parent, single relative, single grandparent) compared to 23% of similar European-American families. Davis, *supra* note 170, at 5.

213. *Id.* at 6.

214. Davis, *supra* note 170, at 28; Short et al., *supra* note 204.

215. Short et al., *supra* note 204; Davis, *supra*, note 170, at 28. Of poor individuals, 36% of European-Americans are uninsured compared to 35% of African-Americans. Of low-income individuals, 31% of European-Americans are uninsured compared to 30% of African-Americans. Finally, of middle/high-income individuals, 9% of European-Americans are uninsured compared to 16% of African-Americans. *Id.* African-Americans are more likely to be uninsured because they are more likely to be unemployed or employed in low paying positions which do not provide health care benefits. For instance, in 1989, 30.7% of African-Americans were poor, compared with 12.8% of European-Americans. In 1990, the African-American unemployment rate (11.3%) was 140% more than European-Americans (4.7%). Finally, the mean earnings of European-Americans males were 36% higher than African-American males. U.S. House of Representatives, Committee on Ways and Means, 1991. *Green Book, Background Material and Data on-Programs within the Jurisdication of the Committee on Ways and Means*, Washington, D.C.: U.S. Government Printing Office, May 7 (1991).

Expanding insurance coverage so that everyone will have either employer-based or government-based insurance is one proposal for addressing the inequities in the health care system.[216] During the 102nd Congress, more than thirty proposals were introduced to expand insurance coverage and reform the health care system.[217] The proposals under consideration fell into five major categories: market-reform, employer mandate plus Medicaid, employer choice of Medicare or private, Medicare for all, comprehensive public plan. (See Table 1).

- *Market-reform.* Small group health insurance reform is a targeted approach to extend insurance to the working uninsured.[218] It proposes reforming the small group market to make coverage affordable and easier to purchase and to then sell private health insurance to small firms.[219] The reforms include: requiring private insurers to make coverage available to all firms, employees and dependents in the group, limiting pre-existing condition waiting periods for coverage, limiting variation of premiums based on group risk, limiting the extent to which premiums could be increased.[220]
- *Employer-mandated basic coverage plus Medicaid.* Similar to market-reform, this proposal would require employers to offer coverage and to contribute at least 75 to 80% toward the premium cost.[221] In addition, Medicaid would be expanded to cover all poor persons not encompassed under an employer policy.[222]
- *Employer choice of Medicare or private.* The "play or pay" option would provide employers with the alternative of acquiring private health insurance coverage for employees and dependents or contributing

---

216. Numerous policy responses have been suggested for increasing insurance coverage. The three main proposals are employer mandate coverage which require all employers to provide health insurance, expansion of Medicaid cover-age or a combination of employer mandated and expansion of Medicaid. Long, *supra* note 168, at 200–12. It is estimated that even with a combined employer mandate and Medicaid expansion some 2.1 million African-Americans will remain uninsured. *Id.* at 211. Thus, a fourth proposal, universal health insurance, has been suggested.

217. *This Week with David Brinkley* (ABC television broadcast, Feb. 2, 1992).

218. Davis, *supra* note 170, at 11–12.

219. *Id.* at 11.

220. *Id.* at 11–13.

221. *Id.* at 13.

222. *Id.*

toward their coverage under a public plan similar to Medicare.[223] If a person is not covered under a private insurance plan, he or she would automatically be covered under the public plan and assessed a premium based on income.[224]

- *Medicare for all.* This alternative would broaden the present Medicare program to the whole population. Employers would be required to contribute financially toward the coverage of their employees. States would also be required to contribute current Medicaid funding for acute care benefits to the poor.[225]
- *Comprehensive public plan.* This option provides comprehensive health benefits to the entire United States population through a single public plan.[226] This plan would replace all private health insurance.[227]

Table 1. Expanded health insurance options[228]

	Market-reform	Employer mandate plus Medicaid	Employer choice of Medicare or private	Medicare for all	Comprehensive public plan
Coverage	20–23 million	6 million	Universal	Universal	Universal
Benefits	Limited	Basic	Medicare	Medicare	Comprehensive
Private insurance	170 million	200 million	180 million	Supplemental	None
Cost containment	None	Managed care	All Payer	Single payer	Global budget
Financing	Individual premiums	Employer premiums contributions	Employer premium contributions or payroll	Payroll tax Income tax	Payroll tax Income tax Other

---

223. *Id.* at 15–18.

224. *Id.* Acute benefits for low-income families would no longer be covered under Medicaid. Instead, states would contribute toward the new public plan coverage of acute care benefits. *Id.* However, Medicaid would continue to provide supplemental benefits and long-term care. *Id.*

225. *Id.* at 18–20.

226. *Id.* at 20–21.

227. *Id.*

228. *Id.* app. (chart 2).

2. Policy analysis[229]

Horizontal equity.

To the extent that expanded insurance coverage would provide economic access for all uninsured, it has horizontal equity. In essence, expanded insurance coverage treats equals (the uninsured) as equals. Therefore, options such as employer choice of Medicare or private insurance, Medicare for all, and comprehensive public plan, have horizontal equity.

However, market-reform and employer-mandated plus Medicaid do not provide for coverage for all uninsured. For instance, market-reform options do not require the employer to contribute toward the premiums. Without employer contributions, many employees in low-paying jobs will not be able to afford the premiums. Furthermore, premiums may increase because of availability of coverage to high-risk, sick individuals who had been previously excluded by underwriting practices.[230] Therefore, under the market-reform option almost 40 millions persons will still be uninsured.[231] Similarly, employer mandate only covers two-thirds of the uninsured who are in families with a working adult. It excludes from coverage almost 7 million uninsured,

---

229. The chart below is a visual representation of how well "Expanding Insurance Coverage" meets the various criteria. A minus sign (−) means that the criterion is not met. A plus sign (+) means that the criterion is met. A question mark (?) means that it is uncertain as to how well the criterion will be met.

Horizontal equity	Vertical equity	Economic efficiency	Preference satisfaction	Privacy	Stigma	Political feasibility
?	−	?	−	?	?	+

230. *Id.* at 12; *See generally* Paul Cotton, *Insurance Loss Threatens Medical Gain*, 266 JAMA 2185 (1991) (explaining that healthy people are increasingly unable to get what health care they do need due to severe medical underwriting practices by health insurance companies); *Limits on Medical Coverage May Affect 1 of 3 under 65*, ATLANTA J. & CONST., June 19, 1991, at B3 (detailing how an underwriting guide from an insurer contained 84 conditions—from acne to varicose veins—that it permanently excluded from health insurance coverage); *Private System Places Millions at Risk, Citizen Action Report Says*, 18 Pens. Rep. (BNA) 1048 (June 24, 1991) (discussing how private health insurance policies have lifetime limits on coverage, routinely deny coverage for any treatment or device that they do not recognize as accepted medical practice, exclude from underwriting such conditions as allergies or mild headaches be permanently excluded and deny coverage for pregnancy and cancer).

231. Davis, *supra* note 170, at 12.

such as part-time workers and older adults who are disabled or retire early and are not eligible for Medicare.[232] The groups (including those in low-paying jobs and/or part-time employment) that market-reform and employer mandate plus Medicaid will not cover would include high numbers of African-Americans.

Vertical equity.

A system of universal insurance regardless of coverage fails to resolve the racial difference in access between African-Americans and European-Americans that is not related to insurance coverage. For example, European-Americans have better access to health care even when the insurance coverage is similar.[233] Expanding insurance would not increase community availability of either European-American institutions and providers or African-American institutions and providers. Nor does expanding insurance coverage address the issues of racially disparate treatment. In short, expanding insurance coverage does not address the issue of institutional racism. Consequently, expanding insurance coverage does not provide for vertical equity.

Economic efficiency.

Whether expanding insurance coverage is economically efficient is highly debatable. Without cost controls, expanding insurance coverage could increase health care costs drastically. Historically, the existence of health insurance has played a significant role in increased health care costs. This is so because the insurer's method of reimbursing providers introduced into the health care system a "complex of irrational economic incentives".[234]

In particular, the "fee-for-service basis"[235] system euphemistically called "the free lunch system," has delivered medical care without regard to cost containment, and sometimes without regard to medical necessity. Under fee-for-service, third-party payers pay health care providers for each discrete item of service. In 1980, 50% of active

---

232. *Id.* at 13–14.

233. *See supra* notes 183–86 and accompanying text.

234. Alexander M. Capron, *Containing Health Care Costs: Ethical and Legal Implications of Changes in the Methods of Paying Physicians*, 36 CASE W. RES. L. REV. 708 (1986).

235. Yoder, *Physicians Payment Methods: Forms and Levels of Physicians' Compensation, in* INSTITUTE OF MEDICINE, REFORMING PHYSICIAN PAYMENT: REPORT OF A CONFERENCE 87, 88 (1984).

physicians were compensated by fee-for-service; approximately 20% were salaried and the other 30% received a mixed form of compensation.[236] Similarly, government programs (Medicaid and Medicare) reimbursed providers for most of their costs or charges incurred in treating covered patients.[237] Both reimbursement forms created powerful incentives to over-utilize the health care system.[238] In fact, no one had a rational incentive to economize.

For example, a patient contracted for insurance through the employer for 80% of the usual, customary, and reasonable (UCR) cost of "medically necessary care." Therefore, the patient lacked the incentive to economize because no matter the charges, the patient only paid 20% of the cost.[239] Because the insurance premium was shared with the employer, the patient generally was not directly concerned with future premium increases. Even so, her individual health care choices did not directly influence her insurance premium, since insurers did not typically base health care insurance premiums on "experience rating." In this way the patient did not realize the full financial impact of her health care treatment decisions.

---

236. *Id.*

237. *See supra* text and notes accompanying footnote 200.

238. Capron, *supra* note 234, at 708. In particular, the payers' methods of calculating fees to be paid further complicated the picture. The practice of covering "usual, customary and reasonable (UCR) cost" allowed the provider to charge whatever the market would bear—and they usually did.

> When the maximum payments available under usual and customary became public knowledge, there was a natural tendency on the part of physicians ... to move to the maximum available ... Once that was done, the whole concept of usual and customary, based on physicians' pricing as an independent entity unaffected by their peers or others in the community, was gone. The whole program changed its nature both as to Medicare and as to private, usual and customary.... Prices rose dramatically ... The doctor could find [the maximum UCR] out very readily by simply testing the system by raising his fees until he hit the upper limit, and they did.

Sylvia A. Law & Barry Ensminger, *Negotiating Physicians' Fees: Individual Patients or Society? (A Case Study in Federalism)*, 61 N.Y. U.L. REV. 1, 34 (citing Transcript at 27–98–99 *Kartell v. Blue Shield of Mass., Inc.*, 582 F. Supp. 734 (D. Mass. 1984) (testimony of John Larkin Thompson, president of Blue Shield of Massachusetts)).

239. When insurance induces a person to use more medical care than he or she would use if paying for the services directly, then the insurance is a "moral hazard" with respect to the person's indifference to cost. MARK HALL & IRA ELLMAN, HEALTH CARE LAW AND ETHICS IN A NUTSHELL 8 (1989).

Nor were hospitals and physicians motivated to economize. Because most third-party payers guaranteed providers 80% of their customary charges, fee-for-service or cost-based charges had an opposite and "perverse influence" on health service delivery.[240] Under both reimbursement systems, providers made more when they treated more.[241] This phenomenon had two effects. First, physicians and hospitals tended to de-emphasize preventive care, which was not as lucrative as treatment services. Second, providers tended to place excessive reliance on the use of medical technology because third-party payers paid for discrete procedures, not time spent with patients.[242]

From the patient's point of view, insurance removed the need to ration health care dollars, creating a "moral hazard problem."[243] And, from the insurer's point of view, a payment system that had worked well for auto and life insurance seemed to make sense. In these ways, health care insurance was designed and implemented on the basis of faulty assumptions by all parties.[244]

Extending health care insurance to greater numbers of persons could result in over-utilization unless serious cost containment measures, such as utilization review[245] and financial risk-shifting,[246] are introduced into the health care system.

---

240. Capron, *supra* note 234, at 709.

241. W.G. Manning et al., *A Controlled Trial on the Effect of a Prepaid Group Practice on Use of Services*, 310 NEW ENG. J. MED. 1505–10 (1984).

242. Hall & Ellman, *supra* note 239, at 11 (1990).

243. *See supra* note 234 and accompanying text.

244. *See supra* note 233 and accompanying text.

245. Utilization review is the process by which an organization determines if medical services are appropriate and necessary. In the managed care product, this involves examining providers' authorization and furnishing services to detect variations from the norm that may point to unnecessary or inappropriate care. Pamela S. Bouey, *Peer Review In Managed Care Setting, in* COM. LAW AND PRAC. COURSE AND HANDBOOK SERIES, MANAGED CARE 1988: LEGAL AND OPERATIONAL HEALTH CLASSES (1988). When the third-party payer detects variation, either it does not pay the claim [retrospective utilization management programs analyze data on hospital admissions, patterns of treatment and utilization of certain procedures or refuses to authorize the provision of the service (concurrent and prospective)]. Under a prospective review system, most non-emergency hospital admissions must receive prior approval and an initial approved length of stay is assigned. Richard Hinden & Douglas Elden, *Liability Issues for Managed Care Entities*, 14 SETON HALL LEGIS. J. 1, 52 (1990).

246. If payers did not combine utilization review with financial risk shifting, the review process alone would have limited effectiveness in controlling costs. Consequently, payers use various financial risk-shifting mechanisms. These

(*cont.*)

Neither the market-reform option nor the employer-mandated option is likely to contain substantial cost containment provisions. Small firms and private plans do not typically offer managed care products which provide the mechanism for serious cost containment. While some larger employers may offer managed care products, they represent a relatively small proportion of the newly insured since most larger employers are already covering their employees. There is potential for cost containment with the expansion of Medicaid, since it would extend its tight provider payment limits to a larger number of persons. However, those same payment limits might also act as a deterrent to provider participation which would then limit the actual availability of service. Therefore, expanding insurance is only efficient if the health care system is reformed to eliminate unnecessary medical care, reduce overpriced procedures, and improve administration.

Stigma.
While expanding insurance coverage will not necessarily stigmatize, actions taken to make it workable, that is, cost containment efforts, might lead to stigmatization. The stigmatization may be a result of individuals being treated differently based on the type and amount of coverage they have. Historically, the type and extent of coverage varies among individuals and groups, based on whether it is government or employer-based insurance.

Even among employers, insurance varied among large employers with unions (such as General Motors) and smaller employers without unions. Further, regardless of size of employer, individuals employed

---

(246, *cont.*) mechanisms cause the provider (physician) to change his or her pattern of practice from over-utilization to "appropriate utilization" at best and "under-utilization" at worst.

Financial risk-shifting can arise in a variety of arrangements: ownership interest, joint-venture, or a "bonus" arrangement in which the third-party payer shares the surplus from "cost-effective" care with the physician. *See generally* Paul M. Elwood, Jr., *When MDs Meet DRGs*, 57 HOSP., Dec. 16, 1983, at 62–63; E. Haavi Morreim, *The MD and the DRG*, 15 HASTINGS CTR. REP., June 1985, at 30, 34–35; Capron, *supra* note 234, at 725–29. While the form may vary, the penalities have similar effects. For instance, payers indirectly penalize physicians by giving them less profits or directly penalize them by reducing capitation payments each time they make "inappropriate referrals." However, not all risk shifting mechanisms have the same impact. Some have a greater potential than others for causing the physician to act in a way that is not consistent with the patient's best interests. For instance, because mechanisms, like physician diagnostic-related groups and capitation, require the physicians to bear individual loss, they have the greatest risk.

in minimum-wage positions often have no coverage or minimal coverage with large deductible amounts.

Government programs (such as Medicaid and Medicare) have had lower provider payment schedules and treatment guidelines, which discourage provider participation. In fact, many providers have refused to accept payment from policies that either do not make full restitution or that place restriction on their practices. Individuals who have these policies are likely to be labeled negatively by providers and institutions. Given that many African-Americans are employed in minimum-wage positions (or are covered by government insurance) they are likely to be stigmatized more by providers' refusal to accept certain policies.

Preference satisfaction.

There is no indication that a generalized insurance program will allow for preference satisfaction for all participants. Preference satisfaction implies the ability to exercise choice in providers and treatment. To make expanded insurance coverage workable, patient choice might be limited to control cost. For example, many employers may adopt managed care plans as a mechanism of controlling cost. Managed care plans[247] control cost by having physicians act as "gate-keepers",

---

247. With the stabilization of HMOs as a cost control mechanism, payers were pushed to find more efficient cost control methods or plans. The push resulted in the proliferation of other managed care arrangements, most notably preferred provider organizations (PPOs). PPOs contract directly with an employer through its health benefits department or indirectly through an insurance carrier. Typically, while the choice of providers is limited, the overall expense to the patient is lower than with traditional insurance. Physicians contracting with PPOs agree to accept both utilization review controls and financial risk-shifting structures. Payers give consumers economic incentives to use the PPOs' physicians. National Health Lawyers Association, *Introduction To Alternative Delivery Mechanisms: HMOs, PPOs & CMPs* 11 (Jeanie M. Johnson ed., 1986). Greg de Lissovoy et al., *Preferred Provider Organizations: Today's Models and Tomorrow's Prospects*, 23 INQUIRY 7, 7–8 (1986).

Monetary incentives focused on the patient effectively obviate freedom of choice. If a patient is unable to pay the difference, he or she will have no choice but to utilize the preferred provider. Approximately 20 states have attempted to resolve this issue by passing laws which limit the reimbursement differential between PPO and non-PPO utilization. It is unclear whether such limitations protect "freedom of choice" since to do so would limit the effectiveness of managed care products. Daniel Forbes, *Cut Health Care Costs, Get Sued?*, DUN'S BUS. MONTH, July 1986, at 39; *see also* Edward J. Hopkins & Gary Davis, *Restricted Choice—A Liability of Alternative Delivery Systems*, 58 FLA. B. J. 145, 145–46 (1984); Dr. Norman Payson, *A Physician's Viewpoint on PRO's*, 6 WHITTIER L. REV. 699–05 (1984).

limiting a person's access to certain treatment and to specialist physicians.[248] While expanding insurance coverage in itself will not limit preference satisfaction, the gate-keeping aspects of cost containment programs will. These attempts to have the physician become the gate-keeper to medical care will ultimately change the entire structure of the American health care system[249] and not necessarily for the better. The least articulate, least educated, least financially well-off person will

---

248. Current cost-containment efforts shift the risk of financial loss for health care in whole or in part to the providers of that care. Galen D. Powers, *Allocation of Risk in Managed Care Programs, in* MANAGED HEALTH CARE: LEGAL AND OPERATIONAL ISSUES FACING PROVIDERS, INSURERS, AND EMPLOYERS 279 (1986) [hereinafter *Allocation of Risk*]. Physicians are offered economic incentives to act as the third-party payer's agent—the "gate-keeper" to health care services. Carolyn M. Clancy & Bruce E. Hillner, *Physicians as Gate-keepers: the Impact of Financial Incentives*, 149 ARCHIVES INTERNAL MED. 917, 917–20 (1989). This change shifts the focus of the health care system from the doctor–patient relationship to the doctor–payer relationship. Ultimately, the doctor and payer will determine the quality of care received by the patient and the patient's access to that care. The gate-keeping role is not new to physicians. They have used their position in several ways. For instance, physicians have used their authority as health care gate-keepers to resist hospitals' and insurers' efforts to influence medical treatment. Furthermore, they have generally used their role to obtain more services for the patient, not less. Now, however, they use their position to "save" money for third-party payers by ordering fewer services. *See* Robert Scheier, *Twin City MDs Fight IPA Hospital Contracts*, AM. MED. NEWS, Feb. 28, 1986.

249. No matter how one looks at gatekeeping schemes they will eventually alter the perceptions and expectations of society, physicians, patients and third-party payers. How these parties will feel about what is owed to whom, what treatments are appropriate in what circumstances, and even what qualifies as a disease will be altered. Capron, *supra* note 234, at 730–33. These changes run the risk of injuring individuals merely because they cannot get access to the treatment that they need. When this failure to obtain appropriate medical care is due to cost containment efforts, who shall bear the cost? If cost containment is an important societal goal, then the cost of injuries should be spread throughout the society. Soon payers will routinely withhold (or decline to pay for) certain interventions that might benefit certain patients but that simply cost too much because it is the collective societal attitude not to "check on physicians' temptation to place their own interest ahead of their patient's interests. Instead society [attempts] to use physicians' selfish motivation to restrain full pursuit of patients' interest." Capron, *supra* note 234, at 749. "By asserting incentives that result in the physicians' having their own finances at risk, the new methods of physician reimbursement turn physicians into gatekeepers for [third-party payers]. Their decisions would no longer be based on medical criteria alone (i.e., does this medicine have something to offer this patient?) but would take into account the financial risk if they admit patients into the system whose care costs more than insurance will pay." Capron, *supra* note 234, at 753.

have the most limits imposed by cost containment efforts. If cost containment efforts result in injuries, the poor and minorities will have to bear the cost of restricted access to services. The cost containment efforts that will be associated with expanding insurance coverage could potentially result in *greater* health disparity between African-Americans and European-Americans. This is especially true given physicians' propensity to treat patients differently based on race.

Privacy.

Expanded insurance coverage does not necessarily affect privacy. However, as in preference satisfaction, steps taken to implement the option may negatively affect a person's privacy. In order for governments and third-party payers to carry out utilization review and financial risk-shifting, they must scrutinize the treatment of individual patients. In particular, utilization review examines appropriateness of medical services to detect variations from the norm that point to unnecessary or inappropriate care.[250] When the third-party payer detects variation, either it does not pay the claim (retrospective[251]) or refuses to authorize the provision of the service (concurrent and prospective[252]). Each form[253] requires varying degrees of information about the individual. The plan which will most invade an individual's

---

250. Bouey, *supra* note 245, at 1.

251. "Retrospective utilization management programs analyze data on hospital admissions, patterns of treatment and utilization of certain procedures." Hinden & Elden, *supra* note 245, at 52.

252. "Under a prospective review system, most non-emergency hospital admissions must receive prior approval and an initial approved length of stay is assigned." Hinden & Elden, *supra* note 245, at 52.

253. Utilization review may take several forms:

Pre-admission review for scheduled hospitalization which determines the medical necessity of a scheduled inpatient admission, of expensive procedures, or of outpatient procedures. Initial determination is made by a nurse review coordinator using established criteria. Almost all managed care products use pre-admission certifications. Bouey, *supra* note 207, at 11. A registered nurse usually conducts off-site pre-admission certification. If there is a scheduled admission prior to hospitalization, the patient's physician completes a review form. She describes the patient's medical condition, and the treatment plan, and forwards the form to the nurse review coordinator. The nurse notifies the physician, patient and hospital of the decision regarding the appropriateness of admission and length of stay. Harold Bischoff, *Utilization Review and Health Maintenance Organizations*, 13–14 (1989) (fellowship thesis, American Hospital Association). There is, of course, an appeal process that is conducted by a physician.

(*cont.*)

privacy is the one that employs prospective or concurrent utilization review because it requires information about a current illness for the purpose of denying care.

Political feasibility.
Almost certainly, within the next four years some bill will be passed expanding insurance coverage. The only real question is what shape the reform will take. As noted above, the 102nd Congress introduced more than thirty proposals which include market-reform, employer mandate plus Medicaid, employer choice of Medicare or private, Medicare for all, comprehensive public plan. Given the extensive insurance lobby, it is not likely that a comprehensive public plan or a Medicare-for-all plan will be adopted since both those options would nearly eliminate the role of private insurance. The market-reform option, while the least intrusive into the current system, would also leave many individuals uncovered. Given the pain and agony that many are undergoing to

---

(253, *cont.*)   *Admission review for unscheduled hospitalization* determines the medical necessity of unscheduled in-patient admissions or other admissions not covered by pre-admission review. Most managed care products use concurrent review. The primary exception is hospitals that are paid based upon diagnostic-related groups. Bouey, *supra* note 245, at 10.

Second opinions for elective surgery. Bouey, *supra* note 245 at 11.

Concurrent review (or, length of stay ["LOS"] certification) determines the medical necessity of a continued hospital stay. When the LOS certificate expires either the patient or the provider may request extension. Bouey, *supra* note 245, at 12; Hinden & Elden, *supra* note 245, at 52. A concurrent review is conducted by a nurse reviewing the patient's treatment plan. The nurse conducts the review at the hospital using established medical criteria. If the nurse judges the treatment plan to be appropriate, s/he approves the stay until the next review cycle or the patient is discharged. If s/he does not approve the treatment plan, the nurse refers the case to a physician advisor who either confirms the need for continued treatment or suggests alternate treatment. Bischoff, *supra* note 253, at 11.

Gate-keeping by primary physician determines, in a variety of ways, whether or not a patient should be seen. Bouey, *supra* note 245, at 14.

Retrospective claims review disallows payments of claims for utilization abuses. Since it is not as effective as prospective or concurrent review, use of retrospective claims review is declining. Bouey, *supra* note 245, at 14. However, it is useful as a tool to research provider claims. For example, it would be useful in determining whether the objective laboratory data (biopsy) and subjective data (surgeon notes) coincide with the length of stay or the length of surgery. Bischoff, *supra* note 253, at 15. Consequently, retrospective review can be a very important tool in a managed care agency such as an HMO.

change the system, leaving large numbers uncovered would be political suicide. The most likely reform is some combination of employer mandate plus Medicaid and/or employer choice of Medicare and/or private. While this would leave some individuals uncovered, it would provide the most extensive coverage without radically changing the health care system.

Summary.

The lack of health insurance explains a significant part of the difference in the use of health care services between African-Americans and European-Americans. Expanding insurance coverage is certain to help to increase the use of health care services. For example, in 1977 uninsured African-Americans in the South saw physicians an average of 1.5 times, while insured African-Americans saw physicians an average of 2.8 times.[254] However, it is important to note that, while African-Americans' physician visits almost doubled for those with insurance, the racial differential between African-Americans and European-Americans remained steady.[255] That is, uninsured European-Americans had 150% more visits per year than uninsured African-Americans; insured European-Americans had 132% more visits per year than insured African-Americans.[256]

It seems that expanded insurance coverage is a policy option which will remove major economic barriers to health care. However, this option is not a satisfactory replacement for removing race-related problems with access to health care. Furthermore, it increases access at the risk of increasing health care cost, decreasing preference satisfaction and interfering with an individual's privacy—all of which are areas in which African-Americans will be affected in greater proportion than European-Americans.

Ultimately, the most significant problem with expanding insurance coverage, from the African-American perspective, is that expanding insurance coverage does little more than provide individuals with a piece of paper that says, in effect, that they may obtain health care, *if* they can find someone to accept the coverage. Expanding coverage does nothing to ensure that a provider in the community will furnish health care nor does it address the issues of disparate medical treatment.

---

254. Karen Davis & Diane Rowland, *Uninsured and Undeserved: Inequalities in Health Care in the United States*, 61 MILBANK MEMORIAL FUND Q. 149, 155–58 (1983).
255. Davis, *supra* note 170, at 9.
256. *Id.*

C. Targeting health care services to African-Americans

1. Background

Targeting health care services to African-Americans would focus resources on the specific health problems confronting them. In particular, funds could be allocated to establish community clinics in African-American communities. Such targeting services to specific population groups is not new and has been implemented in other areas: Maternal-Child health, Family Planning and Handicapped Children. Community clinics have been used to serve low income communities.

Congress passed the Disadvantaged Minority Health Improvement Act (DMHIA) to improve the health status of individuals from disadvantaged backgrounds, including racial and ethnic minorities, and to increase the numbers of minorities in the health professions. This was to be accomplished by establishing within the Department of Health and Human Services an Office of Minority Health and by giving the office grant authority.[257] The DMHIA also established a program of primary health care services to residents of public housing.[258] It revived and extended the program of Centers for Excellence in Health Professions Education for Minorities.[259] The Act established programs of loans, scholarships, and loan repayment for individuals from disadvantaged backgrounds who are pursuing a degree in a health profession.[260] It revised and extended the authority for the National Center for Health Statistics, and it created a new program of grants for data

---

257. *See* Disadvantaged Minority Health Improvement Act of 1990, Pub. L. No. 101–527, 104 Stat. 2311. The establishment of the Office of Minority Health within the Office of the Assistant Secretary for Health in the Department of Health & Human Services was codified in Title XVII of the Public Health Service Act. The Disadvantaged Minority Health Improvement Act (DMHIA) provided for a broad range of activities relating to improving the health status of African-Americans and other minorities. For instance, the Office of Minority Health (OMH) is required to establish objectives and to coordinate all activities within the Department of Health & Human Services related to minority health, including disease prevention, health promotion, service delivery, and research. Furthermore, OMH is required to enter into interagency agreements with public health service agencies to increase the participation of minorities in the service and its promotion programs.

258. *Id.* at § 3.

259. *Id.* at § 4.

260. *Id.* at § 5.

studies on the health of ethnic and racial minorities.[261] The DMHIA established a new program of grants for assisting communities in educating minorities to serve as health professionals in those communities.[262] It revised and extended the programs of Community and Migrant Health Centers[263] and created a program of grants for improving the health status of Pacific Islanders.[264] Furthermore, the Congress appropriated funding specifically directed to issues relevant to improving African-American health.

States could take steps to target services toward African-Americans. In 1991–92, only nineteen states had minority health entities. Seven states established the minority health entities by statute,[265] four states established the minority health entities by executive order,[266] and eight states established the entities by the appointed health officer.[267] However, the budgets for these entities indicate that they may be little more than "advisors" on minority health rather than service providers. In 1991–92, only three states had budgets which exceeded $500,000[268] and eleven states had less than $100,000.[269]

2. Policy analysis [270]

Horizontal equity.
Targeting health care services to African-Americans requires treating African-Americans differently than European-Americans even when

---

261. *Id.* at § 6.

262. *Id.* at § 8.

263. *Id.* at § 9.

264. *Id.* at § 10.

265. Arkansas, Illinois, Iowa, Missouri, Ohio, Texas. *Ohio Office of Minority Health, Characteristics of Minority Health Entities by State* (Table 1) (unpublished information on file at Case Western Reserve *Health Matrix Journal of Law-Medicine* office).

266. Delaware, Michigan, Mississippi and New Jersey. *Id.*

267. Alabama, Georgia, Hawaii, Indiana, Massachusetts, Oregon, South Carolina and Virginia. *Id.*

268. Michigan ($900,000), New Jersey ($500,000), Ohio ($1,600,000) and Oregon ($1,838,241).

269. *Id.*

270. The chart below is a visual representation of how well "Targeting Services" meets the various criteria. A minus sign (−) means that the criterion is not met. A plus sign (+) means that the criterion is met. A question mark (?) means that it is uncertain as to how well the criterion will be met.

(cont.)

both have similar health problems. Thus, this proposal fails to promote horizontal equity.

Vertical equity.

To the extent that African-Americans and European-Americans are affected differently by health disorders, it does provide vertical equity. For instance, more African-Americans are affected by diabetes than European-Americans. Consequently, targeting services toward African-Americans would be treating unequal groups unequally to promote equality.

Stigma.

The very act of targeting African-Americans can result in significant stigma. Singling out African-Americans would lead to labeling the beneficiaries of the programs as different. This process could increase racial polarization. Providing greater services to African-Americans could arouse opposition from other groups who perceive their needs as great as African-Americans.

Preference satisfaction.

Whether there would be preference satisfaction depends on how the services are delivered. If the services are delivered through private providers, then certainly there would be no more problems with preference satisfaction than any of the other insurance programs. On the other hand, if the services are delivered through programs that employ a specific staff, there would be limited preference satisfaction since the choice of providers for African-Americans using the services would be limited.

Economic efficiency.

As in expanding insurance coverage, the cost of targeting services to African-Americans is significant. The government would need to allocate additional funds for the provision of the services. However, to the extent that targeting services to specific population attacks the

(270, *cont.*)

Horizontal equity	Vertical equity	Economic efficiency	Preference satisfaction	Privacy	Stigma	Political feasibility
−	+	?	?	−	−	+

problem directly, targeting services could be more efficient (and less costly) than a broader approach (i.e. primary care for all).

Privacy.
To the extent that African-Americans would need to be identified as having specific health issues in order to have their health care problems addressed, issues of privacy exist. Problems also exist if programs would need information from African-Americans to monitor the community health.

Political feasibility.
This choice has limited political feasibility. Given the current deficit, Congress may have difficulty in justifying spending limited health care resources on a narrow population group. Other groups who view themselves as having similar or significant health problems could be angered if their population was not given similar treatment. In this age of racial tension and discord, in-fighting over limited resources is undesirable.

Summary.
Targeting services to African-Americans would address some access issues and treatment disparity problems since it would require availability of services in the African-American community. The treatment disparity between African-Americans and European-Americans is more likely to be addressed in this environment. However, a major drawback to targeting service is that it does not necessarily effect change in the overall system. Assuming that such an approach would be short term, the problems of racial barriers to access and racially disparate treatment would continue. Furthermore, African-Americans not served by the special programs could continue to face those same problems. Other major drawbacks are the significant stigma that might be associated with such programs and the political unpopularity of targeting health care services for a specific ethnic population group.

D. Using Title VI to eliminate institutional racism

1. Background

The Civil Rights Act of 1964 provides the legal force for desegregation efforts in health care. Specifically, section 601 of Title VI provides:

> No person in the United States, shall, on the grounds of race, color, or

national origin, be excluded from participation in, be denied the benefits of, or be subject to discrimination under any program or activity receiving Federal financial assistance.[271]

In short, Title VI prohibits discrimination on the basis of race, color, or national origin. The Office of Civil Rights (OCR) is delegated the responsibility of enforcing Title VI and the Department of Health Education and Welfare (now Department of Health and Human Services (DHHS) and Department of Education) issued the first interpretive regulations.[272] Those regulations provide that:

> A recipient... may not... utilize criteria or methods of administration which have the *effect* of subjecting individuals to discrimination of their race, color or national origin, or have the *effect* of defeating or substantially impairing accomplishment of the objectives of the program as respect individuals of a particular race, color, or national origin.[273]

A recipient is any public or private entity or individual that receives federal financial assistance.[274] Federal financial assistance includes federal money awarded through grant, loan, or contract.[275] In light of

---

271. Title VI of the 1964 Civil Rights Act, Pub. L. No. 99–352, 378 252 (codified at 42 U.S.C. §§ 2000d-200d-4 (1982).

272. *See* H.R. DOC. No. 318, 88th Cong., 2d Sess. (1964). *See generally* Mitchell Rice & Woodrow Jones, Jr., *Public Policy Compliance/Enforcement and Black American Health: Title VI of the Civil Rights Act of 1964*, in HEALTH CARE ISSUES IN BLACK AMERICA: POLICIES, PROBLEMS AND PROSPECTS 100–17 (Woodrow Jones, Jr. & Mitchell F. Rice eds., 1987); Dorn et al., *supra* note 100, at 439–40 (interpreting the Title VI regulations); Sidney Watson, *Reinvigorating Title VI: Defending Health Care Discrimination—It Shouldn't Be So Easy?*, 58 FORDHAM L. REVIEW 939, 943–48 (1990).

273. 45 C.F.R. § 80.3(b)(2) (1991) (emphasis added).

274. 45 C.F.R. § 80.13(i) (1991). DHHS provides federal assistance "to more than 6,800 hospitals, 13,700 out-patient and primary care facilities, various state and local public health agencies, 8,000 day care centers and 37,000 local services agencies.... [T]here are more than 43,000 DHHS recipients serving more than 93 million beneficiaries." Rice and Jones, *supra* note 236, at 100.

275. Although it does not include federal contracts of insurance or guaranty 42 U.S.C.A. § 2000d-1 (1981); 42 U.S.C.A. § 2000d-4 (1981), it does include: Medicare and Medicaid constitute federal financial assistance. *See* United States v. Baylor Univ. Medical Ctr., 736 F.2d 1039, 1046–47 (5th Cir. 1984) *cert. denied* 469 U.S. 1189 (1985) (Comprehensive Citations); Supplemental Security Income Payments are not federal financial assistance. *See* Sobral- Perez v. Heckler, 717 F.2d 36, 38–41 (2d Cir. 1983) *cert. denied*, 466 U.S. 929 (1984); Health planning grants 45 C.F.R. § 80 app. A, pt. 1, at 92; Loans and loan

these two definitions, Title VI has the potential of having a broad range effect. Once a program[276] has been determined to violate Title VI, the program "must take affirmative action to overcome the effects of prior discrimination."[277]

While the statute does not specifically define discrimination, it specifically requires HEW to define discrimination.[278] In particular, Title VI regulations prohibit:

- Criteria or methods of administration which have the effect of subjecting individuals to discrimination because of their race, color, or national origin.[279]
- Criteria or methods of administration which have the effect of defeating or substantially impairing accomplishment of the objectives of the program with respect to individuals of a particular race, color, or national origin.[280]
- Difference in quality of services because of the individual's race, color, or national origin.[281]
- Differences in quantity or the manner in which the benefit is provided because of the individual's race, color, or national origin.[282]
- Locating services with the purpose or effect of excluding individuals because of the individual's race, color, or national origin from the benefits of the program.[283]

Title VI could be used to improve access of African-Americans to health care services. Title VI regulations clearly prohibit policies

---

guarantees for hospitals and other medical facilities, 45 C.F.R. § 80 app. A., pt. 1, at 109 (1991) and Maternal and Child Health Grants and Crippled Children Services grants 45 C.F.R. § 80 app A., pt 1 (1991).

276. The program includes an entire agency or institution if any part receives federal financial assistance. 42 U.S.C. §§ 2000d, 2000d-4a (1982); Civil Rights Restoration Act of 1987, Pub. L. No. 100–259, 102 Stat. 28, 28–29. *See* O'Conner v. Peru State College, 781 F.2d 632, 639–42 (8th Cir. 1986).

277. 45 C.F.R. § 80.3(b) (6) (i) (1991).

278. 42 U.S.C. § 2000d-1 (1982).

279. *Cf.*, 45 C.F.R. § 80.3(B)(1)(vii)(2) (1991) (Health Education and Welfare); 15 C.F.R. § 8.4(b)(2) (1991) (Commerce).

280. *Cf.*, 45 C.F.R. § 80.3(b)(1)(vii)(2) (1991) (Health Education and Welfare) 15 C.F.R. § 8.4(b)(2) (1991) (Commerce).

281. 45 C.F.R. § 80.3(b)(1)(i) (1991).

282. 45 C.F.R. § 80.3(b)(1)–(3) (1991).

283. *Id.*

and practices which result in segregation within and between institutions.[284] Hospitals and nursing homes which engage in restrictive admission practices face discontinuation of their federal funds.[285] Communities can use Title VI to resist major changes in health care delivery that disadvantage African-Americans. For example, the closing of a predominantly African-American inner-city hospital and the expansion of another hospital serving primarily European-Americans could be attacked under Title VI.[286] Similarly, Medicaid and Medicare cutbacks which primarily affect African-Americans also violate Title VI.[287] Thus, Title VI has the potential of forcing health care institutions to evaluate their policies and practices which have a disparate impact on African-Americans.

Title VI can also be used to correct problems of racially disparate health care. Under Title VI, institutions must assure that the quality and quantity of health care services offered to African-Americans are proportionate to their need.

2. Policy analysis[288]

Horizontal equity.

Title VI focuses on assuring that African-Americans who have been treated differently than European-Americans are assured the same access and health care treatment. Using Title VI as a way to eliminate

---

284. For example, referral of white mental patients to individual counseling and blacks to group counseling; or the dumping of indigent emergency room patients from private, largely "white" hospitals to public hospitals would be prohibited under Title VI. Dorn et al., *supra* note 100, at 440–41.

285. Restricted admission practices which have a discriminatory effect include: not having physicians on staff or otherwise available who accept Medicaid patients; or requiring pre-admission deposits as a condition of obtaining care. Dorn et al., *supra* note 100, at 441.

286. *Id.*

287. *Id.*

288. The chart below is a visual representation of how well the "Eliminating Discrimination" meets the various criteria. A minus sign (-) means that the criterion is not met. A plus sign (+) means that the criterion is met. A question mark (?) means that it is uncertain as to how well the criterion will be met.

Horizontal equity	Vertical equity	Economic efficiency	Preference satisfaction	Privacy	Stigma	Political feasibility
+	+	?	+	-	?	?

institutional racism would achieve horizontal equity since it would treat equals (sick individuals) as equals.[289]

Vertical equity.
Meeting vertical equity will depend largely on the types of policies and practices an institution adopts as part of Title VI compliance. Using Title VI to eliminate institutional racism in health care merely requires that African-Americans who are sick and in need of care be given equal access to health care and appropriate medical treatment. However, to the extent that African-Americans now have less access and different treatment, it would require institutions to adopt policies and practices that would assure African-Americans increased access and better treatment. Those policies and practices might treat African-Americans and European-Americans differently. If so, vertical equity would be met.

Stigma.
Using Title VI may not remove the problem of stigma. Whether stigma persists will depend on how the institutions respond to the Title VI challenges and how the community responds to health care policy changes and costs necessitated by Title VI compliance. Individuals using any targeted services would certainly risk labeling. Title VI could generally raise racial hostility among the European-Americans (and other groups) that are experiencing different types of access problems. Such hostility could result in additional stigma on African-Americans. However, to the extent that Title VI compliance assures that no group is discriminated against based on race, Title VI compliance would improve access and treatment for other ethnic groups similarly situated to African-Americans.

Preference satisfaction.
Unlike "targeting services," Title VI could have the advantage of allowing for preference satisfaction. As institutions do away with discriminatory practices which limit access and treatment options, individuals will have increased choice. On the other hand, unless existing facilities are made sufficiently attractive to competent providers, preference satisfaction still may be lacking. To some extent, it is a program's responsibility to expend the resources necessary to assure quality of services to the African-American community. Realistically,

---

289. Although, Title VI does have affirmative action provisions and rules.

the courts are likely to allow programs to balance this goal against other goals.

Economic Efficiency.

If the current system is the most efficient for a significant segment of the population, efficiency may be lost if health care institutions reconsider their administrative policies and their evaluations of physicians to decide the disparate impact that their institution and policies will have on African-Americans. However, evidence indicates that this system is not the most economically efficient. More than $200 billion are wasted each year in unnecessary care and inefficient administration. That $200 billion is enough to assure adequate health care and changes in the health care system to eliminate institutional racism.

Privacy.

While the other options raised issues of patient privacy, this option raises issues of provider privacy. Title VI compliance will require evaluation of physician behavior. For example, treatment decisions must be scrutinized by health care institutions and licensing boards to identify and explain any racial disparity in treatment. Provider attitudinal study may require identification of patients themselves. Even if this latter step is eliminated, individual physician treatment choices and institutional records will be scrutinized in ways not presently undertaken. Thus, privacy criteria are not met.

Political feasibility.

Title VI can be enforced through the administrative complaint process or through a private legal action. The political feasibility of using Title VI to eliminate racism depends in part on the forum chosen.

a. *Administrative complaint process.* The administrative compliance mechanism authorizes the federal agencies that award federal financial assistance to take action against programs which violate Title VI.[290] The administrative process presents several problems. First, the victim of discrimination

---

290. Agencies may refuse to grant funds or terminate funding to any recipient found in violation of the Title VI regulations. The termination is limited to the particular program or part of program. While no court order is necessary, judicial review is available at the request of the fund recipient. *See* 45 C.F.R. § 80.8 (1991); *see generally* Dorn et al., *supra* note 100, at 442–44.

must file a complaint with the Office of Civil Rights within 180 days of the challenged discrimination.[291] A short time period is a particular handicap among the sick and individuals who may not be aware of their rights[292] Unawareness of rights encompasses both ignorance of the statute and ignorance of medical procedures appropriate for treatment of a disease. This leaves the individual unaware both that a treatment did not meet the standard of care and that this difference was the result of racial discrimination. Thus, it becomes difficult to use Title VI if attorneys merely wait for the patient to complain, since the patient may be completely unaware of the injury and the remedy.

Second, the lack of formal participation of complainants in the administrative process[293] leaves the victims with little control over the remedies to be tailored. Third, the process can be unusually long. It is not unusual for the entire process to take over a year.[294] Finally, if the patient later decides to sue, there is the potential that the administrative complaint process will hold up the process of litigation.[295]

Despite these problems, an administrative complaint presents several advantages. First, it can provide important leverage in negotiations with health facilities.[296] Second, the Office of Civil Rights (OCR) can command institutions to retain race-coded statistics which will be crucial to proving discrimination.[297] Third, OCR can collect the facts saving legal services considerable time and expense.[298] Finally, under the OCR guidelines, investigated institutions have the burden of persuasion in responding to a prima facie case of discrimination.[299] This is a significant advantage since the OCR approach to discriminatory effect has been more pro-complaint than the courts.

---

291. 45 C.F.R. § 80.7(b) (1991).

292. One solution to the issue of ignorance of rights may be to require hospitals to give notice to patients that they have the right to file a complaint with Office of Civil Rights if they feel that they have been denied services or that the quality of services has been affected because of race.

293. 45 C.F.R. § 81.23 (1991).

294. Dorn et al., *supra* note 100, at 444.

295. *See* Cheyney State College Faculty v. Hufstedler, 703 F.2d 732, 738 (1983) (holding that a study of action was appropriate as some of the problems could be more readily obtained through flexibility of the ongoing administrative process); *see generally* Dorn et al., *supra* note 100, at 444.

296. Dorn et al., *supra* note 100, at 444.

297. *Id.*

298. *Id.*

299. Dorn et al., *supra* note 100, at 444–46.

b. *Private law suit.* The other approach to enforcing Title VI is through a civil suit. No complaint with OCR is required before an individual Wles a private action under Title VI. An individual can sue to enforce both the statute and its implementing regulations.[300] One obvious drawback to litigating Title VI is that gathering and analyzing relevant statistics can be extremely time-consuming as well as expensive. However, the biggest drawback to litigating Title VI is the lack of meaningful evidentiary burdens on the defendant.

The evidentiary burden that a defendant bears depends on the categorization of the allegations of discrimination: disparate treatment versus disproportionate adverse impact. Disparate treatment discrimination pertains to intentional discrimination. The plaintiff is charged with the burden of proving discriminatory motive. Disproportionate adverse impact involves practices which may appear racially neutral but which have a more significant negative impact on minorities. Most of the practices involved in institutional racism (admission requirements, Medicaid/Medicare cutbacks, hospital relocations, medical treatment disparity) involve disproportionate adverse impact discrimination.

Disproportionate adverse impact analysis requires (1) the plaintiff to establish a prima facie case, (2) the defendant to establish a business justification, and (3) the plaintiff rebutting the defendant's business justification by showing less discriminatory alternatives.[301] The evidentiary burden placed on the defendant's establishment of a business justification is the most significant roadblock to establishing a Title VI violation.

The principal evidentiary problem with Title VI disproportionate adverse impact litigations is confusion with Title VII.[302] Historically, in Title VII cases, the defendant bore the burden of not only coming forth with evidence of business justification but also the burden of proof.[303] In *Wards Cove*, the Supreme Court eliminated the requirement that the defendant bear the burden of proof. Under *Wards Cove*, a

---

300. *See* Guardians Ass'n v. Civil Serv. Comm'n, 463 U.S. 582, 593–95 (1983); Consolidated Rail Corp v. Darrone, 104 S.Ct. 1248, 1252–53 & n. 9 (1984). Plaintiff may recover equitable retrospective and prospective relief. 463 U.S. at 602–03. Court not yet addressing whether plaintiff may recover damages. 463 U.S. at 630.

301. *See, e.g.,* Wards Cove Packing Co. v. Atonio, 109 S.Ct. 2115, 2124–27 (1989) (providing general reference to burdens of proof; International Bd. of Teamster v. United States, 431 U.S. 324, 335 (1977); *see also* Watson, *supra* note 272, at 958–59.

302. Watson, *supra* note 272 at 971–75.

defendant need only introduce some evidence of business justification. There is no longer a requirement that the defendant prove business necessity, that the policy foster safety and efficiency, or be essential to the goal of promoting safety and efficiency.[304] However, the requirement of discriminatory intent has been rejected by the Congress in its employment discrimination legislation.[305] While this is an important development in employment law, it is an open question as to whether the courts will change their focus on Title VI cases.

In the few Title VI health cases which exist, the burden of proof on the defendant to justify a disproportionate adverse impact policy seems to have been lessened even further. Defendants have successfully justified a policy with disproportionate adverse impact by demonstrating that the policy is rationally related to a legitimate need.[306] This standard makes it difficult to challenge racist policies and practices in the health care area. Cost containment is a legitimate goal, and courts are likely to find that any relationship between the policy or practice and cost containment will suffice.

It is through litigation that Title VI will be unhitched from Title VII.[307] The federal government has every right to impose a burden on the acceptance of taxpayer monies. Allowing defendants to overcome the burden with a mere rationally related justification nullifies the purpose of Title VI. Since defendants do not have to accept federal funds they should be held to a "precise compliance with [the] spending power" of Title VI.[308]

> Courts have mistakenly turned to Title VII principles as the starting point for fashioning evidentiary burdens in Title VI cases involving

---

303. *Id.* at 959–60.

304. *Id.* at 960 (*quoting* United States v. Jacksonville Terminal Co., 451 F.2d 418, 451 (5th Cir. 1971) *quoted in* Pettway v. American Cast Iron Pipe Co., 494 F.2d 211, 245 (5th Cir. 1974), *cert. denied* 439 U.S. 1115 (1979).

305. *See* Civil Rights Act of 1991, Pub. L. No. 102–166 (Nov. 21, 1991), 105 Stat. 1071, 102d Cong, 1st Sess. (1991) (codifying interpretation of Civil Rights Act of 1964, Title VII, which had been enunciated in Griggs v. Duke Power Co., 401 U.S. 424 (1971), and repudiated in Wards Cove Packing Co. v. Antonio, 490 U.S. 642 (1989).

306. Bryan v. Koch, 627 F.2d 612, 619–20 (1980) (holding that Title VI does not implicitly require a recipient to consider alternatives to proposed placement of closing of a public facility); NAACP v. Medical Ctr., Inc., 657 F.2d 1322, 1334–37 (3rd Cir. 1981).

307. Watson, *supra* note 272, at 971–75

308. *Id.* at 973.

challenges to facially neutral policies that have the effect of excluding minority patients. Title VII regulates purely private employment decisions ... Title VI is a spending power statute. It does not regulate but places condition on the expenditure of federal money.[309]

Summary.

Hospitals, nursing homes, health care institutions, and health care providers who receive federal funds should bear the burden to justify policies which have the effect of discriminating against African-Americans. If the courts (or the legislators) can be made to see that under Title VI the government has every right to demand that its money be spent in a non-discriminating way, then Title VI has the potential of being a powerful tool to end institutional racism. Unfortunately, the combination of an increased desire to control health costs and the political climate with recent Reagan and Bush appointees to the federal court may mean that getting the courts to hold health care providers to the fire may not be politically feasible now. It remains to be seen what impact the Clinton administration will have on courts. Nevertheless, the Title VI administrative process and threatened litigation could be a powerful tool in getting health care institutions to comply voluntarily.

V. CONCLUSION

Health care institutions have a social responsibility to identify and delineate all causes of disease and disability in a population and then to mobilize the medical resources necessary to attack those causes.[310] Since it has been shown that the health of African-Americans is markedly lower than European-American, it necessarily follows that "this situation would have to be called, in part, a racist consequence of the actions and structure of those health institutions."[311]

Getting rid of the effects of institutional racism is a task for which European-American institutions must accept the responsibility, along with the burden of identifying effecting solutions. Doing nothing is an

---

309. *Id.* at 978.

310. *See* KNOWLES & PREWITT, *supra* note 15, at 96 (placing burden of mobilizing medical resources on health institutions due to their relationship with medical community and patients).

311. *Id.*

unacceptable option. It would allow the continuation of economic and social apartheid based on race. Reform efforts which call for expanded insurance coverage are inadequate not only because it is possible that only a small minority of African-Americans will continue to be uncovered; more importantly, it does nothing to relieve racial barriers to access based on the availability of culturally relevant services in the community or medical treatment disparities. While special health services could be targeted to African-Americans, fiscally and politically this alternative is very unlikely. Furthermore, it still fails to deal with the inadequacy of the system in dealing with racism. Finally, litigators could use Title VI to eliminate racist practices in health care delivery and health care education. This would do little to assure economic access. But more importantly, the courts have adopted a position which makes the use of Title VI politically difficult. However, as the courts' composition changes over the next several years this option may become more viable.

No single approach will adequately address the multi-faceted problem of improving the health care status of African-Americans. It is also clear that the health care system is undergoing enormous changes designed to make it more just. If that reform is to include better health care for African-Americans it will need to do more than assure economic access through expanding insurance. It will need increased availability of providers through Title VI and decreased treatment disparity through Title VI. Strengthening Title VI such that it becomes politically feasible to use through both the administrative and civil process should be the *quid pro quo* for accepting cost containment restrictions. No system can be just so long as vestiges of racism remain. Strengthening Title VI is the only mechanism available to assure that health care in America is no longer racist.

[Racism remains a] prime cause of the unequal and racially discriminatory provision of funds for health services; of the overcrowding of the ill-equipped black hospitals and the underutilization of white hospitals; of miserable housing, gross pollution, poor sanitation, and lack of health care....

[Racism] in consequence, is the underlying structure causing the dreadful burden of excess morbidity and mortality, much of it preventable, that is borne by the black population. These health- specific effects are superimposed on the more general consequences of [racism] which bars the majority of [African-American] citizens from participating in decisions on the allocation of resources for health or other needs.

We believe that the ... [American] health care system is, in consequence, fundamentally flawed. Fragmentation and duplication of services ... is costly and inefficient. ...

For the majority of the black population, the whole spectrum of health services (but most urgently, primary care) is inadequate. Entire generations suffer through much of their lifetimes. ...

Even if ... [racism] ended tomorrow, their effects on health would persist for years, in part because of the health consequences of the profound poverty ... that [racism] itself has engendered and in part because widespread attitudes that encourage racism, elitism, sexism, a colonialist mentality, and prejudice against the poor take time and commitment to change ...

Clearly, ... [America] has the ability to reduce markedly, if not eliminate, the serious health problems that exist among the black population. It can, if it chooses, eliminate the institutionalized system of racism and discrimination that have made the country, for decades, a symbol of human rights violations. The task facing ... [us] is to continue to extend the process that [civil rights reforms] have begun, until profound and lasting improvements in health care ... are a reality.[312]

---

312. This quote is taken from an article about South Africa with merely name changes from South Africa to the US and Apartheid to Racism, it is equally true about the United States of America. Elena Nightingale et al., *Apartheid Medicine: Health and Human Rights in South Africa*, 264 JAMA 2097, 2102 (1990).

Life style, health status, and distributive justice*

Robert L. Schwartz

Only a few years ago the American system for providing health care was considered rather benign—an inevitable consequence of American values. Over the past few years, however, the increased amount of our resources allocated to health care—now about 14% of the gross domestic product[1]—and the consistently high levels of those people

---

* The author appreciates the commentary and editorial assistance offered by Pam Lambert, Margaret Caffey-Moquin, Karen Kingen and Jessica Sutin.

1. George D. Lundberg, *National Health Care Reform: The Aura of Inevitability Intensifies*, 267 JAMA 2521, 2522 fig. 2 (1992). This is a remarkable increase over the 12% figure for the previous year. *See* E. BROWN, HEALTH USA: A NATIONAL HEALTH PROGRAM FOR THE UNITED STATES DEPARTMENT OF COMMERCE, 1991 UNITED STATES INDUSTRIAL OUTLOOK 44-1-11-6 (1991). Dr Lundberg, editor of the Journal of the American Medical Association, views the increase in the resources spent on health care as an "extreme" that is "unacceptable". Lundberg, *supra* at 2522. The amount of our national resources spent on health care has increased regularly and substantially over the past forty years.

National expenditures on health care have increased from $12.7 billion in 1950 to $41.9 billion in 1965 to $647 billion in 1990. Per capita spending on medical care has grown from $82 per year in 1950 to $211 in 1965 to $2511 in 1900 . . . Between 1980 and 1988, the medical care component of the consumer price index increased 85% compared to a general increase of inflation of 43% . . . Americans spend more on health care than they spend on groceries, owner-occupied housing, or transportation.

BARRY R. FURROW ET AL., HEALTH LAW 661 (2d ed. 1991).

Justice and Health Care: Comparative Perspectives. Edited by A. Grubb and M.J. Mehlman. © 1995 John Wiley & Sons Ltd.

not covered by even that very high expenditure—15% across the United States, and up to 25% in some states[2]—have made the system unacceptable. To put it simply, the cost of health care and the widespread lack of access to it have become a national scandal.[3]

As this scandal has unfolded, we have reacted to it just as we react to most other scandals that manifest themselves during political years; we have begun our search for scapegoats. Indeed, we have rounded up the usual suspects—some people blame the problems on insurance

---

2. Medicaid, which is the primary program designed to cover the poor, covers fewer than half of the people under the federal poverty line. FURROW ET AL., *supra* note 1, at 529. *See also* Geraldine Dallek, *Health Care for America's Poor: Separate and Unequal*, 20 CLEARINGHOUSE REV. 361 (1986). New Mexico, the state with the highest percentage of its population without any form of private or public coverage, only recently brought that percentage down to one-fourth of its residents. GOVERNOR'S HEALTH POLICY ADVISORY COMMITTEE, HEALTH FOR THE FUTURE: A PROPOSED HEALTH POLICY FOR NEW MEXICO 9 (1988). *See also* KATHLEEN BROOK ET AL., HEALTH INSURANCE COVERAGE IN NEW MEXICO 10 (1991). When the underinsured are added to the uncovered, the number may rise to one-fourth the population of the entire country. Pamela J. Farley, *Who are the Underinsured?*, 63 MILBANK MEMORIAL FUND Q. 476 (1985).

3. With the American Medical Association and the American Hospital Association joining virtually every other national organization that deals with health care financing in calling for dramatic health care reform, it is hard to find any support for the current structure. Presidential candidates are fighting with each other over the structure that ought to replace the current financing system, but there is no disagreement that the current system provides inadequate access at excessive cost. The only question is which kind of substantial change will be most effective. As Dr. Lundberg points out:

At least 57 national and state legislative proposals for health care reform have been filed; major components of the Republican and Democratic platforms will deal with health care reform. Presidential contenders have already developed their postures regarding health care reform... With President Bush having entered the discussion, the reality of reform seems assured. The only questions now are what, how much, how soon, how incremental, how complete, how effective, and how long-lasting.

Lundberg, *supra* note 1, at 2521. He suggests that "[m]ajor political change in a democratic republic such as ours comes about when a cluster of forces temporally coalesces to form a critical political mass of sufficient strength to power that change," something that has now happened with our health care system. *Id. See also* Robert J. Blendon et al., *Making the Critical Choices*, 267 JAMA 2509 (1992) (discussing substantive questions that must be addressed by any new system).

companies,[4] others blame the problem on lawyers and the legal system,[5] still others blame the problem on greedy, profit driven private enterprise and the existence of the market mechanism for the delivery of health care,[6] and yet others blame it on bureaucratic government regulation of that market.[7] Doctors, medical schools, hospitals, drug companies—all have been alleged to be culpable for the scandal of our health care system.

The newest and most original scapegoat upon which we can place the blame for the high cost of health care are those whose life style choices puts their health or lives at risk. Of course, if our health care cost and access problems are a consequence of unhealthy choices made by autonomous individuals, we are relieved of the obligation of figuring out how to reform our health care delivery system. In that case, the solution to our health care problem is obvious—we merely need to impose appropriate penalties on those who make costly, immoral and unhealthy life style choices.

---

4. *See, e.g.*, Kevin Grumbach et al., *Liberal Benefits, Conservative Spending: The Physicians for a National Health Program Proposal*, 265 JAMA 2549 (1991).

5. Not surprisingly, this is a central part of the American Medical Association's entry into the health care reform sweepstakes. *See* James A. Todd et al., *Health Access America—Strengthening the US Health Care System*, 265 JAMA 2503 (1991) (reviewing problems with current insurance availability in the United States and proposing reforms to improve access and quality of health care). Limited access to health care is also one of the myriad of social ills that President Bush blames on lawyers and the legal system. GEORGE BUSH, THE PRESIDENT'S COMPREHENSIVE HEALTH REFORM PROGRAM 50 (1992).

6. *See, e.g.*, Rand E. Rosenblatt, *Health Care, Markets, and Democratic Values*, 34 VAND. L. REV. 1067 (1981); Bruce C. Vladeck, *The Market vs. Regulation: The Case for Regulation*, 59 MILBANK MEMORIAL FUND Q. 209 (1981); and Robert G. Evans, *Tension, Compression, and Shear: Directions, Stresses and Outcomes of Health Care Cost Control*, 15 J. HEALTH POL., POL'Y & L. 101 (1990). *See also* Arnold S. Relman, *What Markets Are Doing to Medicine*, ATLANTIC MONTHLY 98, 106 (1992) (warning that "if physicians continue to allow themselves to be drawn along the path of private entrepreneurship, they will increasingly be seen as self-interested businessmen and will lose many of the privileges they now enjoy as fiduciaries and trusted professionals").

7. *See, e.g.*, James F. Blumstein, *Rationing Medical Resources: A Constitutional, Legal and Policy Analysis*, 59 TEX. L. REV. 1345 (1981) and James F. Blumstein & Frank A. Sloan, *Redefining Government's Role in Health Care: Is a Dose of Competition What the Doctor Should Order?* 34 VAND. L. REV. 849, 852 (1981). *See also* CLARK C. HAVIGHURST, DEREGULATING THE HEALTH CARE INDUSTRY: PLANNING FOR COMPETITION (1982).

The call for some kind of mechanism that would make people pay for the health consequences of their life style choices is coming from a variety of sources. Some physicians have announced that they will automatically reject alcoholic liver transplant candidates, or put them lower on the priority list, because their moral fault—their alcoholism—caused them to need the transplant.[8] At least one state has attempted to deny Medicaid funding for liver transplants for former alcoholics unless they can prove abstinence for at least two years prior to the transplant.[9]

Employers are cashing in on this trend as a way to save insurance dollars. For example, Circle K stores proposed denying coverage for all employee health claims resulting from self-induced conditions; they would deny coverage for the results of drug or alcohol abuse, self-inflicted wounds, and AIDS (unless it can be proven that it was acquired by transfusion).[10] Several employers pay larger motor vehicle accident death benefits to an employee's family if the employee was wearing a seat belt during the fatal accident.[11] Some companies charge employees who smoke more than other employees to participate in their group health plan;[12] Turner Broadcasting refuses to hire any employee who smokes;[13] and the United States Senate has considered a Medicare Part B premium surcharge for smokers.[14] Haggar Apparel Company pays only 60% of the cost of prenatal care (rather that the 100% otherwise standard) if the pregnant employee or family member delays seeking prenatal medical care after she becomes aware of her pregnancy.[15] The state of Delaware plans to implement a scheme later this year under which it would charge unhealthy state

---

8. Gregory Tetrault, *The Morality of Transplantation*, 266 JAMA 213 (1991). *See also* Carl Cohen & Martin Benjamin, *Alcoholics and Liver Transplantation*, 265 JAMA 1299 (1991).

9. Allen v. Mansour, 681 F. Supp. 1232 (E.D. Mich. 1986).

10. *See* George Will, *Who Should Insure Our Lifestyle Choices?*, WASH. POST, Aug. 11, 1988, at A21 (discussing policy to deny employee coverage for certain ailments). *Also see* Jaime Fernandez, *The Folly of Basing Health Insurance on "Lifestyle Choices"*, WASH. POST, Aug. 20, 1988, at A21 (responding to the article by George Will).

11. Laurie Cohen, *Wanted: Healthier Workers; More Companies Give Rewards for Staying Well*, CHI. TRIB., Jan. 6, 1992, at B1.

12. *Id.*

13. Dan Cordtz, *For Our Own Good*, FIN. WORLD, Dec. 10, 1991, at 48.

14. David Durenburger, *Financing Health Care for an Aging Population*, WASH. POST, April 14, 1987, at Z14.

15. Cordtz, *supra* note 13.

employees more for group health insurance than it charges other employees.[16]

The courts have already confronted some of these attempts to hold individuals responsible for their health status. Turner Broadcasting has not been required to hire smokers.[17] Michigan may not impose a two year sobriety rule to refuse liver transplants to Medicaid patients who were alcoholics. All Medicaid recipients must be treated on the basis of medical necessity.[18] Other attempts to make patients, employees, aid recipients, and the insured financially responsible for their medical conditions or to deny them care for these conditions altogether are certainly bound for Congress, state legislatures, the courts, and union–management negotiation tables.

I. THE RANGE OF LIFE STYLE CHOICES AND THEIR CONSEQUENCES ON HEALTH STATUS

If all of those whose life style choices have health consequences were required to bear the full burden of those consequences, there would be few of us (and few diseases or injuries) that would not be implicated. While the medical hazards of smoking and alcohol consumption are well known,[19] the medical consequences of other kinds of action are less established or less obvious. Helmetless motorcyclists[20] and bicyclists[21] and drivers who do not wear seat belts put

16. Cohen, *supra* note 11.

17. Christine Woolsey, *Off-duty Conduct: None of the Employer's Business?*, BUS. INS., Feb. 17, 1992, at 10.

18. Allen v. Mansour, 681 F. Supp. 1232 (E.D. Mich. 1986).

19. The Office of Technology Assessment estimates the cost of smoking in the United States at over $65 billion per year, with $22 billion attributable to health care costs and $43 billion attributable to lost productivity. For an analysis of the costs of alcohol to society *see William R. Miller*, THE EFFECTIVENESS OF ALCOHOLISM TREATMENT MODALITIES: TESTIMONY TO THE U.S. SENATE COMMITTEE ON GOVERNMENTAL AFFAIRS, in 2 CAUSES AND CONSEQUENCES OF ALCOHOL ABUSE 158 (1989). Willard G. Manning et al., *The Taxes of Sin: Do Smokers and Drinkers Pay Their Way?*, 261 JAMA 1604 (1989) (discussing the consequences of smoking and alcohol use and their costs for society).

20. Allen Short, *Collision Course; State Must Pass Helmet Law for Motorcyclists or Face Funding Cut*, MINN. STAR TRIB., Mar. 1, 1992, at A1 (citing estimates by the General Accounting Office that indicate that motorcycle riders with helmets have fatality rates as much as 70% lower than those without helmets).

21. According to one study done at Allegheny General Hospital in Pittsburgh, 50,000 children were injured in bicycle-related accidents in 1990, and

(*cont.*)

their lives at risk;[22] obese and sedentary people put their health at risk.[23] Those who consume excess fat or insufficient fiber have increased risk of some kinds of cancers[24] (and, possibly, heart disease). Even former President Bush risks some kinds of cancer when he refuses his broccoli. On the other hand, those who eat too many carbohydrates run the risk of the most common disease, dental cavities.[25] Those who engage in unprotected sex run the risk of several different illnesses;[26] those who engage in protected sex run risks from certain types of protection;[27] those who engage in no sexual activity may run yet another set of physical, emotional, and psychological risks.

(21, *cont.*) over 1000 died. Eighty-five percent of the injuries could have been avoided through the use of bicycle helmets. *Asides and Insides in Healthcare*, CHI. TRIB., Dec. 8, 1991, at 44. *See also* Robert Thompson et al., *A Case—Control Study of the Effectiveness of Bicycle Safety Helmets*, 320 NEW ENG. J. MED 1361 (1989). *See generally* A JONES ET AL., COST OF INJURY IN THE UNITED STATES; A REPORT TO CONGRESS 115–16 (1989).

22. The Chairman of the National Transportation Safety Board has estimated that 18,087 lives were saved in 1990 as a direct result of mandatory seat belt laws. *See* Bill McAllister & Evelyn Richards, *Nine States Targeted on Seat Belt Laws*, WASH. POST, Sept. 20, 1991, at A25.

23. *See* W.B. Kannel & Tavia Gordon, *Physiological and Medical Concomitants of Obesity: The Framingham Study*, reprinted in OBESITY IN AMERICA 125 (George A. Bray ed., 1979).

24. The increased risk is not just the risk of colon cancer, a risk that is fairly well known. *See* Kara Smigel, *Fewer Colon Polyps Found in Men with High-Fiber, Low-Fat Diets*, 84 J. NAT. CANCER INST. 80 (1992). There is an association between saturated animal fats and breast cancer, too. *See* David P. Rose, *Effect of Dietary Fat on Human Breast Cancer Growth and Lung Metastasis in Nude Mice*, 83 J. NAT. CANCER INST. 1491 (1991). *See also* David P. Rose, LIPIDS, OBESITY AND FEMALE REPRODUCTIVE CANCER, in LIPIDS AND WOMEN'S HEALTH (Geoffrey P. Redmond ed., 1991). David I. Gregorio et al., *Dietary Fat Consumption and Survival Among Women with Breast Cancer*, 75 J. NAT. CANCER INST. 37 (1985).

25. *See* Rosie Schwartz, *It's Time To Put A Stop to Sugar-Filled Breakfasts*, OTTAWA CITIZEN, March 11, 1992, at E2.

26. The Centers for Disease Control reports that 11,609 people have contracted AIDS through heterosexual contact. The number who contracted it this way in 1990 (2289) is up 30% from those who contracted it by heterosexual contact in 1989. In addition, the Executive Director of the American Social Health Association reports that 12 million new sexually transmitted disease cases are reported each year. *See* Beth Sherman, *Its A Scary New World for Those Re-Entering the Dating Scene after Divorce or Death of A Spouse*, NEWSDAY, Jan. 25, 1992, at 17.

27. *See* Sharon Snider, *The Pill—Thirty Years of Safety Concerns*, 24 FDA CONSUMER 8, 10 (1990). *See also* Robert Stein, *Spermicides Linked to Urinary Tract*

People who choose to live far enough away from where they work or shop so that they have to drive to those sites substantially increase their chance of death or serious bodily injury in an automobile accident. Those who choose to work as miners or police officers or loggers run a greater risk of violent or accidental death than do the rest of us,[28] although being unemployed also substantially shortens ones life expectancy.[29] Those who participate in certain sports (including skiing, boxing, hang gliding, and statistics suggest, baseball and football) risk severe injury.[30]

People who do not become vaccinated against measles are at risk for

---

Infections, UNITED PRESS INT'L, Jan. 2 1991, and Ridgley Ochs, *The Latest in Birth Control Methods; Researchers; Reliable, Safe Forms on the Market*, NEWSDAY (Nassua and Suffolk), Apr. 28, 1992, at 61.

28. *See* RUTH GASTEL, OCCUPATIONAL DISEASE: INSURANCE ISSUES (1992) (discussing generally occupational illnesses).

29. Harold Gilliam, *Mend Your Ways or Count Your Days*, SAN FRANCISCO CHRON., June 9, 1991, at 13/Z1. Not surprisingly, health is also closely related to homelessness; the indigent homeless are worse off than the indigent with homes. *See* Lillian Gelberg et al., *Health, Homelessness and Poverty; A Study of Clinic Users*, 150 ARCHIVES INTERNAL MED. 2325 (1990).

30. Data from the National Athletic Injury-Illness Reporting System indicate that most drownings, many firearm fatalities, 10% of brain injuries, 7% of spinal cord injuries, and 13% of facial injuries are related to sports. Susan G. Gererich, *Sports Injuries; Implications for Prevention*, 100 PUB. HEALTH REP. 570 (1985). A Vermont study on cross-country skiing revealed an injury rate of 0.72 per 1000 skier days. Per Renstrom & Robert J. Johnson, 8 SPORTS MED. (6) 346 (1989). A study of elite Alpine skiers in Quebec estimated the injury rate at 17 per 1000 skier days. Ross E. Anderson & David L. Montgomery, *Physiology of Alpine Skiing*, 6 SPORTS MED. 4, at 210 (1988). A recent estimate ranked boxing fatality rates (about 0.13 deaths per 1000 participants annually) at or less than those for hang gliding. Robert G. Morrison, *Medical and Public Health Aspects of Boxing*, 255 JAMA 2475 (1986). A study conducted among high school athletes participating in male football, baseball, and soccer, and female basketball and track and field, reported injuries to 39.5% of the participants. R. Durant et al., *Findings from the Preparticipation Athletic Examination and Athletic Injuries*, 146 AM. J. DISABLED CHILDREN 85 (1992). On the other hand, rule changes in football, together with better training and coaching techniques, reduced the occurrence of permanent cervical quadriplegia from 34 in 1976 to 5 in 1984. Joseph S. Tong et al., *The National Football Head and Neck Injury Registry; 14-Year Report on Cervical Quadriplegia, 1971 Through 1984*, 254 JAMA 3439 (1985). Running, a sport widely engaged in for its fitness benefits, poses risks, although generally of a less serious nature. A study of 1680 runners in two community road race events in Canada reported that 48% of the participants experienced at least one injury during the 12-month follow-up period; 54% of those injuries were new. Stephan D. Walter, *The Ontario*
(cont.)

that disease,[31] and those who forgo their winter flu shots put themselves at greater risk of that sometimes fatal disease.[32] Those who allow themselves to live with high blood pressure put themselves at risk for a whole range of diseases.[33] Those who do not participate in a symptomatic screening for breast cancer, colon cancer, lung cancer, heart disease and other diseases are at greater risk of death from those diseases.

Poverty is a life style with adverse health consequences.[34] Those who are poor are at much higher risk of illness than those who are rich. Those who choose to live in Chicago or New York City rather than Minneapolis or Salt Lake City are also choosing a life style that, according to statistics, is likely to result in a shorter life.[35]

The rich variety of life style choices for which individuals may bear moral responsibility and the various health consequences of those

---

(30, *cont.*) *Cohort Study of Running-Related Injuries*, 149 ARCHIVES INTERNAL MED. 2561 (1989).

All of the dangers of these athletic endeavors are exacerbated when the athletes look for a competitive advantage through the use of medicine. *See* Virginia S. Cowart, *Ethical, as Well as Physiological, Questions Continue to Arise Over Athlete's Steroid Abuse*, 261 JAMA 3362 (1989).

31. The Centers for Disease Control reported 27,672 measles cases in the United States in 1990, a 52.1% increase over the incidence reported for 1989. Among the 1990 cases were 89 suspected measles-associated deaths. Division of Immunization, Center for Prevention Services, Centers for Disease Control, *Measles—United States*, 1990, 265 JAMA 3227 (1990). In 1983, the disease reached its nadir in the United States with 1497 cases. The dramatic rise in incidence has been attributed to a failure to vaccinate. Laura L. Fisher & R. Gordon Douglas, *Infectious Diseases*, 265 JAMA 3130, 3131 (1991).

32. Annual deaths from influenza and its complications range from 20,000 to 40,000; yet only 30% to 40% of high-risk people are vaccinated each year. Kristin L. Nichol et al., *Influenza Vaccination; Knowledge, Attitudes, and Behaviour Among High-Risk Outpatients*, 152 ARCHIVES INTERNAL MED. 106. (1992).

33. Hypertension (high blood pressure) currently places about 58 million Americans at increased risk for stroke, heart disease, and kidney failure. Morbidity and Mortality Weekly Report, Centers for Disease Control, *Progress Toward Achieving the 1990 High Blood Pressure Objectives*, 264 JAMA 2192 (1990).

34. *See* Gelberg et al., *supra* note 29, at 2325. Poverty appears to be one of the primary reasons African-Americans are at a higher risk for cancer than whites. *See* Suzanne P. Kelley, *Blacks at Higher Risk for Cancer; Myths, Mistrust and Poverty Are Among Factors*, STAR TRIB., Dec. 8, 1991, at B1.

35. This increase in longevity is thought to be due, in part, to the high proportion of Mormons in the population of Utah. Because of their abstinence from tobacco, alcohol and caffeine, together with good general health practices, active Mormons have been recognized as a population at very low risk for cancer. James E. Enstrom, *Cancer Mortality Among Mormons*, 36 CANCER INST. 805 (1975). *See also* James E. Enstrom. *Health Practices and Cancer Mortality Among*

choices suggest that no analysis of the propriety of imposing that responsibility may apply to every person or every condition. Some relevant life style choices involve health care decision making; some involve career choices; some involve leisure time choices. Should we treat the responsibility that accompanies these different kinds of decisions differently? Is there more culpability attached to a leisure time choice that to an employment choice? Is there more culpability in making an "unhealthy" work choice than in making a risky decision about medical treatment?

To determine when, if ever, it might be appropriate to make someone pay for her self-induced health status, we should determine what the reasons for imposing such a responsibility could ever be.

II. ARE INDIVIDUALS RESPONSIBLE FOR THEIR HEALTH STATUS?

The idea that one is responsible for one's own health status is not new. It is recognized in virtually every form of ancient medicine, and it provides the basis of many systems of folk medicine.[36] For centuries people have believed that illness is a form of divine retribution, and that the unworthy are proven so by their disease state.[37] This historical approach is reflected in the current belief that "clean living" is the way to health (and, thus, ill health must be the consequence of unclean living).[38] If you are sick, it is likely to be because you deserve it. You

---

Active California Mormons, 81 J. NATL. CANCER INST. 1807 (1989). Actually, the states with the longest average life spans are Minnesota and The Dakotas; Nevada (which also has a large Mormon population) has the shortest average life span. *See* Gilliam, *supra* note 29, at 13.

36. *See* Erik Eckholm, *AIDS and Folk Healing, a Zimbabwe Encounter*, N.Y. TIMES, Oct. 5, 1990, at A10 (describing one current example where the belief that one is responsible for personal health is present in folk medicine).

37. *See* Peter Sedgwick, *Illness—Mental and Otherwise*, in CONCEPTS OF HEALTH AND DISEASE: INTERDISCIPLINARY PERSPECTIVES 119, 125–26 (Arthur Caplan et al. eds., 1981). As Sedgwick points out, "[i]n a society where the treatment of the sick is still conducted through religious ritual, the notion of illness will not be entirely distinct from the notion of sinfulness or pollution." *Id.* at 126. *See also* Henry Cohen, *The Evolution of the Concept of Disease*, in CONCEPTS OF HEALTH AND DISEASE: INTERDISCIPLINARY PERSPECTIVES 209 (Arthur Caplan et al. eds. 1981).

38. Indeed, this twentieth century phenomenon is remarkably similar to nineteenth century developments. Presbyterian minister Sylvester Graham's mid-nineteenth century notions that we should avoid alcohol, meat, and overly

(cont.)

got your cold, just as your mother promised, because you walked out in the rain without a warm coat and rubbers, which, your mother assured you, was a moral failing. Radio talk show hosts and their callers all know exactly which kinds of people have AIDS, and what kinds of immoral conduct gave rise to their affliction.

Are those who need medical care because of their moral choices less deserving of our health care resources than others? There are three ways that those who have made "unhealthy" choices could be required to bear the burdens of those choices. Those with "unhealthy" life styles could be denied health care (for the conditions their improper conduct abetted, or for all conditions); they could be given lower priority for scarce health care resources than those whose need is independent of their conduct; or they could be charged comparatively more than deserving others for their health care (either at the point of the health care services, or earlier through higher insurance premiums or additional taxes).

Whatever burden might be attached to "unhealthy" conduct is generally justified on three grounds. First, the additional burden deters others from making the same improper life style choices. Second, the burden appropriately punishes the morally wrongful conduct. Third, it is not equitable to distribute scarce health care resources to those who choose to create health risks (and who thus could choose to avoid them).[39] Each of these

---

(38, *cont.*) refined grains—and that spiritual health is necessarily closely related to physical health—is reflected in the current interest in "natural" foods, even if the nineteenth century Christianity that provided the underpinning to Rev. Graham's theory is now replaced by a more general and less sectarian notion of spirituality. The cracker invented by Rev. Graham has its analogue in the shelves of whole grain crackers now available in the natural food stores. His spiritual and physical Puritanism also touched off a conversion to "biological living" in nineteenth century cereal magnates John Harvey Kellogg and C. W. Post, who espoused and expanded Graham's principles through writing, lecturing, and product development.

For a more thorough account of the relationship between religious movements and health movements in the nineteenth century, *see* James C. Whorton, *Traditions of Folk Medicine in America*, 257 JAMA 1632 (1987); JAMES C. WHORTON, CRUSADERS FOR FITNESS: THE HISTORY OF AMERICAN HEALTH REFORMERS (1982); and STEPHEN NISSENBAUM, SEX, DIET, AND DEBILITY IN JACKSONIAN AMERICA (1980). Indeed, the anti-medicine culmination of the nineteenth century "do it naturally" movement—Christian Science—may have its equivalent in the mistrust of medicine that seems to underlie the current interest in "natural" foods.

39. A fourth justification, that of efficiency, suggests that imposing the risk on one who can control it is the cheapest way of reducing that risk. In fact, this justification is really a combination of the justifications based on deter-

propositions is based on three presumptions: first, that the life style in question is truly voluntary; second, that the life style actually brought about the condition that now demands treatment; and third, that the life style is not warranted by other countervailing social interests. In fact, in most cases the voluntariness, causation and countervailing social interest elements are subject to a great many uncertainties.

III. VOLUNTARINESS

Before imposing any burden on those life style choices which result in the need for medical care, one must be sure that the life style choices are truly voluntary. It is impossible to deter conduct that is not within a person's control by imposing sanctions on that conduct; aging, for example, cannot be deterred by threats of punishment. No one would suggest that retributive justice permits the imposition of a punishment on one whose conduct was involuntary. Punishment requires moral responsibility, and moral responsibility is premised upon free will. Finally, principles of distributive justice require that people in like situations be treated in like ways. Two patients with identical medical conditions, each the consequence of a process beyond the patient's control, are in like situations with regard to their medical needs.

There are, however, few conditions that are purely voluntary. The choice to take a drink appears to be voluntary, but alcoholism, we know, is a product of several forces. Alcoholism does not occur in a vacuum. There is a genetic component, which may be race linked.[40] There certainly is a social component, and the alcohol use patterns of an alcoholic's family seem to have a substantial effect on the chances that one will become an alcoholic.[41] There is also a gender component of alcohol related diseases.[42] Alcoholism is more likely to lead to

---

rence and the equitable distribution of scarce resources. For an excellent discussion of each of these justifications, and for the best analysis of how voluntary health risks might be considered by public policy, *see* Gerald Dworkin, *Taking Risks, Assessing Responsibilities*, HASTINGS CENTER REP., Oct. 1981, at 26. Much of the organization of this article is drawn from Professor Dworkin's excellent analysis.

40. Cohen & Benjamin, *supra* note 8, at 1299.
41. *See* Miller, *supra* note 19.
42. Cohen & Benjamin, *supra* note 8.

cirrhosis in women than in men, and any decision not to provide liver transplants to alcoholics will disproportionately affect women.[43]

Indeed, it is hard to find a life style "choice" or a health condition that is not, at least in part, a consequence of genetics, family environment, social environment, gender, life trauma, ethnicity, community, education (and, especially, health education) and, probably, most significantly, wealth. As one union official pointed out when his employer proposed a life style health insurance premium differential, the rich and the poor have different ways of dealing with stress. The rich may choose an occasional weekend in Barbados or on the slopes; the poor are more likely to choose "a six-pack and a smoke."[44] Is an impoverished person's choice to live in a poor neighborhood, miles away from the new suburban job belts, a voluntary act? Are the risks that arise from the eating habits of someone who has never been taught about the consequences of consuming fats, and who does not know what a complex carbohydrate is, voluntarily undertaken? Is a coal miner who knows no other way of feeding his family making a voluntary choice when he decides to go down into the mine? Is one who has become addicted to drugs or alcohol (or food or sex, for that matter) acting voluntarily while satisfying that addiction?

Obviously, there is some voluntary element to each of these kinds of conduct. Some kinds of conduct are more clearly the consequence of free choice than are others; arguably the failure to wear seat belts after a company-wide seat belt campaign is a truly voluntary act. Most life style choices, though, are the consequences of a variety of factors, and most commonly we do not know the significance of the different factors. The problem is not that we have yet to research the genetic, social, or family influences on alcoholism, for example, it is that we do not know the relative consequences of those influences despite our research. We do know that most life style choices—including those that have adverse health consequences—are the result of more than a series of simple voluntary choices.

---

43. *Id.* M. Berglund, *Mortality and Alcoholics Related to Clinical State at First Admission: A Study of 537 Deaths*, 70 ACTA PSYCHIATRICA SCANDINAVICA 407, 415 (1984).

44. *See* Cohen, *supra* note 11, at C1 (quoting Vance Sulsky, Chief Negotiator in Newcastle for the Delaware Public Employees Council 81 of the American Federation of State, County, and Municipal Employees).

IV. CAUSATION

One is responsible for one's health status only if it is actually (and perhaps proximately) caused by one's voluntary conduct. However, while it is possible to define general risks from identifiable kinds of conduct, it is difficult to draw a direct link between an example of that conduct and a particular health consequence.[45] We know that the use of seat belts generally decreases the risk of death in automobile accidents, but it is not so easy to determine that the use of a seat belt in a particular accident would save the life of the driver.[46] While we know of the connection between lack of exercise and heart disease, we also know that hundreds of thousands of physically fit people die of heart disease each year while hundreds of thousands of the unfit live.[47] It is usually impossible to trace an individual's death to that individual's exercise habits. While homosexual sex carries with it a risk of HIV, so does heterosexual sex.[48] We can say that having seven lottery tickets gives you a better chance to win than having only one; it is harder to say that someone won the lottery because she bought seven tickets. Similarly, while we can define conduct that increases the risk of illness or injury (and we all engage in a variety of conduct that does so in many different ways), it remains very difficult to conclude that an identifiable health event was actually caused by a life style choice.

V. COUNTERVAILING SOCIAL INTEREST

Even where voluntary conduct results in a causally proximate way in an adverse health consequence, society may wish to encourage that arguably dangerous conduct. In some cases the justification for such

---

45. For an excellent discussion of the relationship between causation, voluntariness, and moral responsibility in this arena, *see* Dworkin, *supra* note 39.

46. While the National Transportation Safety Board says that 18,087 lives were saved in 1990 because of mandatory seat belt laws, no one can determine precisely who was saved because of the existence of those laws. *See* McAllister, *supra* note 22, at A25.

47. Indeed, some of the generally encouraged "healthy" behaviors appear to have no effect on some kinds of risks. *See* I-Min Lee et al., *Physical Activity and the Risk of Developing Colorectal Cancer Among College Alumni*, 83 J. NAT: CANCER INST. 1324 (1991).

48. *See* Sherman, *supra* note 26, at 17.

conduct is quite obvious; we want soldiers, police officers, firefighters and others to undertake those occupations even though they face danger when they do so. Some justifications are less apparent, however. We acknowledge the talents of daredevil stunt artists, NFL tackles, and great boxers because of the pleasure those entertainers bring to the entire society; it is worth it for all of us for those with particular skills to undertake those health risks.

While driving across town to work is more dangerous than walking down the street to work, there is a social value in being able to choose your place of work and being able to maintain your home community and neighborhood even when you change your place of work. This social value may be a countervailing social interest that justifies the substantial voluntary health risks undertaken by commuters.

For many kinds of social justifications, the quality of the allegedly countervailing social interest is a matter of real and intense social debate. The first African-Americans who risked integrating their schools also faced physical danger to themselves. This voluntarily undertaken risk is justified and appropriately applauded by our society. Civil rights workers in the 1960s faced real health risks when they marched in the South; we now think of those risks as justified by the nature of their cause and the ultimate outcome of their endeavors. Will we feel that way about others who now risk their own safety to demonstrate, for example, in support of the right to life or the right to choose?

How are we to treat the person who refuses to wear a seat belt because he views it as an inappropriate intrusion by government into his private realm of decision making? How are we to evaluate the motorcyclist who does not wear a helmet as a matter of political expression—as a part of the Hell's Angels uniform, for example?[49] While smoking, eating "unhealthy" foods, playing high risk sports, and participating in identifiable social activities are all leisure life style choices, they also may have expressive political content. It is difficult to determine the appropriate level of generality upon which we would base a justification for voluntarily undertaking health risks. Consequently, it is not easy to determine whether particular voluntary conduct which actually causes an adverse health result is justified on the basis of principles important to the rest of society.

---

49. LAURENCE H. TRIBE, AMERICAN CONSTITUTIONAL LAW 939–40 (1st ed. 1978) (raising the issue of how high the appropriate level of government intervention into private lives should be).

VI. ARGUMENTS FOR ASSESSING INDIVIDUAL RESPONSIBILITIES

A. Deterrence

One argument for denying coverage for health care that is caused by voluntary conduct, or for charging more for such health care, is to deter undesirable conduct. We may wish to deter the conduct because it is costly or unpleasant for the one engaging in the conduct or her family. If someone knows that he will be denied treatment for lung cancer if he smokes, the argument goes, he will stop smoking. If someone knows that she will be denied bypass surgery if she is obese or has not exercised regularly, the argument continues, she will lose weight and begin an exercise regimen. If someone knows that health care is generally not available for HIV related conditions, the argument concludes, he will avoid intravenous drug use, and homosexual sex (and, perhaps, heterosexual sex).

In fact, there is no evidence that these kinds of incentives are of any value. It is hard to believe that the added cost of health care, or the risk that it will not be available, will add much to the deterrence value of the health risk itself. Lost health care coverage simply comes too late to be an effective deterrent, and, as a general matter, its consequences are too insignificant to add anything to the incentive of good health itself.[50] If the risk of death from lung and cardiovascular disease does not discourage a person from smoking, it is hard to believe that the

---

50. In applying deterrence theory to criminal behavior it has been asserted that "an individual will engage in proscribed conduct as long as the 'perception of the possibility that he ... will suffer a sanction' is less that the 'expected private benefit' provided by that conduct." Thus, deterrence as a theory applied to life style choices, ranging from criminal activity to diet and health care, presumes that people engage in cost-benefit analysis before they act. *See* A. Morgan Cloud, *Cocaine, Demand and Addiction: A study of the Possible Convergence of Rational Theory and National Policy*, 42 VAND. L. REV. 725, 767 (1989).

The courts have recognized this principle in malpractice cases where the defense of comparative or contributory negligence of the patient is based upon the patient's unhealthy life style and the resultant need for medical treatment. For example, in Ostrowski v. Azzara, 545 A.2d 148, 150 (N.J. 1988), the doctor alleged that the diabetic plaintiff had smoked cigarettes and had failed to maintain her weight, diet, and blood sugar at acceptable levels. The Supreme Court of New Jersey reversed the trial court decision allowing this evidence of pre-treatment health habits to go to the jury on the issue of causation. *See also* Sawka v. Prokopowycz, 306 N.W.2d 354 (Ct. App. Mich. 1981), where the court determined that smoking did not constitute contributory negligence in an

(cont.)

cost or availability of treatment for these conditions will make a difference. For those who participate in behaviour that puts them at risk of HIV infection, the nature of the health care available for that disease five or ten years hence is simply too removed to be a meaningful deterrent.

The argument that the absence of good health care for a disease leads people to avoid the risk factors of that disease also suggests that making health care more available for particular diseases will encourage people to run the risks of those diseases. The development of new and widely available techniques for treating heart disease has not encouraged people to engage in behavior that puts their heart at risk, however.[51] The attention this medical care has brought to the health risk has resulted in healthier behavior—presumably the result of greater knowledge of and concern about the health consequences of the behavior. Needle exchange programs do not lead to an increase in the number of people who use drugs; they have simply made it safer for those who already do so.[52] There simply is no example of a health status that has become more common because it has become more successfully treatable. Indeed, in some cases the result of this deterrent approach, which would provide treatment for those who did not cause

---

(50, *cont.*) action for failure to diagnose lung cancer, and Jensen v. Archbishop Bergen Mercy Hospital, 459 N.W.2d 178. 187 (Neb. 1990), where the Supreme Court of Nebraska held that the failure to lose weight was not contributory negligence in an action for malpractice for treatment of the embolism, even though the failure to lose weight may have been causally related to the creation of the embolism. *But see* Musachia v. Rosman, 190 So. 2d 47 (Fla. Ct. App. 1966). For an analysis of these cases, *see* Madelynn R. Orr, Comment, *Defense of Patients' Contribution to Fault and Medical Malpractice Actions*, 25 CREIGHTON L. REV. 665 (1992). Of course, deterrence is not the only reason for the existence of the criminal law or tort law.

51. The death rate from major cardiovascular disease in the United States has fallen from 510 per 100,000 population in 1950 (its peak) to 410 per 100,000 in 1985 to 366 per 100,000 in 1990. DEPARTMENT OF HEALTH AND HUMAN SERVICES, NATIONAL CENTER FOR HEALTH STATISTICS, MORTALITY: DEATH RATES FOR SELECTED CAUSES, INFORMATION PLEASE ALMANAC ATLAS & YEARBOOK 814 (1992). *See also* P. Gunby, *Cardiovascular Disease Remains Nation's Leading Cause of Death*, 267 JAMA 335 (1992).

52. *See* Philip J. Hilts, *AIDS Panel Backs Efforts to Exchange Drug Users' Needles*, N.Y. TIMES, Aug. 7, 1991, at A1. For an interesting perspective on the variety of needle exchange programs, *see* Arnold S. Trebach, *Lessons From Needle Park*, WASH. POST, Mar. 17, 1992, at A17 (discussing why some needle exchange programs are more effective than others).

their own health status but deny it to those who did, is nothing more than to drive underground the behavior or life style choice that created the problem.[53] Where the deterrent is not the denial of treatment, but rather a surcharge on current health coverage costs, this consequence is likely to be exacerbated. One result of driving this behavior underground is that education and health promotion campaigns—which may effectively deter unhealthy conduct—cannot reach those with the greatest need.

The use of a higher charge for medical coverage for those who have voluntarily put their health at risk, and denial of health care for voluntarily acquired illnesses or injuries, is not likely to provide much of an incentive to engage in healthier behavior. These deterrents add little to the fear of the adverse health outcome and, in fact, they may undercut the success of health education, which is more likely to be of value. In any case, there is no reason to believe that they would be as effective as incentives as other more direct approaches—including paying people to stop smoking, making physical fitness activities more available to people where they work and live, and assuring that cars are equipped with adequate safety devices.

B. Punishment

The second argument for imposing the burden of voluntary health risks on those who create them is based in the notion of retributive justice. There are two parts to this argument—the first is that voluntarily acquiring illness or injury is punishable conduct, and the second is that the limitation of access to health care is an appropriate form of punishment.

Illness and injury are evidence of immorality, the argument goes, because we are the stewards of our own bodies, and it is immoral in some fundamental way for any person to despoil the body he has been given.[54] This is a moral responsibility recognized, for example, in the Bible: Do you not know that you are a temple of God, and that the Spirit of God dwells in you? If any man destroys the temple of God, God will destroy him, for the temple of God is holy, and that is what you are.[55]

---

53. See Trebach, *supra* note 52.
54. See Sedgwick, *supra* note 37, and the accompanying text.
55. 1 *Cor.* 3:16–17 (New American Standard Bible). A few chapters later the same book includes a somewhat softer exhortation:

(*cont.*)

It is, of course, recognized in entirely nonreligious literature also. To the extent this unhealthy state is caused by voluntary conduct, it is as subject to punishment as any other culpable conduct. On the other hand, this ancient and new age sense of moral culpability for one's health status runs counter to another development over the past thirty years; for the most part we have stopped treating health status as criminal. Private drunkenness cannot be criminal,[56] being addicted to narcotics cannot be criminal[57] and we no longer bring attempted suicides to the police station and book them as soon as they are stabilized (although, until the 1950s, this was common).[58]

There can be little doubt that the deprivation of adequate health care is viewed as an appropriate part of criminal punishment, even when the underlying culpable conduct is not health related. The deplorable condition of our prison health systems is one way in which the morally culpable are provided with much lower quality medical care than the righteous majority.[59] The practice of providing virtually unlimited resources to treat innocent newborns, the only fully nonculpable among us, also suggests that moral status is a relevant consideration in the distribution of health care resources.[60]

(55, *cont.*)   Or do you not know that your body is a temple of the Holy Spirit who is in you, whom you have from God, and that you are not your own? For you have been bought with a price; therefore glorify God in your body.

1 *Cor.* 6:19–20 (New American Standard Bible). *See also* Gerald J. Gruman, *Death and Dying: Euthanasia and Sustaining Life—Historical Perspectives, in* ENCY-CLOPEDIA OF BIOETHICS 261 (Warren T. Reich ed., 1978).

56. Powell v. Texas, 392 U.S. 514 (1968). Although Justice Marshall, writing for a plurality, declined to find the Texas statute that criminalized public drunkenness unconstitutional, he emphasized that the Texas court's conviction was for a public, not a private, act.

57. Robinson v. California, 370 U.S. 660 (1962) (holding that a California statute which made it punishable for any person to be addicted to the use of narcotics was cruel and unusual punishment in violation of the Eighth and Fourteenth Amendment).

58. For a good history of the legal treatment of suicide, *see* GEORGE PATRICK SMITH, FINAL CHOICES: AUTONOMY IN HEALTH CARE DECISIONS (1989).

59. *See* B. Jaye Anno, *The Role of Organized Medicine in Correctional Health Care,* 247 JAMA 2923 (1982), and Iris F. Litt & Michael I. Cohen, *Prisons, Adolescents and the Right to Quality Medical Care: The Time is Now,* 64 AM. J. PUB. HEALTH 894 (1974). *See also* Andrew Skolnick, *Government Issues Guidelines to Stem Rising Tuberculosis Rates in Prisons,* 262 JAMA 3249 (1989).

60. Child Abuse and Neglect Prevention and Treatment, 45 C.F.R. § 1340.15 (1991). *See also* Iafelice v. Zarafa, 534 A.2d 417 (N.J. Super Ct. App. Div. 1987).

Of course, there are problems in using the availability of health care as a punishment, whether for health-related quasi-crimes or for other misdeeds. We do not deny any other necessities to those who have committed crimes; why should this necessity be denied to those who have not? Is the denial of treatment that is necessary to preserve life (or to make it more bearable) proportional to the immoral conduct? Are isolation and hastened death the right punishment for intravenous drug use or unprotected homosexual sex? Heterosexual sex? Would you impose a penalty on either? Would you impose the same penalty on both? Is death at the side of the highway, while the paramedics look on, the proper punishment for failure to wear a seat belt or a motorcycle helmet? Is the decision to deny affordable health care coverage to a family the proper punishment for a smoking employee? What, exactly, is the proper punishment for choosing to live outside of Utah?

If punishment is a justifiable reason for denying care to those who have created the need for medical care as a result of their voluntary conduct, we will have to develop a quasi-criminal system to define medical quasi-crimes and their appropriate punishments. Someone will have to define these quasi-crimes and determine when risks to health are justified by other concerns. In fact, some high risk activities seem to bring little moral condemnation in this society, and others are almost universally condemned. High risk activities of the rich and famous—skiing, high stress life styles, flying private planes, scuba diving—seem acceptable. High risk activities of the poor—smoking, overeating, drinking—seem to be morally unacceptable. We can presume that invidious discrimination that affects the rest of the health care system will also have an effect on the description and punishment of culpable health states. If race and gender seem to play some subtle role in the selection of liver transplant candidates when those attributes are formally irrelevant,[61] and if they play a very substantial role in the selection of bypass surgery candidates,[62] we should expect that they will

---

61. *See* Cohen & Benjamin, *supra* note 8. *See also* Philip J. Held et al., *Access to Kidney Transplantation; Has the United States Eliminated Income and Racial Differences?*, 148 ARCHIVES INTERNAL MED. 2594 (1988).

62. Indeed, race seems to play a significant role in determining access to a whole range of medical interventions, from primary care through tertiary care. For a summary and account of the role in determining who has access to care, *see* Durado D. Brooks et al., *Medical Apartheid: An American Perspective*, 266 JAMA 2746 (1991). *See also* Vernellia R. Randall, *Racist Health Care: Reforming an Unjust Health Care System to Meet the Needs of African-Americans*, 3 HEALTH
(*cont.*)

play some role in determining those who are morally qualified to receive health care.

In the end, defining health conditions that deserve punishment, and prescribing health-related punishments for those conditions, is unlikely to be done in a way that will fairly serve the underlying purposes of punishment in this society.

C. The equitable distribution of health resources

Probably the most often expressed and politically expedient reason for imposing the cost burden of voluntary health risks on those whose conduct gave rise to the risks is that it more equitably distributes scarce health resources by more equitably distributing their costs. It is only fair that a person who creates a health risk should have to pay for it. After all, people who choose to wear fancy clothes, drive fast cars, attend expensive colleges or influence important state legislators pay more for their pleasure; they pay more to get more. Those who choose to live in a way that requires the expenditure of additional health care resources ought to pay more because they are getting more.

While it is fair for society to pool its resources to pay for chance occurrences that afflict its members, it hardly seems fair to require those who take steps to avoid illness and injury to subsidize those who voluntarily undertake the risk of illness and injury. Those who choose to run health risks cost the rest of us money, and they should pay it back—either by paying larger health insurance premiums, or forgoing health care for their self-induced conditions.

Of course, these assertions presume that those with unhealthy life styles actually *do* cost us money and this attempt to shift costs to them is not simply an attempt to blame the increasing costs of health care on those with offensive looks or unpopular habits. In fact, there is good reason to believe that, at the very least, people with some unhealthy life styles actually save us much more than they cost. One unreleased 1971 British government study evaluated the financial consequences of imposing a large enough excise tax on cigarettes to substantially reduce smoking—one of the most socially unacceptable

---

(62, *cont.*) MATRIX 127, 131–32 (1994) reproduced in this volume at p.147. *See also* Stepan G. Rostand et al., *Racial Differences in the Incidence of treatment for End-Stage Renal Disease*, 306 NEW ENG. J. MED. 1276 (1982), and Council on Ethical and Judicial Affairs, *Black-White Disparities in Health Care*, 263 JAMA 2344 (1990).

life styles.[63] The simplistic notion that former smokers would be healthier and require less care from the national health service proved true—to a point. At first, there would be an improvement in health status and health care resources would be preserved. But non-smokers get sick and die, too, and while they may live longer than smokers (on the average), there is no evidence that their final illnesses are less expensive than the final illnesses of smokers. While there is an initial savings, there is a substantial additional long-term cost that arises out of the increase in the number of elderly patients and their delayed illnesses. The British study suggested that a 20% fall in smoking would save four million pounds (based on 1971 prices) ten years after it was put into effect, but would cost an additional two million pounds after thirty years.[64]

In addition, smoking may save society money in a host of other ways. The years smoking takes off of one's life always come off the

---

63. Howard Leichter, *Public Policy and the British Experience*, HASTINGS CENTER REP., Oct. 1982 at 32, 36–38.

64. *Id.* at 36. There would be a substantially greater differential if there were a 40% fall in smoking. That would save 16 million pounds over a decade, but cost the British government 29 million pounds (still in 1971 pounds) after 30 years. The 29 million pound additional cost reflects a net increase in social security payments of 24 million pounds. The relative change in the cost of health care and social security associated with 20% and 40% falls in cigarette smoking are indicated in the following chart.

Estimated changes in health care and social security expenditure (based upon 1971 prices)

Fall in cigarette smoking	Net change in health care costs	Net change in social security payments	Net overall change (£ million)
20% fall			
1981	−4	− 4	− 8
1991	−4	+ 1	− 3
2001	+2	+10	+12
40% fall			
1981	−7	− 9	−16
1991	−1	+ 5	+ 4
2001	+5	+24	+29

Source: *Cigarette Smoking and Health*, Report by an interdepartmental Group of Officials, London: October 1971.

back end; indeed, smoking leads to disease that is likely to cause death around the time the smoker ends her working life and about the time she begins retirement. The additional social security costs required to support a non-smoking society would be enormous; even in the short run they would probably exceed the financial savings provided to the health care system. In the United States the consequences of a dramatic reduction in smoking without an accompanying change in the age of retirement could include bankruptcy of the social security system, a politically unbearable increase in the cost of the Medicare program, and the failure of many retirement plans. Because much long-term care for the elderly is provided through state Medicaid programs, that state expenditure, which is already the fastest growing item in most state budgets, would grow even faster if people were living longer. This would require either additional tax revenue or a further decrease in the availability of health services to the non-elderly poor.

As the British study points out, there are further financial consequences of a decrease in smoking. A decrease in smoking (which would decrease tax revenue derived from cigarettes, of course) would be accompanied by an increase in the purchase of other goods, many of which would be imported. This would lead to a further trade imbalance. If smoking were reduced by the imposition of an additional tax on cigarettes, the tax revenue from that source could remain stable, but the consumer price index would go up, and that would require additional government expenditures.[65]

It is not surprising that the British analysis of this issue looked primarily to government costs, which include social security payments and costs incurred by the national health care system. Any analysis of the cost of smoking in the United States would be more complex. The only attempt to do this analysis looked at the external costs of smoking—those costs borne by the society and not the smoker—in order to determine whether the current taxes on smoking were economically efficient.[66] The external costs considered in the study were derived from collectively financed programs, including health insurance, pensions, sick leave, disability insurance, and group life insurance. The study separately considered such external costs as property loss from fires associated with cigarette smoking and employer-paid sick leave occasioned by cigarette smoking.

65. *Id.* at 36–38.

66. Willard G. Manning et al., *The Taxes of Sin; Do Smokers and Drinkers Pay Their Way?*, 261 JAMA 1604 (1989).

The study found that "each pack of cigarettes increases medical costs by thirty eight cents, but saved one dollar and eighty two cents in public and private pensions. . . . Over all there is a net savings of ninety one cents per pack in undiscounted costs."[67] If all costs are discounted at 5%, there is a net external cost per pack of about fifteen cents, considering both medical cost savings and the pension cost reduction.[68] As the study points out, "our estimate of the external cost of smoking, fifteen cents per pack, is well below the current average (state plus federal) excise and sales taxes of thirty seven cents per pack."[69] Only if lives lost to passive smoking and fires are included as external costs does the external cost of smoking approach the current tax on a per-pack basis.[70]

---

67. *Id.* at 1606.

68. *Id.* at 1606–07.

69. *Id.* at 1608.

70. *Id.* at 1605, 1607. An interesting summary of the consequences of alternative discount rates on the net external cost of smoking is provided in a table included in the publication of this study:

External costs per pack of cigarettes*

External costs	Discount rate		
	0%	5%	10%
Costs per pack ($) Medical care**	0.38	0.26	0.18
Sick leave	0.01	0.01	0.01
Group life insurance	0.11	0.05	0.02
Nursing home	−0.26	−0.03	0.00
Retirement pension***	−1.82	−0.24	−0.02
Fires	0.02	0.02	0.02
Taxes in earnings to finance above programs ($).	−0.65	−0.09	−0.02
Total net costs per pack ($) §	−0.91	0.15	0.24
Life expectancy at age 20 y per pack, min	−137	−28	−6

  * The number of packs of cigarettes are corrected for underreporting. Costs (in 1986 dollars) per pack are calculated by dividing by the discounted number of packs smoked.

 ** Includes all but maternity, well, and dental care.

*** Includes disability insurance.

  § The sum of costs minus taxes on earnings, e.g., costs at 5% equals 0.15 =0.26 + 0.01 + 0.05 − 0.03 − 0.24 + 0.02 − (− 0.09).

While this American study was designed to evaluate tax policy, not the imposition of other burdens on smokers, it suggests that smokers already bear a financial burden that compensates for any they impose upon the rest of society. Of course, this conclusion is based upon several variously supported assumptions about retirement age of smokers and non-smokers, other health habits of smokers, the underreporting of smoking, the discount rate on pensions and other costs, the distribution of external and internal costs, and the value of life, which was set at one million, sixty-six thousand dollars, or about ten dollars per hour.[71]

In other words, smokers do not cost the rest of us money; in fact, they save us money. If fairness were to require that smokers be charged more for health insurance than non-smokers, then fairness also requires that non-smokers be charged more for social security and make larger contributions to retirement plans. Similarly, those with unhealthy eating habits or inadequate exercise habits may be the patriots who are saving our social security system and keeping the Medicare tax contribution financing scheme effective and politically acceptable.

While it is unclear that others with different unhealthy life styles provide the rest of us with a subsidy, as smokers do, it is hardly clear that they cost us anything as a consequence of their habits. Whether helmetless motorcyclists are imposing a financial burden on the rest of us by engaging in their risky behavior depends upon which stereotypical view of this subgroup of motorcyclists is closer to the truth; are they healthy young people entering their working prime, or ne'er-do-wells who are unlikely ever to contribute to society?

Of course, there may be some kinds of choices that clearly impose a cost on society—the failure to wear seat belts, perhaps. However, the principle that costs should be equitably distributed would not permit imposing an additional cost on those who engage in this probably costly behaviour without also imposing an additional cost on those who engage in other probably costly behaviours like driving (rather than walking) to work or skiing or not smoking—behaviors unlikely to be made the subject of any sanctions.

---

71. *Id.* at 1607–09 (concluding that the taxes on liquor do not come close to paying the external costs that the use of liquor imposes on society. Of course, this conclusion is based on another series of rather arbitrary assumptions).

VII. CONCLUSION

It is difficult to assess which health-related life style choices are truly voluntary; in fact, it is a mistake to ask that question as if there were an unambiguous answer in any case. While some behaviors are more voluntary than others, most are a consequence of a combination of voluntary action and genetic predisposition, ethnic background, wealth, geographic location, and a host of other factors. Even if we could assess the voluntariness of health-related behavior, we should not impose the cost of its consequences upon the actor unless we can conclude with some certainty that the unhappy result was actually caused by the identified behavior. However, causation is as ambiguous and as difficult to establish as is the element of voluntariness. Finally, we ought not impose the cost of health consequences actually caused by voluntary conduct on the person who decided to run the risk of the consequence if the risk was justified by a countervailing social interest. Whether there is a countervailing social interest is also marked by uncertainty, ambiguity and ambivalence in most cases.

Even if we could identify some truly voluntary conduct that were clearly and causally connected to some adverse health condition, and even if we could conclude that this conduct were not otherwise socially justified, we could not base an argument for imposing the cost of the conduct—whether it be by denying access to health care for that condition, by giving lower priority to that health care claimant, or by charging that person a higher premium for health insurance—on any of the three bases usually advanced to justify that result: deterrence, punishment, and the equitable distribution of resources. This form of incentive is not likely to deter the unhealthy life style choices to which it may be applied; it will unfairly and improperly punish those who are not deserving of punishment, and it will do so without any regard for a sense of proportionality; and, finally, it will not lead to the equitable distribution of scare societal resources.

In fact, the recent call to impose the costs of health care on those who voluntarily create risks that result in those costs is a way to blame patients for the increase in health care costs. It is a way to avoid dealing with the real reason for the rise in those costs—reasons that include an irrationally structured health care delivery system and a highly subsidized market that can command almost any amount of resources.[72]

---

72. *See* Barry Furrow et al., *supra* note 1, at 661–66.

It is hardly surprising that the punish-the-smoker mentality surfaced first in England and Canada when the costs of those centralized health care systems began to rise precipitously in the 1970s.[73] It is not surprising that the same mentality has arisen in this country at the same time that smoking, consuming a diet high in saturated fats, driving without a seat belt, and several other unhealthy life styles are on the decline. We should not allow ourselves to be drawn away from serious evaluation of the justice of our health care system by focusing on the life style of patients. We should not be diverted from dealing with patient and community education and other proven ways of promoting and encouraging good health (which is certainly a valuable social end, even if it *costs* money) by figuring out how to impose sentence on those with life style related health problems. Even is we could, we ought not make patients pay for their life style choices.

---

73. *See* Leichter, *supra* note 63.

Principles and power in the health care arena: reflections on the Canadian experience

Carolyn Hughes Tuohy

As a political scientist who has devoted considerable attention to the Canadian health care system, I have two purposes in this article. One is to describe the evolution of the Canadian health care system in comparison with that of some other systems, notably those of Britain and the US, and in brief comparison with another component of the Canadian welfare state—the public pension system. The other is to explain this evolution by making a central argument. Welfare states institutionalize principles of distributive justice. In so doing, they translate those principles into structures of power. It is through those power structures that principles of distributive justice will be expressed and will have their impact. The central feature of the power structure of the Canadian health care system is an accommodation between the providers of health care, most particularly the medical profession, and the state. In this accommodation, the medical profession has traded off a substantial part of the entrepreneurial, economic discretion of physicians in order to preserve their clinical autonomy. This accommodation itself is evolving over time, but it will continue to be central to the development of the system in the future.

Justice and Health Care: Comparative Perspectives. Edited by A. Grubb and M.J. Mehlman © 1995 John Wiley & Sons Ltd.

I. PRINCIPLES UNDERLYING THE WELFARE STATE

If you seek to understand the prevailing principles of distributive justice in a given nation, look to the structure of its welfare state. In terms of the principles of distributive justice which underlie them, one can identify four types of welfare states in advanced capitalist nations: social democratic, corporatist, residualist and what, for want of a more descriptive term, might be called the "Beveridge" model.[1]

Social democratic welfare states have universal and generous programs whose benefits are available on uniform terms and conditions to all citizens.[2] Entitlement to benefits is on the basis of membership in the national community—in this sense there is a citizen's "right" to benefits—and programs are designed to be attractive to all members of the community, not just those who have no private alternatives.[3] Indeed, the assumption is that there will be little recourse to private markets for social or health services or for insurance against income disruption or decline.[4]

Corporatist welfare states offer differentiated benefits through social insurance for defined groups (primarily occupationally defined) within the population. These programs tend to be generous overall, but the level of generosity varies within "a labyrinth of status-specific insurance funds."[5] Entitlement is based on contribution, and levels of both contribution and benefits are determined by occupational status.[6]

The residualist welfare state is market-oriented. The underlying assumption is that the market is the primary mechanism of allocation and distribution.[7] Health and social services as well as income ought to accrue to individuals not on the basis of a social entitlement, but primarily according to the individual's "marginal rate of productivity." Welfare state programs are directed primarily to those most disadvant-

---

1. *See* GØSTA ESPING-ANDERSEN, THE THREE WORLDS OF WELFARE CAPITALISM 26–27 (1990) (describing what I have termed as the "corporatist" and "residualist" types of welfare states as "conservative" and "liberal" respectively). Epsing-Anderson does not identify a separate "Beveridge" type.

2. *Id.* at 27.

3. *See id.*

4. *See id.* at 28.

5. *See id.* at 24.

6. *Id.* at 22.

7. *Id.* at 26–27.

aged in the market—hence, the term "residualist." Means-tested programs predominate, benefits are relatively low so as not to draw labor
out of the market, universalism is limited and the middle and upper
classes turn to the market, not the state, for health and social services
and income protection.[8]

Finally, the Beveridge model combines elements of each of the other
three types. From the corporatist model comes the social insurance
principle that benefits are to be based on contributions.[9] But contributions and benefit schedules are not status-specific; rather, they are
based on the social-democratic principle of universality.[10] Finally, like
the programs of the residualist welfare state, Beveridge-type programs
are limited in their generosity. The underlying principles assume that
all individuals have a citizenship right to participate in a social
insurance plan providing a minimum level of benefits, but that any
individual ought to be able to substantially improve his or her position
through participation in the market.[11]

These four models represent pure types. In the real world, each of
these models has been subject to strain and evolution over time. The
social democratic model has been most closely approximated by
Sweden, although the level of generosity of the Swedish welfare state
has become increasingly contested in the late 1980s and 1990s.
Germany most closely corresponds to the corporatist model, and
the US to the residualist model.[12] And, of course, the empirical
expression of the Beveridge model is identified in his name, referring
to the vision of the Beveridge report of 1942 on which the post-war
reform of the British welfare state was based.[13] But the growth over
time in the relative importance of means-tested "supplementary
benefits" has given the British welfare state an increasingly residualist
cast.

Some systems, moreover, combined elements of at least three of
these models. Japan, for example, arguably combined corporatist,
residualist and Beveridge models in the design of its health insurance

---

8. *Id.* at 22.

9. *See id.* at 22.

10. *Id.*

11. *See id.* at 23.

12. *Id.* at 27.

13. WILLIAM BEVERIDGE, U.K. INTER-DEPARTMENTAL COMM. ON SOCIAL
INS. AND ALLIED SERVS., SOCIAL INSURANCE AND ALLIED SERVICES, REPORT
BY SIR WILLIAM BEVERIDGE (HMSO 1942).

and pension systems.[14] And Canada presents the joint phenomena of a social democratic health insurance system, a quasi-Beveridge-style pension system and a residualist system of income maintenance.

I want to focus in this article on the Canadian case, first to consider the distinctive character of the Canadian health insurance system, then to view the health insurance system in comparison with some other national systems and with the Canadian public pension system. The Canadian case suggests that quite different models of distributive justice can coexist in different components of a given welfare state, even when those components came into being at the same time and within the same institutional structures. I will argue that the answer to this apparent anomaly lies in the evolution of the welfare state over time, an evolution shaped only indirectly by the principles of distributive justice that the system embodies. Any set of principles of distributive justice, once institutionalized in a set of programs and structures, implies a structure of power. And it is that power structure, at least as much as the principles and ideas embedded in the system, that will determine the system's evolution.

In the case of health insurance systems, a central component of the power structure is the role of the medical profession. In the Canadian case, I will argue, much of the "success" of the system—its universality, its comprehensive coverage and its record of relatively moderate rates of increase in costs over time—is attributable to the particular nature of the accommodation between the medical profession and the state.

II. PRINCIPLES UNDERLYING THE CANADIAN HEALTH INSURANCE SYSTEM

State-sponsored health insurance was first introduced in Canada at the provincial level, as various provincial governments introduced different models of hospital and medical insurance in the 1940s through the 1960s.[15] The contemporary universal Canadian health insurance system,

---

14. *See* Samuel H. Preston & Shigemi Kono, *Trends in Well-Being of Children and the Elderly in Japan in* THE VULNERABLE 277, 285–86 (John L. Palmer *et al.* eds., 1988) (describing the Japanese health insurance system).

15. *See generally* Malcom G. Taylor, *The Canadian Health Insurance Program* PUB. ADMIN. REV. Jan./Feb. 1973, at 31 [hereinafter *Canadian Health*]; MALCOM G. TAYLOR, INSURING NATIONAL HEALTH CARE: THE CANADIAN EXPERIENCE (1990) [hereinafter INSURANCE NAT'L HEALTH CARE].

however, had its genesis in the province of Saskatchewan, under the social democratic New Democratic Parity.[16] The (NDP) introduced universal comprehensive hospital insurance in 1944,[17] and universal comprehensive medical care insurance in 1962.[18] Each of these models was in due course replicated at the federal level, with the passage of the Federal Hospital Insurance and Diagnostic Services Act in 1958[19] and the federal Medical Care Act in 1966.[20] By 1971, all provinces had universal medical and hospital services insurance plans eligible for federal cost- sharing.[21] To be eligible, provincial programs had to meet five essentially social democratic general criteria: universal coverage (at least 95% of the population), comprehensive coverage of medical and hospital services, provision of coverage on uniform terms and conditions, portability across provinces and public administration.[22] These criteria were consistent with the "Health Charter for Canadians"[23] that had been set out by a federal Royal Commission on Health Services that had reported in 1964, recommending a universal comprehensive state- sponsored system of health insurance.[24] Notably, the Health Charter also included commitments of "freedom of choice" for patients in the selection of physicians and *vice versa*, and to "free and self-governing professions."[25] While these latter two principles in the Health Charter were not specifically enshrined in legislation, they were clearly embedded in the system that resulted.

Indeed, the advent of national health insurance in Canada essentially froze in place the delivery system that existed in the 1960s, by underwriting its costs. One has only to compare Canadian developments with those in Britain on the one hand and in the US on the other to appreciate this point. In Britain, massive organizational change was inherent in the establishment of the National Health Services in 1948. In the US, organizational change flowed from the very *absence* of national health insurance in the 1970s and 1980s.[26] In Canada,

---

16. *See* INSURING NAT'L HEALTH CARE, *supra* note 15, at 7.
17. *Id.* at 7, 67–68.
18. *Canadian Health, supra* note 15, at 34 n. 13.
19. R.S.C., ch. H-8 (1956–57) (Can.).
20. R.S.C., ch. M-8 (1970) (Can.).
21. *Canadian Health, supra* note 15, at 31.
22. *Id.* at 36.
23. Contained in 1 CAN. ROYAL COMM'N ON HEALT SERVS. REPORT (1964).
24. *See* INSURING NAT'L HEALTH CARE, *supra* note 15, at 134–39.
25. *Id.* at 135 (quoting the Health Charter).
26. *See* Paul Starr. *The Social Transformation of American Medicine* 419 (1982).

organizational change was forestalled by the introduction of a system of financing which essentially underwrote the costs of the existing delivery system without changing its structure.

The health care delivery systems of Canada and the US were very similar in the 1960s; medical services provided by physicians in private fee-for-service practices; hospital services provided in non-profit institutions owned by voluntary societies, religious orders, municipalities and universities; extended care facilities owned by such non-profit groups or by private independent for-profit operators. In the 1990s, the delivery system in the US appears transformed. In the absence of national health insurance, public policy has elaborated both categorical programs and regulatory constraints. The resulting complexity has given a competitive advantage to providers with the resources to invest in understanding the system and responding strategically. Public policy has thus fostered organizational change not only directly (as in the case of health maintenance organizations, preferred provider organizations, etc.) but also indirectly (as in the case of large multi-institutional changes, many of them for-profit, which have sprung up in response to the increasing complexity of the system).[27]

In Canada, organization change has been much more modest. The proportion of large group practices has increased, and there have been a number of hospital mergers; but Canada has seen nothing like the "coming of the corporation" to the health care arena on the scale that has occurred in the US.[28] Organizational change is, however, on the agenda of the 1990s—a point to which I shall return below.

The proportion of total health care spending in Canada that flows through the public treasury, at just under three-quarters, is close to the Organisation for Economic Cooperation and Development (OECD) average.[29] Canada differs from most OECD nations, however, in the *pattern* of public and private expenditure. In most other nations public and private expenditures are divided on a "tiered" basis—with private alternatives to publicly funded services within each category of service. In Canada, however, public and private expenditures are segmented. Certain segments—notably medical and hospital services—are almost

---

27. *Id.* at 428.

28. *Id.* at 419, 420, 428.

29. CAROLYN TUOHY, SOCIAL POLICY: TWO WORLDS IN GOVERNING CANADA: INSTITUTIONS AND PUBLIC POLICY 275, 285 (Michael M. Atkinson ed., 1993).

entirely publicly funded; others, such as dental care, drugs and eyeglasses and other prostheses, are in the private sector.[30]

Canada, then, interpreted the social-democratic principle of universality as implying *the removal of financial barriers to access to an established health care system.* Accordingly, it provides universal first-dollar coverage for a comprehensive range of medical and hospital services, within delivery structures that preserve the patient's choice of physician and vice versa. And it has done so at relatively "generous" levels. Government spending on health care, which ranged between 6% and 7% of GDP in the 1980s, is comparable to Western European levels, and well above that in both Britain and the United States.[31]

III. THE EFFECT OF CANADIAN MEDICARE

The medical and hospital system which Canadian governments undertook to finance in the 1960s was a relatively expensive one, in international perspective, due in large part to the intensive use of hospital services. And it is still relatively expensive: per capita costs are second (albeit a fairly distant second) to those in the US.[32] But the rate of cost escalation has been relatively moderate. Canadian health care expenditures (both public and private) increased 70% faster than GDP from 1960 to 1985, as compared with 120% in Britain, 130% in the US, 200% in Sweden and an OECD average of 90%.[33]

The removal of financial barriers to care, moreover, appears to have had its intended effects. There have been a number of studies of the impact of Medicare on the utilization of medical and hospital services

---

30. U.S. GENERAL ACCOUNTING OFFICE, REPORT TO THE CHAIRMAN, COMMITTEE ON GOVERNMENT OPERATIONS, HOUSE OF REPRESENTATIVES, CANADIAN HEALTH INSURANCE: LESSONS FOR THE UNITED STATES, DOC. NO. GAO/HRD-91-90, 102d Cong., 1st Sess. 23 (1991) [hereinafter GAO REPORT]. Various provinces have plans covering drugs or dental care for certain categories within the population, such as children's dental care or drugs for those over sixty-five. *Id.* In the hospital sector, various amenities such as private rooms, can be purchased on an individual basis.

31. New Orientations for Social Policy, OECD Social Policy Studies No. 12, at tbl. 2 (1994); *see also* Michael O'Higgins, *The Allocation of Public Resources to Children and the Elderly in OECD Countries, in* THE VULNERABLE 29, 214–15 tbl. 9.6 (1988).

32. CAROLYN J. TUOHY, POLICY AND POLITICS IN CANADA: INSTITUTIONALIZED AMBIVALENCE 105 (1992).

33. *Id.* (citing Schieber & Poullier 1987).

across income classes. Despite some methodological difficulties, and some modest variation in the findings, a recent comprehensive review of these studies could fairly conclude that "a notable policy achievement [has] been realized resulting in the progressive redistribution by class in the use of health care."[34]

As the issue of national health insurance has waxed and wanted on the policy agenda of the US, the "Canadian model" has periodically been raised in that context by both enthusiasts and skeptics. Many of the perceptions of the Canadian system are based on anecdotes or misinformation. One benefit of the increased American interest in the Canadian system, however, at least from an academic perspective, has been an increase in the number of comparative studies of the two systems.

A. Cost control and access

There is little debate that the Canadian system provides access to a wide range of medical and hospital services to a far larger proportion of its population while remaining less costly than the American system.[35] The Canadian system provides first-dollar coverage of medical and hospital services for all residents; and while the range of services covered varies somewhat from province to province, the range of services covered is extensive.[36] In the US, about 15% of the population has no health insurance coverage;[37] and for the remainder the extent and terms of coverage vary widely between public and private plans and among private plans.[38] In Canada, charges to patients in excess of the government benefit for insured services are banned, and there are no deductibles or co-payments.[39] In the US, "co-payments and deductibles are common, and it is not unusual for health care providers to bill the patient for charges in excess of the standard insurance reimbursement."[40]

As for cost, total per capita health care expenditures in Canada (including public and private expenditures) are about two-thirds of

---

34. Robin F. Badgley, *Social and Economic Disparities Under Canadian Health Care*, 21 INT'L J. HEALTH SERVS. 659, 662 (1991).

35. *See* GAO REPORT, *supra* note 30, at 20–24, 28–29 (1991).

36. *Id.* at 23.

37. *Id.* at 23–24.

38. *Id.* at 24.

39. *Id.* at 23.

40. *Id.* at 4.

those in the US.[41] As a proportion of the GDP, total health care expenditures rose from 8.5% to 10.0% between 1985 and 1991 in Canada, for a compound annual increase of 2.7%.[42] In the US in the same period, total health expenditures rose from 10.5% to 13.2% of GDP, for a compound annual increase of 3.9%.[43] (It should be noted here that the US and Canada have the two most expensive health care systems in the OECD.[44] The fact that Canada is a distant second to the US[45] is of great interest in the context of North American debates over health care policy; but it should not obscure the expensiveness of the Canadian system.)

Canada achieves its lower costs in a number of ways. In the first place, the administrative costs of the "single payer" Canadian system are considerably lower than those of the US.[46] For Canadian public insurers, "there are no marketing expenses, no costs of estimating risk status in order to set differential premiums or decide whom to cover, and no allocation for shareholder profits; the process of claims payment, although not free of costs, is greatly simplified and much cheaper."[47] For Canadian providers, the single-payer system means less administrative overhead. In 1987, for example, office expenses for physicians in Canada amounted on average to about 36% of their gross billings, as compared with 48% in the US.[48] The General Accounting Office of the US Congress (GAO) has estimated that difference in insurers' overhead accounts for about 17% of the difference in cost between the two systems.[49] Others have estimated that if provider overheads related to the costs of the multi-payer system in the US are included, differences in administrative costs may account for more than half of the difference between the two systems.[50]

---

41. George J. Schieber et al., *Data Watch: Health Spending, Delivery and Outcomes in OECD Countries*, 12 HEALTH AFFAIRS 120, 121 (1993) (utilizing 1991 statistics).

42. *Id.*

43. *Id.*

44. *Id.* at 121–22.

45. *Id.*

46. Robert G. Evans et al., *Controlling Health Expenditures: The Canadian Reality*, 320 NEW ENG. J. MED. 571, 573 (1989).

47. *Id.* at 572–73.

48. GAO REPORT, *supra* note 30, at. 5.

49. *Id.* at 29.

50. Evans et al., *supra* note 46, at 572–73.

B. Payments to providers

Canada's lower expenditures on health care also reflect lower levels of payment to health care providers. In 1987, Canada spent 34% less per capita on physician services and 18% less per capita on hospital services than did the US, despite the fact that Canada had roughly the same number of physicians and about 40% more hospital beds per capita.[51] Differences in spending on physicians reflects two factors: a different specialty mix (the US has a higher specialist: general practitioner ratio) and the level of physician fees.[52] In the decade following the introduction of Canadian Medicare, real physician fees rose much faster in the US than in Canada; indeed in Canada (with the exception of British Columbia and Alberta), real fees declined over that period.[53] Between 1971 and 1985, real fees declined 18% in Canada and rose 22% in the US.[54] Differences in net income are less than might be expected, however, partly due to lower practice expenses. Because of the different specialty mixes in the two countries, income comparisons are best made by specialty. One such comparison related US physicians to their counterparts in Ontario.[55] In 1986, average net incomes in general practice and family practice were marginally higher for the US than for Ontario physicians.[56] The differences were more pronounced in obstetrics and gynecology, with US physicians earning on average one-quarter to one-third more than their Ontario counterparts.[57] In pediatrics and internal medicine, however, the net earnings of Ontario physicians were on average marginally higher than those in the US.[58] In this respect, as in a number of others shortly to be discussed, the

---

51. Morris L. Barer & Robert G. Evans, *Riding North on a South-bound Horse!: Expenditures, Prices, Utilization and Incomes in the Canadian Health Care System, in* MEDICARE AT MATURITY 53, 78–80 (Robert G. Evans & Greg L. Stoddart eds., 1986).

52. *See* GAO REPORT, *supra* note 30, at 35–38.

53. *See id.* at 35.

54. *Id.*

55. John K. Iglehart, *Canada's Health Care System Faces Its Problems,* 322 NEW ENG. J. MED. 562 (1990). Ontario physicians represent about 40% of all Canadian physicians; and both net professional incomes and medical fees are close to the Canadian average. *See* Barer & Evans, *supra* note 51, at 78, 94; Iglehart, *supra,* at 563, 568.

56. *See* Iglehart, *supra* note 55, at 568.

57. *See id.*

58. *See id.*

most pronounced differences between the two systems are related to areas of intensive care.

C. Hospital utilization

Differences in hospital expenditures reflect in part different mixes of hospital activities: the US favors intensive, high-technology services while Canada leans toward long-term chronic care.[59] (Hence, hospital costs can be lower in Canada than in the US even while hospitalization rates are higher.) But even after allowing for such differences, a study of hospital costs in California, New York, British Columbia and Ontario found that "the cost of an average intensive care day in California in 1985 was more than twice that of a corresponding day in a Canadian hospital... Canadian hospitals appear to combine lower treatment intensity with longer inpatient stays."[60] Even with longer stays, Canadian costs per discharge were about 30% lower than those in New York hospitals and 38% lower than those in California in 1985.[61] It is worth noting, however, that Canadian and American hospitals were much more similar with regard to the costs of outpatient visits.[62]

D. High technology and queues

These cost advantages of the Canadian system have led American skeptics to look for the potential downside; in particular, restrictions on the availability of high-technology service, and waiting times or "queues" for service. It is with regard to such allegations that the relevant data tend to become more anecdotal and less systematic; but some work has been done to provide a basis for comparison.

There is little doubt that the US exceeds Canada in the availability of high-technology procedures. This is consistent with the general phenomenon that the diffusion of technology has been greater in systems with high proportions of specialists and less centralized cost control.[63] As a matter of public policy, Canadian provincial

59. Evans et al., *supra* note 46, at 574.

60. Jack Zwanziger et al., *Data Watch: Comparison of Hospital Costs in California, New York, And Canada*, HEALTH AFF. Summer 1993, at 130, 137.

61. *Id.* at 135.

62. *Id.* at 134.

63. *See* J. ROGERS HOLLINGSWORTH ET AL. STATE INTERVENTION IN MEDICAL CARE: CONSEQUENCES FOR BRITAIN, FRANCE, SWEDEN AND THE UNITED STATES, 1870–1970 (1990).

governments control the diffusion of medical technology. Operating funds for certain types of equipment such as imaging machines will not be provided unless acquisition of the equipment has been approved by the government.[64] Furthermore, under the hospital global budgeting system, any significant change in the volume of service, including high-technology services, must be approved in order for the hospital to receive the necessary additional operating funds.[65]

Neither nation systematically collects data relating to the availability of high-technology services; but a study by a senior policy analyst for the American Medical Association, based on interviews and the review of relevant documents and literature, compared the availability of selected technologies in Canada, the US and Germany.[66] He found "(1) nearly eight times more MRI [magnetic resonance imaging] and radiation therapy units per capita in the United States than in Canada; (2) over six times more lithotripsy centers per capita in the United States; (3) roughly three times more cardiac catheterization and open-heart surgery units per capita in the United States; and (4) slightly more availability of organ transplantation units per capita in the United States."[67] German ratios were intermediate between Canada and the US in the case of cardiac catheterization, radiation therapy, lithotripsy and MRI, and were below Canadian ratios for open-heart surgery and organ transplantation.[68]

Other comparative work has focused on one of these technologies— open-heart surgery, and in particular, coronary bypass surgery ('CABS'). A survey of California, New York, British Columbia, Manitoba and Ontario hospital discharge data found that in 1989 the age-adjusted CABS rate in California was 27% higher than in New York and 80% higher than in the three Canadian provinces combined.[69] In the two American states, however, CABS rates were higher in high-income areas; while in Canada, rates varied little by the income of the area of residence.[70] Earlier work comparing hospital discharge

---

64. GAO REPORT, *supra* note 30, at 48.

65. *Id.* at 48–49.

66. Dale A. Rublee, *Data Watch: Medical Technology In Canada, Germany, And The United States*, 8 HEALTH AFFAIRS 178 (1989).

67. *Id.* at 178.

68. *See id*, at 180 Exhibit 1.

69. Geoffrey M. Anderson et al. *Use of Coronary Artery Bypass Surgery in the United States and Canada*, 269 JAMA 1661, 1661 (1993).

70. *Id.*

data for Manitdoa and Ontario with Medicare data from the US for 1983 found markedly higher rates of CABS for elderly patients in the US than in Canada.[71] For the 65 to 74 age group, US Rates were over twice as high as in Canada; and for patients over 75 the US rate was four times the Canadian rate.[72] In the case of other surgical procedures for the treatment of ischemic heart disease, however, differences were much less pronounced. The rate of cardiac-valve procedures for all patients over 65 years of age was only 20% higher in the US than in Canada; and with regard to other major reconstructive vascular surgery and pacemaker implantation, Canadian rates were higher.[73]

The lesser availability of some high-technology services in Canada has given rise to concern about waiting times or "queues" for various services. There is a plethora of anecdote, as well as a dearth of systematic data regarding waiting times for service on both sides of the Canada–US border. Press coverage of waiting times for certain procedures in Ontario reached a mild crescendo in the late 1980s. The US GAO in the context of a study of the Canadian health care system, conducted a survey of selected specialty units in Ontario's 26 teaching hospitals in October 1990 (by which time some steps had already been taken to shorten waiting times in a number of areas, as noted below) to determine the extent of queuing for services in eight areas of high-technology: CAT (computerized axial tomography) scan, MRI, (Magnetic Resonance Imaging), cardiovascular surgery, eye surgery, orthopedic surgery, lithotripsy, specialized physical rehabilitation and autologous bone marrow transplants.[74] The GAO found virtually no queues for "emergent" cases, except in the case of lithotripsy, for which, at the time of the GAO study, there was only one unit in the province.[75] It did, however, find considerable variation in waiting times for urgent and elective cares. (Another study also found considerable variation in the classification of CABS cases as "emergent," "urgent" and "elective."[76]) The longest queues for elective cases existed for

71. Geoffrey M. Anderson et al., *Hospital Care for Elderly Patients with Diseases of the Circulatory System: A Comparison of Hospital Use in the United States and Canada*, 21 NEW ENG. J. MED. 1443, 1447 (1989).

72. *See id.*

73. *See id* at 1446–47.

74. *See* GAO REPORT, *supra* note 30 at 55 tbl. 4.1.

75. *Id.* at 56.

76. C. David Naylor, *A Different View of Queues in Ontario*, 10 HEALTH AFFAIRS 110, 114 (1991).

lithotripsy (24 months) and for MRI (up to 16 months).[77] For cardiovascular surgery, waiting times in urgent cases ranged from one day to one week, and in elective cases from one week to six months.[78] It should be kept in mind that these data were collected from hospital administrators at a time when the provincial government was responding to queues in part by providing hospitals with additional funding, and as the GAO noted, there was no independent source of data from which it could verify these figures.[79] The GAO did not present comparable data for the US.

The existence of such queues brought about responses on the part of provincial governments. Some of the responses involved the approval of additional equipment and facilities. In Ontario, a second lithotripsy unit was approved,[80] and open-heart surgery capacity was expanded, including the opening of an additional unit.[81] Bottlenecks in related areas such as intensive care units were also addressed with additional funding.[82] In addition, responses focused on the better management of queues on a regional basis and greater attention to case selection and classification and to the use of alternative techniques.[83] The backlog of CABS patients was also reduced by referring about 16% of waiting patients for treatment in the US.[84] This combination of responses led to a dramatic decline in waiting times. By January 1991, waiting times in elective CABS cases had been reduced to a few weeks, down from three months or more in some facilities a year earlier.[85]

As noted, some of the backlog of CABS cases was cleared by referring patients to US facilities. This raises the question of the extent to which the US functions as a "safety valve" for the Canadian system. In a recent cross-national survey of physicians, nearly one-third of the Canadian respondents (as compared with 19% of respondents in western Germany and 7% of American respondents) reported referring a patient outside the country for treatment.[86] But the number of

---

77. *Canadian Health, supra* note 15.
78. *Id.*
79. *Id.* at 54.
80. *Id.* at 56 n.h.
81. Naylor, *supra* note 76, at 115–16.
82. *Id.* at 116.
83. *See id.*
84. *Id; see also* GAO REPORT, *supra* note 30, at 60–61.
85. Naylor, *supra* note 76, at 115, 116.
86. Robert J. Blendon et al., *Physicians Perspectives on Caring for Patients in the United States, Canada and West Germany*, 328 NEW ENG. J. MED. 1011, 1014 (1993).

patients involved is relatively small. Informal surveys of border hospitals by the Pepper Commission in the US and by the American Medical Association in the late 1980s suggest that Canadians accounted in most cases for less than 1%, and in no case more than 3% of admissions.[87] Large numbers of Canadians vacation in the US particularly in the winter months, however; and the high cost of reimbursing them for medical and hospital care received in that context has led some provincial governments, notably Ontario, to limit the rate of reimbursement.[88]

The constrained availability of high-technology services is only a problem, of course, to the extent that such services are not available for cases for which they are truly indicated, and in which they will be efficacious. And in this regard, there is still much research to be done. In commenting on his findings of the differences in the availability of high-technology services in Canada, the US and Germany noted above, Dale Rublee pointed out that 'the differences can be interpreted to suggest overprovision in the United States rather than underprovision in Canada or Germany.'[89] And, noting the wide variation across geographic areas within as well as between the US and Canada in the utilization of CABS, the GAO cautioned that, "Canada's lower rates for certain procedures do not conclusively represent underservicing, nor do US rates conclusively represent over-provision of service."[90]

E. Patient and provider satisfaction

As most comparative studies of health care systems suggest, different systems entail different trade-offs. The Canadian system offers much broader accessibility and generally less service intensity than is the case in the US. These trade-offs have resulted in a system which, while not

---

87. GAO Report, *supra* note, 30, at 60.

88. It should be noted that there is also a flow of patients in the other direction, both legally and illegally. Hospitals in Ontario have been directed by the Ministry of Health to ensure that their acceptance of US patients does not restrict the availability of facilities for Canadian patients. The issues of the fraudulent use of government health care insurance cards by non-residents has also received considerable attention both within the Ministry of Health and in the press.

89. Rublee, *supra* note, 66, at 181.

90. GAO Report, *supra* note 30, at 51.

without its critics, is overwhelmingly popular. Medicare has virtually become a defining element of the Canadian identity. During the heated and wrenching public debate over the Free Trade Agreement ('FTA') with the United States in 1988, politicians opposing the agreement repeatedly invoked Medicare as one of the things that distinguished Canada from the US, and alleged that it was threatened by the agreement. Public opinion polls showed that this allegation was the most effective way of galvanizing opposition to the FTA.[91] Polls have consistently demonstrated that Medicare is by far the most popular public program in Canada.[92] And a 1988 cross-national poll showed that Canadians were more satisfied with their health care system than were either American or British respondents, and that they overwhelmingly preferred the Canadian system to the British or the American systems.[93] A large majority of American respondents, on the other hand, preferred a Canadian-style system to their own.[94] Subsequent polls have reinforced these results.[95]

What is perhaps more surprising is the relatively favorable light in which the system is viewed by health care providers. Even in briefs critical of government policy, medical groups, for example, typically present the Canadian system as one of the best in the world, while expressing some concerns about its future.[96] The twin specters of the US system (intrusive regulation, corporate dominance, inadequate coverage) and the British system (inadequate resources, excessive rationing) are frequently evoked. Attitude surveys of physicians find large majorities are satisfied with their conditions of practice and positively oriented toward Medicare—although sizable pockets of discontent remain. A 1986 survey of Canadian physicians, for example, found less than one-quarter dissatisfied with medical practice and less than one-third dissatisfied with the functioning of Medicare.[97] Sixty

---

91. Richard Johnston & Andre Blats, *A Resounding Maybe*, THE GLOBE AND MAIL. (TORONTO), Dec. 19, 1988.

92. Robert J. Blendon, *Three Systems: A Comparative Survey*, 11 HEALTH MGMT. Q. 2–10 (1989).

93. *Id.* at 5.

94. *Id.*

95. *E.G.*, GALLUP CANADA, THE GALLUP REPORT, August 1, 1991 (Toronto 1991).

96. *See*, e.g., TUOHY, *supra* note 32, at 144–45.

97. Michael H. Stevenson, Eugene Vayda & A. Paul Williams, MEDICAL POLITICS AFTER THE CANADA HEALTH ACT. PRELIMINARY RESULTS OF THE 1986 PHYSICIANS' SURVEY, Paper Delivered at the Annual Meeting of the

percent believed that Medicare had positively influenced health status, but 75% believed that it had reduced the individual's personal sense of responsibility for health.[98]

A more extensive comparative survey in 1991 shed light on the judgments of physicians in Canada, the US and western Germany regarding the trade-offs implicit in their health care systems. In general, although a majority of physicians in each country believed that some fundamental changes in their health systems were necessary, satisfaction with the health system was higher among Canadian and German physicians than among American physicians.[99] When respondents were asked to identify the most serious problems with their system, the sharpest differences arose between Canadian and American physicians, whose judgments of their respective systems appeared virtually as mirror images of each other. American physicians were much more likely than Canadian physicians to identify the following as serious problems with their system: delays or disputes in processing insurance forms and in receiving payment, the inability of patients to afford some aspect of necessary medical care, external review of clinical decisions for the purpose of controlling health costs and limitations on the length of hospital stays.[100] On the other hand, Canadian physicians were much more likely to complain of limitations on the supply of well-equipped medical facilities.[101]

IV. ACCOMMODATION BETWEEN THE MEDICAL PROFESSION AND THE STATE

These observations point to a central feature of Canadian Medicare: its birth may owe much to social democracy, but its ongoing maintenance and development depends upon an accommodation between the medical profession and the state. It is useful here to distinguish, as Patricia Day and Rudolph Klein[102] have done in the British case,

---

Canadian Political Science Association, McMaster University, Hamilton, Ontario (1987).

98. Id.

99. Blendon et al., supra note 86, at 1012.

100. Id. at 1015.

101. Id.

102. Patricia Day & Rudolph Klein, Constitutional and Distributional Conflict on British Medical Politics. The Case of General Practice, 1911–91. 11 POLITICAL STUDIES 462, 462 (1992).

between the "constitutional" politics that surrounded the *establishment* of Canadian Medicare, and the ongoing *distributional* politics that have flowed in its wake. The establishment of the system had more to do with partisan and federal-provincial politics than with the relationship between the medical profession and the state. The social democratic NDP government of Saskatchewan pioneered both hospital and medical insurance, and it has been argued that it was the growing popularity of the NDP at the federal level that prompted the governing federal Liberals to introduce a wave of welfare-state legislation, including the Medical Care Act, in the minority parliament of 1964–68.[103] Furthermore, the medical profession did not enter the Medicare era without protest: medical strikes accompanied the introduction of universal medical care insurance in both Saskatchewan and Quebec.[104] But the terms of the "constitutional" understandings reached by the profession and the state surrounding the introduction of Medicare ensured that the medical profession would play a central policy-making role. The medicare era itself has been marked by an accommodation between the profession and the state.

The particular nature of that accommodation varies across provinces, for it is at the provincial level that health care policy has been made, within broad federal guidelines. In some provinces, notably British Columbia and Manitoba, the profession-state relationship has been adversarial; in Quebec it has been more "statist"; and in other provinces it has been more collaborative, albeit marked by episodes of conflict.[105] But each of these accommodations has revolved around two pivotal trade-offs for the medical profession: one between the entrepreneurial and the clinical discretion of physicians; the other between their individual and their collective autonomy.

The first of these trade-offs arises from the principles embodied in the Canadian health insurance system: the removal of financial barriers to access to medically necessary services. The removal of financial barriers at the point of contact with the system implies that the state assume the costs of medical and hospital services. The state thus

---

103. *See, e.g.*, INSURING NAT'L HEALTH CARE, *supra* note 15, at 142–43.
104. *See id.* at 117.
105. JONATHON LOMAS, CATHY CHARLES & JANET GREB, THE PRICE OF PEACE: THE STRUCTURE AND PROCESS OF PHYSICIAN FEE NEGOTIATIONS IN CANADA 168–69 (McMaster University Centre for Health Economic and Policy Analysis Working Paper #92–17, 1992). For an analysis of the fee negotiation in each province, territory and generally, see *id.* generally.

acquires a direct interest in those costs, an interest that brings it into conflict with the traditional entrepreneurial discretion of the physician to set the price, as well as to determine the volume and mix of the services that he or she provides.

Almost all of the conflict between the medical profession and the state that followed in the wake of the adoption of Medicare concerned the price of medical services. Under Medicare, as the federal government progressively withdrew from cost-sharing agreements, provincial governments became the primary bearers of the costs of medical and hospital services. In seeking to control these costs, provincial governments turned first to prices: fees for medical services, and charges for hospital patient days. Rather than paying the medical fees that were "usual and customary" in particular localities as did US third-party payers, provincial governments at first agreed to pay physicians on the basis of the fee schedules set by the provincial medical associations,[106] prorated by a given percentage. Soon, however, the schedule of payments was set through negotiations between the government and the medical association in each province. In most cases they negotiated overall increases in the payment schedule, leaving the allocation of these increases across individual items in the fee schedule to be carried out internally by the medical associations themselves.[107] In making these internal allocations, medical associations have typically been more concerned with smoothing income differentials across specialty groups than with measuring the relative costs or benefits of given procedures.[108] In reaching their accommodations with the state, that is, medical associations have had to manage delicate internal accommodations, a point to which I shall shortly return.

Over time, the agenda of these negotiations has broadened to include the establishment of more-or-less firmly fixed caps on total expenditures on physicians' services under the government plans.[109] The rationale for the establishment of these limits was to take account of utilization increases.[110] In fact, however, a comprehensive survey of the negotiation process in all ten provinces concluded that the purpose of government was to establish global limits: arguments about

---

106. *Canadian Health, supra* note 15, at 36.
107. *See* LOMAS, CHARLES, & GREB, *supra* note 105, at 184–85.
108. *Id.*
109. *See id.* at 178.
110. *Id.*

increased "utilization" simply provided a politically feasible way of doing so.[111]

As a result of these negotiations, then, the entrepreneurial discretion of individual physicians has been limited. Prices are established centrally, and the economic pay-off from varying volume and mix may bump up against either individual or global caps. One effect of Medicare, then, has been to increase substantially the role of organized medicine. This brings us to the second, and indeed more basic trade-off with which physicians are faced under Canadian Medicare. In order to retain some power over the price of their services, individual physicians have had to cede their ability to set prices to the central association. This process was not without conflict; and each provincial association has had to manage a complex and delicate internal accommodation.

For a time, there was an option for physicians to escape these constraints to some extent by "extra-billing" their patients, that is, by billing patients over and above what the government plan would pay. Only about 10% of physicians exercised this option, and the amount of extra-billing was estimated at only about 1.3% of total physician billings under Medicare.[112] In no province did this amount exceed 3%.[113] The economic and political significance of extra-billing was increased, however, by the fact that it was "clustered" in certain specialties and localities.[114] Even more important in political terms, extra-billing flew in the face of one of the fundamental principles underlying Canadian Medicare—the removal of financial barriers to access medical and hospital care.

In the early 1980s, a federal Liberal government declining in popularity and facing non-Liberal governments in each of the provinces, sezied upon the issue of extra-billing as a way of symbolizing its commitment to preserving the universality of the nation's most popular social program. It portrayed non-Liberal governments in the provinces as allowing the principle of universality to be eroded by condoning extra-billing, and passed legislation, the Canada Health Act of 1984,[115] penalizing those provinces by providing for federal transfer payments to be reduced by an amount equal to the estimated

111. *Id.*
112. TUOHY, *supra* note 32, at 116–17.
113. *Id.*
114. *Id.*
115. R.S.C., ch. C–6 (1984) (Can.).

amount of extra-billing in any given province: a dollar-for-dollar penalty.[116]

In one sense, at least, the federal strategy back-fired. The federal Conservatives, whom the Liberals had hoped to tar with the same brush as their siblings in power in several provinces, supported the Canada Health Act in parliament.[117] With its passage in 1984, the politics shifted to the provinces and were shaped by the relationship between the medical profession and the government in each province. In all cases but one, the process of negotiating the ban on extra-billing was relatively non-conflictual, and the medical profession achieved substantial gains in the form of fee schedule increases and binding arbitration mechanisms for future fee schedule disputes.

The exception was Ontario, where the banning of extra-billing occasioned unprecedented conflict between the Ontario Medical Association (OMA) and the government, culminating in a four-week doctors' strike.[118] This conflict was largely the result of the disruption of the accommodation between the OMA and the provincial government resulting from the accession of the Liberals to power after 43 years of Conservative rule. The episode poisoned the relationship between the OMA and the government for a time, but in 1991 a wide-ranging agreement between the OMA and the social democratic NDP government, which had by then replaced the Liberals, inaugurated a new era of profession–state accommodation.[119]

Throughout this process, the *clinical* discretion of individual physicians—the ability of the individual physician to exercise his or her clinical judgment in individual cases according to professionally-determined standards—has remained virtually untouched. Financial constraints have been global and across-the-board; within those constraints, physicians experience relatively little second-guessing by third parties. Utilization review committees established in several provinces to monitor physicians' practice patterns have focused on only the most aberrant cases, identified by volume of billings.

It can legitimately be argued that the clinical autonomy of physicians is constrained to the extent that the diagnostic and therapeutic options

---

116. R.S.C., ch. C–6, 66, 18, 20.

117. *See* TUOHY, *supra* note 32, at 129, Peter Ward, *Medical Care Laws are Likely to Change*, BOSTON GLOBE, Dec. 18, 1983, *available in* LEXIS, Papers Database.

118. Iglehart, *supra* note 55, at 565; TUOHY, *supra* note 29, at 122–23.

119. TUOHY, *supra* note 32, at 131.

open to them are limited by available facilities and equipment. It must be remembered, however, that the facilities subject to the greatest constraint in Canada are those involving certain high-technology procedures;[120] and there is considerable debate among clinical epidemio-logists as to the range of conditions for which such procedures are in fact indicated. As for other resources such as hospital beds and nursing staff, Canada has fewer hospital beds per capita, but more employees per bed than the OECD average. (In the US, the bed population ratio is even lower, while the employee bed ratio is higher.) In the three-nation survey of physicians cited above, Canadians were not significantly more likely than Americans to complain of a shortage of competent nursing staff.[121]

The point remains that within gross over-all constraints, the clinical autonomy of the individual physician, and of the profession as a whole, has been maintained. As the agenda of health policy evolves in Canada, the various accommodations between the medical profession and provincial government that underlie the preservation of clinical autonomy will be tested. So far, these accommodations have proved remarkably resilient. This can be seen by considering the course of development of several major items on the health care agenda of the 1990s: user fees, de-insurance, clinical guidelines and organizational change.

V. THE EVOLVING AGENDA

A. User fees

The issue of "user fees" for insured services was put to rest for a time with the passage of the Canada Health Act and the compliance of all provinces with that federal legislation. The issue of user fees has re-emerged, however.[122] The Canada Health Act, which bans such charges, has become increasingly toothless. In its efforts to reduce spending, the federal government is progressively withdrawing from

---

120. See *supra* notes 63–64 and accompanying text.
121. See Blendon et al., *supra* note 86, at 1015.
122. The federal government in 1994 reduced its transfer to the British Columbia government as a penalty for allowing extra-billing by a local group of physicians. It has also established a deadline for provinces to cease allowing private clinics to charge "facility fees" in addition to the amount covered by governmental insurance.

sharing the cost of provincial health insurance plans. With the end of federal contributions in some provinces toward the end of this decade,[123] the federal government's ability to enforce the provisions of the Canada Health Act will come to an end as well, unless funding is restored or some other enforcement mechanism is introduced.

Without the discipline of the federal legislation, it is possible that some provincial governments will reintroduce user fees. Any government that sought to reintroduce extra-billing would do so at a great political risk, however, for little political or fiscal gain.

B. De-insuring

So far, provincial governments appear to be more attracted to the option of de-insuring some services than to the imposition of user fees as a cost control measure. This response is, indeed, more consistent with Canada's "segmented" rather than "tiered" approach to the role of the public and private sectors. The Canada Health Act made even more explicit the premises of its predecessor legislation: on its face, it requires provincial health insurance plans to cover fully all "medically required" physician services and a broadly defined set of "necessary" types of hospital services in order to qualify for federal financial contributions. Provincial governments, in complying with the federal legislation, have either *de facto* or *de jure* accepted "medical necessity" as the standard for coverage under their respective plans.[124] The determination of which physicians services are "medically required" and which hospital services are "necessary," however, has not been defined in legislation.

In the hospital sector, the operational definition of "necessity" has been negotiated by government and health care providers. Through a process of prospective global hospital budgeting, provincial governments have, since the 1970s, been negotiating with individual hospitals about how many beds, imaging machines, etc. are "necessary." Differences of opinion in this regard resulted for a time in hospitals breaching their budgets to adopt non-approved programs.[125] The resulting deficits were tolerated and forgiven for a time by governments,

---

123. Kenneth Norrie, *Social Policy and Equalization, in* THE FUTURE OF FISCAL FEDERALISM 163 (Keith G. Banting et al. eds., 1994).

124. R.S.C., Ch. C–6, 62.

125. Tuohy *supra* note 32, at 120.

but the limits of that tolerance were reached in the late 1980s.[126]

The question of what physicians' services are "medically required" has, until recently, not been a matter of negotiation between providers and governments. As noted earlier, fee schedule negotiations between medical associations and provincial governments have generally focused on the overall percentage increase in fees, not the relative value of items nor the scope of the services covered, which has changed little since a broad base of coverage was established in each province upon the establishment of Medicare.[127]

There have been, however, recent attempts to de-limit the scope of coverage under Medicare. Under the letter and the spirit of both federal provincial legislation, services can be de-insured only if they are deemed not to be medically necessary. Negotiations to identify potential candidates for de-insuring have been undertaken between the medical profession and government in a number of provinces. To date, there has been very little effect on the comprehensiveness of coverage, but the discussions around these issues are worth briefly considering here for what they can tell us about the shape of future developments.

Most of the services and procedures considered for "de-insuring" are related to cosmetic surgery, mental health and reproduction. The selection of these procedures for consideration has resulted in part from the ideological agendas of governments, and in part from a consideration of income differentials within the medical profession. In Alberta in 1985, as part of the negotiations between the Alberta Medical Association and the provincial government pertaining to the banning of extra-billing, it was decided that several services be "de-insured," including family planning counseling, tubal ligations, vasectomies and mammoplasty. This selection was driven largely by the conservation social policy ideology of the governing Conservative Party of the day. From the perspective of the medical profession, however, it focused with few exceptions on fairly lucrative procedures performed by relatively high-earning specialists. Furthermore, the de-insurance of such services freed physicians to bill privately at rates of their own choosing. As an internal accommodation within the profession, it allowed for some smoothing of differentials in Medicare earnings while allowing a "safety valve" for the specialties affected. This agreement

---

126. *See id.*
127. Notes 105–11. and accompanying text.

did not survive the public protest that ensued, however, and funding for most of these services was restored.

In Ontario, a number of services have also been proposed for de-insuring. In this case, the list includes some cosmetic procedures, and *in vitro* fertilization (IVF) in some circumstances (Ontario is the only province in which IVF is a publicly insured service.) Again, these are lucrative services and procedures are performed by relatively high-earning specialists. Their de-insurance would allow them to be offered in private markets. The OMA, however, was initially less disposed to enter into this type of accommodation than its Alberta counterpart had been. The response in Ontario was essentially a procedural one; the provincial government and the OMA came to an agreement on the structures through which decisions would be made about the efficacy of various procedures through health services research and determined that decisions about insurance coverage would be made on that basis.

As part of the wide-ranging 1991 agreement between the Ontario government and the OMA noted above, a Joint Management Committee (JMC) was formed between the Ontario government and the OMA, and under its aegis an Institute for Clinical Evaluation Sciences was established, based at a Toronto teaching hospital. The process of developing a list of procedures to be de-insured went on for over a year until it became entailed in the government's broad expenditure control agenda in the spring of 1993. The unfolding of that episode casts further light on the evolving nature of the profession–state accommodation, and merits some elaboration here.

As part of a broad expenditure control package in June 1993, the NDP government of Ontario introduced legislation giving it broad powers to de-insure services, and to limit payments under the government health insurance plan on the basis of the utilization profile of the patient, the practitioner or the facility involved.[128] The OMA reacted strongly and vociferously against these provisions, accusing the government of preempting the JMC process, and mounting an extensive public relations campaign. The government, for its part, stated that the

---

128. That is, payment for a given service could be reduced or denied if the number of services provided to a given patient, or by a given physician, or within a given facility, exceeded a prescribed maximum during a particular time period. The legislation also granted the government broad regulatory powers to control expenditures, limit the number of practitioners, and affect the geographic distribution of practitioners and facilities.

legislation provision constituted a "fail safe" to take effect only if a negotiated agreement with the OMA could not be reached. In the result, the OMA and the government reached an agreement on a range of cost-control measures, including a three-year freeze on medical fees and a "hard cap" on total physicians' billings. The JMC process for determining which services were to be de-insured was reinstated, tied to tighter deadlines, given a set dollar volume (420 million) by which billings were to be reduced through de-insurance, and augmented by an advisory panel including "members of the public" as well as medical and governmental representatives and tied to tighter deadlines.

There are at least three points worth noting about these developments in Ontario for what they suggest about the evolution of the profession–state accommodation. First, they suggest that governments may be more willing to flex their legislative muscle to establish a "shadow" within which their negotiations with the profession can proceed. Second, they suggest the resiliency of the profession–state accommodation even under conditions of growing fiscal constraint. And third, they suggest that the government's approach to accommodation may be shifting the balance of power within the medical profession over time. In the past, academically-based physicians were at the core of profession–state accommodation; and the OMA played a varying role depending upon the vagaries of its internal politics.[129] The NDP government of Ontario has preferred, however, to deal primarily with the OMA as the legitimate "bargaining agent" for the profession.[130] For its part, the OMA has worked its way through a wrenching internal process which has left it more open to accommodation with the state. In 1991 for the first time a body central to the profession–state relationship, the JMC, had no academically-based medical members.

This new accommodation between the OMA and the provincial government in Ontario has not been without controversy within the profession. There is still a minority body of opinion which holds that the OMA has been too concerned with the preservation and enhancement of the power of organized medicine at the expense of the autonomy of the individual physician. The 1991 agreement, which not only established the JMC but also provided for an automatic check-off

---

129. *See* TUOHY, *supra* note 32, at 126.
130. *Id.* at 151.

of membership dues to the OMA from each individual physician's payments under Medicare, was strongly contested by this minority. The agreement was finally ratified at a highly publicized mass meeting of the OMA membership in a Toronto hockey arena.

C. Clinical guidelines

The tension between the collective autonomy of the profession and the individual autonomy of the practitioner is raised even more squarely by the development of clinical guidelines. The issue of using clinical guidelines developed by professional bodies to shape the behavior of individual practitioners has been on the agenda of Canadian health policy, to very little effect, for well over a decade. In the early 1990s, however, this mechanism has achieved greater prominence. A number of provinces have developed joint profession–government bodies to develop clinical guidelines, although the fiscal sanctions associated with the guidelines vary considerably. Ontario's Institute for Clinical Evaluation Sciences, under the aegis of the Joint Management Committee, is one such mechanism, and the status of the guidelines it is to develop is as yet unclear. An earlier initiative in Ontario in which guidelines on the use of Caesarean sections were widely distributed to obstetricians were unsuccessful in modifying behavior.[131] In Saskatchewan, however, guidelines on thyroid tests issued by the Health Services Utilization and Research Commission resulted in a marked drop (65–79%) in the ordering of certain tests in circumstances in which the guidelines suggested they were not indicated.[132] In British Columbia, an undertaking to develop clinical guidelines backed by legislation and fiscal sanctions formed the centerpiece of an agreement negotiated between the British Columbia Medical Association and the British Columbia government in August 1993. As governments and professional bodies thus move slowly in the direction of "managed care," relations between the profession and the state, and between individual practitioners and professional bodies, will be under increasing pressure.

---

131. Donathan Lomas et al. "Do practice guidelines guide practice? The effect of a consensus statement on the practice of physicians," *New England Journal of Medicine* 1989, 321: 1306–1311.

132. Rod Mickleburgh, *£1-Million to be Saved by Cuts in Thyroid Tests*, THE GLOBE AND MAIL (Toronto), Aug. 31, 1993, at A1–2.

D. Organizational change

These relationships will also be strained as the health care system increasingly confronts issues of organizational change. These issues have been on the agenda of Canadian health policy since the 1970s, but outside Quebec there has been very little action in this regard. Now these issues are rising on the agenda in a number of provinces, although the response has varied depending on a mix of factors including the partisan complexion of the government and the degree of populism or statism in the political culture. Under NDP governments, for example, both British Columbia and Saskatchewan have recently announced plans to decentralize policy-making structures by establishing systems of local (and, in British Columbia, regional) health authorities with greater budgetary and managerial powers than have been granted to similar bodies in the past. In less populist Ontario, the NDP government has made a number of decisions centrally, such as the decision to regularize the practice of midwifery, that have important implications for the reorganization of health care delivery, and has not expanded the powers of district health councils beyond their traditional advisory functions. Quebec and New Brunswick, under Liberal governments, have established or reorganized regional boards with somewhat more limited scope and more constrained powers than those proposed in British Columbia and Saskarchewan. Organizational reforms in Nova Scotia, begun under a Conservative government and continued under a Liberal government, established a system of regional planning agencies with advisory powers only. In Manitoba, under a Conservative government, proposals for a restructuring of the delivery system have emanated from the provincial government without the creation of local or regional councils.[133]

There is, then, at least in theory, considerable scope for variation across provincial plans: the definition of "medical necessity" and the structure of the health care delivery system have been determined in the context of an accommodation between the medical profession and the state in each province. And it is true that costs, supply and utilization vary considerably across provinces.[134] What is remarkable is

---

133. JEREMIAH HURLEY, JONATHAN LOMAS & VANDNA BHATIA, IS THE WOLF. FINALLY AT THE DOOR? PROVINCIAL REFORM TO MANAGE HEALTH-CARE RESOURCES (McMaster University Centre for Health Economics and Policy Analysis Working Pages 93–12, 1993).

134. TUOHY, *supra* note 32, at 137.

that the variation is not greater than it is, given the loose constraints of the federal legislation. This variation is limited because the interests of the medical profession are fundamentally similar across provinces; and, if clinical discretion is to be maintained while entrepreneurial discretion is limited, these interests militate in favor of a comprehensive and generously funded scheme. For the same reason, the progressive withdrawal of the federal government, which is likely to continue over the rest of this decade, will not lead to substantially greater variation across provinces.

In summary, the Canadian health insurance system has removed financial barriers to the access of a comprehensive range of services, while leaving the definition of that range essentially to the medical profession. These defining principles of the system imply a distribution of power and its flip side, autonomy. It places physicians in a position of power/autonomy to determine the range of services provided while limiting their economic power and autonomy.

The "social democratic" character of Canadian Medicare is not simply a function of its founding principles. Rather, it is a function of the expression of those principles in power structures. Let me further develop this point by drawing two contrasts: one, international, between the Canadian and British health systems, and the other, intra-national, between the Canadian health care system and the Canadian public pension system.

VI. HEALTH CARE IN BRITAIN AND CANADA

First, let us contrast the Canadian and British health care systems. In Britain, governmental health costs amount to about 5.5% of the GDP, and about over 80% of total health care costs.[135] Most accounts of the British system, before the 1990 reforms, suggest that physicians retained considerable clinical discretion within broad budgetary constraints, although the balance between individual and collective autonomy might have been tilting more toward the collective end of the scale over time. A study of medical decision making under conditions of "rationing" in Britain made this point.[136] They observed that

---

135. TUOHY, *supra* note 29, at 285, & n. 7.
136. William B. Schwartz & Henry J. Anton, *Rationing Hospital Care: Lessons from Britain*, 310 NEW ENG. J. MED. 52 (1984).

although governmental budgetary decisions regarding equipment and staffing established overall budgetary constraints, there was virtually no regulatory control over the diagnostic and therapeutic decisions of individual physicians.[137] In cases in which those decisions resulted in "excessive" expenditures, "actions were taken by senior [medical] staff which led to voluntary curbs by the physicians responsible."[138] Arnold Heidenheimer, in contrasting the British and German systems, argued that British physicians have even more clinical autonomy than do German physicians, precisely because the British National Health Service, with its greater control of broad budgetary parameters, can tolerate greater freedom within individual practices."[139]

The 1990 reforms do not substantially change this characterization. As in the Canadian case, however, public policy changes may bring about shifts in the balance of power *within* the medical profession. In Britain, the establishment of fund-holding general practices (GP) may change that balance by subjecting consultants to closer questioning by GPs (Interestingly, the funding-holding reforms have reintroduced a dimension of entrepreneurialism to general practice, a feature which explains much of its appeal to the "first wave" of GP fund-holders.) But a potential shift in the balance of power between GPs and consultants does not threaten the clinical discretion of physicians *per se*. Furthermore, there is some evidence that referral patterns have not changed as a result of these reforms.[140] Nor have District Health Authorities so far proved to be a threat to professional autonomy; rather, they have shown themselves, if anything, to be more cautious about disputing the professional judgments of providers in the hospital sector than are GPs.[141]

The budgetary constraints within which physicians must operate in Britain, however, are considerably more stringent than those which exist in Canada, as is apparent in the lower overall levels of governmental spending on health care in Britain.[142] In the face of these

---

137. *Id.* at 54 (mentioning the only possible control as the intervention of other staff physicians).

138. *Id.*

139. ARNOLD J. HEIDENHEIMER ET AL. COMPARATIVE PUBLIC POLICY: THE POLITICS OF SOCIAL CHOICE IN EUROPE AND AMERICA 61 (2d ed. 1983).

140. Angela Coulter & Jean Bradlow, *Effects of NHS Reforms on General Practitioner's Referral Patterns*, 306 BRIT. MED. J. 433–37 (1993).

141. Howard Glennerster & Manos Matsagaris, *The U.K. Health Reforms: The Fundholding Experiment*, 23 HEALTH POLICY 179, 189 (1993).

142. *See supra* notes 33, 135 and accompanying text.

constraints, and in contrast to the Canadian case, a private market in medical and hospital services has been maintained as a kind of "safety valve."

In order to understand the differences between the Canadian and British systems, we need to go back to the genesis of the programs, to the prevailing policy ideas and power structures of the time. The NHS was born in the era of Beveridge reforms, in a context in which the medical profession was organizationally divided between general practitioners and specialists who held different views about the appropriate direction of public policy. In such a context, the trade-off between economic and clinical discretion was made on terms more unfavorable to the profession than was later to be the case in Canada.

National health insurance was first considered in Canada at the time the NHS was being born in Britain. In 1945–46, the federal government presented a set of proposals for a cost-shared national health insurance problem to the provinces, proposals that had been shaped in part by the observation of contemporary developments in Britain.[143] At the time, there existed a remarkable consensus among medical, hospital and insurance interests favorable to the establishment of a comprehensive health insurance plan in the public sector.[144] Viewing such a plan as "necessary ... and probably inevitable,"[145] these groups supported it in principle and sought to maximize their influence over its development and implementation. The sense of inevitability arose in no small part from their observation of events in Britain. Had national health insurance been adopted at that time, it would undoubtedly have borne a closer resemblance to the NHS than did the scheme that ultimately resulted.[146] As it was, however, the federal proposals went down to defeat, tied as they were to a broader package of proposals for federal–provincial fiscal arrangements that were unacceptable to the provinces.[147]

The resulting delay gave time for private plans to develop and expand, and for various provincial governments to experiment with different models of governmental health insurance plans. By the late

---

143. *Canadian Health, supra* note 15, at 32–33.

144. *Id.* at 33.

145. INSURING NAT'L HEALTH CARE, *supra* note 15, at 49.

146. *See,* INSURING NAT'L HEALTH CARE *supra* note 15, at 33 (discussing the historical background and development of the Canadian Medicare system); TUOHY, *supra* note 32, at 144–45.

147. *Canadian Health, supra* note 15, at 33.

1950s and 1960s, when a federal–provincial climate more favorable to the launching of a national plan had developed, a substantial proportion of the population had become accustomed to relatively generous and comprehensive coverage under private insurance plans.[148] Furthermore, opinion within the medical profession had come to favor governmental subsidization and supplementation of private plans.[149] Although its view ultimately did not prevail, the medical profession presented a relatively united front, and could establish a policy price for its participation in the program. The system was hence launched on an economic and political base favorable to more generous financing and a greater degree of medical influence than had been the case in Britain.

VII. HEALTH CARE v. PUBLIC PENSIONS IN CANADA

If Canadian Medicare has a social democratic character, the Canadian public pension system clearly does not. As the system developed over time, means-tested pensions introduced at the federal level in the 1920s were replaced by a three-tiered system of universal, contributory and income-tested supplemental benefits.[150] The universal tier, the Old Age Security (OAS) pension, was introduced in 1951.[151] It provides a flat-rate benefit and is financed from general revenues.[152] The OAS plan is not designed, however, to provide sufficient income for a pensioner. The pension scheme also includes a contributory tier, the Canada Pension Plan (CPP), introduced in 1965.[153] CPP benefits are related to contributions and both are related to earnings, up to a maximum. Finally, for those with income below a certain level, there

---

148. *Id.* at 33–34.
149. *Id.* at 34.
150. *See* Paul D. Pierson & R. Kent Weaver. *Imposing Losses in Pension Policy, in* DO INSTITUTIONS MATTER? GOVERNMENT CAPABILITIES IN THE UNITED STATES AND ABROAD 110, 124–25 (R. Kent Weaver & Bert A. Rockman eds., 1993). JOHN MYLES, OLD AGE IN THE WELFARE STATE, 38, 46–47 (rev. ed. 1989); KEITH BANTING, THE WELFARE STATE AND CANADIAN FEDERALISM 7–11 (1982).
151. *See* MYLES, *supra* note 150, at 77–78.
152. *See* BANTING, *supra* note 150, at 7.
153. *Id.* at 9.

is a Guaranteed Income Supplement (GIS), introduced in 1966, as well as other supplementary provincial plans.[154]

With its limited universal benefit, supplemented either by the means-tested GIS or the contributory CPP or both, this is a "quasi-Beveridge" system. As of the early 1980s, it performed relatively well, in international perspective, in raising the low-income elderly out of poverty.[155] But it performed relatively poorly in replacing the income of the average worker upon retirement,[156] and even more poorly in the case of upper-income earners. Hence, it encouraged both middle-and upper-income individuals to turn to private alternatives. It must be noted that as the contributory CPP matures, replacement rates are rising.[157]

As in other industrialized states, the Canadian public pension system underwent some reform in the 1980s. After an abortive attempt in 1985 to reduce OAS benefits by partially removing inflation protection, the federal Conservative government in 1989 introduced a "claw back" of the OAS pension from higher-income earners.[158] Accordingly, the OAS pension is now progressively taxed back at higher levels of income, and is taxed back completely for the upper 5% of income earners.[159] This "universal" tier was thus effectively converted to an income-tested plan. These changes, together with an enhancement of the GIS in the early 1980s, increased the focus of the Canadian public pension scheme upon low-income individuals.[160] The contributory CPP underwent less structural change, although modest reforms in 1986 resulted in greater flexibility in the retirement age, improvement in the rights of surviving spouses, enhancement of disability benefits and an increase in the contribution rate.

The Canadian public pension system was put into place in the 1950s and 1960s, roughly the same period in which the medical and hospital

---

154. *Id.* at 13; Pierson & Weaver, *supra* note 150, at 124–25.

155. *See* Timothy Smeeding et al., *Patterns of Income and Poverty: The Economic Status of Children and the Elderly in Eight Countries, in* THE VULNERABLE 89, 111 (John L. Palmer et al. eds., 1988).

156. *See* Jonathan Aldrich, *The Earnings Replacement Rate of Old-Age Benefits in 12 Countries,* 45 SOC. SECURITY BULL., 3, 8 (1982); MYLES, *See* note 150, at 56.

157. *See* Keith G. Banting, *Economic Integration and Social Policy: Canada and the United States, in* SOCIAL POLICY IN THE GLOBAL ECONOMY 29–30 (Terrance M. Humsley ed., 1992).

158. *See id.* at 30.

159. *See id.* at 29.

160. *See id.* at 30.

insurance system was taking shape. Why did the Canadian political system, at the same period in its history, yield a social-democratic health insurance system, and a Beveridge-style pension system? And why, in the 1980s, did fiscal pressures lead to an erosion of universality in the pension system and not in the health care system? The answer lies in the structure of interests in these two arenas. There is, in the pension arena, no group comparable to the medical profession. The pension system involves a transfer of incomes, not services. There is no other group of service providers whose income and careers are as tied up with the generosity of the system. In both arenas, the consumer interest is diffuse.[161] And although the "consumers" of pensions lobbied effectively against an across-the-board reduction of the basic pension in 1985, claw-backs from upper-income pension recipients occasioned much less consumer protest.[162]

In the absence of a strong "provider" interest, public pension policy is shaped almost entirely by the interests of governments. Banting has pointed out the extent to which income maintenance policies in Canada are shaped by the interests of "governments as governments," essentially, jurisdictional and fiscal concerns.[163] This means, in the first place that, since change in a number of key income maintenance programs entails a complex set of implications for the fiscal responsibilities of various levels of government, governmental interests have accordingly acted as a brake on policy development. Hence, there were few changes to the Canada Pension Plan, which involves a complex set of federal–provincial arrangements, in the 1980s. Second, governments frustrated by federal–provincial entanglements tend to turn to those instruments over which they have exclusive control. This explains the focus on Old Age Security pensions by the federal Conservatives in the

---

161. Organized labor, which has been an effective proponent of generous social programs in other nations, is too organizationally decentralized and ideologically divided to play a similar role in Canada See David Cameron, Social Democracy, Corporation *Labour Quiescence and the Representation of Economic Interest in Advanced Capitalist Society, in* ORDER AND CONFLICT IN CONTEMPORARY CAPITALISM (John Goldthorpe ed., 1984); Rodney Haddow, *The Canadian Labour Congress and the Welfare State Debates,* paper presented at the *63rd Annual Meeting of the Canadian Political Science Association,* Queen's University, Kingston, Ontario, June 4, 1991.

162. Banting, *supra* note 157, at 29–30.

163. *See* KEITH BANTING, THE WELFARE STATE AND CANADIAN FEDERALISM 43, 51 (2d ed. 1987).

same period.[164] In addition, the interest of "governments as governments" comes into play: the way in which governments use the instruments at their command will be determined not so much by group pressure as by partisanship and ideology. This will cause the erosion of the universality of the OAS pension as part of the Conservative agenda of deficit reduction.

VIII. CONCLUSION

Medicare is Canada's social policy success story. Its social democratic character has been attributed by a number of observers to the presence of a social democratic party within the Canadian political system. The significance of the NDP in this respect should not be slighted. After all, it was the NDP government of Saskatchewan that first introduced governmental hospital insurance in 1944 and government medical insurance in 1962, and it was arguably the electoral threat from the NDP that led the minority federal Liberal government to press ahead with the introduction of national medical care insurance in 1966. In the same era, however, the Canadian system generated a public pension system which, with its limited universal and contributory benefit tiers, and its means-tested supplemental tier, is a hybrid of Beveridge and residualist welfare state models. In the 1980s, the universality of the health care system was preserved, and indeed enhanced, while the limited universality of the pension system was eroded. The evolution of the health insurance system, then, cannot be understood with reference to social democratic principles alone. It has depended as well on the presence of a medical profession willing to enter into an accommodation with the state, an accommodation which trades off economic power to preserve the clinical autonomy of the profession as a whole, and to a large degree of individual physicians too.

Any set of principles of distributive justice implies a distribution of power, and it is through that structure of power that the principles will be implemented. The Canadian system places physicians, as the interpreters of the "necessity" of care, in a central role. Although the

---

164. Tuohy, *supra* note 29, at 294–95; Paul D. Pierson & R. Kent Weaver, *Imposing Losses in Pension Policy, in* DO INSTITUTIONS MATTER? GOVERNMENT CAPABILITIES IN THE U.S. AND ABROAD 148 (R. Kent Weaver and Bert A. Rockman eds., 1993).

Canadian medical profession has resisted change at a number of key junctures, it has accommodated those changes.

The Canadian system is not without its problems. It remains the second most expensive system in the industrialized world.[165] Geographic maldistribution of facilities and services remains a problem. The treatment of the elderly, particularly as the population ages, presents an enormous set of challenges.[166] Both the medical profession and the state, as the central shapers of the system, are part of these problems. But they are also part of the solutions. Such strengths as the system has, and they are considerable, can be attributed to both parties, and both will continue to shape the system in the future.

---

165. *See supra* notes 43–44 and accompanying text.

166. Morris L. Barer *et al. Aging and Health Care Utilization: New Evidence on Old Fallacies,* SOCIAL SCIENCE AND MEDICINE, 24, 10: 851–862 (1987).

A right to health care? A comparative perspective

Dieter Giesen

I. INTRODUCTION

The existence of a right to health care has been one of the most problematic and debated issues in medical ethics and medical law. In a world of scarce resources, budgetary constraints and ever-increasing demand, the value of asserting a right to health care has become apparent to those who seek to shield existing services from cutbacks and to extend access to medical care to disadvantaged groups in society. In the course of this article, some of the practical legal implications of recognizing a right to health care will be examined from a comparative perspective. At the outset it is important to distinguish between (1) claims made by individuals upon society in general to ensure access to health care, and (2) claims made by those in need of treatment upon individual doctors to ensure that vital medical assistance is afforded, especially in times of emergency. In establishing the

Editors' Note: In conformity with the 'Blue Book' citation system adopted in the USA, a number of the citations to European materials have been changed. The editors wish to thank the author for his indulgence in allowing this departure from the conventions he normally adopts.

The author gratefully acknowledges the valuable cooperation received, throughout the preparation of this article, from John Harrington, LL.M, B.C.L., Research Assistant at the Working Centre, 1992–93.

Justice and Health Care: Comparative Perspectives. Edited by A. Grubb and M.J. Mehlman. © 1995 John Wiley & Sons Ltd.

general structures for the provision of health care and in determining the extent of a doctor's liability for refusal to treat a patient in need, the law plays a pivotal role in enforcing the ethical norms of any given society. A comparison will show that, at first blush, the relevant legal rules vary considerably, reflecting differing political and philosophical priorities. In many common law countries, especially the US, an austere individualism is favored at the expense of the elementary obligations of common humanity and solidarity which are acknowledged by almost all the civil law jurisdictions. Nonetheless, the extreme libertarianism of the Anglo-Saxon world has been considerably tempered and modified such that at the societal and individual levels, access to medical services has been expanded, albeit in an indirect fashion. In spite of these advances, a comparative analysis will also highlight outstanding deficiencies in the legal rules governing access to health care in a number of jurisdictions, deficiencies which are at odds with the expressed value-commitments of these societies.

Once a discussion of the question of access to health care as a matter of rights and obligations has begun, consistency demands that the issues arising within the therapeutic context also be considered from a normative perspective. The individual who submits himself to medical procedures does not for that reason forfeit any of the fundamental rights which the law of all civilized nations recognizes him as holding. This view of the patient, *qua* an autonomous subject of the law, as central to the health care system has important implications for contemporary medical practice and for judicial attitudes thereto.

II. THE HEALTH CARE SYSTEM: RIGHTS AND OBLIGATIONS

Article 25 of the Universal Declaration of Human Rights[1] states that:

> Everyone has the right to a standard of living adequate for the health and well-being of himself and his family, including food, clothing, housing and medical care and necessary social services, and the right to security in the event of unemployment, *sickness*, disability, widowhood, old age or other lack of livelihood in circumstances beyond his control.[2]

---

1. (1948), *reprinted in* INTERNATIONAL LAW: THE ESSENTIAL TREATIES AND OTHER RELEVANT DOCUMENTS 437 (I. Von Munch & A. Buske eds., 1985).

2. *Id.* (emphasis added). The Universal Declaration of Human Rights was adopted by the General Assembly of the United Nations on December 10,

Although this provision has been strongly influential in the post-war world, its identification of an affirmative right to health care can at best be seen only as aspirational. The assertion of a right to medical services founders upon difficulties of political philosophy, and such a right is not recognized by the legal system of any democratic society. Unlike the classic rights to "negative" liberty, as first embodied in the US Constitution and the French Declaration of the Rights of Man, which restrain the state from the arbitrary and oppressive use of its powers, a right to health care would allow the individual plaintiff, by means of litigation, to oblige the state to allocate resources to a specific extent and for a specific purpose. Yet the availability of such a remedy would clearly overturn the collective decision-making process as performed by the legislative arm of government. It is for this reason that courts in many jurisdictions have been firm in rejecting claims for an affirmative right to health care services, as beyond the scope of the adjudicative function.[3] As the English Court of Appeal stated, "it is not for this court, or any court, to substitute its own judgment for the judgment of those who are responsible for the allocation of resources.... The courts of this country cannot arrange the [waiting] lists in the hospital...."[4]

It was the open-ended and inchoate nature of the putative right to health care that led the US President's Commission to agree that, as long as the ethical and jurisprudential debate on access to health care was focused upon attempts to assert and refute a right to medical services, it could provide no useful guidance to those involved in formulating law and policy in the health care sector.[5] This admission does not, however, exhaust ethical and legal consideration of access to health care, for the concept of a moral right clearly must be distin-

---

1948. *See* LOUIS B. SOHN & THOMAS BUERGENTHAL, BASIC DOCUMENTS ON INTERNATIONAL PROTECTION OF HUMAN RIGHTS 33 (1973).

3. *E.g.*, R. v. Central Birmingham Health Authority, *ex parte* Collier, (Eng. C.A. Jan. 6, 1988) (LEXIS, Enggen library, Cases file); R. v. Central Birmingham Health Authority, *ex parte* Walker, 04 3 B.L.M.R. 32 (Eng. C.A. Nov. 25, 1987), *available in* LEXIS, Enggen library, Cases file; Harris v. McRae, 448 U.S. 297 (1980); Maher v. Roe, 432 U.S. 464, 469 (1977) ("The Constitution imposes no obligation on the States to pay the pregnancy-related medical expenses of indigent women, or indeed to pay the medical expenses of indigents." (cite omitted)). *See also* IAN KENNEDY & ANDREW GRUBB, MEDICAL LAW: TEXT WITH MATERIALS 415–29 (2nd ed. 1994) (providing excerpts from several British cases).

4. R.v. *Central Birmingham Health Authority, ex parte Collier*, at *3.

5. 1 US PRESIDENT'S COMM'N FOR THE STUDY OF ETHICAL PROBLEMS IN MEDICINE AND BIOMEDICAL AND BEHAVIORAL RESEARCH, SECURING ACCESS
(*cont.*)

guished from that of a moral obligation. While all moral *rights* necessarily entail moral obligations (i.e., to ensure that the appropriate entitlements are met), the existence of moral *obligations* does *not* in every instance imply the existence of correlative moral rights. Thus, as the President's Commission said, most appositely, "a person may have a moral obligation to help those in need, even though the needy cannot, strictly speaking, demand that person's aid as something they are due."[6]

The autonomy of the individual citizen has been recognized as the core value of the legal and constitutional order, both in civil law and common law countries.[7] In addition, it must be acknowledged that individuals require a minimum level of health and physical well-being in order to develop autonomously their life-styles and to fulfill their goals in accordance with their value commitments. As such, health may be viewed as a basic good, an essential prerequisite to the exercise of personal autonomy and an irreducible condition of human flourishing.[8] To the extent that any society *denies* access to basic health care services, it disvalues individual autonomy and thereby exposes itself to serious moral criticism.[9]

Among the democratic states of the developed world, the moral force of this obligation is borne out by the prevalence of state-funded health care systems. Thus, the British National Health Service Acts require the Secretary of State to provide such accommodation, facilities and staff as are necessary to meet the reasonable requirements of the health service.[10] In Sweden, a directly funded national health care

---

(5, *cont.*) TO HEALTH CARE: A REPORT ON THE ETHICAL IMPLICATIONS OF DIFFERENCES IN THE AVAILABILITY OF HEALTH SERVICES 34–35 (1983) [hereinafter SECURING ACCESS].

6. *Id.* at 34; *see also* R. v. Instan, [1893] 1 Q.B. 450, 543–44 (Coleridge, L., Eng.).

7. In England: Sidaway v. Bethlem Royal Hosp. Governors, [1985] 1 All E.R. 643, 649. In Germany: GRUNDGESETZ [Constitution] [GG] art. 1, 2; Judgment of Dec. 9, 1958, BGH, 29 Entscheidungen des Bundesgerichtshofes in Zivilsachen [BGHZ] 46. In the U.S.: Schloendorff v. Society of New York Hosp., 105 N.E. 92, 93 (N.Y. 1914). For comparative references, see Dieter Giesen, *From Paternalism to Self-determination to Shared Decision Making*, 1988 ACTA JURIDICA 107 (S. Afr.).

8. Although a detailed philosophical discussion is beyond the scope of this article, the following may be profitably referred to: JOHN FINNIS, NATURAL LAW AND NATURAL RIGHTS 100–160 (1980); JOSEPH RAZ, THE MORALITY OF FREEDOM 400–429 (1986); John A. Hayes, *Health Care as a Natural Right*, 11 MED. LAW 405, 406–407 (1992).

9. SECURING ACCESS, *supra* note 5, at 34.

10. National Health Service Act 1977, ch. 49, § 3 (Eng.) obliges the Secretary of State to provide accommodation, medical, dental, nursing and

system is also in place. A differently funded, but no less comprehensive coverage is achieved in Canada through government financing of privately run health care structures. A duty upon the state to provide for medical assistance also may be inferred from Article 20(1) of the German Federal Constitution which states that: "The Federal Republic of Germany is a democratic and *social* federal state."[11] This concept of a *Sozialstaat* is implemented by the provision of a state-run health insurance scheme, in addition to a range of private health insurance programs, which ensures that *all* German citizens have access to medical attention and hospital care when it is necessary.

Of course, it must be acknowledged that aspects of these various systems have been rightly criticized as often wasteful and inefficient.[12] A combination of rising public expectations, the expansionist dynamic of medical science and increasing demands upon finite public resources have necessitated careful scrutiny of health care expenditures.[13] Furthermore, it has been shown that a concentration upon highly expensive medical technology of limited use has reinforced pre-existing inequalities of access.[14] Thus, in Britain, the *Black Report*, which regrettably did not receive adequate attention from health policy makers, noted marked discrepancies between the health of different income groups and regions and found that mortality levels rose

---

ambulance facilities, facilities for expectant and nursing mothers, facilities for ill persons (i.e., preventive care, active care and after care) and services for the diagnosis and treatment of illness. Similar provisions apply in Scotland under the National Health Service (Scotland) Act 1978, ch. 29, Part II, § 18.

11. GRUNDGESETZ [Constitution] [GG] art. 20(1) (F.R.G.) (emphasis added), *reprinted & translated in* CONSTITUTIONS OF THE COUNTRIES OF THE WORLD 90 (Albert P. Blaustein & Gilbert H. Flanz eds., 1991).

12. *See* CLARK C. HAVIGHURST, HEALTH CARE LAW AND POLICY: READINGS, NOTES, AND QUESTIONS chs. 1, 2, 8–10 (1988); Harry Schwartz, *Access, Equity, and Equality in American Medical Care, in* 2 U.S. PRESIDENT'S COMM'N FOR THE STUDY OF ETHICAL PROBLEMS IN MEDICINE AND BIOMEDICAL AND BEHAVIORAL RESEARCH, SECURING ACCESS TO HEALTH CARE: THE ETHICAL IMPLICATIONS OF DIFFERENCES IN THE AVAILABILITY OF HEALTH SERVICES 67 app. D at 74–76 (1983) [hereinafter APPENDICES: SOCIOCULTURAL AND PHILOSOPHICAL STUDIES].

13. For a compelling critique of "medical imperialism" and its often disastrous consequences, see IVAN ILLICH, MEDICAL NEMESIS: THE EXPROPRIATION OF HEALTH (1976).

14. *See* DIETER GIESEN, INTERNATIONAL MEDICAL MALPRACTICE LAW: A COMPARATIVE LAW STUDY OF CIVIL LIABILITY ARISING FROM MEDICAL CARE ¶¶ 1470–93 (1988).

inversely with falling occupation rank or status.[15] The development of efficient and more equitable strategies for the *prevention* of ill-health has been hindered by many doctors' view of themselves as "scientist problem solvers and curers"[16] and their correspondingly insatiable desire for costly new techniques and equipment.[17] Notwithstanding these forceful criticisms, it is clear that the moral obligation to provide access to adequate medical facilities *is* honored to a significant extent in each of the countries mentioned. This is made especially clear when the existing health care structures in the US are examined.

The authors of a leading American health law textbook have correctly asserted that "virtually every developed nation in the world except the United States assures universal access to health care."[18] The strong tradition of individualism in American political culture emphasizes that health care is largely a matter of private interest, the allocation of which is best left to the market. This tradition has, however, been modified by the acknowledgement of certain community obligations to provide minimal facilities and, indeed, a statutory or constitutional duty to provide at least some services for the indigent is recognized in all but three states.[19] Consequently, the coverage available to individuals in the event of ill-health is made up of an uneven patchwork of individual insurance schemes, employment-related schemes and a number of federally sanctioned initiatives to assist the needy.[20] The latter are chiefly comprised of the Medicare scheme, which provides for the health needs of the elderly and the "medically needy", and the Medicaid scheme, which makes treatment available to the "deserving" poor.[21]

---

15. SIR DOUGLAS BLACK ET AL., INEQUALITIES IN HEALTH: THE BLACK REPORT 63–64. (1982); *see also* IAN KENNEDY, THE UNMASKING OF MEDICINE 58 (1981). Note: the recent British Government White Paper, SECRETARY OF STATE FOR HEALTH, THE HEALTH OF THE NATION: A STRATEGY FOR HEALTH IN ENGLAND (1992), while commendably emphasizing the need to strengthen preventive medical practice, ignores many of the criticisms contained in the *Black Report*.

16. GIESEN, *supra* note 14, at ¶ 1446.

17. *Id.* at ¶¶ 1442–1513; *see also* KENNEDY, *supra* note 15, at 70–75.

18. BARRY R. FURROW ET AL., HEALTH LAW: CASES, MATERIALS AND PROBLEMS 602 (2nd ed. 1991).

19. *Id.* at 601.

20. SECURING ACCESS, *supra* note 5, at 115–182 (detailing various health insurance and medical assistance schemes). *See also* FURROW ET AL., *supra* note 18, at 529–599.

21. A rare and useful philosophical exploration of the concept of the "deserving" poor is provided by George Sher, *Health Care and the "Deserving Poor"*, *in* APPENDICES: SOCIOCULTURAL AND PHILOSOPHICAL STUDIES, *supra* note 12, at 293 app. L.

While Medicare generally has been successful, this has not been true of Medicaid.[22] The exacting criteria for Medicaid assistance, whereby most single persons and couples without children are excluded as "undeserving" poor, have meant that only about 50% of persons below the federal poverty standard are covered.[23] This in turn has led to the alarming statistics that approximately 14% of the US population were completely uninsured in 1992 and approximately 6% were under-insured.[24] Indeed, one commentator has noted the emergence of a new category of "medically excluded" persons, whose incomes are insufficient to meet the costs of private insurance, but sufficiently high to put them just beyond the reach of the Medicaid program.[25] In addition, escalating price inflation in the medical sector as a whole has meant that levels of reimbursement to doctors attending to Medicaid patients are generally viewed as inadequate,[26] with the result that large numbers of badly needed physicians have forsaken the inner cities and poorer rural areas for more lucrative practices in the suburbs.[27] These difficulties have been exacerbated by economic measures which have crudely

---

22. *See* Daniel Callahan, *Medical Futility, Medical Necessity: The-Problem-Without-A-Name* 21 HASTINGS CTR. REP., Jul.–Aug. 1991, at 32.

23. SECURING ACCESS, *supra* note 5, at 95 (noting that "[t]he income eligibility limits for Medicaid . . . are generally more restrictive than the national poverty guidelines").

24. *Bush, Clinton Health Care Plans Analyzed in Families USA/Lewin-ICF Analysis Performed Under Auspices of Bipartisan Committee*, HEALTH NEWS DAILY, Oct. 2, 1992, *available in* WESTLAW, HND Database (citing U.S. Dep't of Labor estimates); *see also*, SECURING ACCESS, *supra* note 5, at 92–100. As it was put recently, "[i]nstead of rationing medical services themselves, as the United Kingdom does in order to provide everyone basic care, United States health insurance mechanisms simply 'ration' uninsured individuals away from medical treatment altogether." Frances H. Miller, *Denial of Health Care and Informed Consent in English and American Law*, 18 AM. J.L. & MED. 37, 42 (1992).

25. *See* Paul Starr, *Medical Care and the Pursuit of Equality in America*, *in* APPENDICES: SOCIOCULTURAL AND PHILOSOPHICAL STUDIES, *supra* note 12, at 3 app. A (discussing the development of marginal inequality in medical care and the rise in employee health benefit plans). *See also* HAVIGHURST, *supra* note 12, at 40–46; *see generally id.* especially at 65, 111, 140.

26. *See* SECURING ACCESS, *supra* note 5, at 183–197 (recognizing a growing concern by the American public that rising costs do not result in increased benefits).

27. For an examination of the wide variations in the ratio of physicians to population in the US and the corresponding differences in levels of health, see John L.S. Holloman Jr., *Access to Health Care, in* APPENDICES: SOCIOCULTURAL AND PHILOSOPHICAL STUDIES, *supra* note 12, at 79 app. E at 84–85.

reduced the number of services available to Medicaid recipients, rather than tackling the root causes of medical expansionism in general.[28] It is, therefore, no surprise that the US President's Commission found that levels of ill-health were considerably higher among low-income groups and traditionally disadvantaged minorities in American society.[29] Bearing this in mind, it is hoped that President Bill Clinton will remain true to his undertaking to effect a far-reaching reform of the US health care system.[30]

III. MEDICAL EMERGENCY AND THE DUTY TO RESCUE

The absence of a comprehensive health care system in the US, with access predicated upon need, is felt most acutely in cases of medical emergency. In this context, this article is most appropriately focused upon the existence and extent of the moral and legal duty upon medical professionals and hospital authorities to effectively rescue an individual whose health and life is in grave danger by affording urgently required treatment. In dealing with the question of whether the moral duty to render emergency medical assistance as embodied in the parable of the Good Samaritan[31] is to be converted into a legal duty, the approaches of the common law and civil law jurisdictions have diverged considerably.

The individualist bias already noted in this article in connection with the US health care system is also manifested in the refusal of courts in common law countries to impose liability for failure to act to prevent harm or nonfeasance as distinguished from affirmative misconduct or misfeasance.[32] In the medical context, this has meant that a doctor

---

28. Thus, while the recent reforms of the Oregon Medicaid program have expanded the number of persons covered, it has been shown that the state's novel system of "fluid prioritization" of available health care benefits will disadvantage children and pregnant women considerably. *See* Sarah Rosenbaum, *Mothers and Children Last: The Oregon Medicaid Experiment*, 18 AM. J.L. & MED. 97 (1992).

29. SECURING ACCESS, *supra* note 5, at 49–113.

30. " 'A compassionate government', says Clinton, 'must extend care to the 37 million people in the U.S. who have no medical insurance.' " George J. Church, *His Seven Most Urgent Decisions*, TIME, Jan. 25, 1993, at 30.

31. *See* ST. LUKE 10: 25–37.

32. W. PAGE KEETON ET AL., PROSSER AND KEETON ON THE LAW OF TORTS §§ 3, 56 (5th ed. 1984).

"may flout his Hippocratic oath and deny aid to a stranger, even in an emergency like a road accident."[33] Indeed, in a leading decision of the High Court of Australia, it was stated that in the parable of the Good Samaritan "both priest and Levite ensured performance of any common law duty of care to the stricken traveller when, by crossing to the other side of the road, they avoided any risk of throwing up dust in his wounds."[34] By contrast, the civil law jurisdictions have not been so timorous about obliging rescue in emergency situations, and failure to do so in certain clearly defined circumstances will incur criminal and civil sanctions.[35]

Supporters of the common law position have argued that to impose such a duty upon doctors would deprive them of their right to contract freely for the provision of medical services and, thereby, would amount to a morally unacceptable appropriation of their labor.[36] This analysis, however, ignores significant aspects of the relationship (1) between doctors and society and (2) between doctors and their individual patients. Fundamentally, the practice of medicine is subject to the licensing powers of state authorities and is confined to a select and well-remunerated body of professionals. Furthermore, the newly-graduated doctor owes a considerable debt to society—his training having been funded by enormous state investment and his clinical experience having been gained through practice upon willing patients, a disproportionate number of whom will themselves have been indigent.[37] Clearly, a doctor required to provide vital treatment in an emergency situation is not "giving something for nothing." In addition, the characterization of the doctor–patient relationship as a series of arms-length transactions solely rooted in the law of contract is wholly at odds with existing law and with the ancient ethical traditions of the medical profession.[38]

---

33. John G. Fleming, The Law of Torts 147 (8th ed. 1992).

34. Jaensch v. Coffey, 155 C.L.R. 549, 579 (Austl. 1984).

35. Code pénal [C. Pén.] art. 63 (Fr.); Code pénal [C. Pén.] art. 422 (Belg.); Strafgesetzbuch [StGB] (Penal Code) § 21 (Aus.); Strafgesetzbuch [StGB] (Penal Code) § 323c (F.R.G.). See also Giesen, supra note 14, ¶¶ 713–29 (1988).

36. See Robert M. Sade, Medical Care as a Right: A Refutation, 285 New Eng. J. Med. 1288 (1971).

37. Holloman, supra note 27, at 92–93.

38. It is submitted that a covenant based analysis of the duties of the individual doctor and of the medical profession as a whole more faithfully represents the realities of social practice and ethical understanding. See William F. May, Code, Covenant, Contract, or Philanthropy, 516 Hastings Ctr. Rep. Dec. 1975, at 29.

Fiduciary duties of disclosure, confidentiality and respect for the patient's fundamental human interests, imposed upon doctors by law, recognize the heightened vulnerability and dependency of patients.[39] This position of patient weakness is at its most extreme in emergency cases, where it is impossible, as a matter of fact, for individuals to negotiate contractual terms or to seek alternative sources of care.

There have, however, been a number of attempts to modify the common law position to the advantage of patients in need through a range of legislative strategies and a significant body of case law designed to "force rescue" in emergency situations. Thus, in the US the Hill-Burton Act of 1946,[40] which provided federal funding for the construction and expansion of hospitals, authorized the federal agency responsible to require assurances from applicants for funding that a measure of hospital care would be provided free of charge to indigent patients.[41] Furthermore, over half of the US state governments have enacted legislation requiring all general and surgical hospitals to provide emergency care as a condition of their being licensed to operate.[42] Regrettably, however, it must be admitted that these measures have *not* had a very substantial impact due to widespread non-compliance and under-enforcement.[43] The Consolidated Omnibus Budget Reconciliation Act of 1985[44] requires all hospitals participating in the Medicare scheme, which have appropriate facilities, to provide

---

39. For a comparative analysis with copious references, see GIESEN, *supra* note 14, ¶¶ 482–729 (1988) (duty of disclosure); *id.* at ¶¶ 833–90 (duty of confidentiality and patient-physician communication). This analysis is illustrated by recent North American case law from the US and Canada. *See, e.g.*, Moore v. Regents of the Univ. of Cal., 793 P.2d 479 (Cal. 1990) (doctor required by law to disclose any financial or scientific interest he may have in a patient's course of treatment); Norberg v. Weinrib, 92 D.L.R. 4th 449 (Can. 1992) (doctor required by law not only to protect a patient's narrow legal and economic interests, but also fundamental human interests).

40. 42 U.S.C. § 291 (1982).

41. FURROW ET AL., *supra* note 18, at 628–629 (synopsis of legislative history and of litigation concerning subsequent regulations for the Act.). Note also that discrimination on grounds of race, color or national origin under any program or activity receiving federal funding is subject to review under 42 U.S.C. §§ 2000d to 2000d–6 (1982).

42. *E.g.*, ILL. REV. STAT. ch. 111.5, para. 86 (1969); CAL. HEALTH & SAFETY CODE §§ 1317.2–.2a, §§ 1798.170–.172 (West 1990).

43. *See* KAREN H. ROTHENBERG, *Who Cares?: The Evolution of the Legal Duty to Provide Emergency Care*, 26 HOU. L. REV. 21, 54, 59 (1989).

44. 42 U.S.C. § 1395dd (1988).

treatment to stabilize an emergency condition, to provide assistance to a woman in active labor or to provide for an appropriate transfer of either type of patient to another medical facility (i.e., where the benefits of transferring the patient outweigh the burdens of doing so). The effectiveness of this statute is increased by the inclusion of a "civil enforcement" provision allowing a patient who has been injured by a hospital's violation of the provisions of the statute to obtain damages and equitable relief.[45]

Although in the absence of a contractual agreement a doctor is under no common law duty to render emergency treatment as was found in the Arizona case of *Hiser v. Randolph*,[46] courts have shown a notable desire to circumvent the harsher implications of this rule.[47] Thus, it has been held in both England and the US that, when a patient presents himself at a health care facility in reliance upon the established custom of that facility to afford emergency treatment, a doctor who refuses to attend to him will be liable for medical malpractice,[48] as will the hospital itself by way of vicarious or direct liability.[49] Similarly, a doctor who discontinues a necessary course of treatment without making adequate provision for his replacement by another physician will be liable under the law of negligence for abandonment.[50] In an expansive interpretation of *when* such a course of treatment can be said to have commenced, the Supreme Court of Mississippi has held that where the plaintiff "was recorded as an emergency room patient, and remained there two hours . . . the Hospital and its employees had a duty to use reasonable care in protecting his life and well being."[51] It has also been

---

45. 42 U.S.C. § 1395dd (d)(3)(A) (1986) (current version at 42 U.S.C. § 1395dd (d)(2)(A) (1988)). *See* Owens v. Nacogdoches County Hosp. Dist., 741 F. Supp. 1269 (E.D. Tex. 1990) (successful invocation of this provision by a woman who had been transferred, just prior to going into labor, by defendant to a distant hospital solely on the basis of her indigence).

46. Hiser v. Randolph, 617 P.2d 774 (Ariz. 1980) (holding defendant-doctor was bound by his contract of employment which obliged him to render emergency treatment).

47. *See* ROTHENBERG, *supra* note 43 (providing a thorough discussion of American developments in this regard).

48. Barnett v. Chelsea & Kensington Hosp. Mgmt. Comm., [1969] 1 Q. B. 428 (Eng.) (denying claim, however, because plaintiff was unable to establish an adequate causal link between omission to treat and death of decedent); *see also* Wilmington Gen. Hosp. v. Manlove, 174 A.2d 135, 140 (Del. 1961).

49. For a comparative discussion of the vicarious and direct liability of hospital authorities, see GIESEN, *supra* note 14, at ¶¶ 50–106.

50. *See id.* at ¶ 724.

51. New Biloxi Hosp., Inc. v. Frazier, 146 So. 2d 882, 887 (Miss. 1962).

held that, where state regulations and licensing conditions require hospitals to maintain emergency rooms, access to these facilities cannot be denied solely on the basis of an inability to pay.[52]

The enactment in many American jurisdictions of so-called Good Samaritan statutes is a further development intended to ameliorate the situation of patients in urgent need of treatment.[53] These statutes, which only apply outside the hospital context, are intended to provide an incentive to doctors to fulfill their ethical obligations in this regard by generally imposing liability upon them only where they have been *grossly negligent* in the provision of emergency treatment.[54] As Professor and now Justice Linden stated, this affirmative action rule "does not inhibit would-be rescuers while at the same time is not too inviting to bunglers."[55] It is submitted, however, that these statutes, which are the result of "active lobbying by medical associations,"[56] represent a wholly anomalous and unacceptable exception to the general law of negligence. While it has been widely affirmed that in determining whether a defendant is liable in negligence courts must take into account the objective circumstances in which he found himself,[57] this does not mean that at common law a different, lower standard of care is applied to conduct in emergency situations. Rather, it has been held in England for example that, once a rescue attempt has been commenced, the rescuer must comply with the standard of care of the reasonable man in the particular circumstances.[58] There would appear to be no principled reason for extending favorable treatment to the medical profession in this regard. Furthermore, doctors' fears of a flood of litigation are wholly misplaced, since no single case has been found in the US or Canada where a physician was actually sued for malpractice arising out of treatment rendered at the scene of an emergency.[59]

---

52. *E.g.*, Guerrero v. Copper Queen Hosp., 537 P.2d 1329, 1331 (Ariz. 1974); *see also* Thompson v. Sun City Community Hosp. Inc., 688 P.2d 605, 609 (Ariz. 1984) (endorsing the decision in *Guerrero*).

53. For a state-by-state survey of 'Good Samaritan' statutes, see GIESEN, *supra* note 14, at ¶ 720.

54. But cf. Colby v. Schwartz, 78 Cal. App. 3d 885 (1978) (holding that physicians are not protected by such statutes when working on an emergency case as part of normal hospital routine).

55. ALLEN M. LINDEN, CANADIAN TORT LAW 227 (4th ed. 1988).

56. KEETON ET AL., *supra* note 32, at § 56.

57. GIESEN, *supra* note 14, at ¶ 133.

58. Harrison v. British Rys. Bd., [1981] 3 All E.R. 679 (Eng. Q.B.).

59. GIESEN, *supra* note 14, at ¶ 721.

It thus emerges that in common law countries, in the absence of an affirmative duty to provide emergency medical assistance, a mosaic of statutory and common law obligations and incentives has been put in place to give effect to the basic humanitarian duty[60] to assist another in peril. Unfortunately, we have also seen that each of these incremental measures has met with but partial success and, indeed, John Fleming's criticism that the "remnants of excessive individualism [in the common law] are apt to evoke invidious comparison with affirmative duties of good neighbourliness in most countries outside the common law orbit"[61] remains valid. It is submitted that a clear, though sharply delimited and defined duty to rescue individuals in grave need of attention should be imposed upon doctors and hospital authorities who are in a position to do so. The cautious judicial development of the defence of necessity, which raises similar fears of undue intrusion upon individual liberty,[62] would provide a useful model for the shaping of a common law duty to rescue.[63] Furthermore, judicial interpretation of Section 323c of the German Penal Code demonstrates that the problems of identifying the appropriate defendant and of establishing causation, which are often cited by Anglo-Saxon commentators as reasons for not imposing liability for omissions, are not insurmountable.[64] Indeed, a number of German decisions indicate that, so far from there being a reduction in the standard expected of doctors in rescue situations, as is the case under the aforementioned Good Samaritan statutes, the extent and quality of the assistance which they are required to provide may be increased in the light of their special training and skills.[65]

---

60. As embodied in the parable of the Good Samaritan itself. *See* ST. LUKE 10: 25–37.

61. FLEMING, *supra* note 33, at 147.

62. Southwark London Borough Council v. Williams, [1971] 1 Ch. 734 (Eng. C.A.) (rejecting claim of a deference of "economic" necessity to an action in trespass, confined the defence to urgent situations of imminent peril). *See also* FLEMING, *supra* note 33, at 94–8.

63. For a masterful exposition of the analogical basis for a common law duty to rescue and a demonstration of the compatibility of such a duty with the two main philosophical traditions of the common law, see Ernest J. Weinrib, *The Case for a Duty to Rescue*, 90 YALE L.J. 247 (1980).

64. *See* ADOLF SCHÖNKE ET AL., STRAFGESETZBUCH: KOMMENTAR notes 1–36 to § 323c St GB (Penal Code) (24th ed. 1991).

65. Judgment 3 Ss 396/74 of Sept. 6, 1974, OLG Hamm, 1975 NEUE JURISTISCHE WOCHENSCHRIFT [NJW] 604 (F.R.G.); Judgment Ss 532/56 of July 1957, OLG Köln, 1957 NJW 1609 (F.R.G.); Judgment Ss 5/48 of Dec. 12,

(*cont.*)

IV. ETHICS, LAW AND THE PATIENT'S RIGHTS

We have seen that the failure of certain states to provide at least a minimum of health care to their indigent members, and the reluctance of the common law to impose a duty upon doctors to render aid in emergency situations, are both open to harsh criticism in the light of ethical principles generally accepted in society. However, these principles, which generate rights to receive and obligations to provide certain forms of medical treatment, are applicable with equal normative force to the therapeutic relationship itself, once access to the health care system has been obtained.

The overwhelming propensity of medical professionals to view their task as the scientific application of all available technology to the patient has already been identified as a significant cause of increasing costs in the health care sector. Correspondingly, on this model "[d]isease manifests itself as a malfunction in a specific area; it can be corrected or ameliorated with proper diagnosis and reparative techniques. These techniques usually consist of a chemical or biological agent specifically suited to attack and render harmless the germ or biological malfunction that caused the disease."[66] Under this conception the individual, although gaining access to medical services, loses all rights on becoming a patient and becomes merely the passive object of those procedures which the attending physicians deem to be in his best interests.[67] But if the law is to faithfully embody the value of individual autonomy, which is at the core of any civilized society[68] and

---

(65, *cont.*) 1948, OLG Koblenz, 1948 NJW 489 (F.R.G.). *See also* Arthur Kreuzer, *Die unterlassene ärzliche Hilfeleistung in der Rechtsprechung*, 1967 NJW 278–281 (F.R.G.); Hans Welzel, *Zur Dogmatik der echten Unterlassungsdelikte, insbesondere des § 330c* [now § 323c] *StGB*, 1953 NJW 327–329 (F.R.G.).

66. Sally Guttmacher, *Whole in Body, Mind, and Spirit: Holistic Health and the Limits of Medicine*, 9 HASTINGS CTR. RPT., April 1979, at 15, 16.

67. This is also the focus of the scathing criticism to be found in KENNEDY, *supra* note 15, at 70–75.

68. The central importance of individual autonomy in the legal and political order has been widely acknowledged. *See, e.g.*, Sidaway v. Bethlem Royal Hosp. Governors, [1985] 1 All E.R. 643, 649g–h (Eng.) (Scarman, L., dissenting); Scholendorff v. Society of New York Hosp., 105 N.E. 92, 93 (N.Y. 1912); GRUNDGESETZ [Constitution] [GG] arts. 1–2 (F.R.G.); Judgment VI ZR 203/57 of Dec. 9, 1958, BGH, 29 Entscheidungen des Bundesgerichtshofes in Zivilsachen [BGHZ] 46, 54 (F.R.G.).

which, as we have seen, generates the moral obligation upon society to provide for access to *necessary* medical care, it cannot allow the medical profession to play God in this manner.[69]

As Lord Scarman stated, in his formidable dissent in *Sidaway v. Bethlem Royal Hospital Governors*:

> The doctor's concern is with health and relief of pain. These are the medical objectives. But a patient may well have in mind circumstances, objectives and values which he may reasonably not make known to the doctor but which may lead him to a decision different from that suggested by a purely medical opinion. The doctor's duty can be seen, therefore, to be one which requires him not only to advise as to matters of medical treatment but also to provide his patient with the information needed to enable the patient to consider and balance the medical advantages and risks alongside other relevant matters, such as, for example, his family, business or social responsibilities of which the doctor may be only partially, if at all informed.[70]

The patient's full and valid consent is an unavoidable prerequisite of the legality of any diagnostic or therapeutic procedure to which he is submitted.[71] In this regard, in so far as courts in England (or Scotland) have allowed the medical profession itself to set the standard of disclosure in consent cases, they have abdicated their constitutional function to develop objective standards of care and thereby have failed to vindicate and protect the patient's right to self-determination.[72] In so doing, the English and Scottish courts are out of step not only with their counterparts in the civil law world, but also with all the other major common law jurisdictions.

In adopting a patient-centered approach to the question of standards of disclosure in medical malpractice actions, the Supreme Court of South Australia has stated that the law must respect "the right of every human being to make decisions which affect his own life and to

---

69. *See* Sidaway v. Bethlem Royal Hosp. Governors, [1985] 1 All E.R. 1018, 1028a (Eng. C.A.) (Sir John Donaldson); *see also* GIESEN, *supra* note 14, at ¶ 133.

70. *Sidaway*, [1985] 1 All E.R. at 652d–f (Scarman, L., dissenting).

71. *See* GIESEN, *supra* note 14, at ¶¶ 482–832 (1988) (providing a full comparative discussion of disclosure requirements in medical law).

72. *Sidaway*, [1985] 1 All E.R. 643; Gold v. Haringey Health Authority, [1987] 3 W.L.R. 649 (Eng. C.A.); Hunter v. Hanley, 1955 Sess. Cas. 200 (Scot.); *see also* Dieter Giesen & John Hayes, *The Patient's Right to Know—A Comparative View*, 21 ANGLO-AM. L. REV. 101 (1992). *Contra Sidaway*, 1 All E.R. at 645 ff (Scarman, L., dissenting).

determine the risks which he is willing to undertake."[73] While the *patient-centered* perspective of Australian and Canadian jurisprudence regarding consent to medical treatment avoids the most lamentable shortcomings of the deferential *doctor-centered* approach in Britain vis-à-vis the medical profession, it is submitted that the qualification of this approach by the adoption of a "reasonable patient" test[74] *fails* to extend due protection to the patient's fundamental right to self-determination. The application of a test based upon reasonableness means that the patient's "supposedly inviolable right to decide for himself what is done with his body is made subject to a standard *set by others*. The right to base one's consent on proper information is effectively vitiated for those with fears, apprehensions, religious beliefs or superstitions outside the mainstream of society."[75] These words have been echoed by the German Federal Supreme Court, which has imposed the optimal requirement that the extent of disclosure required of the attending doctor be determined by the *subjective* informational needs of the *particular* patient.[76] As it stated, to "respect the patient's own will is to respect his freedom and dignity as a human being."[77]

Ethical and legal issues of the most profound significance are also integral to treatment decisions at the "edges of life."[78] A proliferation of new techniques in the field of artificial reproduction presents the serious threat that the pursuit of the novel and the fashionable by

---

73. F. v. R., 33 S.A. St. R. 189, 191 (Austl. 1983).

74. *See, e.g.,* Rogers v. Whittaker, [1992] Austl. Torts R. § 81–189 (Austl.); F v. R., 33 S.A. St. R. 189 (Austl. 1983); Reibl v. Hughes, [1980] 1 S.C.R. 880 (Can.); Hopp v. Lepp, [1980] 2 S.C.R. 192 (Can.); Canterbury v. Spence, 464 F.2d 772 (D.C. Cir. 1972); Cobbs v. Grant, 502 P.2d 1 (Cal. 1972).

75. McPherson v. Ellis, 287 S.E.2d 892, 897 (N.C. 1982) (emphasis added) (holding that jury should consider what patient's decision would have been had she had been properly informed of risk of paralysis).

76. Judgment VIZR 203/57 of Dec. 9, 1958, BGH, 29 Entscheidungen des Bundesgerichtshofes in Zivilsachen [BGHZ] 46, LM § 276 [Ca] BGB No 8, 1959 NEUE JURISTISCHE WOCHENSCHRIFT [NJW] 811, 1959 VersR 153 (F.R.G.). *See also* DIETER GIESEN, ARZTHAFTUNGSRECHT 112–120, 171, 259 (3rd ed. 1990) (F.R.G.).

77. Judgment VI ZR 203/57 of Dec. 9, 1958, BGH, 29 BGHZ 46, 53–56, LM § 276 [Ca] BGB No 8, 1959 NJW 811, 1959 VersR 153; *see also* Judgment BvR 878/74 of July 25, 1979, BVerfG, 52 Entscheidungen des Bundesverfassungsgerichts [BVerfGE] 1313 (F.R.G.).

78. *See* PAUL RAMSEY, ETHICS AT THE EDGE OF LIFE: MEDICAL AND LEGAL INTERSECTIONS (1978). The importance of the ethical issues at the end of life are discussed in GIESEN, *supra* note 14, at ¶¶ 938–983, 1324, 1328, 1360–1375, 1391, 1405–1416, 1424–1441, 1460–1493.

medical researchers will leave the law lagging behind and unable to fully implement society's *fundamental* ethical values.[79] The price of medical prowess in this area has been the destruction of countless human embryos through cryopreservation and experimentation. In the face of this, the law must insist that artificially conceived human life is nurtured in the child's own interests and emphasize that that which is medically possible is not always morally or legally acceptable. As Professor Krause has explained it, "a child is not 'medication' to be prescribed lightly to frustrated, would-be parents ... the greatest responsibility is owed directly to the child."[80] Put bluntly, the law cannot allow doctors, under the guise of fulfilling societal obligations to provide health care, to take up the glittering stones of human genes and embryonic life and piece together mosaics at random, in accordance with their scientific whims or curiosity.

Similarly, at the other "end of life," technological developments have enabled doctors to prolong the lives of many terminally and hopelessly ill patients (i.e., those in a persistent vegetative state).[81] In these circumstances it is again essential that the medical profession is not allowed to play God with human life. The law must reflect its strong commitment to both individual autonomy *and* the sanctity of human life in regulating this area of medical practice.[82]

V. CONCLUSION

It has been seen that an ethically consistent approach must inform both provisions for initial access to health care and the legal regulation of treatment once this access has been achieved. Discussion of patients' rights is of little significance if individuals are excluded *in limine* from necessary medical services due to poverty or geographical happenstance. But correspondingly, individuals must be ensured the full enjoyment of their basic human rights once they have entered the system. Common to our consideration of issues of access, consent to treatment and procedures undertaken at the edges of life was the tendency noted among medical professionals to conceive of themselves

---

79. The legal and ethical aspects of artificial reproduction are discussed in GIESEN, *supra* note 14, at ¶¶ 1343–1416.

80. Harry D. Krause, *Artificial Conception: Legislative Approaches*, 19 FAM. L.Q 185, 206 (1985).

81. GIESEN, *supra* note 14, at ¶¶ 932–987.

82. These were the central concerns of the US Supreme Court in its recent decision in *Cruzan v. Director, Missouri Dep't of Health*, 497 U.S. 261 (1990).

as the agents of an ever-advancing science, free from ethical and legal constraints. This self-image is fostered by the process of "socialization" and "role modelling" which doctors-in- training undergo. A firm *ésprit de corps* is generated and indeed a doctor's primary duty, as embodied in the Hippocratic Oath,[83] is not to his patient or to society *but to his fellow practitioners*.[84] In the words of Ian Kennedy of King's College at London, a result of this veneer of scientific invincibility: "we [the public] have come almost to believe in magic cures and the waving of wands. The reality has been a constant disappointment. The promised or expected cures are not there."[85] Doctors are, therefore, better advised to view their relationship with their individual patients and with society as a whole as one of fiduciary partnership in the furtherance of the basic human values of life and personal autonomy through the promotion and preservation of health. As was said by three of the eight judges on Germany's highest court, the German Federal Constitutional Court, in a landmark medical malpractice decision:

> Trust cannot be demanded one-sidedly by the physician alone. Endeavors are right to place the burden of a physician–patient relationship not only on the shoulders of the physician but to distribute them more evenly by making the patient co-operate and assume his own part of responsibility for his health ... Co-operation, a real physician–patient dialogue and a general strengthening of the patient's sensitivity of their own responsibility will only be possible where the patient first of all is made an active participant and thus has received the information relevant to his medical care ... What is required then is that the physician shares with the patient all the inherent uncertainties and risks, unless the patient has made it clear that he does not want more information. In this way the patient will be made privy to the knowledge about his situation and the inherent risks, a consequence which he will not escape anyway if he consents to treatment. This makes him a responsible partner of the physician.[86]

---

83. An English translation of the Oath is printed in STEDMAN'S MEDICAL DICTIONARY 716–17 (25th ed. 1990).

84. For a discussion of the tendency of professionals to follow one another, see GIESEN, *supra* note 14, at ¶¶ 1471–1527.

85. KENNEDY, *supra* note 15, at 46.

86. Judgment of July 25, 1979, BVerfG, 52 Entscheidungen des Bundesverfassungsgerichgts [BVerfGE] 131, at 171 ff (Hirsch, J.) (F.R.G.); *id.* at 179 (Niebler & Steinberger, J.J.). For a more comprehensive discussion of the text-related issues, see Giesen, *supra* note 7 (comparative references).

Distributing health care rationing and the role of the physician in the United Kingdom National Health Service

Alan Maynard

The policy issue is not whether to allocate or "ration" health care, but how, i.e., what rules will be used by society to determine access to care? These rules will decide who will receive treatment, who will live in pain and discomfort and who, in extremes, will be left to die. Such decisions are never easy for consumers, providers, purchasers and policy makers.

This article will review these issues in the context of the United Kingdom National Health Service (NHS). In the first section, the goals of the NHS will be examined in terms of the principles enunciated in legislation. The next section will look at the practice of rationing in the NHS, processes with characteristics well-known to all who are familiar with the practice of medicine! In the third section the role of physicians in the rationing processes will be examined.

Justice and Health Care: Comparative Perspectives. Edited by A. Grubb and M.J. Mehlman. © 1995 John Wiley & Sons Ltd.

I. THE GOALS OF THE NHS: THE PRINCIPLES OF RESOURCE ALLOCATION

The White Paper of the Churchill government in 1944 stated that:

[T]he Government...wants to ensure that in the future every man, woman and child can rely on getting...the best medical and other facilities available; that their getting them shall not depend on whether they can pay or on any other factor irrelevant to real need.[1]

In 1946, an outline of the Labour Government's NHS Bill stated that the Service

...imposes no limits on availability, e.g., limitations based on financial means, age, sex, employment or vocation, area of residence or insurance qualification.[2]

Even for these Labour Party legislators there were limits to the generalization that services were to be free. The exceptions in the initial legislation were threefold:

1. Charges were to be levied for the repair of spectacles and appliances broken as a result of negligence.
2. Payments were to be made for services and appliances provided at levels or standards above the general service level (e.g., amenity beds and private NHS hospital beds).
3. Charges were to be made for domestic help and some related services.[3]

Aneurin Bevan, the Labour Party's left wing architect of the NHS, resisted amendments to make domestic help and related services free during the passing of the legislation. This dedicated socialist argued in an almost Thatcherite fashion:

I really must resist this amendment. Does the Hon. Member suggest that everything shall be free?...It is a perfectly reasonable proposition that,

---

1. MINISTRY OF HEALTH, A NATIONAL HEALTH SERVICE, CMD. 6502, *reprinted in* RUDOLF KLEIN, THE POLITICS OF THE NATIONAL HEALTH SERVICE at 10 n. 10 (Longman 1983).
2. MINISTRY OF HEALTH, THE NATIONAL HEALTH SERVICE BILL: A SUMMARY OF THE PROPOSED SERVICE, 1946, CMD. 6761.
3. *Id.*

where domestic help of this sort is needed and the persons concerned are able to provide it for themselves, they should do so, and where they are able to make a contribution, they should make it ... it seems to me to be wholly unjustified that we should provide a service of this sort without any payment whatever.... Our objection to the means test was that it was devised for the purpose of withholding money from people. This means test is for the purpose of giving services to people who are in need of these services ... and where people can make a contribution towards the cost, they should make it.[4]

Rhetoric and ambiguity are the hallmarks of political debate and the precise definition of what is being rejected and what is being accepted is usually absent. Such vagueness makes it difficult to hold elected officials accountable and makes the monitoring of their performance and that of health care managers and clinicians very difficult.

It is perpetrated in more recent times. The ideology of the Thatcher government was libertarian. Normally, this would mean that the government would regard access to health care as part of society's reward system, with people permitted (if not encouraged) to use their income and wealth to gain better health care, if they wish, than their fellow citizens in similar circumstances. The logical consequence of the libertarian ideal would be that private practice would predominate, with a "residual" NHS providing a minimum standard of care for the poor. Inequality in access to care is an inevitable consequence of the market. Indeed, it is a sign of its success!

In this market "ideal," the consumers would judge the system's success by its ability to do what they demand at a time and place, and in a quantity and quality they require. Producers would judge the market's success by their ability to make a good income out of it.

However, the "real" health care market does not work like this. Doctors act as the patients' agent, mediating their demands for health care. The consumers' capacity to access care is determined by the reimbursement rules of the insurers and utilization is constrained by anxieties about "medical indigency" and the fear that insurers will adjust the risk rating of those consumers who demand "too much" care.[5]

The complexities of how the "real" health care market works and

---

4. Committee State of the National Health Service Bill, House of Commons Debates, June 18, 1946 HANSARD cols. 1561–62.

5. *See* A. Maynard & A. Williams, *Privatization and Health Care, in* PRIVATIZATION AND THE WELFARE STATE (J. LeGrand et al. eds., 1984).

the political popularity of the NHS constrained the pro-market element in the Conservative government and, as a consequence, Margaret Thatcher argued, at the Conservative Party Conference in Brighton on October 8, 1982 in the 1983 Election Manifesto, that "the principle that adequate health care should be provided for all, regardless of their ability to pay, must be the foundation of any arrangements for financing health care."[6]

During the debates in 1989–90 about the reform of the NHS, Mrs. Thatcher argued that an efficient NHS would drive the private health care sector out of business.

If scarce health care resources are not to be allocated (i.e., rationed between competing patients) in a private market according to the willingness and ability to pay of patients and private insurers, what criteria are to be used? The founding fathers (and mothers) of the NHS wished to allocate health care according to need. This is set out clearly in the legislation.[7] But how does one define "need?"

Doctors and managers in the NHS treat patients who are present due to accident or illness, or because physicians, as a matter of policy, seek out patients for care (e.g., breast cancer screening). More patients present for care than can be treated.[8] Furthermore, due to demographic change and technological innovation, the number of potentially beneficial treatments is increasing and, as a consequence, the gap between what can be done technically and what can be afforded financially is widening.[9]

The rationing process in the NHS ideally should consist of two steps:

1. A technical judgment: Which patients would benefit most from care in terms of enhanced duration and quality of life (e.g., quality adjusted life years = QALYs)?[10]
2. A social judgment: Is it worthwhile to treat patients (i.e., how much will society pay to purchase an additional QALY)?

---

6. Margaret Thatcher, Speech to the Conservative Party Conference, October 8, 1982.

7. *See supra* notes 1, 2 and accompanying text.

8. *See, e.g.,* Jeffery Haller, *Britain's Labour Party Launches Offensive on Health Service*, REUTERS, January 6, 1988 ("Thousands of Britons have been waiting for operations for more than a year. . . .").

9. KLEIN, *supra* note 1, at 81–82.

10. *See Rationing Health Care*, THE ECONOMIST, April 23, 1994, at 17 (explaining QALY analysis); *see also* Ray Robinson, *Cost Utility Analysis; Economic Evaluation and Health Care*, 307 BRIT. MED. J. 859 (1993).

The medical experts should provide technical information about the comparative QALY performance of competing therapies (Step 1). In a society with a national health service, the politicians, as representatives of the taxpayer, should decide how much treatment to fund (Step 2). Technical judgments would prioritize competing treatments, identifying the "best value for money." Funding judgments would decide how far down this league table it will be possible to fund treatments. Below some "plimsoll line," beneficial treatments would not be funded and patients should be left in pain and discomfort, and to die. Treatment in an ideal NHS, therefore, would be allocated according to the patient's capacity to benefit from care and in a manner similar to that attempted in Oregon,[11] discussed in the Netherlands and explored in New Zealand.[12] It also may involve, as in Oregon, the use of truth, those patients refused access to care being told it is due not to the absence of effective therapies, but to the lack of finance.[13] Such honesty may increase pressure for increased funding of, hopefully, cost-effective care.

II. THE GOALS OF THE NHS: THE PRACTICE OF RESOURCE ALLOCATION

The principle of resource allocation, the benefit principle, distilled from the legislation and the legislators' statements requires the clinicians and managers in the NHS to identify what works (i.e., the cost-effectiveness of competing interventions) and deliver, with the assistance of suitably designed incentive systems, those services which give the "biggest bang for the buck."[14] This is easier said than done!

The health care system in the UK is similar to that in any other country: cost data are poor, there are large variations in clinical practice, the few effectiveness data that exist tend to be ignored, often

---

11. *See, e.g.*, THE BROOKINGS INSTITUTION, RATIONING AMERICA'S HEALTH CARE: THE OREGON PLAN AND BEYOND (Martin A. Strosberg et al. eds., 1992).

12. *See* Chris Ham, *Priorities: When Health Care Goes on the Ration*, THE GUARDIAN SOCIETY PAGE, Nov. 9, 1994, at 7; GOVERNMENT COMM. ON CHOICES IN HEALTH CARE, NETH. MINISTRY OF WELFARE, HLEATH AND CULTURAL AFFAIRS, CHOICES IN HEALTH CARE, DUNNING REPORT (1992); HEALTH CARE REFORMS GROUPS, N.Z. COMMUNICATIONS UNIT, HEALTH CARE REFORMS REPORT No. 9 (Apr. 29, 1992).

13. *See* Ham, *supra* note 12; THE BROOKINGS INSTITUTION, *supra* note 11.

14. KLEIN, *supra* note 1, at 81–82; *see also id.* at 102 n. 44.

for many years, and the majority of health care services in use have no proven scientific basis.[15]

The NHS is seen by many Americans as a socialized system of health care delivery. While it may be fun to use such rhetoric in the polemics of the political market place, it has little basis. Until recently there has been an implicit agreement, described by Rudolf Klein, between the doctors' trade union otherwise known as the British Medical Association (BMA) and the government that the BMA would not challenge on funding issues provided the government did not challenge on issues of clinical practice.[16] This concordat survived until the 1980s and meant that clinicians determined both who they treated and how.[17] This discretion remains even after a decade of Thatcherism and means that the freedom of UK clinicians is generally greater than that of their American peers working in a "free market."[18]

Clinical freedom in a broad sense is complemented in the NHS by poor data about costs. In the US there are price data (which do not reveal costs, of course!), but in the UK the finance systems until recently were designed solely to facilitate expenditure control and adherence to cash limited budgets; they were not designed to inform anyone about the cost of procedures.

This absence of cost data is accompanied by poor process data. There are many hospitals in the UK that still do not have efficient patient administration systems and, as a result, it is not easy to identify bed occupancy characteristics.[19] Until 1985 there was a national system of activity data—the hospital activity analysis. This was "redisor-

---

15. *See* Steve Iliffe & Ulrich Feudenstein, *Fundholding: From Solution to Problem: United Kingdom's NHS Funding Reforms*, 308 BRIT. MED. J. 3 (1994); Chris Ham, *Priority Setting in the NHS: Reports from Six Districts; The United Kingdom's National Health Service*, 307 BRIT. MED. J. 435 (1993).

16. KLEIN, *supra* note 1, at 16–17 (describing the origins of the National Health Service); *id.* at 22–23 (detailing BMA discontentment); *id.* at 23–24 (describing the history of Bevan's concessions to physicians in 1948); *id.* at 86–90 (detailing the 1966 compromise and the implementation of the "Family Doctor Charter").

17. *Id.* at 121.

18. SHIRLEY ROBIN LETWIN, THE ANATOMY OF THATCHERISM 216–19 (1992) (describing the "internal market" of the National Health Service).

19. *See* PAUL KIND, HOSPITAL DEATHS—THE MISSING LINK: MEASURING OUTCOME IN HOSPITAL ACTIVITY DATA 2–4 (University of York, Centre For Health Economics, Health Economic Consortium, Discussion Paper 44 1988) (describing the inadequacies of current data collection methods). *See also id.* at 1, 27 (further illustrating the impact of the lack of hospital outcome data).

ganized" in 1986 when the Korner information system was introduced, and as a result there have been no national data since![20]

The data from ad hoc studies show, as in the US from Wennberg's work, large variations in activity rates.[21] Some surgical activity data from McPherson's work are shown in Table 1. Remarkable variations exist, even for so-called "emergency" procedures such as appendectomy. A recent study of the use of diagnostic dilation and curettage ("D&C") in young women showed that D&C rates in England were over six times the US rate: a large proportion of this activity is believed to be ineffective.[22]

Table 1. Variations in surgical activity rate[23] (rate per 10,000 population—age and sex adjusted)

Procedure	Districts		Region	
	Low	High	Low	High
Hernias	10.0	20.0	8.5	14.5
Hemorrhoids	1.0	4.6	1.3	3.0
Prostatectomy	4.5	9.5	5.8	13.2
Cholecystectomy	7.0	11.0	5.7	9.7
Hysterectomy	7.5	15.0	18.1	28.7
Appendectomy	14.0	21.0	12.9	19.4
Tonsillectomy with and without adehoidectomy	7.5	27.5	14.0	25.0

Reviewing the effectiveness literature shows that not only do UK doctors "assault" young women with unnecessary D&C procedures, but they also "assault" young children with hearing loss and "glue ears."[24] It has been concluded that for the majority of patients

20. *Id.* at 1 ("there is little or no information on the impact of health care services on the health of individual patients or the community at large").

21. *See, e.g.,* John E. Wennberg, Jean L. Freeman & William J. Culp, *Are Hospital Services Rationed in New Haven or Over-Utilized in Boston?*, THE LANCET, May 23, 1987, at 1185–89 (1987).

22. *See* Angela Coulter, Anne Klassen, Ian Z. MacKenzie & Kim McPherson, *Diagnostic Dilation and Curettage: Is it Used Properly?*, 306 BRIT. MED. J. 236 (1993).

23. D. SANDERS, A. COULTER & K. MCPHERSON, VARIATIONS IN HOSPITAL ADMISSION RATES: A REVIEW OF THE LITERATURE, tbl. 3 (Project Paper 79, 1989).

24. Nick Freemantle et al., *The Treatment of Persistent Glue Ear*, EFFECTIVE HEALTH CARE, Bulletin No. 4, at A.1 at 2 (Centre for Health Economics

(*cont.*)

"watchful waiting" was the best treatment policy, since for many the hearing loss remedied itself.[25]

Another study by the same group has shown that the efficacy and acceptability of two competing medications for the depression are not statistically different.[26] However, the latest treatment (selective serotonin reuptake inhibitors: SSRIs) is up to thirty times more expensive but is growing in use due to strong marketing.[27] The SSRIs, unlike their rivals the tricyclics, are not toxic in overdose, but the cost of using SSRI to minimize suicide risks may imply a value of life of hundreds of thousands of pounds.[28] This may be an inefficient use of resources because the most cost-effective treatment may be tricyclics.

Table 2. Plausible sources of variation at different levels of aggregation[29]

Variation between	Morbidity	Supply	Clinical	Demand
GPs	S	O	L	S
Districts	M	M	L	S
Regions	L	L	S	M
Countries	L	L	L	L

L = large; M = medium; S = small; O = no effect relative to others in row.

The example of the shift in use from tricyclics to SSRIs based on the results of small studies and vigorous marketing by the industry demonstrates that clinical behavior can be changed quite rapidly with well-designed policies.[30] Often practice is very difficult to change as in

---

25. *Id.* I. 2 at 10.

26. *See* Freemantle et al., supra note 24 at D. 1 at 3–4. *See also* Fujian Song et al., *Selective Serotonin Reuptake Inhibitors: Meta-analysis of Efficacy and Acceptability*, 1215 BRIT. MED. J. 683 (1993); N. Freemantle et al., *The Treatment of Depression in Primary Care*, EFFECTIVE HEALTH CARE, Bulletin No. 5 (Center for Health Economics (York) and School of Public Health (Leeds) 1993).

27. Freemantle et al., *supra* note 26; *see also id.* at D. 12, 13 at 6.

28. *Id.* at D. 6 at 5.

29. Kim McPherson, *Why Do Variations Occur?*, in THE CHALLENGE OF MEDICAL PRACTICE VARIATIONS 29 (T.F. Anderson et al. eds., 1989).

30. *See supra* notes 26–28 and accompanying text.

the case of both glue ears and D&C interventions where these practices have been questioned before, but practices have been maintained. This outcome is due to the lack of attention to the issue of incentives.

In part, this is a function of the focus of the majority of the health care "actors" on spending and activity. It is unusual for clinicians in health systems to produce outcome data.[31] Indeed, it can be seen that throughout history "externals" to clinical practice (non-physicians or radical doctors) have sought to collect this data.

Saddam Hussein's ancestors argued:

> If a surgeon has made a deep incision in the body of a man with a lancet of bronze and saves the man's life, or has opened an abscess in the eye of a man and has saved his eye, he shall take 10 shekels of silver.
>
> If the surgeon has made a deep incision in the body of a man with his lancet of bronze and so destroys the man's eye, they shall cut off his forehand.[32]

A little more recently, the physician to the Prince of Wales wrote that:

> In order, therefore, to procure this valuable collection, I humbly propose, first of all, that three or four persons should be employed in the hospitals (and that without any ways interfering with the gentlemen now concerned), to set down the cases of the patients there from day to day, candidly and judiciously, without any regard to private opinions or public systems, and at the year's end publish these facts just as they are, leaving every one to make the best use he can for himself.[33]

Note that even in those days (over two hundred and sixty years ago) "the gentlemen now concerned" had to be placated!

By the nineteenth century, Thomas Wahley, the editor of *The Lancet* was arguing:

> All public institutions must be compelled to keep case-books and registers, on a uniform plan. Annual abstracts of the results must be

---

31. *See* KIND, *supra* note 19, at 1–5; Paul Kind, *Outcome Measurement Using Hospital Activity Data: Deaths Following Surgical Procedures*, 77 BRIT. J. SURGERY 1399 (1990).

32. STANLEY A. COOK, THE LAWS OF MOSES AND THE CODE OF HAMMURABI 246–47 (London 1903) (quoting §§ 215–218 of Hammurabi's Code).

33. FRANCES CLIFTON, THE STATE OF PHYSIC, ANCIENT AND MODERN, BRIEFLY CONSIDERED: WITH A PLAN FOR THE IMPROVEMENT OF IT (London, 1732).

published. The annual medical report of cases must embrace hospitals, lying-in hospitals, dispensaries, lunatic asylums and prisons.[34]

And this advocacy affected policy making. In 1844, the Lunacy Act required all public psychiatric hospitals to collect outcome data and distinguished "success" in three categories: dead, relieved and unrelieved.[35] This they did throughout the nineteenth century.[36]

It was this classification which Florence Nightingale adopted. She argued:

> I am fain to sum up with an urgent appeal for adopting this or some uniform system of publishing the statistical records of hospitals. There is a growing conviction that in all hospitals, even those which are best conducted, there is a great and unnecessary waste of life. . . .
>
> In attempting to arrive at the truth, I have applied everywhere for information, but in scarcely an instance have I been able to obtain hospital records fit for any purpose of comparison. If they could be obtained, they would enable us to decide many other questions besides the ones alluded to. They would show subscribers how their money was being spent, what amount of good was really being done with it, or whether the money was doing mischief rather than good.[37]

Despite this history of advocating the collection of outcome data, the practice is still unusual. Most NHS hospital activity systems aggregate discharges so that it is difficult to distinguish between "horizontal" (dead) and "vertical" (walking) discharges![38] Where data are available they show large variations in mortality[39] which have to be interpreted with care.

---

34. THE LANCET 650–51 (1841).

35. *See generally* Alison Patrucco Barnes, *The Randolph W. Thrower Symposium: Elder Law: Beyond Guardianship Reform: A Reevaluation of Autonomy and Beneficience for a System of Principled Decision-Making in Long Term Care*, 41 EMORY L. J. 633, 652 (1992). ("In the late 1800s, changes in society and treatment practices produced changes in the law. In England, the increasing use of institutional care led to passage of the Lunacy Act of 1890 which consolidated mental health legislation and attempted to limit the number of individuals subject to compulsory services by narrowing legal definitions and increasing legal barriers. For the first time, the treatment of the mentally ill was subject to legal constraints regardless of the need for property management.")

36. *Id.*

37. FLORENCE NIGHTINGALE, SOME NOTES ON HOSPITALS (3rd ed. 1863).

38. KIND, *supra* note 19, at 4–5; *see also id.* at 7.

39. *Id.* at 27 ("Differences in mortality rate may be accounted for, at least in part, if allowance is made for qualitative or quantitive variations in resources provided by Health Authorities"). *See also* Kind, *supra* note 31.

The major problem in determining treatment success is that there are few trial data to demonstrate effectiveness and cost-effectiveness. It is not unusual to select a therapeutic area (*e.g.*, rehabilitation or mental health) and from a literature search identify less than a dozen studies in total.[40] All too little has changed in the period since 1972 when it was argued that the majority of therapies had no proven scientific basis.[41] Victor Fuchs summarized the problem nicely arguing that 10% of health care expenditure damaged patients' health, 10% had no effect on health, and 80% of expenditure improved health.[42] The problem is, as Fuchs noted, that no one knows which therapies lie in the 10% and 80% categories.[43]

The principles of resource allocation which can be derived from legislation are not translated into practice in the NHS. Clinical autonomy in the NHS remains very strong and the Thatcher health care reforms have yet to impact significantly on inefficient practice and inefficient practitioners.[44]

III. RESOURCE ALLOCATION: THE PHYSICIANS' ROLE

John Hampton, a cardiologist, wrote over ten years ago that clinical freedom was dead if it meant the freedom to allocate resources regardless of its impact on the patient's health.[45] However, the translation of this principle, that care should be demonstrably cost-effective, into practice is difficult despite the articulate advocacy of leaders of medical opinion.[46] What are the prerequisites of the translation of the principles of resource allocation into efficient clinical practice?

---

40. *See, e.g.*, MIKE MCKENNA, ALAN MAYNARD & KEN WRIGHT, IS REHA-BILITATION COST EFFECTIVE? (University of York, Centre For Health Economics, Health Economics Consortium, Discussion Paper 101 1992); Owen O'Donnell, Alan Maynard & Ken Wright, *Evaluating Mental Health Care: The Role of Economics*, 1 J. MENTAL H. 39 (1992).

41. A.L. COCHRANE, EFFECTIVENESS AND EFFICIENCY 9 (1972) (referring to proof in the forum of data from randomized controlled trials).

42. Victor R. Fuchs, *The "Rationing" of Medical Care*, 311 NEW ENG. J. MED. 1572, 1573 (1984).

43. *Id.*

44. *See generally* LETWIN, *supra* note 18, at 199–227.

45. John R. Hampton, *The End of Clinical Freedom*, 287 BRIT. MED. J. 1237, 1237–38 (1983).

46. *See, e.g.*, BRYAN JENNETT, HIGH TECHNOLOGY MEDICINE: BENEFITS AND BURDENS 249–50 (1984).

The first step is to use the available literature to set standards or benchmarks of appropriate medical practice. This requires the "distilling" of the literature and its analysis by expert groups so as to identify indications for particular interventions. Some nice examples of this approach have been published by the Rand Corporation for therapeutic areas involving angioplasty, coronary artery bypass grafts, abdominal aortic aneurysm surgery and other areas.[47]

The definition of appropriateness benchmarks facilitates the investigation of practice; e.g., case notes and computer files can be interrogated to determine whether practice was appropriate. The results of this can be used to inform future practice via the processes of medical audit and management review. Such an investigative approach can identify inappropriate practice and avoidable deaths.[48]

Appropriateness defined as effective practice may not be cost-effective practice. This can be illustrated with a simple example: an elderly person with muscle pain due to rheumatism can use drug X which gives five hours of pain relief or drug Y which gives ten hours of pain relief. Drug Y is clearly more effective. However, if drug X costs 25 pence per dose and drug Y costs 120 pence per dose, and neither has any side effects, drug X is preferred as it is the most cost-effective: 5 pence per hour of pain relief from drug X as opposed to 12 pence per hour of pain relief from drug Y.

While the number of economic evaluations in health care is increasing exponentially,[49] their quality is uneven.[50] As a consequence while

---

47. L.H. HILBORNE ET AL., CORONARY ARTERY BYPASS GRAFT: A LITERATURE REVIEW AND RATINGS OF APPROPRIATENESS AND NECESSITY (1991); L.L. LEAPE ET AL., PERCUTANEOUS TRANSLUMINAL CORONARY ANGIOPLASTY: A LITERATURE REVIEW AND RATINGS OF APPROPRIATENESS AND NECESSITY (1991); D.J. BALLARD, ABDOMINAL AORTIC ANUERYSM SURGERY: A LITERATURE REVIEW AND RATINGS OF APPROPRIATENESS AND NECESSITY, Series JRA 04 (1992); D.B. MATCHER, CAROTID ENDATERECTOMY: A LITERATURE REVIEW AND RATINGS OF APPROPRIATENESS AND NECESSITY, Series JRA 05 (1992).

48. See, e.g., E.A. CAMPLING, H.B. DEVLIN & J.N. LUNN, THE REPORT OF THE NATIONAL CONFIDENTIAL INQUIRY INTO PERIOPERATIVE DEATHS (London 1990) (providing a description of the confidential enquiry into perioperative deaths ("GEPOP") carried out by the Royal College of Surgeons and the Association of Anaesthetists).

49. M.E. Backhouse et al., An Economic Evaluation Bibliography, 1 HEALTH ECON. 4 (Supp. 1992).

50. Standards of "good practice" to appraise such evaluation can be seen in Alan Williams, The Cost Benefits Approach, 30 BRIT. MED. BULL. 252–56 (1974);

effectiveness data are poor, the knowledge of cost-effectiveness is generally worse!

Yet, the physician is the key agent in resource allocation: it is she who determines access to care. In the NHS the general practitioner acts as the "gate-keeper" to the hospital system, both for diagnostics and for treatment.[51] The hospital consultant, and her firm of juniors, assess general practitioner referrals and offer advice and treatment as they judge appropriate.[52] The waiting list, approaching one million,[53] is used to ration access for non-emergency care, much of which is cost-effective. Emergency demands are met by open access and the "imperative of rescue" often leads to cost-ineffective interventions. Without guidelines of appropriateness, the clinician cannot resist patient and relatives' pressure to "do something" when a 76-year-old man appears in casualty with a bleeding tumor at 3:00 a.m.! The dictum of Florence Nightingale from the 1860s not "to strive officiously" to keep the patient alive[54] tends to be ignored!

Such responses are complicated by the agency relationship. It is argued that there is an asymmetry of information in the health care market such that the doctor is the expert with superior ability to diagnose, treat and predict the outcome of disease. As a consequence of this, the consumer, after making her initial decision to enter the health care market, delegates decision making to the "expert." Thus, the primary agent on the supply side of the market becomes the agent who makes demand-side decisions. If those decisions were based on the predicted marginal productivity of the intervention (the marginal effect), this agency relationship would produce efficient treatment patterns. However, if the doctor pursues other targets, such as income enhancement and empire building, resource allocation will be inefficient.

Many markets such as law, real estate and vehicle repair have some degree of asymmetry in information. After this problem has been

see also MICHAEL F. DRUMMOND, GREG L. STODDART & GEORGE W. TORRENCE, METHODS FOR THE ECONOMIC EVALUATION OF HEALTH CARE PROGRAMES (Oxford University Press 1987); Alan Maynard, *The Design of Future Cost–Benefit Studies*, 3 AM. HEALTH J. 761 (1990).

51. *See* LETWIN, *supra* note 18, at 214; *see also id.* at 217.

52. *See* KLEIN, *supra* note 1, at 44; *see also id.* at 113–14.

53. *Dr. Brian Mawhinney announces latest waiting time figures*, UK DEP'T OF HEALTH (Press Release) 94/218, May 6, 1994.

54. *See* NIGHTINGALE, *supra* note 37.

recognized by corporate attempts to control practices, these are often defeated by the self-interest of the regulated who capture it and use it to enhance their income and power: regulation favors the regulated.[55] These adverse effects can be dissipated by the production of knowledge to question practices and the creation of institutions (*e.g.*, health care purchasers in managed care) to challenge the corporations. However, both the creation of such competition and its sustainment are costly and difficult.

The problems created by agency relationships may be compounded with providers having an increasing commercial interest in the inflation of demand for health care. It has been argued that doctors "are not, and should not be businessmen," but that market reforms are forcing them to behave in this way.[56] The American Medical Association recognizes that problems exist when physicians own the medical facilities for whom they recruit patients.[57] Its Council on Ethical and Judgment Affairs recommended no referrals by physicians to self-owned facilities and that they should invest in facilities only if no alternative funding is available.[58]

The physicians' role in resource allocation is central. Typically, the physicians' scientific training is limited in terms of their capacity to question and evaluate existing practices. Medical schools tend to inculcate "facts," but place too little awareness on the experimental nature of practice and the shallow knowledge upon which it is established. They are exposed to strong pressure to treat because, although aware of the social perspective (*i.e.*, opportunity costs exist for all decisions), they are trained to treat the individual patient in front of them, with all the pressures created by the imperative of rescue.

While the profession has regulated itself extensively, those processes

---

55. G. Stigler, *The Theory of Regulation*, BELL J. ECON. & MGMT. SCI. 1, 3–21 (1971).

56. Arnold S. Relhman, *What Market Values are Doing to Medicine*, THE ATLANTIC MONTHLY, March 1992, at 98–106.

57. *See* Dana Priest, *AMA Delegates Spar Over Self-Referral*, WASH. POST, Dec. 7, 1992, at All; Dana Priest, *AMA Decrees 'Self-Referral' is Unethical*, WASH. POST, Dec. 9, 1992, at A1; *cf.* Brian McCormick, *AMA Reverses Self-referral Stance*, 35 AM. MED. NEWS 1, Dec. 21, 1992, ("In addition, delegates rescinded a six-month-old policy that conflicted with council's ethical stance. That policy said self-referral arrangements were ethical so long as referring physicians disclosed their investment interests and patients were informed of alternative sites for receiving care.").

58. *See* Council on Ethical & Judgment Affairs, *Conflicts of Interest: Physician Ownership of Medical Facilities*, 267 JAMA 2366, 2368 (1992).

are poorly informed by good science about costs and outcomes. All too often regulatory bodies such as the UK General Medical Council serve as a mechanism to discipline deviant practitioners who sleep with their patients, but do not address the issue of those physicians who are unusually successful in killing or disabling their patients! The UK Royal Colleges can, by withdrawing membership from practitioners, leave them unable to practice in the NHS, but this tends to be a discipline rarely used to control inefficient practitioners. Furthermore, any such discussions are conducted in secret, as was the CEPOD inquiry.[59]

The "managers" of institutions controlling the practice of medicine are seeking to change the ways in which medical activity is conducted. The speed with which they are changing is slow but not inconsiderable. However, the "market" is requiring non-clinical managers to move more rapidly and there are risks both of duplication and conflict, particularly with regard to the acquisition and use of data about clinical practice. Such "competition" may be harmful. The naïve belief that markets are primarily driven by greed and self-interest was refuted by the alleged creator of such arguments, Adam Smith, over 200 years ago:

> Those general rules of conduct when they have been fixed in our mind by habitual reflection, are of great use in correcting the misrepresentations of self-love concerning what is fit and proper to be done in our particular situation. . . . The regard of those general rules of conduct, is what is properly called a sense of duty, a principle of greatest consequence in human life, and the only principle by which the bulk of mankind are capable of directing their actions.[60]

If conflict develops about the governance of medicine in the managed care/internal markets in the 1990s, arguments about quality may lead to a deterioration in the physician–patient relationship. Traditionally, patients have believed physicians "do good."[61] If knowledge of practice variations, ineffective care and unproven practice spreads, and patients recognize the scope of physician-induced demand, there many be substantial effects on physician–patient relation-

---

59. CAMPLING, DEVLIN & LUNN, *supra* note 48. *See also* KLEIN, *supra* note 1, at 114 n.25 (describing the UK Royal Colleges).

60. ADAM SMITH, THE THEORY OF MORAL SENTIMENTS 160–62 (D.D. Raphael & A.L. Macfie eds., Oxford 1976).

61. *See* Victor R. Fuchs, *The Counterrevolution in Health Care Financing*, 316 NEW ENG. J. MED. 1154, 1155 (1987) ("Physicians have traditionally idealized the ethic of duty to their patients, and patients have derived considerable comfort from believing that physicians hold to this ethic").

ships and resource allocation, notably a reduction in the placebo effect created by, *inter alia*, physician trust![62] Trust that is merited, that is earned by the use of truth for those who wish to know, can create shared decision making which may improve the cost-effectiveness of medical practice.

For the "ideal" NHS to work efficiently, priorities must be determined by where the greatest improvements in caring and curing can be produced at the margin. Producers will judge the success of the NHS, in this ideal world, by their ability to produce cost-effective care.[63] To achieve this ideal, the knowledge base needs to be increased and the results of such evaluative work used by professional bodies, purchasers and providers to create a cost-effective health care system.

IV. CONCLUSION

The arguments in this article are in the utilitarian tradition favored by many economists. Implicit in these arguments has been an acceptance of the principle of justice of "equality of treatment for those who are in all relevant respects equal"[64] and the interpretation of need for treatment as the capacity of the patient to benefit at the margin.

The consequence of this is that those with limited capacity to benefit will be denied care. This may have unfortunate implications for groups who, for reasons such as genetic endowment, income, age and education, may have limited capacity to benefit. If society decides that it wishes to redistribute care to these needy groups, the opportunity costs of doing so will be apparent and this will enhance public debate and the accountability of policy makers.

An important problem in the discussion of resource allocation rules is, of course, the divergence between the principles which emerge after much debate, and their implementation. In the NHS, the rules implicit in legislation nearly fifty years ago still have little impact on decision making and market transactions. In the NHS there are regular "redis-organizations" to achieve the Holy Grail of efficiency, equity and

---

62. *See* PETER SKRABANEK & JAMES MCCORMICK, FOLLIES AND FALLACIES IN MEDICINE ch. 1 (1989).

63. MAYNARD & WILLIAMS, *supra* note 5, at 5.

64. J.M. Stanley, *Developing Guidelines for Decisions to Forgo Life Prolonging Medical Treatment*, J. MED. ETHICS, Supp. 1992, at 18.

justice, but all too often rhetoric dominates substance just as in the time of the Emperor Nero:

> We trained very hard, but it seemed that every time we were beginning to form up into teams, we would be reorganized. I was to learn later in life that we tend to meet any new situation by reorganizing, and a wonderful method it can be for creating the illusion of progress, while producing confusion, inefficiency and demoralization.[65]

---

65. Caius Petronius, AD 66, quoted in Kevin Townsend, *New Zealand: Study Finds "Illusion of Progress"—Health*, N.Z. HERALD, Feb. 11, 1993.

Legal issues arising out of medical provision for ethnic groups*

David Pearl

I. INTRODUCTION

The black and ethnic minorities[1] now account for approximately 6.2% of the population of the United Kingdom (UK),[2] and it is interesting

---

* I should like to thank Mr. F.J. Holding of the School of Law, University of East Anglia for his critical comments on a draft of this article.

1. This article is not concerned with the difficult problem of the definition of an ethnic group. Such issues create major problems in the race relations field; for example, it has now been held by the UK. Court of Appeal that Rastafarians do not form "a separate ethnic group for the purposes of the Race Relations Act of 1976" and therefore "a Rastafarian who was denied a job as a van driver because he wore his hair long and refused to cut it had not been the victim of racial discrimination as defined in the Act." Paul Magrath, *Law Report: Rastafarians Not an Ethnic Group*, THE INDEPENDENT (London), Feb. 16, 1993, at 22 (reporting on Dawkins v. Department of the Env't Sub nom Crown Suppliers PSA, [1993] I.C.R. 517 (Eng. C.A.). *See also* Mandla (Sewa Singh) v. Dowell Lee, [1983] 2 A.C. 548 (Eng.).

2. UK DEP'T OF HEALTH, ON THE STATE OF THE PUBLIC HEALTH: THE ANNUAL REPORT OF THE CHIEF MEDICAL OFFICER OF THE DEPARTMENT OF HEALTH FOR THE YEAR 1992, at 139 (HMSO 1993). The proportions of the population of the UK by ethnic group are generally stated to be as follows: White 93.81%; Black (Caribbean/African/Other) 1.86%; Indian/Pakistani/Bangladeshi 3.05%; Chinese/Other Asian 0.70%; All Others 0.58%. *Id.* at 139, 140 tbl. 5.2. The 1991 census reveals just under 3 million people from minority ethnic groups. *Id.* at 140 tbl. 5.2.

Justice and Health Care: Comparative Perspectives. Edited by A. Grubb and M.J. Mehlman. © 1995 John Wiley & Sons Ltd.

to observe that for the first time, the Chief Medical Officer has included a chapter on the "Health and Black and Ethnic Minorities" in his Annual Report for 1991.[3]

It is perhaps not surprising that no detailed analysis has been made hitherto of the health problems, defined in the context of Western medicine, of ethnic groups. After all, it was only in 1991 that the Census of Population included a question on ethnic group of the respondents.[4] It is hoped, perhaps a little over-optimistically, that this information will provide more accurate information about the numbers of Blacks and ethnic minorities in the UK. Previous censuses failed to collect similar information and the question on "country of birth" in the 1971 and 1981 censuses was obviously of only limited value to demographers and policy makers.

An important consideration for policy makers in the health service is that the regional distribution of ethnic minorities should be understood. There are many reasons why particular communities have chosen to congregate in certain parts of the country.[5] It is of interest that the Chief Medical Officer himself is aware that these "variations, together with religious and cultural differences, are taken into account when considering the health care needs of a local population."[6]

There is clear evidence of prevalence of particular diseases usually associated with diet, such as non-insulin-dependent diabetes mellitus and coronary heart disease among certain ethnic groups, including both Asians and Caribbeans. Medical literature suggests that one reason for

---

3. UK DEP'T OF HEALTH, ON THE STATE OF THE PUBLIC HEALTH: THE ANNUAL REPORT OF THE CHIEF MEDICAL OFFICER OF THE DEPARTMENT OF HEALTH FOR THE YEAR 1991, at 54 ch. 3 (HMSO 1992) [hereinafter CHIEF MEDICAL OFFICER 1991].

4. See Mark R.D. Johnson, A Question of Ethnic Origin in the 1991 Census, 19 NEW COMMUNITY 281–89 (1993) (discussing the background leading to the eventual acceptance of an "ethnic question" in the 1991 census).

5. See generally Verity S. Khan, The Pakistanis: Mirpuri Villagers at Home and in Bradford, in BETWEEN TWO CULTURES (James L. Watson ed., 1977). For example, the former mill towns of northwest England held a powerful attraction to the early settlers from the subcontinent once employed in similar activities at home. P. Werbner, From Rags to Riches: Manchester Pakistanis in the Textile Trade, 8 NEW COMMUNITY 84–95 (1980).

6. CHIEF MEDICAL OFFICER 1991, supra note 3, at 56.

7. See CHIEF MEDICAL OFFICER 1991, supra note 3, at 65, 66 (citing P.M. McKeigue et al., Coronary Heart Disease in South Asians Overseas: A Review, 42 J. CLINICAL EPIDEMIOLOGY 597 (1989)). See also R. Balrajan, Ethnic Differences

this prevalence is that a central distribution of body fat is a characteristic particular to Asians.[7]

One must accept at the outset the resource implications for the
Health Service for adopting a proactive policy in this area. In the
support context, provision for translation services[8] and special dietary
advice[9] are but two examples of labour intensive activities which need
to be provided by certain health authorities.

Equally important, and perhaps of major consequence for medical
lawyers, are the ethical questions which emerge on a fairly frequent
basis. Some of these dilemmas have been resolved, at least from the
legal perspective, by a process of criminalization. For example, the
Prohibition of Female Circumcision Act 1985[10] provides a legal
framework within which the practice of female circumcision, excision
and infibulation, which is practiced in certain parts of Africa and Arab
countries, has been made the subject of criminal sanction if performed
in the UK.[11] However, the response of individual health care workers
to that practice still requires a sensitive and informed appraisal by
Ethical Committees.

Thus, this article is concerned with two interconnected issues. First,
the article will consider the questions relating to the provision of health
services to ethnic minorities. Secondly, the article will consider ethical

---

in *Mortality from Ischaemic Heart Disease and Cerebrovascular Disease in England and
Wales*, 302 BRIT. MED. J. 560 (1991) (illustrating that Caribbeans have a higher
rate of hypertension and stroke).

8. In a different context, a Nuffield Foundation report identifies an alarming
lack of properly qualified interpreters in the courts which puts non-English
speakers at risk of injustice. *See* Scrivenor, *Lost for Words*, TIMES (London), Feb.
9, 1993.

9. CHIEF MEDICAL OFFICER 1991, *supra* note 3, at 75 (referring to the need
to make dietary messages include examples from the diet of the community
being addressed). *See* HIGHER EDUCATION AUTHORITY, ENJOY HEALTHY
EATING: AN INDEPENDENT INTRODUCTION TO FOOD AND HEALTH (London
1991).

10. *See generally* SEBASTIAN M. POULTER, ENGLISH LAW AND ETHNIC MI-
NORITY CUSTOMS 152, 156–60 (Desmond de Silva ed., 1986).

11. Prohibition of Female Circumcision Act 1985, ch. 38, § 1(1) (Eng.) It is
"[a]n offence for any person—(a) to excise, infibulate or otherwise mutilate the
whole or any part of the labia majora or labia minora or clitoris of another
person; or (b) to aid, abet, counsel or procure the performance by another
person of any of those acts on that other person's own body". *Id. See generally*
K. Hayter, *Female Circumcision—Is there a Legal Solution?*, 1984 J. Soc. WELFARE
L. 323.

questions which are either peculiar to the ethnic minorities or are of frequent occurrence in that context. Overriding both questions, of course, is the important resource question.

II. THE PROVISION OF HEALTH SERVICES

The evidence supporting the statement that the ethnic minority population is not as healthy as the indigenous population is overwhelming. The Chief Medical Officer in his report for 1991 identifies an excess coronary heart disease mortality in those born in the Indian subcontinent of 36% for men and 46% for women aged 20–29 compared with the rate for England and Wales as a whole.[12] This statistical data is based on a study of the period 1979 to 1983.[13] There is clear evidence in the literature that those figures will rise further as a result of demographic changes.[14]

The Chief Medical Officer identifies high ethnic data which is no less worrying, for example rubella infections in pregnancy,[15] tuberculosis[16] and hepatitis B.[17] It is well known that inherited blood diseases, especially sickle cell disease, primarily affect the Afro-Caribbean community.[18] The number of people with the sickle cell disorder, estimated to be about five thousand,[19] hides the fact that there is a larger number

---

12. CHIEF MEDICAL OFFICER 1991, *supra* note 3, at 64.

13. Balarajan, *supra* note 7, at 562.

14. A.G. Lowy et al., *The Effects of Demographic Shift on Coronary Heart Disease Mortality in a Large Migrant Population at High Risk*, 13 J. PUB. HEALTH MED. 276, 279 (1991). *See also* UK DEP'T OF HEALTH, THE HEALTH OF THE NATION: A CONSTRUCTIVE DOCUMENT FOR HEALTH IN ENGLAND 57–59 (1991).

15. In England in 1991, there were only 16 rubella infections in pregnancy, but six of these (or 37%) were in Asian women. CHIEF MEDICAL OFFICER 1991, *supra* note 3, at 66 (stating that the promotion of selective rubella immunization in the Asian community needs to be continued).

16. Here again the data is worrying. In the first six months of 1988, nearly 40% of the patients notified as having tuberculosis ('TB') were of Indian, Pakistani or Bangladeshi origin. *Id.* at 67. Even more troublesome is the observation that the decline of TB notifications from these groups is less than that recorded in the White population where the rate of infection is 25 times lower. *Id.*

17. *Id.*

18. *Id.* at 68.

19. *Id.* (citing M. Brozovic et al., *Acute Admission of Patients with Sickle Cell Disease Who Live in Britain*, 294 BRIT. MED. J. 1206 (1987); Ass'n for Consumer Research, *Sickle Cell Disease and the Non-Specialist*, 27 DRUG THERAPY BULL. 9 (1989)).

with the trait. Thus, there are considerable risks in pregnancy, and screening programs have been instituted for all neonates in certain health authorities in areas with a large concentration of Afro-Caribbeans.[20] The Chief Medical Officer reports also on the questions relating to mental health, diabetes mellitus, cancer,[21] osteoporosis and perinatal mortality rates.[22] In all these cases, the position is less than satisfactory, especially when it is realized that the ethnic minority population is concentrated in particular urban areas.

The UK government itself is concerned by these findings and is now beginning to develop health promotion strategies.[23] The Chief Medical Officer identifies "two major elements."[24] The first element is to ensure that Black and ethnic minorities "understand the health service, what it offers, and when and how they can use it."[25] Particular concerns appear in an article written on behalf of a Community Care project in the Central Birmingham Health Authority.[26] It states: "From the Asian person's perspective, services are inaccessible. We have seen that many are not told about services. The services on offer are often not

---

20. *See* CHIEF MEDICAL OFFICER 1991, *supra* note 3, at 68 (reporting that the Standing Medical Advisory Committee has established a Working Party to look at the clinical management of sickle cell disease).

21. M.G. MARMOT ET AL., IMMIGRANT MORTALITY IN ENGLAND AND WALES 1970–78: CAUSES OF DEATH BY COUNTRY OF BIRTH 35–36, 38 (London HMSO 1984) (stating that the standardized mortality ratio is low for breast cancer and cervical cancer among persons of Indian origin, and high for cancers of the gall bladder among the Caribbean and Indian communities); R.M. Barker & M.R. Baker, *Incidence of Cancer in Bradford Asians*, 44 J. EPIDEMIOLOGY COMMUNITY HEALTH 125, 125–29 (1990).

22. CHIEF MEDICAL OFFICER 1991, *supra* note 3, at 68–71.

23. Baroness Cumberlidge has been given a special responsibility for ethnic health. She is reported to have said: "We are finding that people with ethnic minority backgrounds do not get the full benefit of NHS services. We are not saying 'you have to conform.' We are saying 'please can you tell us how to help you access the services.'" Celia Hall, *NHS to Act on Unequal Service to Minorities*, THE INDEPENDENT (London), Dec. 29, 1992, at 4. A task force has been established to examine existing good practices in health care delivery to ethnic minorities and on January 6, 1993, the health minister arranged the first conference on the subject with ethnic group leaders. *Id. See generally* ACCESS TO HEALTH CARE FOR PEOPLE FROM BLACK AND ETHNIC MINORITIES 1–20 (Anthony Hopkins and Veena Bahl eds., 1993) [hereinafter ACCESS TO HEALTH CARE].

24. CHIEF MEDICAL OFFICER 1991, *supra* note 3, at 73–74.

25. *Id.* at 73.

26. K. Atkin et al., *Asian Elders' Knowledge and Future Use of Community Social and Health Services*, 15 NEW COMMUNITY 439 (1989).

appropriate and generally not geared to ethnic minority people's needs."[27] The second element is to ensure that all health services are appropriate to the health care needs of the local population, including the black and ethnic minority community, and to ensure that these services are delivered in a culturally sensitive manner.[28] A particularly important initiative is the establishment of Services in Health and Race Exchange ("SHARE") by the King's Fund Center to serve as a resource and information center for black and ethnic minority communities and organizations working with these groups.[29]

These statements of intent by the Chief Medical Officer, together with the type of initiative represented by SHARE, are of course all positive indicators. Another important development is the invitation on hospital admission forms to identify patients by ethnic group. This practice was initiated in April 1993.

However, lawyers still have reason to view with some concern aspects of the provision of health care to the ethnic communities.

The question which must be addressed is whether the wider community is ready, through its resource provision, to allocate additional provision for the health needs of the ethnic minorities in the UK. Continuing evidence of discrimination within the criminal justice system has led to the enactment of Section 95 of the Criminal Justice Act 1991.[30] Section 95 states: "The Secretary of State shall in each year publish such information as he considers expedient for the purpose of ... (b) facilitating the performance by such persons of their duty to avoid discriminating against any such persons on the ground of race or sex or any other improper ground."[31]

The first official report has now been published.[32] A similar provision is lacking in any recent legislation on the health service. District Health Authorities are required under the National Health Service and Community Care Act 1990 to carry out "needs assessments" in their areas.[33] This will enable health planners to identify areas of need, but there is still no specific provision in the Act to identify the special health needs of the ethnic groups. Yet, if there is evidence that the

---

27. *Id.* at 443.

28. CHIEF MEDICAL OFFICER 1991, *supra* note 3, at 73–74.

29. *See* CHIEF MEDICAL OFFICER 1991, *supra* note 3, at 74.

30. ch. 53 (Eng.)

31. Criminal Justice Act 1991, § 95(1).

32. KENNETH CLARKE, UK HOME OFFICE, RACE AND THE CRIMINAL JUSTICE SYSTEM (HMSO, 1992).

33. National Health Service and Community Care Act 1990, ch. 19 (Eng.).

ethnic minority population is not as healthy as the indigenous population, a strong case could be made for the enactment of a provision similar to Section 95 of the Criminal Justice Act 1991.

Is there, at the present time, a frame within which the law can provide, either on an individualized basis or as part of a wider group action, additional resources for certain sections of our community? Lawyers need to know whether there is a legal framework within which to begin to address the disturbing facts highlighted in this article. Comparisons, of course, should be made with the position in the US where the argument has been made that its health care system fails to provide for the needs of Afro-Americans.[34]

The Chief Medical Officer identified a number of possible positive actions that should be taken to prevent discrimination in the delivery of services:

- Appropriate diet, such as Halal meat or vegetarian meals.
- Respect and facilities for religious observance and access by spiritual advisers, such as imams, pandits etc.
- Ready availability of women doctors for women patients.
- Ready availability of link workers, interpreters and advocates.
- Information in black and ethnic minority languages.
- Respect for the patient's standards of dignity and privacy, for example the provision of long nightdresses, long-sleeved clothing etc.[35]

It might be thought that these are actions which can be initiated without any difficulty or major cost.[36] Of course, all initiatives have a resource implication, and Health Authorities' purchasing plans reflect the priorities which are communicated to them in a number of ways, including community pressure. Sadly, there are clear indications that budgetary constraints have produced reductions in what can be perceived as "peripheral services."[37] Competition for resources within

---

34. *See* Vernellia R. Randall, *Racist Health Care: Reforming an Unjust Health Care System to Meet the Needs of African-Americans*, 3 HEALTH MATRIX 127, 131–32 (1994) (arguing that health reform in America should ensure complete access and eliminate institutional racism to provide just health care for African-Americans). Reproduced in this volume at p. 147.

35. CHIEF MEDICAL OFFICER 1991, *supra* note 3, at 73 tbl. 3.7.

36. *See* Jay Ogden, *Seasoned Workers*, SOCIAL WORK TODAY, Feb. 20, 1992, at 18 (describing the provision of Halal food and other special food to the ethnic elderly in Birmingham); G. KARMI, LONDON: NORTH WEST & NORTH EAST THAMES REGIONAL HEALTH AUTHORITY, THE ETHNIC HEALTH FACTFILE (1992).

37. In 1992, the Government gave only £500,000 towards help in this area. ACCESS TO HEALTH CARE, *supra* note 23, at 7.

"types of injury," for example spinal injury as opposed to head injury, and within "types of patients," for example young patients as opposed to old patients, is almost certainly going to result in a further marginalization of ethnic minority needs. It must be observed that few Health Authorities have made much progress on developing procedures to ensure that their new contracts will improve the delivery of services to ethnic minorities.[38]

One can predict a future case where a Health Authority fails to provide Halal meat, for example, and an action is brought to court by an aggrieved individual or individuals to force the particular Health Authority to make such provision. One must assume that such an action is likely to be faced with the immediate difficulty that a court would consider such issues as being insusceptible to legal control, bearing as they do on resource allocation.

Similar issues were raised in *R. v. Secretary of State for Social Services, ex parte Hincks*,[39] *R. v. Central Birmingham Health Authority, ex parte Walker*[40] and *R. v. Central Birmingham Health Authority, ex parte Collier*.[41] In all three cases, the courts declined to intervene. As Sir John Donaldson MR said in *Central Birmingham Health Authority, ex parte Walker*:

> This court could only intervene where it was satisfied that there was a prima facie case, not only of failing to allocate resources in the way in which others would think that resources should be allocated, but of a failure to allocate resources to an extent which was *Wednesbury* unreason-

---

38. For a detailed and informed discussion, see Mark R.D. Johnson, *Chartering for Black Citizens' Rights*, 18 NEW COMMUNITY 316, 317 (1992). However, notwithstanding a generally negative report, Johnson does state that some action is now being taken in some authorities to examine what the specific service delivery needs of minorities might be and "to write those rights and legitimate expectations into the contracts." *Id.* Johnson cites as an example the "King's Fund project to promote ethnic sensitivity in contracting with Coventry H[ealth] A[uthority]." *Id.*

39. [1980] 1 B.L.M.R. 93 (Eng. C.A.), *available in* LEXIS, Enggen library, Cases file (involving orthopedic patients at a hospital in Birmingham who had waited for treatment for periods longer than was medically advisable). *See also* IAN KENNEDY & ANDREW GRUBB MEDICAL LAW 387–89, 423–26 (1994).

40. 1987 3 B.L.M.R. 32 (Eng. C.A. Nov. 25, 1987), *available in* LEXIS, Enggen library, Cases file (where health authority lacked sufficient resources to carry out an operation on a "hole in the heart" baby). *See also* Craig Seton, *Heart Baby's Surgery Success*, TIMES (London), Nov. 26, 1987 at 1, 44.

41. (Eng. C.A. Jan. 6, 1988) (LEXIS, Enggen library, Cases file) (concerning a "hole in the heart" baby). *See also* KENNEDY & GRUBB, *supra* note 39, at 428–29 (discussing the case).

able, . . . , or, in simpler words, which involves a breach of a public law duty. . . .[42] Even then, of course, the court has to exercise a judicial discretion. It has to take account of all the circumstances of a particular case with which it is concerned.[43]

A private negligence action is also almost certainly bound to fail on similar public policy considerations. In *Knight v. Home Office*,[44] Mr. Justice Pill said, "In making the decision as to the standard [of care] to be demanded the court must, however, bear in mind as one factor that the resources available for the public service are limited and that the allocation of resources is a matter for Parliament."[45]

However, it is at least arguable that both a public law action directed against a Health Authority and a private negligence claim could succeed in certain situations. The germ for a legal assault in this area is obtained from a fascinating case, *R. v. Ethical Committee of St. Mary's Hospital Ex Parte H.*[46] This case concerned a very different factual situation from the one under discussion. A decision by the ethical advisory committee of the hospital to support the doctors' refusal to provide in-vitro fertilization (IVF) treatment was unsuccessfully challenged on judicial review.[47] The plaintiff had been rejected by the local Social Services Department as a prospective adopter and as a foster mother because she had previous criminal convictions for prostitution.[48] The judge found that the grounds considered by the ethical committee for regarding her to be unsuitable were reasonable.[49] However, in the

---

42. *See* Associated Provincial Picture Houses, Ltd. v. Wednesbury Corp., [1947] 2 All E.R. 680 (Eng. K.B.) (holding that under a review of reasonableness a court is only entitled to investigate the actions of local executive authorities "with a view to seeing whether it has taken into account or . . . has neglected to take into account matters which ought to be taken into account").

43. *Central Birmingham Health Authority, ex parte Walker. Id.*

44. [1990] 3 All E.R. 237 (Eng. Q.B.).

45. *Id.* at 243. *But cf.* Law Reform (Personal Injuries) Act 1948, 11 & 12 Geo. 6, ch. 41, § 2(4) (Eng.) ("In an action for damages for personal injuries (including any such action arising out of a contract), there shall be disregarded, in determining the reasonableness of any expenses, the possibility of avoiding those expenses or part of them by taking advantage of facilities available under the National Health Service Act, 1946, or the National Health Service (Scotland) Act, 1947, or of any corresponding facilities in Northern Ireland.").

46. [1988] 1 Fam. L.R. 512 (Eng. Q.B.), *available in* LEXIS, Enggen Library, Cases file.

47. *Id.*

48. *Id.*

49. *Id.*

course of the judgment, the judge did say that if the IVF treatment had been refused for a wholly irrational reason, for example if the couple were Black or Jewish, then such a refusal should have been struck down by a review court as unlawful.[50] Thus, the refusal of treatment on non-medical grounds is clearly reviewable by a court. As one commentator has said in connection with this case, "A patient denied renal dialysis or surgery because the consultant in charge refused to treat divorced people or Labour Party members might well have a remedy."[51]

This hypothetical illustration enables us to construct the parameters of a legal framework which in effect provides the Health Authority with broad discretion in the medical field. This enables it to take into account resource implications which are unchallengeable in a court, but which refuse to allow wholly irrational decisions.

The difficulty of such a model, of course, is simply that it leaves too much to chance. Discrimination is often not openly acknowledged. When it is, it can be dealt with by current legislation. More difficult to deal with is the attempt to tackle the different health needs of the ethnic minorities.[52] In this context, the law operates perhaps only at the margins.

III. ETHNIC MINORITIES AND ETHICS OF MEDICINE

The following advertisement appeared in the *Law Society Gazette* for January 27, 1993:

Transcultural Medicine

Medical Practitioner specializing in Transcultural Medicine (dealing with patients from different cultural, religious, and ethnic background) available to assist in relevant cases.

---

50. *Id.*

51. MARGARET BRAZIER, MEDICINE, PATIENTS AND THE LAW 23 (1992).

52. *See* Kamila Hawthorne, *Asian Diabetics Attending a British Hospital Clinic: A Pilot Study to Evaluate Their Care*, 40 BRIT, J. GEN. PRAC. 243 (1990). In addition, it is also important to identify some disturbing evidence of discrimination within the health service with respect to the recruitment and employment of health personnel. *See* CRE INVESTIGATION INTO THE REORGANIZATION AND REGRADING OF NURSING (1992).

A number of issues are raised when considering this and similar advertisements appearing elsewhere. First and foremost, it is necessary to consider exactly what is meant by "transcultural medicine." Presumably, the writer of the advertisement is offering to provide alternatives to Western medicine, perhaps the "traditional" medicines such as Ayurvedic, Chinese, or at least offering information to respondents on where such alternative medicines can be obtained. Does the phrase suggest, for example, that certain medical-cosmetics such as "surma"[53] will be available by the process of a single telephone call?

The Chief Medical Officer in his Report for 1991 identifies the necessity for health professionals to be aware that some Black and other ethnic minority patients will be using "alternative medicines" as well as, or as a substitute for those prescribed.[54]

Practitioners of alternative methods of treatment are not registered under or regulated by the Medical Act 1983[55] and alternative medicines are not registered under the Medicines Act 1968.[56] Thus, a practitioner of alternative medicines cannot call himself a medical doctor, and anyone who "wilfully[57] or falsely pretends to be or takes or uses"[58] that name is committing a criminal offence under Section 49(1) of the Medical Act 1983. However, the existence of alternative medicine provides a hidden dimension to the provision of health care in the UK for members of the ethnic minority groups, and it is as well that this dimension is understood. At the present time, this provision is unregulated and not susceptible to any control by the professional bodies or any other institutional framework. There is certainly a case

---

53. "*Surma*" is "a fine powder which looks rather like mascara, but instead of being applied to the outside of the eyelids it is painted on to the conjunctival surfaces of the eye. From there it is washed by tears from the eyes, swallowed through the back of the throat and hence absorbed into the blood. Asian parents appear to be applying it . . . to the children's eyes not only for cosmetic purposes but also to relieve eye-strain and soreness, as well as to ward off evil spirits. . . . [*S*]*urma* . . . often contains lead sulphide . . . [and] [n]umerous children are being admitted to hospitals every year suffering from lead poisoning as a result of using [*surma*]". POULTER, *supra* note 10, at 287–88.

54. *See, e.g.*, David & Leslie, *Eastern Treatment and Eastern Health*, 6 J. COMMUNITY NURSING 16 (1979).

55. ch. 54 (Eng.).

56. ch. 67 (Eng.).

57. Wilson v. Inyang, [1951] 2 K.B. 799, 804 (Eng.) (holding that an African did not wilfully use the title because he honestly held the belief that he could call himself "Naturopath Physician, N.D., M.R.D.P.").

58. Medical Act 1983, § 49(1).

for the suggestion that such practitioners should be controlled by some regulatory provision. Notwithstanding a certain level of apprehension, it is thought that the understanding of the alternative methods of treatment will have a more positive effect on the health of the ethnic minorities than any insensitive attempt to undermine the efficacy of such alternatives. At one level, of course, there is here an important principle of the freedom for individuals to attempt alternative cures, if they so wish, to those available in Western medicine.

It is obviously true that some "traditional" remedies may be injurious to health, including as mentioned earlier the toxicity of "surma."[59] For example, it has been argued that the paramount concern is the health of society as a whole and therefore the State is under a duty "to intervene in the public interest."[60]

In this context there is a particular problem surrounding the use of certain drugs such as cannabis which are illegal at the present time. Such use is often portrayed as ethnic-based, in particular, among West Indian Rastafarians who use it for religious and medicinal reasons.[61] Cannabis is a controlled drug whose use was criminalized under the provisions of the Misuse of Drugs Act 1971.[62]

Attention must be directed also to so-called "cannabis psychosis." Black support groups say that labelling certain mental disorders as being brought about by "cannabis psychosis" is an easy option for diagnostic difficulties in relation to the mental health problems of Black patients. Thus, the argument goes, psychiatrists in particular look no further than cannabis smoking as a cause for mental disturbance among young Black Rastafarians.[63] From the legal perspective, there is necessarily an identification with psychiatrists who follow this approach. Yet, such simplistic and all-embracing attitudes may well hide other expla-

---

59. *See supra* note 53; Ali, Smales & M. Aslam, *Surma and Lead Poisoning*, 2 BRIT. MED. J. 915 (1978); M. Aslam, S.S. Davis & M.A. Healy, *Heavy Metals in Some Asian Medicines and Cosmetics*, 93 PUB. HEALTH (London) 274 (1979).

60. POULTER, *supra* note 10, at 287.

61. Some doctors, such as Joycelyn Elders the Surgeon General of the US, have gone on record as saying that they will back the medical use of cannabis, especially in relieving pain in relation to patients with cancer, AIDS and Multiple Sclerosis. *See, e.g., Health: Cannabis: Why Doctors Want It to be Legal*, THE INDEPENDENT (London), Feb. 23, 1993, at 14.

62. ch. 38 (Eng.).

63. *See* Chris Ranger, *Race, Culture and the 'Cannabis Psychosis': The Role of Social Factors in the Construction of a Disease Category*, 15 NEW COMMUNITY 357, 360 (1989).

nations which still require research and analysis. It is too easy to erect a concept of a "cannabis psychosis" for an illness which is not easily understood. It is almost certainly dangerous to stereotype illness on the basis of race in this context.

Other practices have been criminalized. For instance, attention already has been given to outlawing the practice of female circumcision through the Prohibition of Female Circumcision Act 1985. Not all commentators welcome such interventions. For example, one writer in an article published in 1984 prior to the legislation prohibiting female circumcision, but during a period of intense media coverage of this issue, identified the dilemma when he wrote:

> Purely elective cosmetic surgery is an obvious case where the right of the individual to consent to treatment is not seriously questioned. Breast reduction, for example, is an unnecessary and mutilating operation involving considerable pain and scarring for the patient. If justification for its performance were called for, medical evidence of anxiety and depression brought on by the woman's dissatisfaction with her body would undoubtedly be sufficient to outweigh the injury inherent in the treatment.... Precisely the same justification would be pleaded in support of the legality of female circumcision and should, by analogy, in the absence of further justification for its prohibition, be sufficient. In both cases the women's perception of themselves reflects the demands of the social group to which they belong. This justification is the greater in the case of female circumcision where its necessity extends beyond mere aesthetic appeal, being crucial to the women's status with the group.[64]

One may seriously challenge the analogy with breast reduction or enhancement. Such cosmetic surgery is usually a matter of free choice, whereas female circumcision is imposed on young girls by their elders. However, there is some strength in what the writer implied in the above comment for one should not underestimate societal pressures on some women to conform to stereotypes. One must consider what lies ahead for the girls who are not circumcised in accordance with their community practices.

The writer's argument could, of course, also be used to justify other "marginal" activities such as the acceptance of "gender selection,"[65] yet here again the perceived advantage of such a procedure in certain

---

64. Hayter, *supra* note 11, at 325.

65. A private member's bill outlawing such activities was defeated in the House of Commons, Feb. 23, 1993. Children (Prohibition of Sex Selection) Bill 1993, Hansard, 219 H.C. Official Report col. 769–772.

sections of the community might be tested against the ethical values to be adopted by society as a whole in this controversial area.

Another topical illustration of the same dilemma, but going beyond simple questions relating to ethnic groups so as to include religious minorities, is the issue of autonomy in medical decision making. This problem is most acute in relation to attempts to provide blood transfusions for Jehovah's Witnesses or "Born Again" Christians and their children, some of whom are followers of the fundamentalist approach to the sanctity of blood.[66] There have been a number of recent instances where members of the Jehovah's Witnesses have bled to death after hemorrhaging during a routine operation where the doctor is aware of the patient's view on blood transfusions but the patient's religious beliefs prevented the patient from having transfusions.[67]

Thus, the question of diverse medical practices raises ethical questions regarding self-determination and autonomy together with critical questions of resources.[68]

IV. CONCLUSIONS

We return to the dominant question identified in this article, namely that of resources. The current ideology in the UK places on budget-holders the primary responsibility to ensure that resources are used in accordance with the priorities laid down by the budget-holder in question. This is as true of health providers as it is of education providers or any other provider of services. This Thatcherite ideology

---

66. *See Re* T, [1992] 4 All E.R. 649 (Eng. C.A.) (holding that T did not give consent due to her medical condition and that her mother had undue influence in T's decision to refuse a blood transfusion); *Re* S, [1992] 4 All E.R. 671, 672 (Eng. Fam.) (declaring "that a Caesarian section and any necessary consequential treatment which the hospital and its staff proposed to perform on the patient was in the vital interests of the patient and her unborn child and could be lawfully performed despite the patient's refusal to give her consent"). *See generally* Andrew Grubb, *Treatment Decisions: Keeping It in the Family*, in CHOICES AND DECISIONS IN HEALTH CARE 37 (Andrew Grubb ed., 1993).

67. *See, e.g., Woman Dies*, THE INDEPENDENT (London), Feb. 5, 1993, at 2 (reporting that a Jehovah's Witness died because she refused to have a blood transfusion after suffering a hemorrhage during a routine operation).

68. For example, in relation to blood substitutes, there is no doubt that the alternatives, which are available, are likely to be substantially more expensive than blood or blood products themselves.

inevitably makes minority groups and interests more vulnerable than they would be if services were based solely on needs. Inevitably ethnic groups' needs are marginalized within such an environment; however, it is to the law that such groups turn in the extreme situations. Judicial review procedures require refinement to enable class actions to be more readily available; *locus standi* rules need to be reappraised, and strategies similar to Section 95 of the Criminal Justice Act 1991 need to be introduced into the health arena. The law must learn to be more proactive, since at the present time there has been little legal activity in this arena. The message is simple: there is plenty for law and lawyers to do.

Index

significant risk
  determination of, 133
  proof required by ADA, 134
  severity of harm, 137
Sloan v. Metropolitan Health Council of Indianapolis, 81
smokers, Medicare surcharge, 228
smoking, financial consequences of decrease in, 246
social interest, countervailing, effects of life style on health, 237–9
social responsibility, of health care institutions, 222
society, effect of transplantable organ market on, 34–8
socioeconomic class, effect on health status, 167–9
stigma
  'do nothing' policy option, 194
  expanded insurance coverage, 204–5
  policy analysis, 217
subsidies, government, through Medicaid, 99
Supreme Court
  against forced medical testing, 112
  move towards constitutional review, 111

targeting services
  family planning, 210
  handicapped children, 210
  maternal/child care, 210
  policy analysis, 211–13
tax
  on cigarettes, 246
  exemptions for hospitals, 90
tax collector, health care financing, 89–92
Tex. v. Cleburne Living Center, Inc., 111
third parties
  refusal to reimburse for experimental treatment, 92
  rescuing from exposure to risks, 61
Title VI, 213–18

tort duties, expansion of, 75–84
transcultural medicine, awareness of, 332–3
translation, provision for services to ethnic groups, 325
transmission, mode of, 135–6
transplantation, kidney, *see* kidney disease/transplantation
Truman v. Thomas, 60
tuberculosis, 'direct threat' standards, DOJ regulations, 125

Uniform Anatomical Gift Act (UAGA), 14–16
  overcoming family veto, 35
uninsured, emergency rooms last resort for, 85
United Kingdom, health promotion for ethnic groups, 327
United Network for Organ Sharing (UNOS)
  national system of control, 22
  survey on compensation for donors, 23–4
United States Constitution, 24–6
urban areas, concentration of ethnic minorities, 327
urine tests, and Fourth Amendment, 112–14
Urrutia v. Patino, 56
Utah County v. Intermountain Health Care, 91

vaccination, compulsory
  cases of, 115–17
  right to refuse, 114–15
vertical equity
  'do nothing' policy option, 192
  expanded insurance coverage, 201
  policy analysis, 217
vicarious liability
  of institutions, 79
  limitations of, 78
  principle of agency law, 78
video shops, *see* adult video shops
voluntariness, of life style choices, 235–7

Index compiled by Campbell Purton